GANGSTERS
OR
GUERRILLAS?

Representations of Irish Republicans
in 'Troubles Fiction'

by
Patrick Magee

First published 2001
by
Beyond the Pale
BTP Publications Ltd
Unit 2.1.2 Conway Mill
5-7 Conway Street
Belfast BT13 2DE

Tel: +44 (0)28 90 438630
Fax: +44 (0)28 90 439707
E-mail: office@btpale.com
Website: http://www.btpale.com

British Library Cataloguing-in-Publication Data.
A catalogue record for this book is available from the British Library.

ISBN 1-900960-14-1

Cover Photograph: Agnieszka Martynowicz
Printed in Dublin by Colour Books Ltd.

CONTENTS

Dedicated to my father, John Magee, 1929-1995

Acknowledgements

The reading and research for this book began while I was in Maghaberry and was completed in the H-Blocks. The general intuition is that incarceration provides an ideal opportunity for study and reflection. However, as any lag or Lifer will verify, prison has its own peculiar, hothouse pressures, with many an essay deadline missed because of a bad visit, Dear John, lockdown or some other distraction.

The obverse of that pressurised reality is the comradeship and support of fellow prisoners. At the risk of offending those not included, for I am indebted to many, I would like to thank the following for their opinions on various drafts, the loan of books, sage advice, and for allowing me 'space' to do the work: Rab Fryers, Jim McVeigh, Ciaran Morrison, Terry Perry, John Tumelty and Pádraig Wilson.

There are many others outside those confines, some of them ex-prisoners, who supplied texts and information that I may not otherwise have obtained, among them Ronan Bennett, Danny Morrison and Sean P. Murphy (who died last year). I am particularly grateful to Aly Renwick for conducting an interview on my behalf with Peter Berresford Ellis, and indeed to Peter for his contribution, which I use liberally in my 'closing argument'.

I am also grateful to Prof. Robert Welch, the School of Language and Literature, University of Ulster, Coleraine, for his patient advice and regular, encouraging visits to the Blocks as my academic supervisor. Bill Rolston, Tom McGill, Aaron Kelly and David Butler were also helpful in discussions and supplying material about some of the theory that informs the thesis.

I would also like to record my gratitude to individuals from the Education Departments of both prisons for their practical support, particularly during my time in Maghaberry.

I doubt if there is a study of the politics, history and/or culture of the North that doesn't acknowledge the unique resources of the Linen Hall Library, Belfast. This will be no exception: my thanks to Yvonne Murphy and her colleagues at the 'Political Collection'.

With so much wise counsel availed of, it is nevertheless necessary to add that the views expressed and the conclusions reached herein are my own.

And finally, though primarily, I wish to express an especial thank you to my wife, Barbara, for her input, wisdom, and for putting up with it all.

Pat Magee
Autumn, 2001

Foreword

In 1974 when Pat Magee was interned in Cage Two, Long Kesh, he can remember reading Jack Higgins' thriller, *The Savage Day*. It was much later before he realised that the novel fell into the category of what came to be termed, 'Troubles fiction'.

When next he was in jail, from 1985 until his release under the Belfast Agreement in 1999, having served fourteen years out of five life sentences for the bombing of the Grand Hotel in Brighton, he took an Open University degree in politics and modern literature.

In 1994 Pat was transferred from England to Maghaberry Prison in County Antrim where he studied as a postgraduate student, attached to the University of Ulster. He produced the first draft of his doctoral thesis on the subject of 'Troubles fiction', ironically, in the H-Blocks of Long Kesh, a prison which had undergone much change in the interim, and had been at the epicentre of a showdown between republicans and the British government. It was here that ten Irish republicans died in a seven-month long hunger strike in 1981, an event which Pat argues had an impact beyond the defeat of Britain's criminalisation policy and the subsequent resurgence in support for the Republican Movement.

Pat's forensic analyses of the texts under review (a representative 150 out of some 700 published since 1969) reveals that in the use of language, staple plots, the stereotypical depictions of the various protagonists (IRA baddies/SAS goodies), most of the authors are actually witting or unwitting 'players' in the propaganda war. Pulp fiction PROs for the British establishment or – as he ingeniously puts it, they represent 'the paraliterary wing of Brit propaganda'.

And so we have a gallery of caricatures almost unchanged since the *Punch* magazine depictions of the mad, fighting, drinking, dangerous Oirish of the nineteenth century. A nation incapable of running their own affairs and in need of a civilising agent. This notion, successfully planted in the English psyche, was to become the seedbed of racist attitudes for subsequent generations and facilitates the belief that British imperialist involvement in Ireland is a noble enterprise.

The Irish get their madness from their mother's milk or while sitting on their granny's knee. Read about the mad bombers sporting tattoos of the Sacred Heart on their arms, with names like, The Skull or Kevin 'Machine-gun' McNally of

Kilkenny, 'one of the hardest and most fanatically anti-British of all the IRA hardliners.' At their meetings, at which they are inevitably drinking bottles of stout, the chairman says, 'I now call this special meeting of the Breakaway Branch of the Unofficial IRA to order.' Or, a Mulholland says, 'Do you know that, Rory, to cleanse ourselves we'll be needing a whole river of blood.'

Of course, none of these novels were planned as immortal literature or would-be masterpieces so, one could argue, why waste time on them? Such pap novels might be laughable or dismissible if it were not for their insidious perpetuation of ignorance, their glorification of British violence and their demonising of Irish nationalists and republicans. Pat Magee quite persuasively argues that, whilst such works are open to ridicule, the influence of popular fiction should not be underestimated in their capacity to form and influence attitudes and opinions, or in perpetuating prejudice, even if that is not how they were conceived. Best-selling novels by writers like Gerald Seymour and Tom Clancy have been powerful in shaping public perceptions of republicans and, more favourably, their British counterparts.

In the way that they offer British readers the assurances that their government's role in Ireland is as a peacekeeper they perform an ideological and political function of cosseting the establishment from domestic criticism and allowing it a free hand. They work almost in the same way as the tabloid press has done in defending 'our boys' in the British army after every state killing. They function in the same way as the 'unofficial' censorship and later the broadcasting ban on Sinn Fein, did by suppressing the discrepant voice whilst supporting the dominant ideology on the causes of the conflict.

His research examines the cultural and political circumstances in which these works were composed/manufactured, published, marketed and distributed. He makes the telling point that, for example, a Seymour novel which had the IRA Volunteer as hero and a denouement concluding that it was time for a British withdrawal would receive a markedly different, and quite negative, reception because of its oppositional position to the established norms.

Few writers can escape being influenced by their milieu; and the role of the *serious* writer in society – with social, moral and/or political responsibilities – is one that has been debated and contested through many periods and fashions. 'Poets are the unacknowledged legislators of the world,' wrote Shelley, rather grandiosely. 'Writers are forged in injustice as a sword is forged,' said Hemingway, though later, he wrote, 'There is no left and right in writing. There is only good and bad writing.' Cyril Connolly was quite clear on the subject: 'The artist should keep himself free from all creed, from all dogma, from all opinion.'

Many of the books under review were written by Irish writers, including Ben Kiely, Bernard McLaverty, Frances Molloy, Mary Beckett, Ronan Bennett, Seamus Deane, Edna O'Brien, Eoin McNamee, Patrick McCabe, Robert McLiam Wilson and Glen Patterson, to name but some, most of who consider themselves, or are considered, as serious and successful *literary* authors. Many of them have been writing post-1981. Pat's favourite book of the period, with a 'troubles' theme, is Dermot Healey's *A Goat's Song*. In my opinion, one of the worst books to be written about Belfast and the IRA was Brian Moore's *Lies of Silence*, an anti-Catholic, anti-republican diatribe, whose plot – which included an IRA Volunteer with a pimply face and his uncle, an IRA messenger-priest – was preposterous. Needless-to-say, it was nominated for the Booker Prize.

Pat argues that the sacrifices of the hunger strikers occasioned an identifiable, though not extensive, discursive shift in the fictional depiction of the conflict which has continued to the present. In other words, as Britain's role as a protagonist and not a neutral party emerged, as stories of state collusion with loyalist paramilitaries were established as fact, the standard black and white, simplistic presentation of the conflict was becoming untenable, and this shift may be increasingly reflected in emergent fiction.

The provenance of this critical study, Pat's doctoral thesis, is clear but it will appeal not just to students of politics and literature but to the general reader, particularly his reminders of how ridiculous and stupid – I would argue, wanton – some writers could be.

Finally, the person who defies the stereotype most, the cipher known simply as 'The Brighton Bomber', as if he sprung up out of nowhere, without family or history or authentic experience, is the author himself, Pat Magee. I first met Pat in Long Kesh internment camp in the early 1970s. In the 1980s, when I was the editor of *An Phoblacht/Republican News*, Pat also worked on the paper (and, in fact, was shot and wounded in our Dublin office by a loyalist gunman in 1981 whilst producing the paper). He was quiet, intelligent, thoughtful and assiduous.

A loyal republican and a supporter of the peace process, Patrick Magee has now established the Causeway Project which seeks to facilitate meetings between perpetrators and victims of any action that occurred during the course of the Troubles.

This book is the product of his diligence, of a fine mind at work, out to understand and reveal one of the many levels at which war was fought, in most of the cases by individuals – I will not say intellectuals – at their desks, far from the discrimination, the suffering and oppression, and the bombs that followed.

Danny Morrison
Belfast, November 2001

1.

Introduction: Misrepresentation and Reality

When I mention having studied 'Troubles fiction' while in prison, that is, prose fiction dealing with the conflict in the North of Ireland since the late 1960s, I often meet with polite silence and a not quite imperceptible downcasting of the eyes. Some awkward mental shuffling is going on in the recipient's head. Partly it's a prejudice against popular culture as a subject worthy of serious academic attention. Any and every textbook or scholarly article on popular fiction in general that I've consulted seems to start with a self-justificatory, almost apologetic explanation about why the subject ought to merit serious attention. Many examples of the Troubles fiction 'genre' are indeed quite dishearteningly awful, judging them not on their literary merit (or lack) but on the basis of their distorted take on the conflict. One critic advised against any extensive reading: 'only a desperate thesis writer – or a masochist – would attempt such a task'.[1] There is also a view afoot that it is frivolous or a conceit that time and energy should be devoted to studying misrepresentations in popular fiction when so many other aspects of the Troubles cry out for the attention of republicans. I find myself at the outset having to justify the endeavour.

I read my first Troubles' novel while interned in Cage Two, Long Kesh in 1974. It was Jack Higgins's *The Savage Day*.[2] I picked it up, doubtless discarded, curious about how the IRA and the war in the North were represented, more particularly, how we, that is, I and others like me, came across in popular fiction. Soul-auditing and self-analysis came naturally in that environment, and here was a chance to get an 'external' view on how the world was being primed to see us. Then, I believed novelists, all novelists, were the fortunate possessors of acute insight into the human condition; and if ever a situation merited imaginative engagement it was that pertaining in the North. I was hoping for, and half expecting, an awareness and perspective beyond the habitual tabloid excesses fostered, we believed, from Thiepval Barracks, Lisburn, the location of the British Army's HQ and heart of its 'black propaganda' operation. So, turning to a work whose blurb promised that Ireland's fate would hang on the outcome of the plot, I expected considerably more than Higgins's war-comic reduction. It is certainly true that the conflict would tax the most creative and articulate. However, as Oscar Wilde said, 'books are well written, or badly written. That is all'.[3] In the novel the

1

main protagonists are members of the Official IRA; the Provos are referred to as 'Bradyites', seemingly a reference to Ruairi O Bradaigh, then president of Provisional Sinn Féin. Two Bradyites, Lucas and Riley, have no redeeming features and are depicted as sectarian thugs. I'll say more about *The Savage Day* in Chapter Three, but I realised that there was no discernible gulf between the fictional and tabloid accounts. Over the years I've read other examples, which for the most part confirmed the impression of ignorance about, and a heavy bias against, the Irish republican perspective. The republicans I knew were politically intelligent, committed and honourable people, not the psychotic scum of tabloid outrage here given fictional ratification.

After a wide reading of this type of fiction for a doctoral thesis, the composite Irish republican to materialise was of a Mother Ireland-fixated psycho-killer, aka a Provo Godfather, readily discernible with recourse to an identikit indebted to Tenniel's 'Irish Frankenstein' and other images from *Punch*[4] redolent of Victorian racism. Various permutations of the formula reveal a blarney-spouting thug with a 'ferrety look' and halitosis, or, as a recent novel puts it, 'the Fenian world of rotten teeth and puffy blotched skin'.[5] Obscured in this murky understanding, the violence attributed to republicans results from an ingrained bloodlust and is not the effect or symptom of a deeper political malaise. And when romantic nationalism, via Pearse's putative call for 'blood sacrifice', doesn't provide the motivation for violence, then personal aggrandisement and enrichment, often through drug trafficking, is frequently the slander of next resort.

More insidiously harmful is the striking uniformity of the novels' underlying assumptions. With few exceptions, the common theme encountered *ad nauseam* is of Britain's role as honest broker in the North of Ireland, a referee between warring factions, or contending atavisms. Britain is rarely depicted as part of the problem; never mind, as republicans would argue, the problem. The narrowness of outlook amounts to a generic bias despite the diversity of the fiction. It is remarkable that across the genre-spectrum comprising these texts we encounter again and again the same sets of tropes and lurid mischaracterisations – a testament to the ubiquitous cultural penetration of Britain's point of view in regard to the conflict.

To read these works uncritically is to accept at face value many assumptions that continue to hinder a resolution of the divisions in Ireland. Gross negatives of the IRA gunman, like the Irish joke or the Cummings' cartoon, offer non-explanations that have befogged the issues central to the conflict and detract from the ongoing search for a just and lasting peace settlement. It is important to counter and correct these misrepresentations for an audience still largely starved of any adequate understanding of the republican perspective. Only when opposing sides see each other clearly, and recognise each other's humanity, will a resolution begin. Why? Because ignorance about any one of the protagonists to a conflict will hamper its resolution and contribute to its prolongation. To allow the distortions prevalent in much of the prose fiction output to go unchallenged would be to collude with, as Franz Fanon observed, 'the racist who creates the inferior'.

Definitions

Two over-lapping definitional parameters need to be established from the outset: what constitutes 'Troubles fiction' and what is meant by 'the Troubles'?[6] Starting with the latter, 'the Troubles' originally was popularly applied to the period stretching from the Easter Rising of 1916 to the end of the Civil War in 1923, and does not appear to have had much of a present-day coinage prior to 1973.[7] The first upper-case example I have come across is in a 1971 edition of *Fortnight*[8] – and incidentally, published the day before the death of the first British soldier during the present Troubles. One commentator has suggested that the terms 'the Northern Situation' and 'the Disturbances' were more in vogue;[9] another referred to 'the Ulster Emergency'.[10] Only as the seriousness and protracted nature of the violence became evident did this resort to an historical epithet achieve a wider currency.

'The Troubles' underlines a continuation – the unfinished business of partition – as well as pointing up the difficulty in defining the situation. Is it civil war, national liberation struggle, insurrection? Or can it be explained away, as the tabloids and the body of fiction in question do, as mindless sectarian terrorism or criminal anarchy?

The use of the term 'the Troubles' was certainly adopted wholesale by those authors for whom the conflict provided a fictional context, and who made do with the hand-me-down rather than fashion a more tailored nomenclature. There are at least 700 works of prose fiction (novels and short stories) that deal either substantially or in part with the contemporary conflict. There is, though, a difficulty in pigeonholing the relevant fiction under a neat generic heading. As one fairly representative definition has it, genre is 'a contingent grouping of texts based on their common internal characteristics'.[11] However, many examples of the texts defy slick categorisation. Much of the output may be accurately described as a hybrid of the thriller, romance and war novel genres. Some of the terms previously used tend to disparage the works, stressing a garish sensationalism: 'Troubles thrillers', 'Balaclava novels', 'Troubles-trash';[12] and for one novelist they represented 'a lucrative sub-genre for tourist Brits and Americans'.[13]

I have opted for describing this thirty-year output of novels and short stories as 'Troubles fiction' because it very usefully defines the whole literary output under discussion in terms of a period and a theme, conveniently eliding a variety of genres and sub-categories and implicitly leaving formal questions (as to estimations of literary value) to the side in order to concentrate critical attention on the role and practice of misrepresentation. Therefore, I use the term 'Troubles fiction' as a generic catch-all or flag of convenience. But, then, as Seymour Chatman argues, 'no individual work is a perfect specimen of a genre... all works are more or less mixed in generic character'.[14]

The Troubles viewed simplistically as a criminal conspiracy or as an outbreak of irrationality may provide the narrative ingredients for a simple detective story.

Often reducible to a struggle between good and evil, right and wrong, black and white, the Crime novel is also capable of exploring psychological, social and cultural motivations. More often than not the tensions over remit and competence of the various 'security forces' involved in an episode provide a rich source for narrative development and plotting. And it needn't be as simple as saying that when the RUC leads an investigation that the generic influence is the Detective story, or that when the British Army run the show that we are dealing with a War novel. The conflict is characterised by so many antagonistic forces and interests, internal and external, that it readily lends itself as a focus for many generic influences. There are subgenres and refinements, and texts which are exceptions to the rules.

The range of the Troubles fiction genre

A brief sampling of the fictional range may illustrate the difficulties alluded to in its categorisation. For example, as might be expected from a literary form as protean and resistant to definition as the novel, responses to the Troubles have been diverse. Encompassed, as already mentioned, are the stock thriller fare of Jack Higgins and Gerald Seymour; international blockbusters, like Tom Clancy's *Patriot Games*;[15] the darkly comic, such as Martin Waddell's brilliant satire *A Little Bit British*[16] and John Morrow's implausibly roguish *Confession's of Proinsias O'Toole*; and on a more consciously literary plane, Dermot Healy's *A Goat's Song*,[17] Edna O'Brien's *House of Splendid Isolation*,[18] Patrick McCabe's *The Dead School*[19] and Seamus Deane's Booker-finalist, *Reading in the Dark*.[20]

The Troubles' theme has also been taken up by writers prominent in genres other than the Thriller and the Detective. Shaun Hutson, for example, a popular writer of horror fiction, has produced at least three novels about the conflict.[21] And the acclaimed Science Fiction author Frank Herbert, more familiar perhaps for his Dune series, has remained within that genre in a novel dealing with the Provos, *The White Plague*.[22]

Novels from political insiders are few. The prominent Tory ex-Cabinet minister Douglas Hurd wrote *Vote to Kill* before his term as Northern Ireland Secretary of State, and more recently *The Shape of Ice*;[23] and Roy Bradford's *The Last Ditch* drew on his experience as a former Stormont minister.[24] Novels written by prominent Irish republicans are also a scarce commodity, the relatively few examples of which were to appear in print much later during the course of the conflict, Danny Morrison's *West Belfast* and *The Wrong Man* being, perhaps, the most notable.[25]

There are also many examples of novels in which reference to the conflict is fleeting, as in Malcolm Bradbury's campus satire *The History Man*, but which, nevertheless, demonstrate to a degree the social and cultural impact of the Troubles at the time of their publication, in this instance offering an insight into apparent levels of extra-curricular support for the Irish republican cause in Redbrick universities during the early to mid-1970s.[26]

The short story format, usually a guarantee of a more imaginative treatment of the Troubles theme, is also well attended, examples of which include, John Montague's 'The Cry',[27] Anne Devlin's 'Naming the Names',[28] and Gerry Adams's collection *The Street*.[29]

Several novels have been written in the last thirty years which deal with earlier historical periods.[30] Some of these are relevant to this argument, nevertheless, as when, for example, the historical narrative is a guise to examine some aspect of the current conflict. At the risk of opening a can of worms, however – for what in history might not be construed as relevant to the present? – with a few exceptions (which I will try to justify as I proceed) I've chosen to exclude novels that do not deal directly with the current context. And of those cited, I hope my choices do not appear too arbitrary.

Appendices

Such a diversity of fictional responses to the conflict requires a systematic approach to their collation and categorisation. In researching the genre, I compiled a bibliography of about 700 works of prose fiction relevant to the subject.[31] That compilation incorporates Bill Rolston and Robert Bell's bibliography of 320 titles, *Literature of the 'Troubles'*.[32] Their list covers titles published between 1969 and the end of May 1996, including short stories and non-English novels. All told, there are some 480 novels in English directly dealing with the conflict and published since 1969, popularly accredited as the year the Troubles began. These novels are listed chronologically in Appendix A.

My bibliography largely recorded the figures for novels published in Britain (necessarily, given the greater access to and familiarity with data from the British market as collated from, for example, the review pages of the British and Irish press). However, from the 1970s the transnational nature of the publishing industry has meant that titles either appeared simultaneously in Britain, Ireland, the United States and the Commonwealth, or shortly after their initial release on this side of the Atlantic, and vice versa. The data therefore is arguably applicable to wider, international trends, though I cannot rule out that a more focused study of the genre in, for example, the United States might elicit different, localised trends, and perhaps particularly from the output of smaller publishers.

I would also refer the reader to Appendix B which gives a breakdown of the information collated for my thesis. As represented, this forms the quantitative basis for my argument that the genre has undergone developments during the course of the last thirty years. Data on the texts is categorised as follows: (a) novels dealing either directly or in significant part with some aspect of the conflict (though excluding the ten novels published prior to 1970; (b) short stories, published as collections, or included in anthologies; graphic novels; (c) non-English fiction: fiction originally published in, for example, Gaelic, French, Dutch, etc; and (d) novels and short stories in which the Troubles is not a significant theme and may amount to a bare reference. Two further categories are given: (e) comprising category (a) fiction written by Irish authors; and (f) category (a) fiction written by women.

Appendix B's lay-out corresponds to the six-year periods mainly used to arrange the chapters (1976-1981, 1988-1993, etc.). There are two exceptions to this format: pre-1970 fiction is dealt with as a decade, and is discussed in Chapter Two; and the six years 1970 to 1975 are split into the two three-year periods covered in Chapters Three and Four, the shorter time-focus in each being merited because of the specific conditions and developments pertaining during the early years of the conflict.

The six-yearly periodisation structuring chapters Five to Eight may appear arbitrary, although the division is broadly contiguous in a pleasing symmetry to many specific developments. A strict periodisation also underlines the longevity of the conflict in a way that an uneven, concertina-ed and varied division may have acted to distract or detract from the sense of temporal continuity. And where no such symmetry presents itself, as for example when a particular event or development will not sit easily within what may seem the artificial nature of the framework, I thought it better for the sake of consistency to impose the division. To give one example, Chapter Seven (1988-1993) might have usefully carried over into 1994, the year which saw the first IRA cessation, instead of ending with the Downing Street Declaration of December 1993. The strict chapter periodisation also puts in perspective some salient events in the republican movement's political development. For example, the gap of nineteen years between the ceasefires of 1975 and 1994, is covered by Chapters Five, Six, and Seven, and corresponds to what has been termed the IRA's 'Long War'. Perhaps more tellingly, the chronological division into six-yearly periods highlights the fact, totally absent in the fiction and largely lost to the media, that the republican movement has been engaged in a peace strategy since the mid-1980s, a matter that therefore arises in Chapter Six and not at the conclusion of this critical history in Chapter Eight, which would conform to the prejudices of those who would diminish Sinn Féin's pre-eminent role in the struggle for peace with justice.

Interpreting the data

Caution is needed in interpreting the data summarised. The task of collating data is not completed. Overlooked or omitted titles continue to surface, suggesting that my figures are not exhaustive. I would hazard that the final tally, from 1969 to 1999 inclusive, might well exceed 800. Additionally, new relevant fiction continues to be churned out, with forty three titles issued in 1996 alone, thirty three of which are category (a) novels, making it the record year for that category. I would estimate, however, that at least in regard to category (a) that no significant further titles are extant and that the distribution by year is therefore a fair representation of market trends, and thus a reasonably firm basis from which to extrapolate narrative trends. Even so, throughout I have focused only on broad trends as discernible from the Appendix B chart. I do not place undue emphasis on the figures in the short story category: the presence in one year, for example, of several titles from different authors taken from one anthology is bound, given the small numbers involved in total, to distort the picture. Likewise, the figures in the other categories are relatively smaller and may therefore also be statistically insignificant. However, categories (e) and (f), referring to Irish writers and women writers respectively, do suggest quite important commercial and social developments which I will discuss where relevant, although again some caution is required because of the fewer examples in either category.

Looking at the figures, the first (quite obvious) point to make is that prior to 1970, prior that is to the levels of conflict commonly associated with the Troubles, very few pertinent novels appeared, and those that are included deal with either the Fifties' Border Campaign or with the burgeoning crisis of the Sixties. In Chapter Two I mention how pre-1970 texts reveal simmering social tensions and establish some of the earlier stereotypes. The twenty pre-1970 titles are not included in the overall sum of 693 texts. That sum relates only to texts issued from 1970 onwards.

As I stated above, only broad trends merit attention given the relatively few texts that the figures represent. The broadest trends are the occasional troughs and booms in publication of category (a) novels. There are four years whose figures represent a trough: 1974, 1983, 1988 and 1997; and five periods that can lay claim to being boom years for the genre: 1973, 1976-1981, 1987, 1989-1996, and 1998. The figures clearly show that boom years are more prevalent than slumps. The genre has been phenomenally successful in publishing terms since 1973; the date in fact coincides with the birth of what amounts to a publishing phenomenon.

I argue also that there is an appreciable extent to which the publication of Troubles fiction reflects contemporaneous levels of social tolerance towards matters Irish. The reduction in numbers of new novels published in the years I have indicated as trough years can be explained by a discursive context of increased hostility to the IRA. Conversely, during periods of a more open climate of debate about the issues surrounding the conflict there is a correspondingly increased tendency in fiction for a more questioning fictional treatment and challenge to dominant or received assumptions.

The following facts are particularly interesting in terms of social and commercial trends. In the course of the 1960s only 20 relevant titles in all categories were published. Focusing on category (a) titles, in the 1970s, 124 novels were published; in the 1980s, 139; and in the 1990s, 217. The rising publication figures indicate an almost exponential growth in the market for and popularity of fiction dealing with the conflict from its inception. Fourteen publishing houses between them handled over half the total of category (a) novels.[33]

The total number of authors is 496, of whom 167 are Irish (I have insufficient biographical information on a further thirty five authors who may be Irish), and eighty five of whom are from the contested northern six counties (or the North as it is commonly referred to by nationalists). This suggests that interest from writers extended quite considerably beyond Ireland.

In terms of works by Irish authors, the output practically doubled in successive decades: six relevant novels out of the eighteen titles in total (novels and short stories) published in the 1960s; and twenty five category (a) novels in the 1970s, forty three in the 1980s, and eighty in the 1990s. Of these, ninety were written by novelists from the North, while fifty seven were by novelists from the South. The figures indicate the healthy state of Irish writing. However, as few as thirty two novels in English by Irish authors were first published in Ireland. Irish publishers such as Blackstaff, Brandon, Poolbeg and Mercier led the way in promoting first-time Irish authors.

At least 71 of the novels are by debut novelists. This substantial number may indicate that the conventions, range of stock assumptions and characterisations found in this body of fiction make it an attractive narrative (and perhaps commercial) option for first-time novelists. On the other hand, these novelists may be simply following a standard piece of advice to aspiring authors to write about what they know: a greater percentage, more than half, in fact, are Irish, and a further ten either reported the conflict as journalists, served with the British forces, or lived in Ireland, and for those reasons, presumably, were closer to events.

Ninety-four of the total number of authors are women. The output reflects the upsurge in women's fiction beginning in the 1980s. Generally, women writers have contributed more reflective, less thriller-based treatments of the Troubles context. In the 1970s, fifteen category (a) novels were by women; in the 1980s, twenty seven; and thirty three in the 1990s. Of these, twenty four are by Irish women, thirteen of whom are from the North.

A surprising feature to emerge from my reading of Troubles fiction is the large number of journalists who have turned their word-processors to fiction. Joseph McMinn notes the 'remarkable proportion of these novels… written by journalists who have spent years covering the North'.[34] He mentions Kevin Dowling, Gerald Seymour, Des Hamill and Jimmy Breslin. One could also add Jack Holland, Joe Joyce, Eugene McEldowney, Colin Bateman, Martin Dillon, Gavin Esler, Gordon Stevens, Malachi O'Doherty, Chapman Pincher and Eddie Shah. At least sixty six authors with journalism or media backgrounds have written a Troubles novel, the latest addition to this fold being the ITN political correspondent Tom Bradby, whose first novel, *Shadow Dancer*, was issued in 1998.[35]

I say a 'surprising feature' because one might, if only for a moment, have supposed this input of research expertise and professional knowledge into narrative form would have resulted in a probing, investigative realism, certainly a better informed fiction. Instead, because there is, arguably, virtually little balance or objectivity in journalistic reportage on the Troubles, why should there be in fiction coming from the same sources? I wish to make it clear that I am not arguing the virtues of 'balance' per se. A journalist may quite validly argue from a given political interest and outlook (while allowing for the demands of professional objectivity). The argument should apply with at least equal force to fictional representations.

The role of the moonlighting journalist, an eye ever out for the lucrative screen adaptation, carries additional clout with the reading public, who may be swayed by journalistic credentials the more readily to accept as authentic a biased view, and, given the perception of partial media coverage of the conflict, thus reinforcing the power of reductive representations.

There are, of course, exceptions. In his first novel, *Loyalties* (1990),Gavin Esler – to single out one journalist – manages to combine a superior thriller with a quite searching discussion of the relative merits and absurdities of the British government's broadcasting ban on Sinn Féin (lifted only subsequent to the IRA's 1994 cessation).[36] Despite Esler's achievement in this novel, he doesn't manage to entirely dispense with clichéd IRA gunmen, beloved of hackdom. He also ascribes corporate infighting and empire-building to the Provos' leadership.

The argument in this study is based on a reading of some 150 works of relevant prose fiction, that is, on about a quarter of the total output represented by the above figures. In addition, I have sought to enhance my grasp of the genre's essential characteristics from gleaning information about the contents of a large number of the remaining titles either reviewed in literary journals and columns or in Irish literary bibliographies.[37]

Irish republican perspectives

A cautionary though unapologetic note is required from the outset. This study entails and attempts a comparison between representation and reality. 'Reality', of course, is a dicey sort of a notion to be fooling around with, and a problematic one in terms of the particular theoretical approaches which inform my task, of which I will say more presently. For now, it is necessary to declare what should be already apparent from my use of the phrase 'the North of Ireland'. I write from the 'lived experience' of being an Irish republican. As such, I believe that the political reunification of the island of Ireland is a prerequisite for the fullest development of democracy. The reader will encounter, therefore, phrases such as 'British rule in Ireland', 'the republican struggle', and doubtless other numerous give-aways as to my political stance vis-à-vis the topic.

Essentially, however, I do not write as a nationalist, that is, one who believes in some myth-bound, spiritual essence called Ireland whose allegiance is owed as a consequence of having been born there. Rather, my political beliefs, like those of most other republicans I have either worked with or known in prison, belong in the mainstream republican tradition rooted in the 18th century Enlightenment values of Theobald Wolfe Tone (1763-98).

My own conception of republicanism centres on Tom Paine's definition. In *The Rights of Man* (1791), written in response to Burke's *Reflections on the Revolution in France* (1790), Paine's definition of a republic stresses purpose, not form.

> What is called a republic, is not any particular form of government. it is wholly characteristical of the purport, matter, or object for which government ought to be instituted, and on which it is to be employed, res-publica, the public affairs, or the public good; or, literally translated, the public thing. It is a word of a good original, referring to what ought to be the character and business of government; and in this sense it is naturally opposed to the word monarchy, which has a base original signification. it means arbitrary power in an individual person; in the exercise of which, himself, and not the res-publica, is the object.[38]

The purpose of government in the above formula must be to represent the legitimate interests of all the people – not an élite, nor a majority, but all the people. Any political arrangement not giving expression to the legitimate interests of all the people is therefore deficient. Paine was one of a number of radical thinkers who provoked in the collective imagination and aspirations of groups such as the United Irishmen and subsequent republican revolutionaries ideas about what true political freedom might entail. It is because of its adherence to this tradition that Irish republicanism has always been at the forefront of progressive forces in Ireland.

When considering the discursive genealogy of Irish republicanism, therefore, consideration should always be given to the crucial role in history of the poorest, grassroots, subaltern sections of the Irish people, those not merely of but for their class, whose agency is often overlooked or written out of the historical account, who at various historical junctures threw their support behind, and leadership into, the struggle for independence from Britain – voices of discontent from below. These are Tone's 'men of no property', who were always a major influence in shaping the wider, more inclusive, discursive formation of Irish republicanism, whether manifest in rural Defenderism or the Irish diaspora's collective recall of dispossession and the call for redress. At salient junctures in Ireland's past there was a sufficient overlap of interests, aspirations and values, an alliance sufficiently broad in terms of class, geographic spread and cultural diversity to be truly representative of the great mass of the disadvantaged and disaffected, and to thus further collective goals against the dominant power. The outstanding lesson from a study of Irish resistance to British rule is that the struggle was most effective when the broad mass of the people had a role and voice. The leadership of that popular will, and whether it truly represented the broad masses, was ever the problematic consideration pointing to past failure. However, it has always been the imperative of the powerful to exclude, marginalise, ridicule and silence the voices of those classes which it would subjugate, or to confuse or incorporate those whose allegiance or consent was required to legitimate the political status quo. Division and co-option were means to weaken resistance. The republican movement had to be ever regardful of the blind alleys of history and to be flexible in the direction of its energies and resources to meet the circumstances of the time.

The contemporary republican movement, by which I mean primarily the Provisional IRA and Sinn Féin, claims a common lineage stretching back to Tone and beyond to embrace the long history of resistance to oppression under the English Crown. The collective experience of Irish republicanism is the distillation of that historical legacy, the essential block concepts of which are democracy, separatism, secularism, non-sectarianism, socialism and internationalism.[39] Although contradictions in this complementary grouping of ideas might seem superficially apparent, there are none. For example, the apparent conceptual gulf between separatism and internationalism is explained by the fact that in Tone's day separatism signified the yearning to reverse the expansionist nationalism of England. A certain pragmatism has always guided the republican project, but separatism, then and now, is a prerequisite. The desire for political independence was judged the means to those other ends. All of these precepts cohere in the outlook, attitudes, values, strategy and aspirations of the present-day movement.

This outlook wasn't forged in a vacuum but was the outcome of struggle, of contested views, of pragmatism and flexibility to meet the exigencies of reality as faced by a movement at war against a powerful enemy. One might argue that Irish republicanism's nature is inherently unresolved. Many internal tensions have vied for supremacy over a century and more of struggle. Thomas Davis's Enlightenment goal of achieving an inclusive nation and national identity was one which embraced different classes; whereas James Connolly's Marxist vision, per se, saw both the goal and its achievement in terms of class struggle. Breaches and inconsistencies when they have occurred correspond to fault lines along the dual co-ordinates of nationalism and socialism, and of internal and external influences. However, there is a consensual trajectory, too, to the republican project; the goal of separatism binds its internal inconsistencies, endowing republicanism with a coherence that hitherto has transcended any apparent division.

The aims and objects of the contemporary republican movement are set down in the separate constitutions of the IRA (known internally as 'Óglaigh na hÉireann') and of Sinn Féin (the former of which is published in the IRA's Green Book).[40] Both constitutions articulate the same objective: to work for the establishment of a Democratic Socialist Republic based on the Proclamation of Easter Week, 1916.

In the Westminster general election of December 1918, the last occasion on which the electorate made its choice on an all-Ireland basis, Sinn Féin won 73 out of the 105 seats, 69% of the votes cast, with a 'political programme of demanding complete independence for the unitary state of Ireland'.[41] With this mandate, the First Dáil proclaimed on 21 January 1919 'the Independence of Ireland and ratified the establishment of the Irish republic proclaimed in 1916, thus founding the Republic on the basis of the free votes of the people of ireland with Dáil Éireann as its government'.[42] It is on this basis that republicans insist, therefore, that Ireland was partitioned against the democratically expressed wishes of the overwhelming majority of its people.

Partition was imposed through the implementation of the Government of Ireland Act, 1920. Britain achieved several long-term ends from partition. The primary reason was strategic; historically, Britain had feared that its enemies – Spain and France – would use Ireland as a backdoor; twice in the 20th century the fear was of Germany. This translated in today's world as a fear of Ireland's western approaches. Hence the need for its strategic foothold in the North. The other is economic, and most definitely selfish; historically the relationship was colonial exploitation; partition – a neo-colonial solution – would continue to disadvantage a potential rival and divide opposition to British interests by thwarting the economic, social and political competition of a free Ireland. But what about political ends? One obvious fear was that the achievement and example of a united Ireland would herald the break-up of Britain itself. But perhaps the biggest political consideration was pragmatic: the narrow and blinkered imperative to contain or 'insulate the issue from the mainstream of British political life', and this, as Jack Holland has observed,

> has been the case since about 1922. Insulation was deemed essential to prevent the Irish problem from once more disrupting British politics on the scale it did from the 1880s onward, when it brought down governments, helped to ruin the Liberal Party, and dragged the nation to the brink of civil war.[43]

Northern nationalists locked into a sectarian, gerrymandered statelet, picked up the tab for a partitionist policy that met Britain's selfish ends. The fifty years of Unionist misrule saw the resort to internment in every decade, and repression and discrimination against the Catholic population, a population that had never consented to partition.[44]

The culmination of resistance to partition was the Provos' military campaign from 1970 to the ceasefires of 1994 and 1997. The Provos withstood the combined might of the British Army, the RUC, and various paramilitary factions which often acted collusively. The military campaign enabled the development of Sinn Féin into a political party which, by June 2001, represented 22 per cent of the electorate and the majority of nationalist voters in the North.

Longevity of the Troubles

Having declared where I am coming from politically, I would ask the reader to bear in mind the crucial consideration of the extent to which the republican movement has developed over the course of the last thirty years. An inadequate appreciation of the thirty-year timescale of the present stage of the struggle for republican goals will shape, or more likely obscure, popular understanding of the changes and developments within republican tactics and strategies. Perhaps what is lacking is a necessary distance and detachment from the immediacy of the historical moment. Irish republicanism, as I've indicated, has a staggered history, at times appearing to lurch within the normative duality of Tone's separatism and James Connolly's socialism, at other times clutching some leaden historical baggage resulting from the pragmatism stressed in the old Fenian exhortation that England's difficulty is Ireland's opportunity. The republican movement, in its various historical manifestations, has undergone considerable shifts between militarism, constitutionalism, urban and rural agitation, and combinations thereof.

A recent novel captures well the sense of historical shifts in the usage of the term 'Irish republican'.

> In the honoured tradition of Irish politics, operating in a perpetual ideological void, Mr O'Shaughnessy has been all things to all men. In the cloak of a Republican, he has been socialist and conservative simultaneously. And that's Republican without the larger, small 'r' sense of the word which allows a plurality of views and the liberty of the individual.[45]

Critics of the contemporary republican movement may either fail to appreciate or to overlook the extent to which the original liberal precepts still guide its trajectory. Irish republicans remain motivated to achieve a plural society: that is, an inclusive social formation in keeping with the vision of Tone and Davis and Connolly, devoid of patronage and privilege and based instead on the most thorough democratic transparency and accountability. Historically this was perceived to be only achievable by first breaking the political connection with England, the seat of that royal patronage which worked against local interests. But republicanism has broadened to absorb other ideas on the creation of a just society.

In relative terms, we may evince no great difficulty grasping the enormity of change that occurred during any similar timeframe from the past. When we consider, for example, any comparable span of years – from 1916 to 1946, say, or from 1939 to 1969 – and of the major, historical shifts and events that occurred in Ireland due to a brew of internal and external pressures, we should not find it so remarkable that the republican movement has undergone similarly radical changes in its fortunes and policies during the years 1969 to 1999. Yet if we were to judge the transformations in the contemporary republican movement since 1970 – the year the Irish Republican Army (IRA or, more properly, Óglaigh na hÉireann[46]) split into the Provisional IRA (the Provos[47]) and Official IRA (the Sticks) – solely from the composite representation to be assembled from a wide reading of fiction based on the conflict, the impression would form of myth-bound stasis, with no forward progression or development, and instead, a bitter harping back over past grievances. The movement's ongoing development and internal debates are not reflected and, instead, misrepresentations of these are widely promulgated in the media, and perpetuated within the literary output in question. The longevity of the contemporary phase of the independence struggle will occupy the foreground throughout this study.

Significance of the genre

To return to the matter I raised at the beginning: why is a study of the genre necessary? On what basis do I defend any expenditure of interest? After all, most of the fictional texts I have looked at are examples of popular fiction, and in many instances might even be termed pulp fiction. There is a prejudicial view that popular fiction does not merit serious study. There are no post-modernist bust-ups, or fall outs among deconstructionists at academic seminars over these novels. Conscious of this sensibility, Tony Bennett defines popular fiction as 'that massive, exceedingly heterogeneous, body of texts which is conventionally defined as residue in relation to 'Literature proper' and which is not normally encompassed within the purview of criticism'.[48] The élitist view that Bennett is criticising is one I would also reject, and I proffer the following reasons for treating Troubles fiction as a serious field for critical attention.

Although it is demonstrable that the conflict has generated a huge and often commendable body of sociological, historical and political research, according to Robert Bell of the Linen Hall Library, Belfast, the sale of fiction dealing with the Troubles is 'read by many people throughout the world – certainly outstripping the readership of social science books on the "troubles".'[49]

As a publishing phenomenon, Troubles fiction is perhaps worthy in quantitative terms alone of some critical attention. No similar political conflict comes to mind as having generated anything like this level of authorial and publishing zeal, nor the resulting international readership. The Israeli/Palestinian conflict, for example, although also the subject of much pulp-fictional attention, has been more destructive of lives and property, and of more geopolitical significance, embroiling neighbouring states and the Cold War superpowers. On a per capita basis the Irish/British conflict can have few rivals in the popular fiction stakes. The area of the six counties, it should be remembered, is roughly the size of Connecticut but with half the population. But my focus is on the output's cultural and political significance, of how fiction has helped shape or constrain perceptions.

It is this very popularity of the genre, the fact of its wide readership, that makes it a powerful medium for assigning or fixing meaning, and thus contributes to the shaping or reinforcement of public perceptions. To the extent that this body of prose largely misrepresents its narrative context, its readers are liable to be misinformed and therefore hold to an erroneous understanding about the conflict. The genre (and for this argument film drama might also be included, for it tends to promote similarly reductive images) may be the only source of signification about the conflict for many readers (and viewers) internationally. Regular readers of the genre may be de-sensitised from appreciating the complexities involved by a steady fusillade of crass simplifications. The global view is more likely to have been influenced by Tom Clancy's *Patriot Games* than by any commensurable wealth of serious academic tomes. To further illustrate this popular reach, in addition to their bestseller status, both Higgins and Seymour are among the most borrowed authors in British public libraries. And the formulaic writing associated with the genre was apparently easy to emulate. As an example of this, a relevant text, Pat Gray's *The Political Map of the Heart*, was joint winner of the World One Day Novel Cup, 1995. At least one text is available on the Internet, Shane Willis's *Zap* (1996): <www.club-king.com/zap>.

Shifting the emphasis more explicitly to theoretical concerns, Troubles fiction is a compact, apprehensible field for study that may more readily elicit general principles for the understanding of all genres – for example, of how and why transformations within genres occur.[50] Allied to this, the study of the genre may help to illustrate how ideology – that is, 'meaning in the service of power', to use John B. Thompson's cogent phrase[51] – works in practice. The relatively smaller reach of Troubles fiction – some 480 novels written contemporaneously within a narrational context of a mere thirty years – may facilitate an analysis of the processes and mechanisms involved in the dissemination and hold of ideology, making the role of ideology potentially more comprehensible or transparent.

Underscoring the merit in pursuing this field of research, some large claims are made for the critical returns from a study of what is essentially popular fiction. Claud Cockburn, for example, argues that such fiction, 'as an expression of the prevailing political and social climate of which it is the product,' can reveal more about society than much sociological research.[52] John Sutherland,[53] Bruce Merry, *et al*,[54] also have pursued this line. Christopher Pawling stresses that 'popular novels are [not] simple repositories of sociological data'.[55] The genre is more than a collection of period pieces of interest only to social historians.[56] If that were the case, then academics might, like the narrator in Michael Foley's novel *The Road to Notown*, read fiction 'checking for anything anti-Catholic'.[57] The arguments summarised are that the popularity of the thriller (and the vast bulk of the works under discussion belong indeed to the thriller genre), with its stock assumptions, conventions, pacy narrative style, and resort to often flimsy characterisations, particularly lends itself to the spread of reductive representations. Thrillers reinforce the prevalence of a simplistic view or help to shape that view, thus ensuring what Alan Titley has claimed is 'a social and political dimension' to the genre's appeal.[58] J. Bowyer Bell goes further in suggesting that 'thrillers on Irish matters may have played a part in the British campaign to restore order' in the North of Ireland.[59]

Bowyer Bell's claim about the counter-insurgency contribution of fiction is difficult to substantiate, let alone evaluate. I would not suggest that the perceived bias against Irish republicans in this output results from overt or even covert intervention by the British state, of the state propagandising, for instance, by suborning 'reliable' hacks to submit suitably jaundiced, anti-republican diatribes, though from a reading of some of the wackier plots to appear in print one could be excused for concluding that the genre acts as the paraliterary wing of Brit propaganda.[60] There is no substantive evidence to pin-point any intrusive, censoring role by the state, in the form, for example, of the shared outlook and interests of well-placed people in the publishing and bookselling world sympathetic or amenable to the promulgation of a pro-government line on Ireland. The evidence for pressure, such as it exists, is anecdotal, amounting to opinion and suspicion among a few writers and critics. The pressures on writers, publishers and booksellers, I argue, are far subtler than direct governmental interference and are a matter of cultural and political environment, not process.

Why then, with notable exceptions, has the 'lived experience' of the conflict as shared by those suffering the brunt of state repression remained unvoiced and largely absent from the fictional account? Several possible factors spring to mind, the foremost being the role of censorship in its various guises, but as I have indicated above this is a difficult charge to investigate let alone substantiate. Another possibly more fruitful area for enquiry and explanation centres on the interdependent relationship between the fiction publishing and bookselling industries. These considerations are more fully aired in Chapter Nine.

The very nature of the medium and its market may act to facilitate the spread of a falsified take on the conflict. Popular fiction is popular precisely because it is escapist. Its British readers in particular (for it is the British reading public, in whose name the British government acts) are most directly disserviced, and arguably do not want to have their comfortable and comforting assumptions in regard to Britain's role in Ireland challenged by the disconcerting expression of an alternative view. Axe-grinding equals low sales.

The tendency repeated by many, indeed most, writers is to reduce Irish republicanism by rubbishing, or diminishing the physical, moral and mental attributes of its representative characters. Little or no recognition is ever given to the injustice of partition or of the repression inflicted upon nationalists by the state. Neither do the stereotypes accord with the ascertainable facts about the social background of republican activists. Two sources particularly undermine the composite misrepresentation, both of which refute many stock assumptions: *Ten Years On in Northern Ireland* cites surveys of the backgrounds of those who have appeared before Diplock courts;[61] and 'Northern Ireland: Future Terrorist Trends' (November 1978), a top-secret report compiled by General J.M. Glover which was intercepted by the Provos and published in *Republican News*.[62] Again, I will draw attention to these where applicable in the study.

Perhaps the nearest parallel in genre fiction of the biased representation of Irish republicans is to be found in the fictional depiction of Native Americans in the Western. Writing in 1978, J. Bowyer Bell commented that 'the common reader is not yet ready for a politically successful 'terrorist' organization as once he was not for the good Red Indian'.[63] The genre of the Western was established as early as the mid-19th century.[64] John Sutherland notes Zane Grey's 'loathing of trade unionism, particularly the 'Wobblies'... [and that] Westerns are traditionally conservative in their political philosophy'.[65] The reader is perhaps familiar with the following composite: the subhuman redskin, a war-painted savage who grunts in a truncated translation – 'heap big medicine man' – whooping and scalping while under the added indignity of a mock Indian name, such as 'Indian Two Feet' or 'Little Chief'.[66] Historically, the diversity of Native American cultures[67] is written out of this account, and instead, the civilising role of the white settler is highlighted.

Racism, then, in the sense of a dehumanising characterisation, is a common denominator linking the fictional portrayal of the Native American and the Irish republican. The dehumanising of any group – whether this is pursued in terms of perceived racial difference and supposed inferiority, whether of class, gender, nationality, religion, political belief – is a means of perpetuating unequal power relations and maintaining the 'system', however defined.

At its most acute, and such was the case in regard to the treatment of Native Americans, the process of dehumanisation may function to justify or mask genocide,[68] a charge which has also been levelled at Britain for its treatment historically of the native Irish. The analogy between the plight of the Native American in fiction and that of Irish republicans is strong, except that the near-genocide of the 'Indians' left them little chance of resisting these misrepresentations, not that one would imagine that unfavourable fictional depictions were high on the list of their immediate concerns while struggling for survival in some wretched government reservation/concentration camp. However, the processes underlying cultural misrepresentations and exploitation are the very same, if different in scale of impact.

Any radical addressing of issues of inequality affecting politically marginalised or disempowered social groups will pose a threat to existing power structures. The role of ideology, specifically the myth of threat from the 'other', is crucial to the maintenance of disadvantage. The race card, the Orange card, reds under the bed, moral panics (whether against AIDS sufferers or single mothers) – these are familiar strategies to harness prejudice and to divide and nullify opposition and thus help to preserve the status quo, or to ensure that change is minimised, cosmetic, and that the underlying inequalities and disparities of wealth and opportunity, seemingly so structurally necessary to capitalism, will continue.

As I mentioned on page one, Franz Fanon asserted that '[i]t is the racist who creates the inferior', paraphrasing Sartre's comment that '[i]t is the anti-Semite who makes the Jew'.[69] In the realm of Troubles fiction, an identical dehumanising process helps to shape public opinion about Irish republicanism. To again invoke John B. Thompson's suggestive phrase, 'ideology… is meaning in the service of power'.[70] It is in this understanding that popular fiction is an ideological instrument. John Sutherland argues, for example, that the

> best-seller expresses and feeds certain needs in the reading public. It consolidates prejudice, provides comfort, is therapy, offers vicarious reward or stimulus. In some socially controlled circumstances it may also indoctrinate or control a population's ideas on politically sensitive subjects.[71]

An author may be unaware that his or her narrative line and character typology reveal deep-seated racism. However, the prevalence of anti-Irish stereotyping in much of the fiction discussed in this study at the very least implies the pervasiveness of racism within British society in general.

The thriller genre has been described as an updating of the morality tale. The profundity of nursery rhymes, myths and legends is credited to their hidden moral thrust, their warning against the breaking of social constraints, codes and taboos. The basic imperative of such tales is didactic. They function as a means of instilling values and respect for a given authority. In the thriller, society's moral centre is threatened. The power and authority vested in that moral centre, unlike in our lived experience of the world, must always prevail. Paradoxically, this is one of the reassuring conventions of the genre, but narrative tension requires this social equilibrium to appear vulnerable from a deviant source for change. Hence the need for the hero, the provider of the eleventh hour solution, to rise to the challenge. In the finale, timed for maximum suspense, the *status quo ante* is ultimately restored.

The IRA is the big, bad 'other' of the modern British morality tale. The conventional, set piece confrontations between good and evil, hero and villain, capitalism and communism, West and East, in Troubles fiction translate into the battle between the forces of law, order and civilisation on the one hand, and on the other, the deviancy and chaos attributed to the Provos. Reduced thus to its absolute underpinnings, and because good triumphs in the denouement, the message is encoded that good will always prevail; evil will never out – a reassuring message in an anxious world, with the reader identifying vicariously with the moral victors.

The lurid characterisations of republicans at times do suggest a crossover into another generic field: Gothic horror. Stephen King has written that

> the horror genre has often been able to find *national phobic pressure points* [my italics]... to play upon and express fears which exist across a wide spectrum of people. Such fears, which are often political, economic, and psychological rather than supernatural, give the best works of horror a pleasing allegorical feel.[72]

King's fertile notion of 'national phobic pressure points' has a parallel in a recent academic study of popular fiction. Homi Bhabha is cited as arguing that the prevalence of stereotypes indicates a problem of representation, and is understandable as both a product and reflection of cultural anxiety.[73] Bhabha's view is one of several theoretical ideas which inform my approach to an explanation, and which together offer an alternative to what might be termed liberal pluralist explanations, that is, from the dominant ideological standpoint that existing political institutions and practices have the capacity to protect the rights of all and are capable of representing all legitimate interests. The limitations of Troubles fiction, generally speaking, are analogous to the inadequacies of those same power relations to give adequate expression to the needs of the weakest in society. The disempowered, the marginalised, all who face discrimination and exclusion, are in essence under-represented, like the voices not heard, or insufficiently allowed expression, or mischaracterised in many examples of the genre. Democratising the genre, striving for inclusivity, is a political as well as an aesthetic quest.

In Troubles fiction the slippage from reality is so routine, the resort to stereotypes so corruptive of the truth, that a comprehensive, theoretically grounded explanation is demanded. This does require a (mercifully) brief discussion of some quite difficult social and cultural theory.

Contending discourses

I will argue from the cultural materialist perspective that different ways of understanding the world are tied to particular political interests, and of how contesting discourses are at play for cultural supremacy.[74] The ideas of the Italian Marxist Antonio Gramsci (1891-1937) and subsequent poststructural interpretations and elaborations of these by cultural studies scholars, such as Terry Eagleton, are formative in this approach. Terry Eagleton explains that 'ideology is a discursive or semiotic phenomenon', a materialist approach that looks at how definitions and 'meaning' are constructed within language, contested at a social level in the play of signs.[75]

The first principles of semiology, the science of signs, were propounded by the Swiss linguist Ferdinand de Saussure.[76] Saussure demonstrated that there is no absolute, one to one correspondence between sign and referent: the words 'tree' and 'arbre', to give his famous example, are signs conceptualising the same physical object. Saussure's recognition of the dual nature of the sign as symbol (signifier) and concept (signified) allowed later exponents to elaborate an objective appraisal of how meanings are culturally generated. Because the relation between symbol and concept is arbitrary, different language groups, and different 'dialects' within the same language groups, have their own words to convey the same signified. The materiality of the signifier, however (for example, the printed word), exists on a temporally different plane from the signified, which as meaning (significance) is prone to a much faster culturally-driven changeability. Words change, and meanings change, but meanings may change more quickly than words. This important principle is the foundation of the poststructuralist understanding that meaning is a matter of cultural negotiation within language, where meanings are generated in relation to one another and where none is fixed. However, this suggests a sort of free market of cultural exchange and change, and doesn't explain the dominance of certain interests over others, and asymmetries of power and influence.

A starting point towards an explanation is afforded through the alignment of various concepts. Particularly pertinent are Louis Althusser's concepts of 'ideological state apparatuses' and 'interpellation'.

According to Althusser, 'ideological state apparatuses', such as the legal and education systems, the church, the media and mass culture, the institution of the family, are the means through which the dominant ideology is validated, and social consensus and the legitimation of the social order achieved. These 'ideological apparatuses' disseminate the dominant account of how things are, and organise compliance with, and thus help to perpetuate, ruling-class dominance. The ideological power invested in this process carries the capacity to name, to define, to set the agenda, to occlude, marginalise and exclude.

Althusser argued that ideology functions by 'interpellating' the subjectivity of the individual in and through language, that is, by 'addressing' or 'hailing' the subject to its side; the individual is persuaded, won-over, by the authoritative, defining voice of the dominant ideas in society. Interpellation is 'a structural feature of all ideology'.[77] In this reckoning, the act of opening a work of popular fiction is equivalent to the persuasive salesman's foot in the door.

Althusser is of further interest in having posited two formalistic effects within discourses, two discursive strategies geared to the construction of meaning: 'closure' and 'fixation'. Closure is a marking-off of discursive territory, of what can and cannot be discussed; fixation is the fixing of meaning, of defining the authoritative terms of debate. These discursive effects make meaning stick, to use John B. Thompson's phrase. Within this field of explanation, ideology is understood to be an accumulative effect within discourses of the prevailing body of conventional wisdom: the interpellating text persuades the reader of the authority of its position as mediated through the strategies of closure and fixation. Ideology, that is, 'meaning in the service of power', becomes common sense. The subjectivity of the individual, by extension, group subjectivity, is shaped within the social interplay of discourses.

Althusser did not claim specifically that fiction is an ideological apparatus, 'but his concept of 'interpellation' has been widely applied to the study of popular fiction'.[78] Popular fiction, in this understanding, isn't a primary site of ideology, like, for example, the educational system; it is a secondary area. The significance of this body of ideas for an understanding of the inherent bias found in Troubles fiction, is that in a poststructuralist analysis Gramsci's concept of hegemony, according to Ashley, 'suggests a distinctive role for fiction in the maintenance of bourgeois dominance and also, potentially, for its subversion'.[79] Roger Bromley is cited as a cultural theorist who argues from a Gramscian base that 'popular fiction has a particular work to do in the maintenance and struggle for hegemony'.[80]

Ideological state apparatuses are privileged because powerful in the structural task of interpellating the subjectivisation of the individual. However, it should be noted that Althusser's concept suggests a deterministic role for ideology with little or no capacity for individual and collective agency. As Bob Ashley explains, 'no single class interest can secure the lasting and unchanging consent of all other groups; hegemony is thus constantly renegotiated and constitutes, Gramsci insisted, "a moving equilibrium".'[81] For Gramsci, it is through 'hegemonic apparatuses', working within civil society, that the dominant ideology becomes habitual and accepted as 'common sense'. In his *Prison Notebooks*, he argued that the 'strangely composite' nature of common sense – the often incoherent and contradictory sets of ideas, whose roots ('an infinity of traces') we are largely unaware of, which we use to make sense of and explain reality – also offers the potential for human agency as the individual transcends common sense with more probing and coherent sets of social explanations in order to truly understand who and what we are, where we are situated historically, and of where our true interests lie.[82]

The 'unstable' nature of hegemony, mediated through discourse, makes it always subject to cultural contention at the level of utterance, the social practice of language. Meaning is contested, and organised in 'historically specific discourses' in service to political, social and economic interests. Therefore, it is argued, language 'becomes an important site of political struggle'.[83] As Chris Weedon succinctly argues, 'discourses represent political interests and in consequence are constantly vying for status and power. The site of this battle for power is the subjectivity of the individual'.[84]

Discourses, which may be considered as dialects within same-language communities, have their own sets of signifiers, radically fixing meaning to the shared signifiers of that same-language community. To give a highly pertinent example, 'terrorists', as applied and understood as a fitting description of the IRA within one discourse becomes a tabloid slur in another discourse within which the IRA would be regarded as 'freedom fighters'. Consider too the different significations given to words such as 'democracy' and 'paratrooper'.[85] Differing interpretations are at play, then, over the same words and different terms are marshalled to affix a contested meaning, for example, 'the principle of consent' versus that of 'national self-determination' (particularly troublesome and loaded terms in the context of political debate on sovereignty in regard to the Good Friday Agreement). Another localised semantic distinction underpins the ascription of 'sectarian' and 'racist' to the nature of the violence here; to describe an attack as 'sectarian' may support the view of the conflict as based on tribal division, thus signifying a parity of culpability ('one side is as bad as the other') which tends to let Britain off the hook, while 'racist' would signal that the resort to violence is designed to perpetuate domination, specifically Orange supremacism, which successive British administrations have turned their backs on in the spirit of 'divide and conquer'.

We all share the same language but not the same meanings; and 'precisely because it forms the common basis of all discursive formations,... [language] becomes the medium of ideological conflict'.[86] In this understanding, unionism and Irish republicanism are traditions of thought inhabiting separate discourses, each drawing on the same linguistic resources but attaching conflicting significance to elements of those resources in line with its own set of cultural, economic and political interests and experience.

The notion of discursive difference is well if ironically configured in the following passage from the novel *Ordinary Decent Criminals* by the American author Lionel Shriver. Like Alice through the looking-glass, Shriver wonders over the seeming incompatibility yet 'essential integrity' of the North's opposing viewpoints:

> The North as an object was an ingenious curio which from one side appeared an ostrich; another, a postman; another, a washing machine. That's why arguments never went anywhere: each picture was true.[87]

Here expressed, then, is the perspective of an at times bemused outsider into our seemingly peculiar political mess, in which the protagonists – Provos, loyalists, unionists, the Irish, the British – are reducible to their exclusive discourses, each clinging vehemently to inherited certainties and to the assertion of their categorically opposed worldviews. Truth, like dust, it seems, is in the eyes of the beholder, and the beholder comprehends the world distortedly or partially.

By the light afforded in this scenario, advocates of a united Ireland will argue that 'Northern Ireland' is a political malformation, a fixed deck rigged to perpetuate inequality no matter what the electoral reshuffle. All constitutional nationalist political parties, North and South, adhere nominally to the principle of reunification of the national territory, though differing with Sinn Féin that violence may be justified in its pursuit. The overriding concern of the political establishment in the South, however, as it has been since partition, is containment, that is, to prevent the North's troubles seeping southward.[88]

Conversely, unionism's bottom line is the assumed democratic integrity of its majority. Theirs is a perverse variation on 'the end of ideology' theory in that 1920 (the year in which the Government of Ireland Act came into force) established the Year Dot, with all preceding history redundant, and no longer a source of precedent and example.[89] British governments, meanwhile, though deeply embroiled as sovereign power nevertheless posture an aloofness, asserting that they occupy the 'moral high ground', from which all the better to sit in judgement over the 'ancient enmities' of two warring tribes.

Moreover, Britain's role as sovereign power over the North with all its centralised, international and clandestine resources, gave and continues to give it a massive start in promoting and propagating a view of the situation in line with its own interests, whether strategic, economic or political. There is a discursive process at play which advantages those with the better resources. The manner in which a particular aspect of the world is perceived becomes the received wisdom due to this advantage.

The same weight, then, is not carried by each discursive position. There are asymmetries and inequalities in the distribution of power and influence in society which reflect the interests of dominant groups. Power-relations are embedded in language, but power is exercised in more direct, concrete relations. Gramsci employed the term 'hegemony' to describe the desired outcome of the various means by which governments construct the consent of those they govern, as distinguished from obedience based on subjugation. Civil society – the church, the media, schools and universities, the institution of the family, newspapers, multifarious civil associations, etc. – binds individuals to the ruling power by consent rather than by coercion. 'Hegemony' differs from 'ideology' in Gramsci's use of the terms in that ideology may be forcibly imposed.[90]

In 'Northern Ireland' the unionists did, in fact, attempt to impose their political outlook. The Special Powers Act, introduced in April 1922, was in force throughout the Stormont years, being made permanent in 1933. Besides the powers to intern, flog, and to impose curfews, one provision of the Act banned the publication and distribution of republican literature. As Michael Farrell has commented, if these draconian measures were not enough, the unionist government also introduced the Public Order Act (1951) and the Flags and Emblems Act (1954),[91] the latter designed to coerce nationalists into abandoning their allegiance to an Irish identity and aspirations for reunification. The often-repeated phrase 'unionist hegemony' (in Gramsci's strict use of 'hegemony') would therefore, in this understanding, be misapplied. Unionists never achieved in the fifty years of their political domination the 'desired outcome' of hegemony, as the history of republican and nationalist opposition, at times violent, attests. The term hegemony, nevertheless, is serviceable for explaining the preponderance outside of Ireland, until recent years, of an understanding of the situation in the North broadly in line with successive British governments' policies, though an understanding not necessarily sympathetic, per se, to unionism.

Britain's highly partial and partisan view had achieved hegemonic status up until, arguably, the 1980s, when a more questioning attitude internationally was roused by what was widely regarded as Britain's intransigent stand on the 1981 Hunger Strike. The power of the British diplomatic mission contributed significantly, as the often first recourse for information, to the creation of the image internationally of the conflict. Britain invested huge resources of money and manpower into propagating to the world its view of the Hunger Strike, particularly via its embassies. Significant political progress would only begin to be made once Sinn Féin effectively challenged Britain's discourse on 'criminalisation'. An additional factor in the weakening of the British discourse was, as Jack Holland points out, 'the growing access that the Irish diplomatic service had to the editorial rooms of major newspapers like the *New York Times* and the *Los Angeles Times*' from the late 1970s onwards.[92] The Irish government had only begun international diplomacy at the end of 1969, and therefore found themselves at a huge disadvantage though, as I have indicated, its priorities throughout were 'containment'. However, the British discourse became more subject to contestation as a complex consequence of the Hunger Strike's aftermath; the defeat of Britain's 'criminalisation' policy, Sinn Féin's growing electoral success, revelations about miscarriages of justice and of dirty tricks, all stem back to the resurgence of resistance resulting from the deaths of the ten hunger strikers, occasioning a discursive shift which has continued to the present, and which, as I will argue in this study, resonated within and through the field of popular fiction. Contradictory or competing moral discourses are held by their respective authors and by their targeted readerships. In much of Troubles fiction the dominant discourse is antipathetic to Irish republicanism.

One commentator has elaborated a definition of discourse that encompasses genres within its comprehension: 'Genres are quasi-objective discourse types generally recognised by a language community or some group within that community'.[93] Troubles fiction in general formally conforms to this description, and the privileged discourse instilled from the genre's inception does not easily translate to a sensibility nurtured from within an oppositional perspective.

Rather than conceive, then, of external pressure for the discursive bias of the genre, despite some evidence of such, it is perhaps more fruitful to register the wider cultural imperatives acting independently and collectively to shape wider, societal perceptions. The register ought also to essentially encompass the role of the reader, what the reader as an interpreting agent brings to the reading, and his or her discursive engagement with the text. This approach might help to explain the uneven reception of Troubles fiction, that despite its indubitable popularity, why much of the output of Troubles fiction is simply not taken seriously by readers more familiar with its narrative context and who consequently cannot abandon the critical distance necessary to go with the narrative flow. And conversely, readers who accept at face value the British line on the conflict, if only for the lack of an alternative, will resist or find novels far-fetched that step outside of the cosy certainties they are used to and for which the genre has predominantly catered. There is always an opportunity cost in terms of truth when public awareness is biased in favour of one explanation to the exclusion of alternative viewpoints. The difference, again, is that with regard to the former a direct comparison with their experience of reality is on offer, while the latter have few objective points of reference to substantiate or refute the official version of events. As Tony Bennett argues,

> the ground on which the text produces its effects consists not of naked subjectivities but of individuals interpellated into particular subject positions within a variety of different – and sometimes contradictory – ideological formations. This further entails recognizing that such positions vary in accordance with consideration of race, class and gender and, concerning their insertion within the system of intertextual relations, on the degree to which, within the educational apparatus, the institution of Literature has borne upon their ideological formation, upon their positioning as readers.[94]

This understanding brings to the fore the contribution of human agency. Subjectivity is 'neither unified or fixed'. Moments of heightened social tension expose conflicts of interest in which a process of questioning occurs, producing 'conflicting subject positions for the individuals involved'.[95] The content and themes of Troubles fiction operate at different levels: often at a crude propagandistic level – the illustration of the concerns of a particular discursive position; but also, and largely unwittingly in terms of an author's role, at a level equivalent to Gramscian 'common sense'. But a crisis of hegemony is reflected in more adventurous, radical, questioning narratives, and arguably also incurs a more questioning readership which in turn loops causatively back into the publishing and distributive fields where largely commercial concerns and decisions can be expected to correspond to changing public perceptions.

The genre spins on dualities: good versus evil, white versus black, 'the free world' versus 'the evil empire', the bi-polar territory of propaganda. Troubles' thrillers fit the mould with their Manichean certainties. There are, as in all genres, variations and transformations, and even honourable attempts to resist and perhaps expand on straitjacketed values. But the overwhelming bulk of novels dealing with the conflict in the North conform slavishly to the formally required simplicity.

Now, if balance were in evidence, reflected in an even-handed and measured appraisal of republicanism in a significant number of instances, and issuing a more exacting probe into the nature of Britain's role in Anglo-Irish difficulties, then there would be little to do other than survey Troubles fiction as a publishing phenomenon. Because, as I argue, such balance is patently lacking, such an approach would be problematic, ignoring as it would, in my view, the real impediment this output poses for awakening readers in Britain and internationally to Britain's oppressive role in Ireland. The very popularity of the genre, with the potential of the best-seller to reach a world-wide readership, can give it a free run in the propaganda stakes when no competing view is on the card. Kevin Whelan quotes fellow historian Robert Gildea: 'What matters is myth, not in the sense of fiction, but in the sense of a construction of the past elaborated by a political community for its own ends'.[96] One could add that the external construction of our understanding of the present is also a remorseless affair, and that Troubles fiction contributes its share to the misrepresentation.

Outline of chapters

Since my topic requires essentially a comparison of representation and reality (as perceived from within the lived experience of this Irish republican), each chapter will open with a summary of the most pertinent developments, setbacks and changes relevant, while drawing a comparison with the unfolding of contemporary events. I have opted for a chronological rather than a thematic approach. As I will attempt to show, Troubles fiction demonstrates the paramountcy of one discursive position in regard to the conflict. Other discourses are at play, and the dominant one has been increasingly under challenge since the early 1980s. The book is structured in an attempt to relate the struggle and role of hegemony to market and fictional trends and to illustrate the changing state of discursive struggle.

In Chapter Two I discuss pre-1970 fiction, most of which was from Irish authors, to determine whether there were any signs of the impending storm, and to discern the derivation of later narrative conventions and tropes.

Chapters Three and Four deal respectively with the periods 1970-1972 and 1973-1975 inclusive. In the earlier period, two factors are striking: the contemporaneity of the fiction; and that more writers from outside of Ireland are represented. 1973 in particular marks the beginning, in quantitative terms, of a publishing phenomenon. An anti-republican discourse was firmly entrenched in the fiction of the latter period.

The focus of Chapter Five (1976-1981) is on the impact of the IRA's bombing offensive in England and the escalation of anti-Irish racism, as evidenced by the publication of many of the most vicious portrayals of the IRA. The genre was accorded some academic interest.

Chapter Six (1982-1987) deals with the changing fortunes of the genre in the aftermath of the Hunger Strikes, Sinn Féin's consequent electoral popularity, the Anglo-Irish Agreement, the increase in the number of women writing, and an increase in the output of film and television drama about the conflict.

Chapter Seven (1988-1993) covers the 1988 slump, the launch of Sinn Féin's peace strategy, the growing input of Irish writers to the genre, the intensification of the IRA's military offensive, the counter to revisionism, and contributing to this, the emergence of republicans publishing fiction. The period ends with the signing of the Downing Street Declaration.

Chapter Eight (1994-1999) brings the account up to date. I discuss the changes in the genre following the ceasefires of 1994, Canary Wharf, and the Good Friday Agreement.

The primary concern of this book is to demonstrate that the bulk of the output conforms to, is informed by, a view of the world in line with a partisan, dominant political discourse. My concern in Chapter Nine is to try to explain how, why and whether the genre's discursive bias is a product of political and commercial pressures. The focus, in other words, will be on the mechanics of a process. From a poststructuralist vantage I will summarise the role of popular fiction in the struggle for hegemony.

2.
A Morbid State: 1960-69

[…]the old is dying and the new cannot be born; in this interregnum a great variety of morbid symptoms appear. (Antonio Gramsci)

It could be said that 'Northern Ireland' was born old: the progeny of grey men, intolerant of change, hitched to the fading certainties and tarnished glory of a British empire already in terminal decline. The statelet was run in a manner to permanently exclude the Catholic/nationalist population from power. Moreover, the formation of the statelet was conceived to give effect to this very intention.[1] Asked why Stormont in January 1946 refused 'one man one vote' in local elections, the Unionist Chief Whip Major L.E. Curran replied that it was to prevent 'Nationalists getting control of the three border counties and Derry City'. Such people, he went on, did not have 'the welfare of the people of Ulster at heart', and the best way to prevent them overthrowing the government was to disenfranchise them.[2] Whenever nationalists refused to acquiesce to Orange supremacy and organised to oppose the injustices of partition, repression was unionism's knee-jerk reaction. Internment was introduced in every decade of the statelet's morbid existence.

The fixity of periodisation in regard to when the Troubles are claimed to have started masks continuities with the past outlined above, for the unionist tradition is loath to accept that discrimination and repression motivated nationalist resistance. A further continuity is evidenced in that a mere seven years separate the official ending of the IRA's Border Campaign in February 1962 and the events of August 1969. This span of time seems like an interlude when considered beside the thirty years, at the time of writing, that have since passed. When one recalls that those seven years of 'peace' were punctuated by incidents of major civil unrest such as the Divis Street Riots of October 1964, and the activities of the re-emergent UVF (Ulster Volunteer Force), then an appreciation of the chronic condition of the artificial entity known as Northern Ireland is further accentuated. The UVF carried out a number of sectarian killings and bombings in response to the imagined threat from resurgent republicanism around the 50th anniversary of the Easter Rising, the most notorious incident being the Malvern Street shooting of June 1966, in which a young Catholic barman was killed. However, the claim of threat from the IRA was a phantom in the minds of loyalist fundamentalists largely concocted to further their political ends by seeking to thwart any notion of reform.

In fact, the republican movement had shifted direction after the failure of the Border Campaign. In 1967, at the annual Bodenstown commemoration, Cathal Goulding, the IRA's Chief of Staff at the time, had urged a turn from the physical force tradition to agitational and constitutional means to achieve the movement's goals.[3] Among republicans there was a distinct gravitation towards the Left, into the tackling of social issues. The movement redirected much of its energies into the nascent civil rights campaign, a development that alarmed unionists but, as Bob Purdie has argued, unionist fears were ill-founded.

> Republicans and Communists were centrally involved in the creation of the [civil rights] movement and that the main civil rights organisation, the Northern Civil Rights Association, originated in a proposal from a Republican group. However, [this article] shows that the evidence does not bear out Unionist assumptions about the subversive intentions of the movement.[4]

The main influences for reform, particularly the call for 'one man, one vote' in local government elections, were externally generated. Perhaps the most significant was the example of the civil rights struggle in the USA. There was no IRA to speak of upon which unionists might allocate blame for the malaise. As mounting political realities further exposed the irreformable nature of the state, the 1960s ended in perhaps the worst violence in the North's history.

The abiding images from the late-Sixties are of the television coverage of RUC men batoning and hosing defenceless civil rights demonstrators, of the 'Battle of the Bogside', and of sectarian confrontations as the North exploded, particularly Belfast and Derry. As Eamonn McCann attests, the early reportage in the British press was at first quite sympathetic regarding the plight of nationalists.[5] Attitudes were to change, though, once the short-lived honeymoon ended between nationalists and the British Army (who arrived on the 14 August 1969). In the British press increasingly blame was directed at republicans for the deteriorating situation despite the fact that the IRA was all but defunct as a military force at this stage.[6] It would later emerge that the UVF were behind much of the escalation in violence, including the bombing of the Silent Valley Reservoir in April, 1969. However, their role in fuelling the tension received little attention in the media. Instead, blame was directed at the IRA – precisely the UVF's intent.

With hindsight we can now apprehend the chasmic depth of the political and social unease ready to explode. However, to read the comments of critics and social observers of the day, one might be forgiven for thinking that a tacit conspiracy existed to downplay the significance of the simmering tensions – a forlorn hope, given the power of television to internationalise a hitherto-contained local problem.

To what extent were these undercurrents and incidents registered in fiction? It is a telling fact that the scattered references to the IRA in the fiction of the 1960s prior to 1969 are usually derisory and mocking. Republicans were exemplified as embittered failures, often physically and emotionally crippled, and not to be taken seriously as a threat to the state. There is really no hint that they posed a tangible threat to the political order of the day. In this respect, the fictionalised account was accurate.

Did writers forewarn of the coming crisis? The evidence is equivocal. John Cronin, in an article entitled 'Ulster's Alarming Novels', criticised local authors for failing in their writing to transcend 'Northern Ireland's dreary doctrinal duality' – a vain cry for an ameliorative 'Ulster' voice, Cronin apparently believing somehow that the North was reformable and could work as a political entity.[7] The poet Michael Longley, in his 'Introduction' to *Causeway: The Arts in Ulster*, cited Brian Moore and Maurice Leitch as examples of novelists who, in his view, warned heedlessly of the gathering storm.[8] Both writers undoubtedly did convey in their work of this period a mood of stultifying unease and social stagnation. However, relatively few novels dealing with the local socio-political realities were published prior to 1969, too few to form a firm opinion as to the weight of their impact on the shaping of public perceptions.

Market factors may assist in explaining the apparent tardy response of local writers to unfolding events. Neil Jordan commented in *New Fiction* (October 1976) that 'in Ireland for some years now it has been almost impossible to publish a novel through the normal channels. Publishers wouldn't touch fiction, saying it doesn't sell etc'.[9] Compared with the phenomenal outpouring of novels with a Troubles theme to appear later, particularly from 1973 onwards, during the 1960s very few examined the subject as then manifest, other than as a peripheral anxiety about change, often unwittingly expressed.

I have managed to collate details on seventeen novels and three short stories written during the period, of which only ten novels and the short stories are strictly relevant in terms of the extent of their focus on contemporary realities. I will begin this critical history by discussing in chronological order six of these – five novels and a short story[10] – which from differing angles and focus illuminate the political and social mood in Ireland in the 1960s up to the widespread public disorder in the North of August 1969, when the British Army appeared on Irish streets, an event which by popular consensus marked the beginning of the contemporary phase of the Troubles. Additionally, I briefly mention one category (d) novel, David Lodge's *The British Museum's Falling Down*.[11]

The range of stereotypes encountered in the fiction of the 1960s to the present shows an emulative descent from certain influential novels written in the 1920s and 1930s, each of which was subsequently filmed, therefore further shaping contemporary and later perceptions of anti-Treaty republicanism: Liam O'Flaherty's *The Informer* (1925) was filmed in 1935; F.L. Green's *Odd Man Out* (1945), in 1947; and Rearden Conner's *Shake Hands with the Devil* (1933), in 1960. Both O'Flaherty and Green refer to the 'Revolutionary Organization' rather than to the IRA. Each conceptualises a collective political and social movement in which their characters have roles. This macro focus at the level of generic 'Organisation' would later, from the mid-1970s onwards, be generally occluded by a narrow and narrowing attention to stereotypes operating externally of the scantiest delineation of wider political forces.

In O'Flaherty's *The Informer*, two interesting types are met. Commandant Dan Gallagher, according to 'the leading organ of the English aristocracy', had trained for the priesthood before his expulsion from an ecclesiastical seminary.[12] He is depicted as a fatally glamorous figure, and women are seduced by 'the web of his conspiracies [and] by the deadly fascination of his face and of his voice, by the romance of his life'.[13] Meanwhile, the corruption and malignancy of Frankie McPhillip, whom Gypo Nolan informs on, is externalised thus:

> His right leg opened outwards in a curve below the knee and he placed the toe
> of his right foot on the ground before the heel when he walked, so that his
> walk had the crouching appearance of a wild animal stalking in the forest.[14]

The author and historian Peter Berresford Ellis goes even further back, citing an Edgar Wallace short story, 'The Man Called McGinnice', published in *Everybody's Magazine* (1918), with a plot involving an IRA squadron flying with the Imperial German Air Force. IRA squadron leader McGinnice 'delights in shooting up his compatriots, the Irish Fusiliers (sic) while, at the same time dropping leaflets to them urging them to 'rise up and destroy the Saxon''.[15] It appears that in Wallace's fervently imperialist imagination the IRA were a force to be reckoned with some eighteen months before the start of the War of Independence.

Harry Patterson, the author of the earliest work in this survey, *Cry of the Hunter* (1960),[16] seems indebted to these dated sources of representation (as does John Broderick, whose novel *The Fugitives* is examined below).

Patterson is more familiar, perhaps, in his regular guise of Jack Higgins. He has also written under the names Martin Tallon, Hugh Marlowe and James Graham.[17] He was born in England in 1929, though raised from the age of two in Belfast where his mother was from originally. They returned to England when he was twelve. In an interview with the critic Ciaran Carty, Higgins relates what must have been quite a traumatic incident from his Belfast childhood which one would suppose helped to shape his attitude to Ireland and perhaps, too, explains the consistency of his interest in the Troubles as a context for his novels.

> When people go on about the Troubles, I say what the hell do you think
> was happening in Belfast in the 1930s. I can remember as a child peering
> around a corner and seeing people being driven out with all their
> belongings, what we'd now call ethnic cleansing.[18]

Within a decade Patterson would become the most prolific writer of thrillers with a Troubles theme or connection, a record he has maintained to date, having published at least seventeen using the Jack Higgins moniker alone. John Sutherland explains that a number of British authors 'had been forced to the expedient of writing under different names finding, as they do, that they need more than one novel a year to live and that the public will not take more than one novel a year from a single identifiable author'.[19] Patterson in fact struggled as a writer until the success in America of his 1976 thriller, *The Eagle Has Landed* (Jack Higgins), after which his previously published novels 'began to rise from the grave in droves'.[20]

Also interesting, in view of what it reveals about market pressures and the appeal of the genre, *Cry of the Hunter* was reissued in 1979 with no mention that the novel's narrative period was the late 1950s, as if the plot dealt with the contemporary Troubles and not the IRA's Border Campaign, which started in December 1956 and officially ended in February 1962. Few reading the later edition would have been aware of its earlier provenance, so successfully does the narrative transpose to the reductive representations devotees of the genre might anticipate during the late 1970s. As John Sutherland notes, there is

> no assurance that the contents of a paperback are as new as its cover. Often it is in the interest of the paperback publisher to blur over any... embarrassing bibliographical facts and encourage thoughtless impulse buying. A glossy paperback may well enclose an old exhausted body resuscitated because the author has some current publicity.[21]

In *Cry of the Hunter*, Patterson employs a narrative device that he is often to return to: drawing a contrast between an older, more humane and honourable type of republican and a younger, unscrupulous and reckless associate. In the novel, republican hero Martin Fallon joined the IRA at seventeen, and at twenty two was 'leader of the organisation in Ulster'.[22] He is on the run in the South, having escaped from Dartmoor Prison. Reluctantly, he agrees to effect the escape of Patrick Rogan who is facing a death sentence for killing an RUC man. Like Fallon, Rogan was a leader of the organisation. Unlike Fallon, Rogan is threatening to squeal on the IRA unless an escape is facilitated: '"He's not to be trusted", O'Hara said. "It could be the end of the organisation in Ulster if he ever stands trial".'[23] However, the moral pressure on Fallon extends further. He is confronted by Rogan's mother.

> She raised her hand and gently touched his face with the tips of her fingers. The skin was drawn tightly over her bones and it was parchment yellow. She looked incredibly ancient and timeless and there was the mark of great suffering upon her face. She said, 'I've given a husband and a son to the cause, Martin Fallon. I've given enough'.[24]

Mrs. Rogan is, of course, 'Mother Ireland' laid on thick, and Fallon's resolve not to return to 'the cause' wilts as he looks into her 'vacant, useless eyes'.[25]

As reincarnated in his later Troubles fiction, the generational comparison works in a rather crude propagandistic fashion to hammer home the message of an almost unbridgeable moral gap between the Romantic idealism accredited here to a previous generation of republicans and Patterson's perception of the depravity of the present-day IRA.

Incidentally, although Martin Fallon is killed off at the end of *Cry of the Hunter*,[26] Patterson does not dispense entirely with his creation, for in *A Prayer for the Dying* (1973) Fallon is pseudonymously 'resurrected' when an IRA man on the run in England assumes the name.

The Irish novelist John Broderick (1927-89), in his 1962 novel *The Fugitives*, provides an example of the concern to examine in fiction the motivations and moral justifications for the use of violence to achieve political ends.[27] As an epigraph, Broderick quotes Blaise Pascal: 'We perceive an image of truth, and possess only a lie' – a sentiment which could well sum up the moral and political difficulties the Troubles apparently pose for writers, and perhaps readers too, of the genre.

Written before the official conclusion of the Border Campaign in 1962, the narrative concerns the killing of a Northern Ireland under-secretary in London. The novel's young Republican protagonist, Paddy Fallon, is on the run in Ireland after his involvement in the minister's assassination.[28] No operation of this magnitude was in fact carried out during the campaign's five-year duration. The inspiration for this plot incident, in terms of parity of seriousness, may have been the assassination in London in 1922 of Sir Henry Wilson, former Chief of Imperial Staff.

In the novel, Broderick makes clear his view that partition was unjust, but this perception is overshadowed by a moral anxiety over the continuing use of violence to further political goals. The author uses a veteran republican, Hugh Ward, as a vehicle to lambaste the alleged corruption of existing political arrangements. This is Ward's rationale for the use of physical force.

> What do you know of this country? And what do you care? Have you ever really given it a thought in the last ten years? Have you ever thought about it at all in the whole of your life? There hasn't been enough bloodshed and it must always be like this until we get what we are fighting for. Forty years ago men died in this country for an ideal. That ideal was a free and undivided Ireland. They have been betrayed. We are not free. We are still divided. And what is being done about it? Nothing. Who cares about the forty thousand people who are exported from this country every year like cattle? A few pious platitudes and then silence. That's all that's done about that. What have those men died for? A smug little corporation, run by a gang of professional politicians who have no interest except self-interest. They have canonised the men of Nineteen Sixteen; written them up like plaster saints in the school-books because every racket needs its martyrs. Not a day passes but one of the racketeers makes a speech about the Border. Nobody believes what they say; they don't even believe it themselves any more. Is it any wonder that Ireland to-day is the most cynical country in the world? It is, you know. I've been around and I know. None of these racketeers want the Border removed. What would happen if we had a large and powerful Protestant minority? Has anything ever really been done about a united Ireland? Aren't they only playing with words? That and a few border posts blown up, a few policemen shot. Who cares about policemen? They don't count with politicians. But now that something has really been done, what do we find? The whole of Scotland Yard working over here with the Irish Government because we dared to do

the same thing that put most of the racketeers or their fathers into power. Because for the first time something irreparable has been done. Something that they can't blow away with words.[29]

Ward's monologue evinces scant motivation other than the implied need here expressed to keep faith with an historical blood struggle: 'There hasn't been enough bloodshed and it must always be like this until we get what we are fighting for'. Also implicit is the thought that *two wrongs don't make a right*, for the author's (if not Ward's) assumption is that the corruption alluded to does not of itself legitimate the strategic use of armed force. Furthermore, in case the reader should miss the point by failing to recognise the inadequacy of the political view expressed, Ward is revealed as a semi-closeted homosexual: a 'monstrous relationship'; 'the filthy thing'.[30] Moral turpitude, as the homophobia of the period would regard homosexuality, is juxtaposed with the supposed baseness of Ward's republicanism.[31] By sleazy association, the younger republican, Paddy Fallon, is prey to the seductive guile of the veteran Ward, both politically and sexually.

Perhaps it is unfair to Broderick to say that he hadn't transcended a certain Civil War myopia regarding the legitimacy of the twenty-six counties since partition. It could be said that the novel was written from the victors' fixity of historical perspective (that is, from a liberal, constitutional perspective) that partition established that only constitutional, legal means henceforth would be valid for settling any political grievances perceived to be outstanding – another application of an 'end of ideology' finality. *The Fugitives* was written in the light of a failed IRA campaign, after all.

Like Patterson's novel, *Cry of the Hunter*, *The Fugitives* was reissued in 1976, again possibly because of its contemporary feel. Both novels feature the assassination of a leading political figure, actions more in keeping with the latter-day IRA's tactics and capacity. *The Fugitives'* underlying political message is anti-partitionist, but it also voices opposition to the use of violence, and this may have been an additional factor in the novel's republication during a particularly violent period of the last thirty years. It should be recognised, however, that while the novel offers a fair account of the political outlook of the 1950s, though one premised on a misunderstanding of the rationale for the use of violence, the republican movement underwent a sea change subsequent to and very largely as a consequence of the failure of the Border Campaign. By giving Ward a platform to expound the 'physical force' outlook, the novel proffers an apparently fair hearing to a point of view that even in its day was ridiculed by a more socially aware generation of republican activists, only then to tarnish that view by denigrating its proponent but without giving voice to the rethink then occurring within republican ranks. Ward, then is a straw man, set up to be knocked down. There is neither acknowledgement nor understanding in the novel that the very nature of extant political arrangements might thwart the pursuit of reform as a strategy for effective change. In 1962, however, Broderick's message was clear: the injustice of partition required new means towards a resolution; and in

Broderick's view the physical force tradition was as corrupt and corrupting as Hugh Ward. Therefore, at the time of the novel's reissue Ward's philosophy was even more inappropriate as a reflection of the then current republican thinking.

The poet John Montague's short story 'The Cry' is written from a Northern nationalist perspective. Published in 1963, 'The Cry' appears in Montague's *Death of a Chieftain and Other Stories* (1964).[32] Peter Douglas, a journalist in London returns on holiday to the cloying piety of his parents' rural home. His father, James, a newsagent, though 'violently anti-English' drinks cocoa from a Coronation mug, a detail the incongruity of which is in itself emblematic of the complexities of Northern identity.[33]

Peter witnesses the brutal beating of a republican suspect by B Specials. This incident sets the scene for a heated discussion between father and son – that is, between a representative of an older, perhaps more apathetic generation and the younger, better informed generation who are no longer prepared to tolerate state brutality and discrimination – on how best to raise the matter. The father, an ex-internee, argues that 'force only recognises greater force'.[34] By extension, because nationalists apparently lack the physical means to effectively counter state oppression, the father is defeatist. Peter believes that Gandhi's example of 'moral protest' is the way forward.

To this end Peter decides to investigate the incident, then write an article for publication in London. This would represent the cry of the title, 'logical but passionate', that would expose the discrimination and brutality experienced by Northern nationalists.[35] Of course, a cry also suggests hurt and a despairing appeal. The short story does, indeed, end on a plaintive note when Peter, by now wavering in his resolution to publish the exposé, is confronted by the stereotypical village idiot brandishing a placard with the scrawled message 'nosy Parker go home'.[36]

While 'The Cry' is an early evocation of the brewing storm, and prophetic in its recognition that change would necessitate an external spotlight of publicity, there is also an ambivalence detectable about the likelihood of change, in that efforts to highlight the endemic discrimination founder on nationalist apathy as much as fear.

A generational theme is also apparent in Maurice Leitch's novel *The Liberty Lad* (1965).[37] The central character is a young Protestant teacher, Frank Glass. The County Antrim-born author, a former primary school teacher and until 1988 a BBC radio producer, has written several fine novels, chiefly preoccupied with examining Protestant identity.

The only republican to be referred to in *The Liberty Lad* is the brother of the clubfoot barman Brendan, who 'went across the water when suspected of having been mixed up with the IRA'.[38] Mention of a clubfoot recalls McPhillip's infirmity in O'Flaherty's *The Informer*, a descriptive device suggestive of an externalised malignancy, which subsequently has often been employed in the genre. By proxy, Brendan appears to represent an infirm, fugitive nationalism constituting no palpable threat to the existing order. That order does appear under threat, however, but through lack of forward momentum rather than nationalist agitation. There is an overwhelming sense in the novel of a stagnant provincialism.

The following excerpt, in which Frank Glass visits his father's place of work, can be read as a metaphor for the decline of unionism's authority: 'For the first time I really understood why the mill *must* close down, why it was useless for this ludicrous garrison of old done men to continue holding on'.[39]

Leitch expands on the image; Frank senses that his father would prefer to be left alone

> with his little forgotten band, his tiny brigade. He might even like it here, [Frank]... thought; his castle, his fortress. I had to force my way in here. I wasn't welcome. Visitors from the outside – the real world – weren't welcome here'.[40]

And it is to that outside world that Frank is drawn; and, we sense from the novel, so were a generation of young, educated Protestants uneasy with the sectarianism inscribed in the status quo, searching for an identity against the background of the North's uncertain future. If Frank remains, the price of advancement in his career is to wheedle up to the homosexual unionist politician Bradley. *The Liberty Lad* was banned in the South of Ireland because of its homosexual theme.[41] Again revealing current attitudes, homosexuality is used as a metaphor for the corruption of the local political scene, with its Orange Order machinations and Masonic handshakes. Bradley equals power; Glass senior represents an exploited, deluded class betrayed by Bradley's. Unionism's historical strength has been its capacity to weld classes together in an arrangement which gave a degree of reflected privilege and prestige to the Protestant working class.

In a further illuminating passage, indicating some sympathy for the plight of Catholics, if patronising in tone, Frank nevertheless appears to misunderstand the nationalist community's relationship to history.

> I began to think about Catholics, not about Catholics I know because I don't really know any, but about them in general. Anything I found out about them has been second-hand, because, living in a community like this, one where the proportions are seventy-five for us, twenty-five for them (an inflammable mixture) division starts early – separate housing estates, then separate schools, separate jobs, separate dances, separate pubs... a people with a past and no interest in the present, because they have been frog-marched back to that past so often that they have long ago given up any claims to right now. A musical, entertaining people (like the Jews) with no neurosis about cleanliness or material wealth... I envy them their calm, inner knowledge of what they are, who they are and where they come from, but not their degrading struggle to keep dignity in a country dedicated to keeping them 'in their place'.[42]

The assertion of the unionist trope that nationalists dwell in the past, having 'given up any claims to right now', was unfortunately timed given that the Civil Rights campaign lay just over the horizon. During the then forty five years' history of the statelet, nationalists had never conceded on their demand for civil equality; on the contrary, nationalists charged unionists with being prisoners of their own siege mentality. Nationalists were *excluded* from any benefits which partition bestowed. If nationalists were in time to outnumber unionists, the logic of the electoral numbers game established by partition dictated that nationalists would be confined to tightly populated electoral wards, such as Derry's Bogside and that discrimination in employment would force more nationalists to emigrate. The author, although clearly opposed to the stultifying complacency of the unionist political order, demonstrates a failure to grasp the dynamic of grievance-spurred nationalism. The passive assertion that 'division starts early' finesses away the reality that divisions were created or fostered.

Leitch is an author who provides insights into the Northern Protestant mind. John Wilson Foster, in *Forces and Themes in Ulster Fiction*, makes the point that this is the best service Northern writers have been able to perform: that they articulate the grievances of their tribe.[43] The literary influence, however, is provincial rather than parochial, in Patrick Kavanagh's formulation of the distinction; that is, the conscious adoption of a metropolitan style rather than one steeped in a localised, rooted culture. Leitch has said that he 'modelled' himself on American writers such as Hemingway, F. Scott Fitzgerald, and particularly Faulkner.[44] Leitch also admits the debt to the literary style and concerns of contemporary English authors such as Alan Sillitoe.[45] Certainly there is a sense of the anger at the conservative social climate inherited by the new generation of English writers such as Sillitoe and Stan Barstow. John Cronin draws a comparison with John Braine, whose *Room at the Top* was published in 1959.[46] *The Liberty Lad* is very much an expatriate appraisal in terms of discursive stance if not narrational location.

David Lodge's 1965 novel, *The British Museum is Falling Down*, though not dealing with events in Ireland, does afford a glimpse of how Ireland was seen from one English perspective. The novel's central theme is the impact of Catholic moral teaching in regard to birth control on the relationship of a young married couple. Again, there is the suggestion that Irish republicanism equals the past, of traditional values having little or no relevance in the modern, hedonistic Sixties. Catholicism is equated with Irish republicanism by Lodge through the very traditional Father Finbarr's ardent support for republican prisoners and, one supposes, their hidebound politics.

> The parish was indeed at least half-populated by Irish, but this was not, in Adam and Barbara's eyes, an adequate excuse for nostalgic allusions to 'Back Home' in sermons, or the sanctioning of collections in the church porch for the dependants of IRA prisoners.[47]

Jack Higgins's thriller *The Violent Enemy* was first published in 1966 as *A Candle for the Dead* (using the pen name Hugh Marlowe and published by Abelard Schuman), perhaps to milk whatever interest there was then current arising from the 50th anniversary of the Easter Rising.[48] The new title and pen name appeared with the 1969 reissue by Hodder and Stoughton, possibly to capitalise on the screen adaptation of that name of the same year. Interviewed by

Ciaran Carty, Jack Higgins has claimed that the film, starring Tom Bell as the republican hero Sean Rogan, 'was banned in the UK because it came out when the Civil Rights campaign was starting in the North'.[49] The ban indicates an extraordinary sensitivity at the time on the part of the British authorities towards any focus of attention on the North.

The plot of the novel, *The Violent Enemy*, involves the break out from prison of Sean Rogan to assist in what he thinks is a fund-raising robbery for the 'Organisation': 'Brains and brawn, that's Sean Rogan. Pound for pound, about the most dangerous man we've had in here'.[50] Higgins thus introduces this fictional rarity, a republican hero, in laudatory, almost reverential, terms. Rogan had '…the face of a soldier, a scholar perhaps. Certainly this was no criminal'.[51] Unlike his 1960 novel, *Cry of the Hunter*, the 'Organisation' now is capitalised. Although not made explicit, we understand that the IRA is meant.

Allowing that the narrative is set in 1964, it is perhaps remarkable (especially when considering the banning of the 1969 screen adaptation) that the novel was reissued in the Hunger Strike year of 1981 without any noticeable fuss, given the opinions expressed in the following two excerpts. In the first, Vanbrugh, the British army officer who helps Rogan escape, consults Rogan's file:

> England's the only country in the civilised world that doesn't make special provision for political offenders, did you know that, Sergeant .[52]

> Sean Rogan's no criminal. He's a political offender. That doesn't mean I think he's right, but it doesn't mean that I have to agree with a system which condemns him to the same treatment as a criminal. In any case, as the IRA has now officially called off its underground campaign, I don't see how any useful purpose can be served by compelling Rogan and men like him to work out their sentences to the bitter end.[53]

In relevant chapters I will look at Higgins's novels written during the 1980s and 1990s in order to contrast later characterisations.

Maurice Leitch won the 1969 Guardian Fiction Prize for his novel *Poor Lazarus* (1969).[54] As in Leitch's 1965 novel, *The Liberty Lad*, discussed above, identity is a central preoccupation.

In a novel of dark humour, Albert Yarr, a Protestant shopkeeper on the Northern side of the border assists a Canadian director, Quigley, to make a documentary in the aftermath of the Border Campaign. Edward P. Quigley, born in Derry, but who left Ireland when five, is now twenty seven and is researching a film on Ireland for a planned series titled 'The Old Country'. It is June, 1967.

No republicans as such feature in the novel; they are a faceless enemy, and the encroaching, claustrophobic presence of the surrounding nationalist, rebel culture makes Yarr feel a stranger in his own land.

> The street door was pulled back – a pair of boots (his new stock of seconds, military green, and not selling, bugger them!) holding it open. He had started the habit of keeping it wide like that all day in all weathers the time the IRA

campaign was at its height on the Border a few miles away, and his predominantly Catholic customers took their trade away from his – the only Protestant and therefore British – shop in the village. But the inviting interior didn't invite. They walked past to Hickey, or Refills, or McAuley's. Now of course the explosions and the siren's shriek from the police barracks on the hill and the tender's rattling rush through the village to the point of attack were night sounds of the past – well two years ago anyway – and business was rising, not much, but rising…[55]

Yarr, drinking in a Catholic midland town bar, ridicules the local drunk, Carbin, who retaliates with a threat: '*Your* time is comin'. Some o' these nights you'll get a bullet in you, niver fear, you British cunt… *Informer!*'.[56]

Quigley keeps a diary, noting that five years after the Border Campaign has officially ended the landscape still bears the scars:

> […]the border cart-track. No man's land. Only recently the spikes marking the line between North and South have been removed. Ripped out like teeth from the tarmacadam. Blotchy scars remaining. Great smuggling country, Yarr tells me, despite the spiked roads.[57]

We get in these works a composite picture of the culture of the day. Hardly a completed picture: there are far too few examples for that. Seven texts are insufficient to do more than touch on some of the complexities of identity and perspective shown therein. Georg Lukacs, in *The Theory of the Novel*, described 'the novel as a 'bourgeois epic' in which the alienated, solitary hero is in constant conflict with his environment'.[58] Paddy Fallon? Peter Douglas? Frank Glass? Sean Rogan? Albert Yarr? Above all, Yarr. In a significant respect, many examples of Troubles fiction to appear subsequently could be called 'epic' because of their shallowness of narrative world, and not merely because of their often one-dimensional characterisations. As David Lloyd claims in *Anomalous States*, the 'epic belongs to a closed and completed world, and characteristically represents the unity of that world and the integration of its exemplary heroes'[59] – an echo here of the way in which characters and plots in certain Troubles fiction are unreflective in their certainties about Britain's right to rule Ireland. To portray Republicans in this light is to ignore the struggle not of isolated individuals but of communities and groups with a common history, grievance or aim. Irish republicanism is ill-served in these novels. Perhaps only when authors are concerned to faithfully represent the viewpoint of a minority, a minority that refuses or resists assimilation and, perhaps, whose aspirations and interests cannot be expressed from a bourgeois or mainstream stand-point, will the 'epic' deficiencies of the genre be transcended. Then, again, perhaps such a comprehensive, inclusive account is an impossibility because of the incomprehension and exasperation generated by the heteroglossia implicit in Leitch's choice of epigraph for *Poor Lazarus*: 'I don't understand you, you don't understand me, and we don't understand ourselves' (Anton Chekhov: *Ivanov*, Act III).

3.
Old Men's Lies: 1970-72

Some quick to arm... walked eye-deep in hell, believing in old men's lies.
(Ezra Pound)[1]

The publication of *Causeway: The Arts in Ulster* (1971) marked the 50th anniversary of the founding of the Northern Ireland state. From the tenor of its contributions the reader would hardly gather that the Orange statelet was a political entity on the verge of collapse. Michael Longley, for example, reflected that 'the abnormality of a cultural apartheid sustained to their mutual impoverishment by both communities is still only gradually being corrected'.[2] Discernible in Longley's expression of regret at the tardiness of social reform is an, at best, muted optimism about the possibilities of writers and artists to heal the wounds of communal division. Furthermore, Longley perceived the conflict primarily in terms of cultural or sectarian antagonism, and of the two communities at each other's throats. This would be a recurring analogy for writers up to the present day, and one that is painfully and regrettably negligent, in my view, concerning what republicans regard as the root cause of the division: Britain's imposition of partition at the insistence of unionists and their Tory backers.

Instead, there is in *Causeway* much earnest discussion about the proper artistic response to events, but little recognition of the depth of seriousness of the situation. John Cronin contributed the 'Prose' section and lamented that, in his opinion, 'of the sanity of laughter there is too little... Ulster writers offer a challenge rather than a reassurance'.[3] It seemed that while Rome was ready for the torch it was the critics in particular who fiddled.

By the late 1960s, as street disturbances became almost a daily occurrence, fears grew concerning the alleged role and culpability of outside or left-wing student agitators. The role of Orange agents provocateurs continued to be overlooked or was unrealised. Even the more astute cultural and social observers failed to recognise the significance of what was happening, of the fault lines ready to open. And when disturbances did erupt there seemed to be an unspoken acceptance that the situation would soon blow over. Hadn't it always done so in the past? For the first anniversary of the eruption of violence that resulted in the arrival of British troops on the streets of the North, the poet Eavan Boland wrote a series of articles for the *Irish Times* entitled 'The Northern Writers' crisis of conscience'. In the final article, Boland supposes 'that the violence must be short-lived and the need for human construction long-lived'. She quoted Brian Friel:

Everybody suspects that when the violence does come it will be very short-lived, quite brutal and very ugly and that it will end, and we're all keeping ourselves in reserve for the situation that will never evolve.[4]

No commentator was projecting the turn of events we were to become familiar with. There had never before been a similar period of such a protracted intensity of violence, no precedent of equal scale or duration from which to draw warning. Certainly no local writer predicted the seriousness of what was happening or imagined the ferocity and complexity of events as they were to unfold. Perhaps, in fairness, no one could have.

And given their proximity to the moment, if Irish writers were found wanting, what criticism is justifiable when writers from elsewhere are deemed to have falsified the nature of the conflict and of its protagonists beyond recognition?

When the balloon went up, events did not at first impact on writers outside of Ireland as a subject for serious imaginative engagement. Instead, the conflict as it initially unfolded occasioned a shallow form of fictional reportage: the conventional thriller with barricades and street riots as a backdrop were to appear in droves, a diversion from or addition to the habitual thriller fare of KGB, CIA and MI6 skulduggery.

The Sixties and early Seventies were a period of intense questioning of received values as a perceived need developed for radical social and political change. This context was the spur for many involved in the civil rights movement and subsequent republican struggle, as the realisation gained ground among republicans that a resort to physical force was necessary in the face of an unyielding, repressive Stormont regime.

However, there is a palpable sense from reading Michael Longley's 'Introduction' to *Causeway* that in the North, Sixties' radicalism was a casualty of the violence.[5] Here was the birth, perhaps, of a new mythology: the Sixties representing an Eden of potential, the serpentine emergence of militant republicanism its downfall. There is no awareness in his writing that for those engaged in the struggle on the streets, the Seventies represented continuity, that rather than rupture there is intensification. For the communities at the front line in the confrontation with the state it was, for all the trauma and sacrifice, a liberating new dawn. Despite the immediate and continual experience of repression, and not merely because of it, people's eyes were opened and many saw for the first time the nature of the relationship between themselves and the state, a relationship tangibly manifested in the presence of armed and aggressive British soldiers. However, even before a British soldier set foot on, for example, the New Lodge Road, Belfast, radical nationalists recognised their enemy, and it sat in Stormont with the connivance of Westminster.

In nationalist working-class areas throughout the six-counties, with few outlets or opportunities for jobs or alleviation from social deprivation, most young people had to face the decision as to whether or not they should participate in the struggle then taking shape in their midst. Few had the luxury of abstaining from the debate, and of opting out from what was happening in their immediate neighbourhoods. The system stank to high heaven and for the first time appeared vulnerable to pressure. It seemed to many in predominantly working-class nationalist neighbourhoods that the republican movement provided the structure and leadership.

For many nationalists the struggle represented a shedding of victimhood; and even for those not directly participating there was a sense of vicarious pride from belonging to communities under siege but refusing to submit. There would be no going back to the bad old days of Orange supremacy. The communities organised: local defence, field hospitals, the provision of accommodation and transport for people forced to flee their homes. Michael Farrell attests that morale was high behind the barricades of the nationalist ghettos, citing as an example the People's Democracy pirate radio station in West Belfast 'pouring out militant propaganda'.[6] No less tangible evidence of this shared sense of pride in resistance was manifested in the flourishing trade in army surplus clothing, and judging by the numbers of youths sporting Bomber jackets, all of whom couldn't have been members of outlawed organisations, a new corporate style for the youth of communities in struggle. The popularity of rebel ballads at this time is particularly illuminating in regard to the mood of resistance in nationalist areas. Without saddling these ballads as a carrier of historical meaning, they did give expression to nationalist pride and grievance, with accounts of escapes and martyrs. May McCann has argued that they expressed what the mainstream established media avoided or wouldn't countenance – the present struggle and the continuities with the past.[7]

None of the novels discussed in this chapter, and few in later chapters, give expression to the sense of liberation felt at the time in nationalist areas. Nevertheless, many do deserve, I believe, academic attention as primary sources for the insights they contain into the political and social atmosphere, attitudes and anxieties of the day;[8] often more so for what is not said or what has been left out of the account. After more than a quarter of a century they merit study as unique historical documents providing unwitting testimony to the perceptions and assumptions of their time and, in some cases, of their role in reinforcing prejudicial discourses.

Generally, however, readers unfamiliar with Irish politics may have turned to popular fiction in the hope that these novels might provide an easy, effortless and entertaining access to the complexities of the situation which bombarded them via the media. Other than through banner-splashed headline reports of the latest outrage, an international audience's only opportunity for a better understanding of the conflict may have been through best-selling fiction.

Unfortunately, what in many instances is on offer in such novels is a travestied account with ludicrous characterisations of the republican protagonists and a simplistic understanding of the political situation. The essential discourse was soon established by the media, quickly assumed the status of 'common sense' and was effectively mirrored in popular fiction: that Britain reluctantly got involved, and that the troops were there only to keep the peace between Protestants and Catholics. Nationalism was downplayed because that might concede a political dimension to the situation. Public opinion in Britain and internationally began to understand the problem in the light of this self-serving discourse. The accumulative influence of popular fiction should not be underestimated in its capacity to form and influence attitudes and opinions. The dark side of this capacity is the potential that Troubles fiction will obfuscate rather than enlighten. That negative potential is unfortunately realised in a majority of the novels studied.

In Chapter Two I discussed the small number of fictional texts published during the 1960s that looked with varying degrees of hindsight and distance at the period from the tail-end of the IRA Border Campaign to the months prior to the arrival of British troops on the streets in August 1969.

There are two notable differences in the novels I survey below. Firstly, their marked contemporaneity is striking, with the narrational focus very largely concentrated on events in the year prior to publication. More usually we might expect a two-year time lag between an actual event and its inspired fictional depiction because of the necessary time needed for a plot to germinate, and because of the needs and processes of the publishing and marketing industries. Indeed, in subsequent chapters many of the novels discussed take a longer, retrospective view of particular traumatic moments of conflict. However, many of the novels in 1970 to 1972 were published within a relatively short period of the real events that appear to have inspired their respective fictionalisation. These novels were meant to convey the immediacy of events in the North, some barely off the front pages, at a time when public interest was at a premium. Key moments and developments are featured: the Battle of the Bogside, the rise of Paisley, the shadowy role of Loyalism in fomenting violence, Burntollet, the disbanding of the B Specials, the Falls Curfew, Internment; and also certain themes that had become the staple concerns of the media, such as hostility to mixed marriages, whether between Catholics and Protestants, or between Catholic women and soldiers; and the often alleged role of reporters in staging or instigating riots.

In several novels reference is made to the factual basis for the story. We should note, as Gabriel Garcia Marquez has observed, that 'in journalism just one fact that is false prejudices the entire work. In contrast, in fiction one single fact that is true gives legitimacy to the entire work'.[9] Some authors supply the reader with background information. For example, Peter Leslie's *The Extremist* (1970) opens with a selection of contemporary press cuttings indicating the themes in his novel.[10] At the conclusion of *A Little Bit British* (1970), Martin Waddell provides 'Explanatory Notes' with sub-headings on *Places* and *People* relevant to the political situation as then presented.[11] There is a journalistic dimension to much of the output, as if the authors have chosen to fictionalise some aspect of the conflict in order the better to explain their perception of realities missed or not capable of being adequately conveyed to the public through a straightforward reporting of events. The often blanket coverage given to the violence at the time may have left the public sated with shallow, surface detail without being much the wiser as to what were the underlying motivations, and perhaps it is in response to this need that the novels were addressed.

On the part of some of the authors the intent is often discernibly didactic, characterised by an earnest desire to inform the reader. Menna Gallie's *You're Welcome to Ulster* (1970) is one example.[12] The term 'thesis novel' might arguably apply in some examples, the author arguing a case or, as in David Brewster's *The Heart's Grown Brutal* (1972), rehearsing many of the then current arguments and political stances.[13] For example, in James Carrick's *With O'Leary in the Grave* (1971), the character Nealis analyses the possible consequences had Jack Lynch's government not stood idly by and instead satisfied the raised hopes of many nationalists that he would send the Irish Army across the border in 1969.[14]

This willingness of some of the authors discussed to imaginatively engage with the historical unfolding of events distinguishes their efforts as superior to the spate of thrillers to appear later, set against a backdrop of urban violence. However, a few eminently worthy novels in terms of their narrative context were exceptions to the foregoing contemporaneity, perhaps because, as Edna Longley states, '1969 re-activated the past in the imagination of writers'.[15] The point is exemplified by three novels which appeared around this time, each dealing with the origins of the conflict: W.A. Ballinger's *The Green Grassy Slopes*, J.G. Farrell's *Troubles*, and Thomas Kilroy's *The Big Chapel*.[16]

The second notable difference between the novels discussed in Chapter Two and those to follow is that writers from outside of Ireland are now more to the fore. With the single exception of David Lodge, the authors surveyed in the previous chapter were Irish or had a close association with Ireland. Perhaps this point isn't surprising because of the increasing international media interest in the conflict at the time. However, the under-representation of Irish writers relative to the previous period should not be construed as a lack of concern about what was happening. Interviewed for *Fortnight* in late 1972 Edna O'Brien, for example, stated that despite her qualms about the British Army's presence in the North she had no desire to write 'a strictly political novel', though she saw this as an abdication of her responsibilities.[17] Her aversion to producing a novel with a Troubles theme seems due, therefore, to artistic rather than political considerations. Richard Deutsch bemoaned the then fact that no well-known, established Irish writers had tackled the conflict. He cited Maurice Leitch's belief that 'some sort of ripening process' needs to occur before local writers could attain the necessary distance and detachment from the situation.[18] Perhaps the incubation period that Leitch implied is the reason so few Irish writers are represented. Arguably, the subject was too close, too personal. But perhaps another factor was that few dared to come off the fence or to risk reputations on half-baked analyses. One critic wryly observed: 'Tolstoy did not publish War and Peace until fifty-seven years after the burning of Moscow'.[19] In this chapter, then, by way of contrast, the concentration will be on a predominantly external take on the Troubles.

I have been able to trace sixteen category (a) novels dealing with the contemporary Troubles published during the years 1970 to 1972. Six were published in 1970; five in 1971; and five in 1972. The small output during these years, relative to the upsurge of novels from 1973 onwards, still represents a quite considerable degree of literary interest when compared to the number of texts published during the decade surveyed in the previous chapter. Of the sixteen novels, I will discuss ten, only four of which, as I have indicated, were written by Irish authors.[20]

In lieu of a foreword to her 1970 novel, *You're Welcome to Ulster*, Menna Gallie provides excerpts from 'The Civil Authorities [Special Powers] Act [Northern Ireland] 1922', the provisions of which warranted detention without trial, the imposition of curfews, the banning of newspapers, films or gramophone records thought subversive. And if these measures were considered insufficiently vigorous, the act also allowed for the arrest of anyone whose behaviour was 'calculated to be prejudicial to the preservation of peace or maintenance of order in Northern Ireland and not specifically provided for in the regulations'.

Gallie, in an elaborate, though dated, plot contrives to expose the repressive nature of the Northern Ireland statelet. She attempts to portray the strangeness and foreignness of the place.

> Ulster, where life, as... [Sarah Thomas, her central character] remembered it, was violent, lived, alive and full of colour; where fights and feuds blew up like squibs, where cynicisms and sentimentalities had the same validity.[21]

The narrative period is the summer of 1969. Allowing for one sympathetically rendered RUC character, the North is represented as a police state, as in the following near encounter at a roadblock manned by B Specials.

> [...]they passed a big, dark, semi-bus parked at the roadside with uniformed men simply gushing out of it, like squished toothpaste. They carried big, clumsy guns and wore flat, uniform hats that shadowed their faces like fascism, like death.

> 'What the hell are those?'

> 'Drive like the wind, in case they halt us. They're the Special Police, the B's, out on their Protestant junketings. Special Powers, remember?'.[22]

The scene functions as a sort of microcosmic interlude – a distillation of the author's core attitude to the situation. Typically, a short gap in the narrative's flow may operate to focus on or encapsulate a particular point. In the above excerpt, the essential sectarianism, that for Gallie necessitates the impartial intervention of Westminster, is set out as in a tableau – for there is a stillness about the depiction, a stepping out of the narrative, the equivalent in fiction of a footnote.

The B Specials were feared by nationalists. In an *Irish Times'* interview Seamus Heaney recollects the attitudes of many nationalists towards the B Specials during the late 1950s:

> I suppose I was 17 or 18 and not at all a political animal, a Northern 'papish' rather than a Republican or anything like that. But I remember being deeply offended and I know the whole Catholic community was deeply offended, by the way in which the B Special constabulary were utilised. The whole Catholic community felt the smart and were meant to feel it, I think. That was the first time I saw, for example, my neighbours

dressed up, with guns in their hands, on the roads at night stopping cars. I myself was stopped because I happened to be at a ceilidhe. It was very easy to pick out the sheep from the goats, you see. You waited on a Sunday night for everyone coming from it. I had my wallet searched, I had my letters read by fairly illiterate men. It's no insult to them to say that as a description – just prejudiced, ignorant Orangemen, who happened to be Protestants and were allowed into this organisation. And they were 'servants of the State'. They were 'defending the Northern Ireland Constitution' by doing that sort of thing.[23]

Sarah, who works for the Ministry of Education, while in Ireland mixes almost exclusively in Catholic professional, academic circles, allowing the reader to eavesdrop on a representative range of middle-class nationalist opinions and attitudes widely held in such company at the time. The accumulative effect is of a cross-sectioned discursive formation, a frozen slice of bias. There is much earnest postprandial discussion about the political situation, and Sarah attests to the 'basic, abysmal, British ignorance about Ireland'.[24] At one such social occasion she hears Una, a student who had demonstrated at Burntollet, reveal her opinion of the IRA.

She declaimed again at Sarah the brutal facts of the persecutions of Catholics; the gerrymandered seats, the discrimination in jobs, in housing, the exclusion of Catholics from State appointments and State agencies, and the vitriolic savagery engendered against Catholics by the extreme right-wing Protestant fanatics, who, like the IRA, could not face the threat of progress.[25]

In the same zealous gush, the IRA is equated with extreme loyalists. Una elaborates on the supposedly typical IRA recruit, an account of whom Sarah compares with the militant attributes of some students in England.

John [Vint] was active in his youth and young Larry's involved in it yet. He's just the type. Never able to hold a job, given to violence, fancying himself, under-educated, frustrated.

How refreshingly old-fashioned. That I can understand, but all the violent young that I know quote Marcuse or Guevara at one, and carry Chairman Mao in their hip pockets. They are usually over-educated and tend to be very affluent.[26]

Sarah suggests that Larry and, implicitly, the typical youth drawn to republican involvement lack political awareness. Una sticks to the line that republicans are a hindrance to reform.

I know the type; they use their patriotism to justify their sadism. Here they bleat about ending Partition, uniting Ireland, as though that, by itself, would provide homes and employment. It's so stupid it has to be fake. They're a menace to the Civil Rights movements. They give the police an excuse to attack, by joining our demonstrations; processions being neither exclusive nor excluding.[27]

Una's contention that the civil rights campaign was being undermined by the actions of republican hotheads doesn't square with the actual accounts of leading activists. One prominent activist, Michael Farrell, founder of People's Democracy, describes how they were

> in constant conflict with the cautious middle-class leadership of NICRA, the Northern Ireland Civil Rights Association who were always afraid of going too far and half astonished that they had been let go as far as they had done.[28]

As Gerry Adams attests, the campaign soon became a means to an end beyond the call for reform.

> The civil rights agenda... became a focus for the emerging differences between the republican leadership and some rank and file activists. The leadership position had by now become clearer. The civil rights struggle was not only seen by them as a serious attempt to democratise the state, but to facilitate this process the national question, the issue of partition, was to be set to one side in order to allay unionist fears, and the movement was demilitarised. This strategy had one serious defect: it underestimated the reactionary and irreformable nature of the state itself and the reluctance of the London government and its Stormont management to introduce reforms. This reality was slowly dawning on many of us who came to believe that the major effect of the civil rights struggle, aside from winning some reforms or partial reforms, would be to show clearly the reactionary and colonial nature of the state and the responsibility of the British government for this situation.[29]

The position that Una is enunciating seems to be that of the republican leadership referred to by Adams above, who became the Officials after the split in 1970.

One of the more interesting characterisations is Mab, a young Welsh nationalist on the run from the RUC after a Twelfth Night riot. In contrast to the Vints, who are loutish rednecks in the novel, Mab is an idealist, and for Gallie it seems that Welsh nationalism epitomised romantic nationalism. Her depiction of his naiveté implicates all the more the violent Irish republican tradition, a tradition which, according to the novel's central premise, is in danger of undermining the development of an effective civil rights movement. Mab confides in Sarah:

> Listen, there's going to be real trouble here. I've seen some of the guns, Sarah; bloody arsenals in Belfast and up and down the country, so I heard. These volunteer blokes are supposed to be running guns from Czechoslovakia; they come via the Congo; by the boatloads, girl. Old-fashioned stuff, mind, working, lethal all right. Snag is the ammo. From what I heard, it's easy enough to buy and run guns, but the ammo is tricky. I've actually handled some of those Czech guns.[30]

'There's going to be real trouble': ringingly obvious, with hindsight. But Mab's claims about having handled weapons would have been seen as lippy posturing by a more informed witness. The author clearly did have her ear to much middle-class speculation concerning republican intentions. However, the evidence is that in

August 1969, the period of the narrative, the IRA was completely swamped by events, unprepared for anything except token resistance. Hence the much referred to wall sloganising of the period: IRA=I Ran Away. As Michael Farrell claims, 'known IRA men had been jeered at in the ghettos because they were unable to defend their own areas'.[31] So much for boatloads of Czech weapons. Another paradox is that the IRA's stock of weapons were allegedly sold or handed over to the Free Wales Army prior to, and possibly in anticipation of, the eruption of violence in the North.

Martin Waddell's novel *A Little Bit British* is an ironic representation of a loyalist bigot, Augustus Harland of 12 Boyne Villas, and of his diary-entries from August 1 to 15, 1969 – a journey into the loyalist psyche.[32] The fact that it reads as fresh and topical today as it must have done in 1970 is a sad, frightening reflection on the lack of progress in certain quarters and of the discourse of loyalist fundamentalism. To read *A Little Bit British* is to prise a rusted lock to re-enter our darker past only to realise we never left. We are given an account of bigotry and intolerance and mindless certitude, and of issues which are as relevant today as then: the targeting of Catholics and the flat misconception of all Catholics as republicans; the role of the Orange Order, and of Orange marches through Catholic areas.

> Mr Paisley's parade will show them where Ulster's heart is. Newry may be an RC town, but it belongs to us, and we intend to make it very plain to them.

> Let them slip off over the border to their RC Republic if they don't like Loyalist Parades.[33]

The same blinkered arguments are aired today to justify supremacy. Waddell deals too with religious stereotyping, and more generally with racism. Catholics: 'like the Blackies… These people are never satisfied with what you give them'.[34] The novel makes the connection, perhaps more relevant so soon after the American Civil Rights period, between religious fundamentalism and white supremacism. It is therefore ironic that Martin Luther King's freedom marches were invoked as a precedent during the press conference to launch The Long March from 'Londonderry to Drumcree', 17 June 1999, by anti-agreement unionists.

Today, under the name Catherine Sefton, Martin Waddell is a highly acclaimed writer of fiction for children and adolescents. Some of his work in this regard is examined in Chapter Six. In September 1996 he visited the H-Blocks to give a lecture on writing for children, and afterwards I took the opportunity to ask him some questions about *A Little Bit British*. His concern in many of his novels is with the effects of the violence on children, and he confided that this concern was earlier expressed by a reference in *A Little Bit British* to the killing of nine-year-old Patrick Rooney by the RUC. During disturbances in the Lower Falls in August 1969 the RUC had raked Divis Flats using Browning machine guns mounted on their Shortland armoured vehicles, also killing an British soldier on home leave.[35] Waddell remembers feeling extremely angry at the news of the boy's death, the news of which shocked him greatly, and of how subsequently he regretted the reference to the killing because of the possible reawakening of the mother's trauma at the tragic loss of her son should she read the novel.

The Extremist (1970), by Peter Leslie, exploits the whodunit format, set against the background of civil unrest in Belfast in late 1969. Leslie, a Belfast man, is good at transcribing the local idiom, using recognisably Northern phrases and expressions such as 'stocious', 'polis', 'by the neck'. Like Gallie and Waddell, he establishes a factual basis for his narrative, in his case a series of press cuttings (8 September 1969 to 19 February 1970) detailing the worsening relations between the British Army and the nationalist communities, as well as recording the resentment felt by loyalists at civil rights reform. A cynic might conclude that the press details were meant to add verismo to the otherwise implausible plot extrapolated from them, implausible because one of the ground rules of the detective thriller (essentially what *The Extremist* is) is the familiarity with, and mobility within, the cultural and social world of the given narrative required if the hero/detective is to get close to solving the mystery. In Leslie's novel, however, a British Army lieutenant, Giles Fleming, turns amateur sleuth when a fellow officer is killed by a sniper while on duty in Belfast. Fleming goes in search of information about the identity of the sniper among extremists on both sides of the political and religious divide. Leslie bestows upon his hero, a British officer doing detective, the necessary moral authority to the extent that he can expect answers of nationalists and loyalists to his questions. He uncovers and prevents a plot by loyalists to masquerade as British Army personnel in order to kill Catholics. Their intention is to provoke the IRA into retaliation against the British Army so as to further unionist calls for tougher security: 'the Unionists will have an excuse to ask the government to bring in stricter measures and cancel all the concessions you... won'.[36]

Two underlying premises are discernible, the first of which is also in Gallie's *You're Welcome to Ulster* – that the bigotry and sectarianism of two sets of extremists is preventing a solution; and secondly, the already settling orthodoxy that the British Army is in the North as a peacekeeping force.

The latter notion is illustrated in the first pages with Fleming's annoyance at a Protestant pastor's intolerance.

> '...Never thought to hear the like,' the clergyman was saying. 'To think I should live to see English soldiers, under the command of an English man, take up arms against loyal subjects of the Queen on behalf of a gang of hooligan Papish...' 'They are not taking up arms,' Fleming snapped. He found it hard to keep his temper in the face of bigotry.[37]

A prostitute, Fran McCraith, is used to suggest the first premise, attesting to the immoral calibre of both sets of 'extremists', whom we suspect she knows professionally – the first refuge of both sets of scoundrels.

> 'I know the bad boys on both sides,' Fran repeated. 'And I don't know which is worse. I suppose you could call the lot of 'em patriots, according to their own standards. But they're rotten in the middle, the both of them.'

> 'Having seen them, I'm inclined to agree,' Fleming said. 'The patriotism of the Orangemen is perverted by narrowmindedness – by bloody ignorance,

if you like. And although the Republicans are far more intelligent, their intelligence is warped by bitterness and refusal to face the facts'.[38]

The character Fleming represents – the decent, fair-minded English officer is a type we first encountered in Jack Higgins's *The Violent Enemy* in which the British Army officer Vanbrugh is similarly cast. The type will be frequently met in Troubles fiction, and very often in contrast to his inferior Irish republican counterpart.

The plot touches on an actual contemporary development: the republican split which created the Provisionals. Fleming makes contact with Deirdre O'Shaughnessy, an Official IRA member ordered to report on a breakaway group led by Riordan [Provos]. It is Fran, however, who describes Riordan to Fleming:

> He's one of the new generation. Some of the Republicans here think the IRA staff down in Dublin has lost its touch. They think it's all theory and no action now. So they've split themselves off and formed a branch up here that's self-supporting, as you might say. Riordan's the boss. He spent five years in the Crumlin Road gaol, 1956 to 1961. The British put him there under the Special Powers Act – you know, no charges and no trial, and you stay as long as Stormont wants you to. He was queer and bitter when he came out – not that I blame him! – and he's that dedicated, nothing matters to him but the Army.[39]

Leslie's descriptions of his republican characters throughout build on the perception of an embittered, narrow-minded atavism. One republican, who might have auditioned for Carol Reed's 1947 film *Odd Man Out*, is described thus: 'He was almost the caricature of the conventional idea of an IRA man, with his pale face, and his belted trench-coat, and his hat with the brim turned down all the way round'.[40] Another is depicted as 'a ferret-faced man with red-rimmed eyes'.[41] It might be an instructive exercise to tally the occasions in Troubles fiction when republicans are endowed with ferrety features. The description usually signals to the reader some outward evidence of a moral shortcoming in the character. However, the author, prefiguring Shaun Herron's later descriptional spleen towards republicans in, for example, *Through the Dark and Hairy Wood* (1972), discussed below, and in *The Whore-mother* (1973),[42] saves his worst for the loyalist, Clancy: 'The man's breath smelled like a camel's – a dreadful mixture of stale beer, cigarette smoke, halitosis and uncleaned teeth'[43] – adjectives and attributes which would become the stock toxic abuse reserved for republicans in fiction as the real violence intensified.

The attention to loyalist paramilitaries, here and in Herron's *Through the Dark and Hairy Wood*, and Martin Waddell's *A Little Bit British* (1970), is in marked contrast to the almost blanket inattention to 'Protestant' violence in the succeeding years. Thereafter, loyalist violence was represented in the media, and by loyalist paramilitaries, as a reaction to republican violence: remove the cause, Irish republicanism, then the raison d'etre of the loyalist groupings would follow. Little or no scrutiny was allowed into the role of collusion between loyalism and the British state – a dirty, hidden war removed from the public mainstream, and not part of the prevalent discourse; and this factor explains, I believe, why so few writers paid it heed. Apart from the few novels cited above, and Maurice Leitch's 1981 novel *Silver's City*, no novel focusing on loyalism was to appear before a spate of novels in the 1990s.

The threat of the new breakaway republican organisation and of its long-term operational capacity is not, at the time Leslie was writing, taken too seriously. After an explosion, we are privy to a conversation in a bar during which other recent bombings are mentioned.

'Students or bloody Papists, it's all the same now.'

'They're on the same side, sure. But it's not the same thing entirely. I'm tellin' you, this was an Army job. It was one of Riordan's specials.'

'– if I'd passed that way just five seconds earlier...'

'– whoever put it there, the bloody Republicans are going to be out of bloody bombs by the end of the month! That was the fourth this week!'[44]

Though striving to be topical, Leslie shows little appreciation of how far the political situation at the time had worsened, of the depth of nationalist grievance and the concomitant support for the newly-emerging Provisional IRA. The narrative suggests that the republican split was between those (the Officials) who were motivated by 'theory' and others (the Provos) who favoured action. In reality, the central issues concerned the matter of the recognition of Leinster House, Stormont and Westminster, and the failure of the IRA to protect nationalist areas from loyalist attack. Instead – and here we have an early fictional example of it – the split has often been simplistically and erroneously portrayed as one between the 'Sticks' as 'politically conscious radicals' with the Provos cast as 'nationalist militarists'.[45] Instead of demonstrating any real understanding that the brewing violence might have a sociopolitical causation, the author constructs a plot in which outside agencies, agents provocateurs, stir things up, easily accomplishable it seems, given the Irish propensity to violence.

Violence was endemic to a country, and a subject country at that, that had been split religiously and politically for nearly four centuries. It was unavoidable in a dispute on both sides of which the protagonists had for so long allowed bigotry and prejudice to cloud reason.[46]

It is telling that this trope of the inherently violent Irish, should appear so soon in Troubles fiction, stressing the tenacity of the stereotype. Rather than look dispassionately for the fundamental causes of what was happening, Leslie has resorted to the use of a characterisation of the Irish firmly rooted in the British psyche, a recourse we met earlier, in Sarah Thompson's 'crazy, Irish, irrational province'.[47] According to David Lloyd, 'no quality has more frequently and repetitiously been attributed to Ireland than violence'.[48] He argues that a more subtle determination of the attribute supports state legitimacy.

Violence is understood as an atavistic and disruptive principle counter to the rationality of legal constitution as barbarity is to an emerging civility, anarchy to culture… [T]he end of violence is the legitimate state formation. By the same token, the end of history is the emergence of the state.[49]

In that understanding, of course, the state has the monopoly of the use of force, and no violent opposition to the state can be tolerated, a view that goes right to the heart of the British discourse. This position forms the basis of Conor Cruise O'Brien's extremely tendentious application of the principle in a 1972 article, written because of his concern with the international support among students for the IRA's campaign.[50]

Conor Cruise O'Brien argued that republicans justified the use of violence on three counts: firstly, the mandate of '1916'; secondly, that the northern statelet was created through the UVF's threat of force in 1912-14; and thirdly, the institutionalised violence of the state. He dealt with these three counts in an often spurious manner. For example, reducing the first count as a 'cult of the dead', he argued that 1916 represented an 'antique and atavistic' obsession, though a 'much less potent' source of legitimation than the existence of social injustice.[51] Likewise, count two is irrational and only accepted by those 'obsessed with the past'. Having dealt with these, he turned his fire on what today would be termed 'the equality agenda'. He argued that inequalities exist in all societies, that institutionalised violence is inherent to varying degrees in all state formations. Acceptance of the principle of the legitimacy of the democratic state necessarily entails, he argued, the condoning of some level of violence. He further argued that in the North mechanisms of redress and accountability existed, not through the local democratic process, which he accepted offered no hope because of the nature of majority-rule; instead, he suggested that 'non-violent agitation, for limited objectives', would have exerted pressure causing Westminster to eventually intervene.[52]

Westminster eventually did intervene, of course. However, the approach advocated by O'Brien failed precisely because even the 'limited objectives' of the Civil Rights Movement threatened the raison-d'être of the statelet. Consider, too, the lessons of recent years. Even with Sinn Féin's considerable electoral mandate, in conjunction with the pressure exerted by constitutional nationalism and the weight of international pressure and opinion, during the period of the IRA's first cessation John Major's government upheld the unionists' veto on progress in the peace process. Major played on what he mistakenly interpreted as the IRA's weakness. Arguably, it took the IRA's resumption of its campaign in England to break the log-jam.

Both Your Houses (1971) is the last published novel of James Barlow, the English popular novelist (*Liner, The Patriots*) who died in 1973. *Both Your Houses* is one of the first, if not the first, contemporary examples of a romantic storyline involving the love affair between a British soldier and a Catholic woman. The novel's 'love-across-the-barricades' theme re-works the Romeo and Juliet story. The star-cross'd lovers are young squaddie, Tom Moody, stationed in Belfast, and Aileen O'Meara, whose family is staunchly republican. The title comes from Mercutio's line in Act III, Scene I: 'A plague o' both your houses'. The choice of title indicates a plot involving the struggle between warring factions, with the British Army caught in the middle, the centre of reason and compromise.

There is some confusion about the exact narrative period. A reference is made to the British Army having been in Belfast two years. However, in the novel, which was published in 1971, though the events described suggest Christmas of that year, the reintroduction of Internment hasn't occurred. Evidently, the author tried to foresee 'security' developments as they may have appeared at the time of writing, probably 1970. I have already alluded to the common belief among many commentators at the time that the violence would be short-lived. The author would not, therefore, have expected that the situation would deteriorate sufficiently to warrant a repressive measure such as Internment.

Nevertheless, allowing for the gap between conception and publication, Barlow may have attempted to capitalise on what he anticipated would be the novel's topicality by locating the narrative a year in advance. If so, this was a quite reckless marketing strategy, given the pace of events in the North. With the reintroduction of Internment on the 9 August 1971 the book was already dated at the time of its appearance in the shops.

Barlow's characterisation of the young squaddie is interesting. Tom is working-class without being class conscious, the product of a culture steeped in racism: 'Deep in Moody's bones was a loathing of foreigners whose miseries and corruption and tortuous arrogant ideologies had to be sorted out by the British soldier'.[53] In this and the following longer excerpt, the author's more politically perceptive voice resonates through Tom's narrower understanding of the natives. Tom's outlook is probably an accurate reflection of the attitude towards and ignorance about the North of many British soldiers at the time.

> Moody knew nothing of Ulster or her agonies of political and sectarian strife, nor of anachronistic string-pulling by the Orange Order, or gelignite smuggling by others; was only half aware of the legacy of hatred and Ireland's history of exploitation, plantation, division and conquest... He had seen the people he was going to protect – seen them on TV screaming like lunatics, seen women beating at soldiers' chests and throwing stiletto shoes at them in a rage meaningless to him but exploited by others. He'd trained in Germany for possible encounters with the hooligans – fighting the Army, whether for kicks or ideology. He was anticipating a hard, ruthless, bigoted mean people, living in back-to-back houses (as thousands did in Small Heath), with poor sanitary conditions: people with pale ignorant faces and, in the older generation, a runt stature, the result of a history as wretched as any peasant from Kerry with his great-grandfather's tales of brutal landlords and starvation'.[54]

'Ideology' is here used in a pejorative sense to suggest a warped understanding. The grudging allowance that ideas, 'ideology', might spur at least some of the 'hooligans' Moody is trained to deal with doesn't detract from the impression of mindless violence. The phrase 'exploited by others' is also telling: 'others' seemingly betokening influences outside of, foreign to, the community. Later we meet the republican subversive O'Mellan, the archetypal ideologue.

As in Leslie's *The Extremist*, and Gallie's *You're Welcome to Ulster*, Protestants are depicted as being resentful towards the British Army's presence. An Orange band is outraged when Tom's patrol prevents them from parading through a 'Cat-lick' area. Some local Catholics, however, are determined to cause trouble. Padric Tumelty, an IRA volunteer, is one of them and is revealed as a bigot and sexist with a curious penchant for Elizabethan raillery, I assume in keeping with the novel's Shakespearean echoes:

'We do not have to bear this insult,' he said loudly. 'These dogs come without their sashes but mock us with their flutes and stupid Orange music... I do not intend to endure it.'

The women made noises of encouragement, and the young man continued: 'These are dogs of the kennel of Prods. I don't take insults from them. Not even from their women. Nor from fools playing silver trumpets. When I've punished their imitations of men, ferocious in the bars with loaded bellies, I attend to their women. They scream then, loving my piece of Fenian flesh'.[55]

This unfortunate parody (suggesting Tybalt?) pretty much sets the tone in the author's attempt at a 'literary' style.

The younger republican hot-head is then contrasted (it could only be unfavourably) with the veteran republican, Mr O'Meara, Aileen's father, who comes on the scene and reasons with the patrol.

Although not tall, the middle-aged man had a certain authority about him – his voice had silenced most others – so that Lance-corporal Small hesitated, presuming that he might be the local Member of the Stormont Parliament, and even the band captain became attentive.

He had a worn face in which there was kindness but no faith in victory; it had a faint residue of bitterness, and was the portrait of a personality which had been beaten, but mostly by circumstances and superior numbers. The face belonged to hopeless causes [...] He looked as if he might be a member of the battered generation of the Irish Republican Army, who had not come to terms with 'reality' as understood by a weaker majority, men who felt that feeding a family, repaying loans, advancing their status at work, had advance claims on a difficult patriotism...'[56]

O'Meara is subsequently revealed to be a member of 'the Provisional Republican Army'.[57] As is Tumelty:

He had joined a Republican club years before in Belfast at the age of sixteen with his mother's approval. Some of his extreme loathing of British troops and Protestants was the product of natural temperament, but the rest of it was due to up-bringing and the memories of a boy of eight of a dead father who had been killed in guerrilla battle. As well, he fulminated with shame because in the big troubles of August, 1969, when the Prods had come burning houses there had been scarcely any IRA activity: just a few old men of the'50s troubles who'd dug up a handful of ancient weapons and helped to stem a massacre. No Republican Army had turned up in Belfast on that day – because one did not really exist...[58]

In the above examples, Barlow demonstrated some attention to the mix of motivations of republicans and the contextual background to the then worsening situation. Sectarianism is rife and street confrontations do bring out hotheads.

Although Barlow does give a nudging allowance towards the influence of nationalist grievances, he fails to show any real understanding of the root causes of the conflict. Instead, the reader is afforded another rendering of the theme of Britain caught between two tribes. Sectarianism is the cause and not an effect in Barlow's interpretation. He also introduces the sinister role of outside revolutionary agitators, even if the portrait is more flattering.

> They called him the big fella because he was huge. He was a man of about thirty-five, and he had come from County Tyrone a year ago to organize things. He was a bachelor and therefore free from the terror of anxiety for others of his blood. He was shrewd and tough, and had got things done. He had a big round humorous face, but it soon hardened. He was no bully or gangster though: he was a professional soldier for that same lifelong ideal of O'Meara's, and in this he had given heart to depressed men.[59]

O'Mellan proves to be a pragmatist as much as an ideological republican. During the rather summarily arranged court martial of the suspected British agent Captain Feeney, O'Mellan mentions British fear of an off-shore 'Cuba', the first reference in fiction, I believe, to an idea which first surfaced in a 1970 Tory Monday Club pamphlet titled *Ireland – Our Cuba?*:[60]

> We know the British are worried about civil war – not in noble sentiments for the Irish but because they fear a Cuban situation which could make Ireland a strategic bombshell. I've even had CIA men talk to me frankly in anxiety about that possibility. We refused arms dealers with American contacts because we know CIA policy is to back the right-wing against the left, and by supplying arms cheaply control that faction or influence it. I had to anticipate penetration at some stage by a British agent. Who but you is a candidate? All these other fellows have been in these streets since birth.[61]

In summary, the novel is a romance set against the backdrop of the Troubles, possibly the first example of a relationship between a British soldier and a Catholic (Leslie's *The Extremist* does have a 'love interest', between the British officer Fleming and Deirdre O'Shaughnessy, an Official IRA member, but this is a twist to the plot, not the novel's main thematic interest). As to why romance appears to have been a strong generic component of these early examples of Troubles fiction, I would suggest that the potency of the image of Ireland as the feminine personified all too easily lends itself to the utilisation of the discourse of romantic fiction as allegory; in the conclusion of *Both Your Houses* a simple resolution of the conflict is offered in the coming together of two ostensible opposites, signifying a possible solution to the conflict. However, depressingly, the potentiality of a resolution between ancient enemies, as symbolised by the thwarted love between a squaddie and a Catholic girl, founders on irrational, because ill-explained, hatred. The love-across-the-barricades theme was given the fullest exploitation in Joan Lingard's 'Kevin and Sadie' novels for teenagers. *Across the Barricades* (1972), the title of the second in a series of five staking a claim to this thematic territory.[62]

The Australian author and biographer Russell Braddon (1921-95), like James Barlow (who, the reader will recall, set his narrative in the near future to anticipate what he imagined might be the turn of events at the time of publication) intentionally located his satirical novel *The Progress of Private Lilyworth* (1971) two or three years ahead. Braddon wrote biographies of Joan Sutherland and of Lord Thomson of Fleet and he even included himself in the narrative as the eponymous Lilyworth's biographer.

The novel's narrative period is August 1973 – again, a risky strategy, and one that didn't pay off in terms of accurately anticipating future events. In order, perhaps, to avoid the libel laws Braddon in the novel killed off Ted Heath, Prime Minister at the time, whose yacht *Morning Cloud* sinks, with the owner and his cabinet, thus releasing them from association or blame for the unfolding plot.[63] There are several other allusions, topical in the period 1970 to 1971, to people who within a year or two had died or whose status had changed; for example, the Beatles are mentioned, supposedly in the assurance of their continuance for many years to come, though unfortunately for Braddon the group disbanded in 1970. More importantly, events, such as the smashing of Stormont are not foreseen. Clearly, Braddon did expect that the violence would escalate, requiring increased troop levels, but he underestimated the seriousness of the deterioration. He predicted troop levels of ten thousand, not the twenty-two thousand at the time of Operation Motorman in the summer of 1972.[64]

Braddon's sub-text is easier to predict: the British Army is in 'Ulster' to keep the two sides from each other's throat. Ecumenism is the worthy solution of the moment. Lilyworth, a naive British soldier, masquerading as a nun, plots to bring the two religious sides together. Another theme, again played for a slapstick effect, is a variation on the old gable-end joke that the letters IRA stand for I Ran Away.

> The reporter turned to the middle-aged man. 'Did you throw anything?'
>
> 'Did he hell,' mocked Brendan. 'He's IRA!'
>
> 'I'm disabled,' whined the middle-aged man [O'Reilly]'.[65]

Braddon persisted in this vein.

> Two miles away, in a dingy bedroom sat four dingy Irishmen: three on an unwholesome looking bed, the fourth on a broken chair. They were drinking stout from bottles.
>
> 'I now call this special meeting of the Breakaway Branch of the Unofficial IRA to order,' said the chairman.[66]

Also predictably, after the meeting they adjourn to the pub. Old racist stereotypes are best, dusted off and introduced for the easy laugh.

The novel also features strongly another concern in the media at the time: the alleged staging of street riots for the media.

> Not a real war, which civilization had made dangerous, but a war in the streets, which television had made glamorous.

So that, as soon as summer arrived – bringing its perfect late light for the cameras – the evening battles began. Ending, of course, in good time for the belligerents (average age, thirteen) to rush home and see themselves on rented or stolen screens.[67]

For Braddon, therefore, there was no 'real' conflict, merely the opportunistically choreographed chance-medleys of the summer months, delinquency, the overspill of fear and anger at the interfaces. The higher incidence of street disturbances during the summer coincides with the raised tensions of the Orange marching season, a long-standing grievance and lived reality of nationalist communities.

Describing a more serious street confrontation, Braddon introduced a new hate figure: the student troublemaker. Passarelli, a political philosophy student from California, who resembles 'a squaw from a Sioux Reservation', directs rioters. And later, 'Rentamob', consisting of 'mostly undergraduates from England', is orchestrated to riot on cue: 'In good time for the commercial television company to edit the film and show it on News At Ten'.[68] The last is a sly dig at independent broadcasters. There was a perception among nationalists at the time that the BBC was more biased against them.

The Irish author John Banville, in a contemporary review of the novel, indicated how out of touch Braddon was with the mood of many in Ireland at the time, who saw little cause for humour in the tragedy by then unfolding daily.

> His ignorance of Northern realities is criminal, romp or no goddam romp, and anyone here caught reading his book should be immediately exiled for treason.[69]

While one may demur now, as perhaps then, from what might seem Banville's rather po-faced verdict, the underlying sentiment bitingly illustrates the yawning gulf in attitudes about the conflict at the time.

Perhaps Braddon's discursive stance was impenetrable to Irish nationalist sensibilities, and he was quite obliviously happy to pander to ignorance about the complexities of the conflict outside of Ireland and to rely on shallow caricature. One does sense in Braddon's novel that he momentarily alighted on the Troubles theme, attracted to its topicality and the opportunity to capitalise on a plethora of stereotypes and pro-British prejudices. Of course, he might actually have believed in the images of the opposing sides he lined up.

> The [British] Army was firing rubber bullets and canisters of gas... The rioters were firing real bullets and hurling Molotov cocktails. The Army was directed by numerous officers, warrant officers, sergeants and corporals: the rioters were encouraged by numerous foreign students and middle-aged militants from an alleged splinter group of the IRA. The Army's officers and NCOs stood ostentatiously in the forefront of the battle; the rioters' supporters skulked furtively at its rear and casualties on both sides were heavy.[70]

The British Army was 'directed'; the rioters were 'encouraged'. With so many officers 'ostentatiously' in front, we must suppose that the casualty ratio between them and ordinary squaddies disadvantaged the former – a detail that strains our credulity, surely?

In an irreverent, and ironic, aside Enoch Powell is accredited with the following novel solution.

> Let all of Ulster's Catholics and Protestants, I say, be rehoused by this Government in Eire and Scotland respectively: and let all of Britain's coloured immigrants, young Liberals, shop stewards and alien agitators be re-settled in Northern Ireland! Then and then only, I submit, shall we be spared religious riots across the water and racial and industrial riots within the moats of this once happy, sceptred isle.[71]

The novel's discursive gravity is centred on the concerns of the English Tory shires. In the closing pages the Prime Minister resigns and Powell takes his place. Who would have predicted that, in real life, Powell would fight and win a seat as an Official Unionist in South Down in October 1974?

Another novel which insists on its basis in fact is James Carrick's *With O'Leary in the Grave* (1971), a point stressed in the 'Author's Note':

> This book is based on something that actually happened, and it follows history to a point. Beyond that point it carries the story into what might have happened if the events described had taken another turn.[72]

Part of Carrick's purpose then is to ask 'What if?'

The central character, Frank Nealis, a policeman and ex-British soldier, returns on leave to his native Derry in August 1969 – just in time to witness the Battle of the Bogside.

Nealis's military experience in Cyprus and other colonial situations affords him a broader worldview and political understanding about the nature of colonialism and of political forces at play which the local republicans appear not to comprehend. Mulholland, for example, is a physical-force republican, hell-bent on blood sacrifice, thus conforming to a common misperception of a strain of influence within republicanism tendentiously attributed back to Padraig Pearse.

> Mulholland leaned forward in a characteristic stance. 'There's only one solution for the troubles of Northern Ireland. Only one solution and that's blood. Until there's a bit of bloodshed then nobody's going to take much notice. Do you know that, Rory, to cleanse ourselves we'll be needing a whole river of blood'.[73]

This brings to mind Hugh Ward's diatribe against alleged corruption in Southern politics in Broderick's 1962 novel, *The Fugitives*, discussed in Chapter Two.

However, the behind-the-scenes direction of the violence described is left to outside agitators, most prominently a 'mono-syllabic American' dubbed 'Larry the Yank' Forrester.

> The men trooped out of the house carrying rifles. The rifles had been made in Czechoslovakia and they had been obtained by the American. They were

streamlined, modern rapid-fire weapons and the men who carried them knew only their theory. None of the men had yet fired one.[74]

The weapons' Czech provenance may be intended to signify by synecdoche the radicalism of the Prague Spring, but perhaps sinisterly, plant a negative association with Iron Curtain communism, despite the American connection. The most likely meaning of the Czech origin, however, were the revelations emerging from the Dublin Arms Trial of 1970, going on at the time Carrick was writing the novel, about the procurement of such weapons for the North. But in reality, the gunrunning allegedly occurred several months after the events in Derry that Carrick depicts, giving a false impression of armed preparedness. However, as Eamon McCann recounts in *War and an Irish Town*, rather than 'a massive subversive conspiracy behind the fighting', the defence of Derry was organised by local people largely through the Derry Citizens Defence Association.[75] No weapons other than petrol bombs and stones appear to have been used to ward off repeated RUC attempts to invade the Bogside.

Regan, the hero of James Wood's *Road to Canossa* (1971), is sent to England on a mission to procure arms for the IRA. Although not a member, Regan was chosen by the IRA for the task because of his English accent, having lived for twelve years in the English Midlands. However, for Regan this 'was a personal commission, something by which he could redeem the wrongs and suffering of his mother'.[76] The suffering of Irish mothers, of course, is a recurrent motif in Irish literature, from 'Cathleen Ni Houlihan' to O'Casey's 'Juno'; and at the outset of this survey there is the example of Mrs Rogan in Patterson's *Cry of the Hunter*. Regan later reveals his motivation.

> 'My father,' Regan said coldly, 'was a policeman. A B Special, a pig with power. He... killed my mother – not murder – he killed her. He used to beat us, for no reason. My father was a beastly sadist. Had he been given the opportunity he would have shot every Catholic in our neighbourhood... He was the' – Regan laughed sourly – 'the leading light in his Orange Lodge. Dressed up and led the annual parades at Easter, carried the banner, led the songs to praise... that was my father. And he came home and belted us with a leather strap – my mother, too'.[77]

During the mission Regan becomes disillusioned by the turn of events in Ireland and because of his perception of the incompetence and lack of trust among the Republicans.

> The Cause was running itself out across the water. [...] The long-haired kids were taking over now, and the CS gas had not deterred them very much. They were even taking it out on the young Scots soldiers who were trying to keep the uneasy peace. The announcer's voice had made it so undeniably clear...

> '...the Springfield Road of Belfast is mainly Roman Catholic... Cardinal Conway deplores the hooliganism... Mainly drunken teenagers, but this can be so sinister in that the trouble can be so easily spread...'

It was about to erupt into a grisly, shattering joke – there would follow the ridicule, and the shabby recrimination, and the women would be the first to suffer as usual. With guns – the guns he could supply for the harried people of the Springfield Road districts – with guns there would be wanton destruction: there would be no question of military observance, of the rules of war, of discretion. It would be another filthy massacre, with children the victims as well as their parents.[78]

Here, again – as in at least two other novels published in 1971, Barlow's *Both Your Houses* and Braddon's *The Progress of Private Lilyworth* – the street disturbances of the time are attributed to the excesses of hooligans. In addition, another theme of the time is encountered, for *Road to Canossa* also shares with Braddon's novel the advocacy of, or reference to, ecumenism as a solution to the North's problems – Catholic and Protestant churches combining or jointly calling for peace.

Regan's apparent disillusionment stems as much from a lack of belief in the ability of nationalist communities to withstand the might of the British Army as it does a lack of faith in the ability of republicans. It seems that the mere mention of that ancient republican bogeyman, the informer, is enough to snuff out any chances of a campaign.

'I… have known members, yes. Some of them very efficient people – men, and women, too – good people, many of them. With a combined purpose. They… elected me to come across and act on their behalf, arrange the business, handle the transportation [...] You can see – by telling you this – that it's all off now.'

'The fight against the rule of law?' The question was forthright.

'The fight to survive and live in one's own country,' he corrected her gently. 'But the time – for the moment, anyway – has passed. It's blown out… like an unpleasant storm. You see,' he went on to explain, 'someone has let us down. Someone has informed the police'.[79]

Even with the qualification 'for the moment', there is again an underlying acceptance that the Troubles will soon blow over, whether wrecked by informers or the excesses of 'extremists'. As in other novels surveyed, there is a clear underestimation of the tenacity and ingenuity in the face of adversity of the IRA and its nationalist base. For O'Meara in Barlow's *Both Your Houses* the Troubles would not last beyond a year or so, while in Leslie's *The Extremist* the operational capacities of the fledgling Provos are doubted.

In Shaun Herron's *Through the Dark and Hairy Wood* (1972), the conflict at that time was fuelled by the fact that 'the whole population of the province[80] is a festering mess of small but deep social humiliations'.[81] Reform would solve nationalist grievances. However, extremists hamper the search for the compromise needed to redress the civil rights' deficit. Herron's main target here is Protestant extremists, although he establishes his loathing for the IRA.

The services of a former CIA agent, Miro, are called upon by Stephen Riada, the Irish Army's Chief of Intelligence, to investigate whether the IRA are in fact behind a communiqué addressed to the British Prime Minister threatening to abduct and execute public figures in the North unless the British Army is withdrawn. The communiqué further threatens that children would also be targeted.

> Children, they wanted it to be very clear, would not be exempt. The same conditions would apply in all cases, including the children… withdrawal or death…

The government appealed to parents everywhere to keep their children off the streets.[82]

The claim may be under investigation but the narrative gives credibility to the notion that republicans are capable of such tactics.

In seeking to investigate the claim, Miro accompanies Riada to a meeting with the IRA in Belfast. At a 'revolutionary tribunal' they meet two republicans.

> Mahood was a big red man with a boyishly freckled face. It was a reckless face, darkened at this moment by politic hostility. I wouldn't want him on my side, Miro thought; he thinks big thoughts and wants to do big deeds; he thinks with his bowels.

> The other man was lean, tall, sharp-faced. There was no humour in his lines… A compulsive conspirator… The roving eyes were peculiarly lifeless, the eyes of an executioner.[83]

If the image thus far might prove insufficiently repellent to his imagined or implied reader, for good measure Herron adds an unsavoury detail: 'Mahood's trouser legs were drawn up. He had pink, hairy calves'.[84]

In retaliation for the first abduction, loyalists kill a Catholic priest, prompting fears of a slide into civil war as the Twelfth approaches. Miro, whose suspicions are roused by the closeness of one action to another, eventually discovers that the communiqué was part of a plot by a unionist MP, Captain Ronald Strong, Doctor of Divinity, intent on plunging the North into chaos rather than countenance the liberalising policies of the government.

David Brewster's novel *The Heart's Grown Brutal* (1972) reads, even today, like a crash course on the Troubles, packed with insights and information on the attitudes and interests of the 'two traditions'.[85] Much of the author's analysis of the power relations between Britain and Ireland stands the test of time quite well.

According to a cover blurb, Brewster is 'the pen-name of a British journalist who has been covering the crisis in Northern Ireland for three years'. Brewster followed the trend established by James Carrick of drawing his title from Yeats: 'We had fed the heart on fantasies / The heart's grown brutal from the fare.'[86]

An English correspondent, Hugh Randall, is sent over to Ireland to cover what is expected to be a tense marching season. (Is there another kind?). It is July 1971. Randall falls under the tutelage of seedy local journalist Horace Blundell. This relationship provides the author with much scope to cram in information about the conflict; as Randall gets to grips with some of the background, so does the reader.

As Blundell explains to Randall, he comes 'of good, landowning, loyalist Anglo-Irish stock', his father having been the 'grand master of his local Orange

Lodge as was his father before him'.[87] It transpires that Blundell later becomes involved with the Provos.

The first encounter in the novel with a republican perpetuates the often encountered imagery of twisted, embittered failure: 'A little man with a club foot clumped up to the bar and tugged at Cafferty's sleeve. Cafferty bent his solid grey head while the man murmured a few words of Gaelic directly into his left ear'.[88] The clubfoot recalls Brendan, Leitch's proxy republican in The Liberty Lad.

Brewster incorporates an actual event into the narrative: the killing by the British Army in Derry on 8 July 1971 of Seamus Cusack and Desmond Beattie. Their deaths led to an upsurge in support and recruitment for the Provos.[89] In the novel, Blundell raises the incident with a Provisional leader.

> 'Presumably, you started this trouble in Derry in the hope of killing a couple of soldiers and drawing off troops from Belfast before the Twelfth. But thanks to the dismal performance of your gunmen the only result has been the death of two Bogside boys.'
>
> 'How then have we been lucky?'
>
> 'Because those two deaths have stirred Catholic Derry up against the British troops till the Bogside's now as hot for them as the Falls, Ardoyne, New Lodge and Ballymurphy districts of Belfast and because they have also stampeded the opposition MPs into announcing a boycott of the Stormont Parliament. You could hardly have expected such a handsome return for so meagre an investment.'
>
> 'Perhaps you underestimate us, Mr. Blundell.'
>
> 'You mean you hoped the troops would get edgy enough to shoot a couple of civilians?'
>
> '"Hoped" is perhaps not quite the word, Mr. Blundell. Let's say it was considered a possibility. Unfortunately, in war, people do get killed, and not necessarily only those who bear arms.'
>
> 'So Cusack and Beattie weren't IRA men?'
>
> 'We've said they weren't, haven't we? And have you ever known the IRA to fail to acknowledge and honour its dead?'[90]

The image projected here is on an IRA willing to put civilians at risk knowing that any British mistakes or retaliatory killings of civilians would assist the republican propaganda war.

Later, a republican spokesperson, Fitzsimmons, attempts to refute the romantic stereotype of the IRA and replace it with a hi-tech version, which must have seemed extravagantly inflated in the early 1970s.

> You know, you really must shed your notion of the Irish Republican Army as a collection of old-fashioned romantics in raincoats with a rosary in one hand and a Thompson gun in the other. We still have such elements of course, but the IRA is an up-to-date movement, ready to employ all the latest innovations, including computer technology, to attain its objects.[91]

Blundell's grudging admiration for the Provos is expressed, following the reintroduction of Internment.

> The security swoop and the battles which followed it had left the Provisionals' command structure virtually intact. The great majority of the IRA men interned were members of the largely non-violent 'Red' or Official faction and all but twenty or so of the remaining internees were members of non-terrorist left-wing political groups like People's Democracy and the Civil Rights Association. The British Army's intelligence had been proved ludicrously inept; their reputation for generally decent behaviour had been severely dented by circumstantial accounts of brutality during and after the roundup; there was little belief left in their impartiality; and their Chief of Staff had made a thoroughgoing ass of himself by declaring that the hard core of the IRA Provisionals had been beaten, just at the moment when one of their top men was giving a news conference to the world's press and television behind the barricades in Ballymurphy. Internment, it seemed, had also completed the polarization of Northern Ireland's two communities and had cut the ground from under the feet of the modern anti-unionist politicians. The British and Northern Ireland governments between them had obligingly dealt the Provisionals a straight flush, just as Fitzsimmons and company had calculated they would if pressed hard enough.

> Rule Britannia! thought Blundell, He'd actually heard a senior British officer say not so long ago that he thought the Provisionals 'weren't very bright'.[92]

Brewster also manages to include a political appraisal from a Southern journalist, Kildare.

> The border will have to go one day, that's for sure, but not until the Prods all go away or until they're willing for it and that'll be a generation at the best and more likely two. So what does the South do about it? I'll tell you. It may not sound very exciting, or dramatic, or noble but it's the only thing a little kiss-me-arse country like this can do and it's to use guile and stealth and deviousness and cunning to get the stupid bloody British to understand the basic realities of the North and then to recognize their own best interests which, surely to Christ, can't be to let the Ulster tail wag the British dog till kingdom bloody come.[93]

The inevitability of reunification is here largely unquestioned; and the tail-wagging-the-dog reference has an echo in the present.

The novel is a rehashing of many of the contemporary political opinions and arguments in support of and against the use of politically motivated violence. It is also a novel about journalistic concerns, being the first Troubles novel to seriously address the demarcation line between objectivity in journalism and political partiality. Blundell's involvement with the Provos contravenes his professionalism. For his pains, his fate is to be thrown from a moving train. Perhaps one of Brewster's intentions in the novel was to provide an antidote to those other novels which portrayed the press largely as fomenters of street disturbances, for example, *The Progress of Private Lilyworth*, 1971. *The Heart Grown Brutal*, while earnestly opinionated and overly didactic, remains a good political thriller of its kind.

The final novel discussed in this chapter, Jack Higgins's 1972 thriller *The Savage Day*, was the first example of the genre I read.[94] As I said at the start of Chapter One, I first read the novel while interned in Cage Two, Long Kesh in 1974. I was curious as to how the republican movement was represented. The blurb promised that Ireland's fate would hang on the outcome of the plot, so I expected considerably more than Higgins's war-comic misrepresentation of a conflict that since the Northern statelet's inception had wrought discrimination, torture, Internment, Special Powers, and the collusive role of murder gangs.

Higgins's depiction of Binnie Gallagher, a member of the Official, not the Provisional IRA, though quite sympathetic was a cartoon cliché, an archetypal throwback to the 1940s or '50s gunman revamped, it seemed, to take advantage of a gullible though lucrative thriller market. Binnie Gallagher would have felt equally at home in either of Higgins's previous Troubles novels published in the 1960s. Binnie's dress-sense struck a false note. Most of the lads in the Cages were teenagers or, like myself, in their early twenties, and with hindsight, image counted for more at that age. Doc Martens, Wranglers and Bomber jackets were the prized look that season, though on parade the odd die-hard Glam Rock victim might be witnessed teetering pluckily on his platform soles. Binnie, sporting a 'dark blue double-breasted Melton overcoat of a kind much favoured by undertakers', would have been immediately suspect. This admittedly superficial detail, then more than the ludicrous Oirish-speak, inaccuracies in the description of location and period, and the ill-researched caricature of our beliefs and values – in fewer words, the stock fare of the genre since – was palpably out of sync with the street-realities we recalled.

Particularly irritating was the episode in which Binnie scared a gang of youths, 'dressed exactly alike in leather boots, jeans and donkey jackets', masquerading as republicans, we were supposed to accept, in order to extort money from a local bar. And how was this accomplished? With not a Branchman in sight to beat it out of him, it took Binnie merely to declare that he was 'a lieutenant in the North Tyrone Brigade'. In the back-street real world, such a declaration would have marked Binnie down as a headcase. Was this how the world was supposed to see us? The reality is, then and now, that 'rank', that is, its outward manifestations, counted for little among the average volunteers who, like normal rebellious youth, demonstrated a healthy disrespect for anyone who took such matters seriously. Instead of the pressures of rank to keep us in line, we were all bound by the collective desire to get the job done. Therefore all those novelistic accounts of IRA volunteers addressing their 'superior' officers as 'Sir' are woefully astray of the mark.

If Higgins evinces a certain empathy for his characterisation of Binnie Gallagher, no such understanding and insight is discernible in his depiction of the Provos, or 'Brady's', 'the Belfast nickname [according to Higgins] for members of the Provisional branch of the IRA', the sighting of whom was sufficient to clear the streets because of their fearsome notoriety and reckless disregard for civilians during attacks on the British Army.[95] A trend already set in his previous novels of offering two opposite republican types – the principled and disciplined versus the sectarian, self-motivated and morally bankrupt – is given a stronger accent here. The two Provos, Lucas and Riley, have no redeeming features, and their actions are depicted as counterproductive to their supposed political ends. In subsequent novels, Higgins sticks to the formula but, because the Official IRA were inactive following the declaration of their ceasefire in May 1972, he reverts to finding his Manichean counterparts solely within the Provos, typically counterpoising the actions of an honourable though disillusioned maverick with those of a bloodlusting psychotic. Binnie Gallagher is therefore stamped from the same narrative fabric as Higgins's earlier positive characterisations, Martin Fallon in *Cry of the Hunter* and Sean Rogan in *The Violent Enemy*. Riley and Lucas are the negatively charged narrative descendants of Patrick Rogan, also encountered in *Cry of the Hunter*.

Ciaran Carty claims that Higgins in *The Savage Day* 'was the first to break the taboo against setting thrillers in the Troubles',[96] a claim that is accurate when Higgins's previous novels are taken into account – *The Violent Enemy* (1966), and prior to that, *Cry of the Hunter* (1960), published under his real name of Harry Patterson – and, additionally, that we accept that the Troubles ran the full course of the 1960s and did not commence at the end of the decade as is generally understood. Taking 1968 as the beginning, a number of thrillers did, of course, appear before *The Savage Day*. Peter Leslie's *The Extremist*, for example, already discussed, appeared in 1970. However, Higgins's distinction is indeed noteworthy because, as I discussed in Chapter Two, the earlier novels dealt with Irish republicanism a decade before the birth of the Provos. If anything, given how prolific an author Higgins is, it is surprising that he did not produce a novel before *The Savage Day* that dealt with the Provos. The threefold increase in the publication of Troubles thrillers after 1972 does seem to refute Ciaran Carty's other point that a taboo existed against the Troubles as a suitable subject for thrillers. These novels appeared practically in tandem with the events they depicted, suggesting not only that the subject drew the interest of many writers but also a keen readership. In 1973, the beginning of the period discussed in the next chapter, more Troubles fiction appeared than ever before.

4.

A Publishing Phenomenon: 1973-75

The period 1973 to 1975 stands out in the history of the conflict as the time in which the republican movement was at its most vulnerable, when British government counter-insurgency tactics came closest to undermining the republican struggle. The reversal in fortunes of the movement is plainly seen when the achievement of its first major strategic objective, 'the smashing of Stormont', is contrasted with the parlous state the movement was brought to during the next three years because of the ill-judged belief that the British were contemplating military and political withdrawal, a belief that resulted in the truce of 1975. In a letter to Harold Wilson, Merlyn Rees is cited as admitting that the British negotiators 'set out to con them and... did'.[1]

We should bear in mind that many examples of the fiction surveyed in this chapter were generated by events in 1972. That year began, as 1971 had ended, with mass resistance and demonstrations by nationalists against civil rights abuses, particularly, at this stage, abuses arising from internment. The Stormont regime and elements within the military establishment panicked into the massive blunder on the streets of Derry on 30 January 1972 when thirteen unarmed civil rights marchers were killed by the British Paratroop Regiment. Bloody Sunday was a turning point. Whatever lingering chance had existed for change through constitutional means vanished. Recruitment to the IRA rocketed as a result. Events that day probably led more young nationalists to join the Provisionals than any other single action by the British. Within weeks the Provisional IRA intensified its campaign and Stormont was prorogued. Even the Official IRA, opposed to a military campaign and on the verge of declaring a ceasefire, retaliated with a bomb at the Paratroops base at Aldershot. In June the Provos negotiated a truce and met with a British government delegation in London. When the truce broke down, the tactics of the British Army in ending the no-go areas may have been seen from Britain and abroad as another turning point in the conflict. John Hume was later to claim that the IRA had squandered a real opportunity to establish itself politically from the success of having negotiated a truce with Britain. From a republican perspective, however, this claim ignores the fact that the British government was not acting in good faith and all along saw a ceasefire merely in terms of its own military and political advantage.

Until this moment there is little sign that the conflict presented a problem in terms of a controversial subject matter for popular fiction. This was to change when it very gradually, it has to be said, dawned that the IRA was not going to be defeated by the new hard-line initiative from the state, and indeed, when the IRA began to take the war to England. At no time during the relevant period do I recall any view among republicans other than that victory was attainable. Outside of republican and nationalist ranks, however, then current public perceptions were that the tide against the IRA was turning; they were going nowhere and in time would be mopped up. Henry Kelly, for example, writing in April 1972, could tentatively predict a sea change.

> There are reasonable grounds for believing that a victory of sorts has been won and that violence may take a breather for a time. It is perhaps the first occasion in three years in the North when prospects look just barely bright for the future.[2]

This optimism was dashed during the next few years as it became clearer that all the political and military machinations of the state would not defeat the IRA and instead the British settled down to the less ambitious goal of achieving, to use Reginald Maudling's phrase, 'an acceptable level of violence'.

The Provisional IRA first targeted England in March 1973 with car-bombs in London. Thereafter, a spate of bombings was carried out, culminating in the Guildford and Woolwich pub bombings in October 1974 and then the Birmingham pub bombing in November of that year. In response, the British government rushed through the Prevention of Terrorism Act, supposedly to curb 'terrorism' but whose 'draconian' effect in the following years was to bludgeon the Irish community, and anyone interested in civil liberty issues, into quiescence. Anti-Irish sentiment reached new depths. The cultural climate was hardly conducive, therefore, to a more tolerant, equitable market for fiction offering a pro-republican explanation or slant – a fact not lost on the many authors since 1973 drawn to the conflict as a background for a commercially-viable subject tailored to the projection of crude absolutes, some of the worst examples of which appeared on the shelves in the mid-1970s. Prior to this period, however, the output was quite wide in terms of discursive perspectives, narrative content and the varied backgrounds of authors. Up until 1974 one senses that there was still a reasonably favourable atmosphere for critical and discursively open fiction. There was less pressure for self-censorship. The years following mark a discursive shift; thereafter, until a further marked discursive shift in the late 1980s, the hegemony of the British discourse would prevail in the genre.

In summary, then, in terms of its literary significance, the period 1973 to 1975 is noteworthy on three counts, which together establish the contribution of popular fiction in the shaping of public perceptions about the conflict. Firstly, 1973 marks the beginning of a publishing phenomenon – the emergence of a discernibly new fictional subgenre. Secondly, the popularity of novels about the

Troubles, as evidenced by the increase in new fiction, contradicts the often claimed and no less often lamented apathy about the subject of 'Northern Ireland' among the British viewing and reading public. Thirdly, the period largely established the anti-Irish republican/anti-Irish thrust of most of the works of fiction in question. Fiction became, wittingly or otherwise, another means of perpetuating a misrepresentation of the conflict, and a misrepresentation broadly in line with the outlook and objectives of successive British governments. In essence, the novels in question very largely replicated the current discourse of the British political establishment in regard to Northern Ireland policy and attitudes to Irish republicanism.

1973 was a record year for the publication of Troubles fiction. Eighteen works of fiction relating to the conflict were published in 1973, sixteen of which were novels in English.[3] Only sixteen category (a) novels had been published during the previous three years, that is, since 1970, and the figure, therefore, represents a triple increase in output and, presumably, interest, both among writers and the reading public. Moreover, compared to the previous years' figures, the sharp rise in publication of this type of fiction continued, except during 1974 when only eight category (a) titles were issued, the reduction more stark given the phenomenal upsurge in published titles during the previous year. In 1975, twelve category (a) novels were published.

What before could be seen as the publication of an occasional novel, a romance, say, or a thriller, set against the background of the Troubles, now was identifiable as the beginning of a publishing phenomenon, a new and distinct subgenre in terms of subject, or, as I mention in Chapter One, a hybrid of the thriller, romance and war novel genres. The traits were in place, of course, in the fiction prior to this period, as discussed in Chapters Two and Three, particularly in the works of non-Irish authors. There were too few titles to talk in terms of a significantly new publishing development, however, until the remarkable increase in titles from 1973 onwards. It is from this date that the salient, archetypal characteristics and concerns of the genre solidified.

The Belfast author Glenn Patterson reckons that fictional representations were set about 1972.[4] It is true that in retrospect the conduct and character of the actual conflict, the war between the Provisionals and the British state, had reached a stark delineation by then. However, 1973 is perhaps the more accurate starting point for the fixed manner in which the conflict came to be depicted. As I've stated, too few novels were produced before then to draw any firm conclusions, while the subsequent upsurge was striking.

The figures merit attention from another angle, for they appear to buck a trend frequently commented upon about a growing public apathy towards media interest in the conflict. John Kirkaldy, for example, in an article highlighting the crude anti-Irish republican bias of British cartoons of the 1970s, argues that media interest underwent a 'pronounced decline' by late 1973, 'the time of the Sunningdale Agreement... the high point of British hopes in Northern Ireland'.[5]

For nationalists, however, suspicion of the media by this time was a widely established condition rather than a trend. Des Wilson notes the dismay of local people in the early 1970s at the typically inaccurate and misleading portrayal of the struggle in magazines such as *Newsweek* and *Time*. Claud Cockburn, he notes, recalled the practice of journalists covering the Spanish Civil War, 1936-1939, who wrote their reports miles from the frontlines, relying on detailed maps of the battle zones lest any exiled Spaniards might note topographical inaccuracies and thereby expose the credibility of the news reports.[6] Wilson claims that

> journalists working from the Europa Hotel and novelists specialising in quick selling novels set in contemporary trouble spots used the same methods. Novelists spent some weeks in Belfast or Derry to get the topography right and then wrote their stories in comfort [my italics].[7]

In *The Irish Novel in Our Time*, Richard Deutsch commented on the 'massive production of third-rate thrillers [that he claimed had]... nearly drowned the literary output in its mediocre flood on the 'troubles''.[8] Deutsch records that there was a readership in 'Britain and in the English-speaking world... attracted by this tribal war in a rather 'exotic' setting'.[9] He claims, however, that the interest soon dissipated when ''war across the sea' extended to the mainland [sic] with the Provisional IRA campaign of bombings during the summer of 1973'.[10] Deutsch does not refer to a comprehensive bibliography of relevant fiction. My own figures, given above, for the number of novels published during the period appear to substantiate his assertion, though it may be that Deutsch only implied that Irish authors and publishers shied away from dealing with the Troubles theme. The noticeable dip in the output of titles in 1974 seems to bear out the comment that the IRA bombing campaign impacted negatively on sales of new fiction dealing with Ireland.

It is pertinent to consider whether the perceptible slump in publication and sales may also in part be attributable to the recession, the effects of which were then being felt throughout the British economy. An article in *The Author* (Winter 1973) is quoted lamenting 'the diminishing market for new fiction'.[11] However, at least in regard to the publication of Troubles fiction, the figures suggest that the genre did not appear to have been negatively affected by the recession. Rather, the evidence of the popularity of Troubles fiction indicates that the authors met with no public aversion to their commodity and that in consequence the genre weathered the recessional tide rather well. This being the case, it is reasonable to conclude that, but for the recession, more titles would have appeared. Any reluctance on the part of publishers and authors referred to by Deutsch apparently did not last long, for he goes on to observe that 'a Belfast publisher [wa]s lately reported to have received more than a hundred novels on the North'.[12] Publishers, of course, are inundated with manuscripts, solicited and unsolicited, and there is no necessary relation between quantity and publishable quality. However, the very fact that so many writers were moved to deal with the North may in itself be significant as an indicator of public concern and interest, a degree of interest which, again, appears to contradict the excuses emanating from the media that the public was fed up with news stories about the North.[13]

I think it is more likely that any degree of public apathy in regard to the news coverage of the conflict arose from the quality of the reportage. The British public was being denied the truth. After January 1971, for example, the BBC introduced a system whereby permission to interview IRA members had to be referred upwards for approval to the Director General, a practice which, more often than not, acted as a ban against such interviews.[14] As Roger Faligot reported, Jonathan Dimbleby revealed during the *Frost Show* (BBC 2, August 1976)

> that the Independent Broadcasting Authority and the BBC had sealed a pact to ensure that the 'enemy' would be unable to speak on British TV, in other words, the British public would not have an opportunity to know what was really at stake in Ireland, and what the views of the Republican Movement were, and then form their own judgement.[15]

Perhaps, though, publishers displayed a certain caution in regard to the contents of some fiction submitted to them at this juncture. Publishers could be forgiven for being cautious when having to judge the commercial merits of novels with a strong topical content. After all, despite Peter Driscoll's rather lame disclaimer at the beginning of his 1974 novel *In Connection With Kilshaw*[16] ('Comparisons with actual political figures in Northern Ireland may be inevitable in the minds of some readers'), the Linen Hall Library, Belfast removed it from the shelf because of an injunction apparently taken out by a leading politician incensed at the supposed libellous resemblance between Kilshaw and himself.

Why then, especially against the backdrop of a recessionary publishing environment, was there a marked rise in the popularity of these works at this time? As part of an explanation, it is possible that these works were satisfying a particular market need other than for fictionalised accounts of an exotic 'tribal war'. The increase in output suggests a growing interest among the public, in Britain and internationally, for insights into what was happening in Ireland that extended beyond the predictable cataloguing of atrocities which formed the staple fare of the daily media coverage. Given fiction's capacity to 'show' rather than 'tell', to enliven staid issues, a reading public sated with the stock tabloid travesties and nevertheless seeking explanations for why British soldiers were being killed may have been drawn to popular fiction as a sort of a crash course on the conflict. Fiction could be a painless way of making the complex intelligible. Here was a target readership for the aspiring and the established thriller writer alike. Unfortunately, an opportunity to dig beneath the surface of the received wisdom and jaundiced media stereotypes was mostly squandered. Few of the novels to appear transcended the official 'bottom line' that British troops were in Ireland to keep warring tribes apart.

As another example of the interest outside of Ireland in the conflict, the period also heralded the first appearance of a number of titles in continental European languages; not translations but Troubles fiction written in the native language of the author.[17] It lies beyond the scope of this survey to ascertain whether these novels differed in terms of their political analyses from the dominant view contained in Troubles fiction in English.

In *Bestsellers: Popular fiction of the 1970s*, John Sutherland has referred to the reluctance of British publishers to reveal insider business. For that reason it is therefore difficult to establish the degree, if any, that oppositional voices in fiction, in terms of plots that take, for example, an anti-British line on the North, were marginalised or silenced in the publishing and market processes. According to Giles Clark,

> [m]ost publishers (including the majors and most medium-sized independent firms) are in London giving them ready access to authors, authors' agents, other publishers, social venues, journalists and producers of the mass-media, and other influential people who decisively affect the life of the nation.[18]

As Sutherland puts it, 'of all literary forms, fiction is most vulnerable to commercial rationalization'.[19] Because of the exigencies of the market, the bigger publishers and booksellers tend to be more conservative and are consumer-led, unwilling to take risks in terms of controversial narrative subject matter for fear of upsetting the market. He argues that the 'creative sector of British publishing has consistently been... the middle- and smaller-sized houses' of which he cites 'Cape, Calder, Chatto, Faber, Secker and Warburg, Deutsch'.[20] Sutherland explains that 'the bestseller is more likely... to have been subjected to negotiation and commercial interference at the 'idea' stage of its existence' than other kinds of novel.[21] The argument is no less true for less-than-bestselling fiction. Even flops are instructive, for they attest to what the book and publishing trades, and indeed the authors, think the public will stomach. The fact that much of the output of Troubles fiction, apart, that is, from the few bestselling authors like Higgins and Gerald Seymour, might be destined for the remaindered list is in itself of less significance than the general bias of the genre. Few alternative perspectives to the establishment take on the conflict are on offer. This is a view implicitly shared by one Irish publisher who claims that

> the greatest difficulties tend not to be associated with acts of censorship or prohibition but to do with the context of the ownership and character of publishing companies and the book trade, which have tended to regard oppositional voices as lying outside the pale.[22]

Thriller writers, always on the lookout for fresh narrative pastures, may have seized on the conflict as a source for the reworking of tired plots and formulaic devices, and for the more imaginative, even 'transformations' within the thriller genre. The structuralist concept of 'transformation' explains developments in the basic narrative elements of a genre. Market interest requires innovative plotting. One author will outplot another; or an author will adjust the formula to produce something new with each novel, by varying, for example, location, narrative period, character types, etc. The conflict in the North provided a zone of action replete with the established fare of the thriller, the romance and the war novel: urban and rural violence in an English-speaking European setting; all the hatred and bloodlust of 'civil war'; religious mania; the revenge meted out to those who broke tribal solidarity; the skulduggery of counter-espionage and the clandestine world of the secret agent.

Disappointingly, instead of realising in their literary endeavours the potential on offer, many authors instead chose to consolidate the heavy bias of the genre around a few salient tropes refurbished from the stock imagery of earlier representations of Irish republicans. In Chapter Two, I give some examples of the stereotypical antecedents for many of these portrayals. As Martin Fallon (not his real name), the repentant maverick republican hero of Jack Higgins's 1973 novel, *A Prayer for the Dying*, says:

> There's a poem by Ezra Pound I used to like. 'Some quick to arm... walked eye-deep in hell, believing in old men's lies.' Well, that was my cause at the final end of things. Old men's lies.[23]

Coincidentally, what at first may pass for a cultured allusion from Fallon by pejorative connotation links Irish republicanism with Pound's madness and association with Fascism, two defining traits of the IRA, as readers of Troubles fiction were given to understand.

Fallon, an IRA man on the run in England (from 'Special Branch, Military Intelligence – even... the IRA')[24] and in need of a passport, agrees to kill a pimp and drug-pusher, Krasko, for undertaker and Manchester gangster, Dandy Jack Meehan. The killing is witnessed by a priest, Father Michael da Costa (ex-SAS). Rather than kill this witness as Meehan orders, Fallon instead utilises the sanctity of the confessional, knowing that the priest cannot reveal what is confided.

Higgins suggests in the novel that Fallon's disillusion with 'old men's lies' and his desire to break from the past is the logical step of any thinking person when faced with the realities of the tired rhetoric and analysis of Irish republicanism.

To counter the notional rhetorical and moral bankruptcy of Irish republicanism Higgins steers the reader to the works of Saint Augustine. Meehan is depicted reading *The City of God*, which the disenchanted but literate Fallon admits he read a long time ago.[25] The British discourse is facilitated in yet another novel guise, for an important facet of Augustine's philosophy invoked the apparent religious and civil legitimacy of government:.

> The good at which all imperfectly just societies throughout history aim is peace and security; this good can be momentarily secured and thus governments of whatever kind must be used as imperfect means of keeping the peace. The civil authority can never be destroyed; it is divinely ordained for men in via, on their way to a hoped-for salvation after all states and all history. In effect, peace and security are of such high value,

according to Augustine, that no amount of civil tyranny can ever justify sedition and insurrection.[26]

If, as discussed in Chapter Three, Higgins's *The Savage Day* set an earlier benchmark for the genre, then *A Prayer for the Dying* continues in that vein. Like all of Higgins's working of the Troubles theme, there is little or no attempt to analyse sociopolitical cause and effect, and instead he proffers the flawed psychology of those drawn to the blood sacrifice supposedly demanded of romantic nationalism, acted out in an atemporal context. If anything, *A Prayer for the Dying* is comfortably relocatable in every regard to the territory of his 1960s' thrillers set in Ireland. With the possible exception of *The Savage Day*, which is cognisant at least of the 1969/70 republican split, many of Higgins's early Troubles thrillers are uncoupled from the actual moment. Narrative time is curiously ahistorical. Thriller writers are more usually concerned that their plots correspond to a degree with the real world. Higgins's novels often appear less concerned to create a credible Northern environment. Instead, he exploits the Troubles' backdrop to rehash yet another exploration of the grey area between good and evil.

Other examples of the genre display a qualitative change, with the appearance of some quite rabidly racist and dehumanising depictions of IRA men, reflecting or playing upon public outrage at bombings and killings attributed to or resulting from the IRA's bombing campaign in the North and, increasingly from April 1973, in Britain.

The prospect of bombs in England underlies the plot of John De St Jorre and Brian Shakespeare's *The Patriot Game* (1973).[27] According to J. Bowyer Bell this collaborative effort was from two 'London journalists... formerly in the British diplomatic service'.[28]

In the novel, James Grogan, a former SAS man who served in Aden, is now a committed IRA man, though he laments their operational inefficiency and tactics and breaks ranks to target Millennium House, London, headquarters of British Intelligence. It is pre-Direct Rule 1972.

Despite a glossary at the front (SAS, SIS/MI6, MI5, SB, RUC, CIA, FBI, 'The Met', Gardai, IRA, The Provos, The Officials, 'Taigs', 'Prod', 'Joe' [agent]), which ordinarily might suggest some attention to detail, the authors misinformedly blame the IRA for the bombing of McGurk's bar, one of several actual incidents referred to; another is the Official IRA's bomb at Aldershot.

The perpetrators of a bomb explosion at a Falls Road bar are described thus:

No men in belted raincoats and wide-brimmed trilbies, the archetypal IRA bombers verging on self-parody who had been involved in other incidents.[29]

An RUC man, Christie, asks the Special Branch Chief Superintendent Barnes whether the Provos are responsible.

'Ah...yes,' replied Barnes noncommittedly.

'Very similar to the explosion at McGurk's. That one destroyed the bar completely and killed fifteen people. Either it's a[n IRA] reprisal against squealers or it could have been an accident... Stupid, murdering bastards.'[30]

Christie is briefed by his tout, Joseph McQuaid.

> [...] I had a drink with a fellow who saw Rory O'Brady a couple of nights ago in Dublin, and the Provisionals say they'll keep the pace going much as it is. They believe there are signs of political movement at Westminster and another six months will see this through.

> Christie snorted. 'In other words, once they get direct rule from Westminster, London and Dublin will negotiate over our heads.'

> 'That's about it,' McQuaid said evenly.[31]

Meanwhile, Grogan advocates a campaign in England, though this is disapproved of by the leadership of the IRA. He reasons that Westminster-initiated reform, and a phased ending of internment, will undermine the IRA's support: 'Then where are you? And where's your united Ireland?'[32] Grogan puts forward his view:

> To prove we are a credible military – and therefore political – force, both in the eyes of our people and the enemy, we've got to strike at the serpent's head. This means identifiable military targets. The bigger the better. Since we know we can't do it in the North, there's only one answer: to take the war where it will really hurt – to England.[33]

Grogan enumerates the types of target he means (though he eventually targets Millennium House).

> [...] sabotage on the Concorde or a government communications centre. We might go for a police or security service headquarters – the type of target the Irgun used to select in Palestine. It could be a member of the Royal Family – say Prince Charles. He's a serving naval officer...[34]

At heart, the novel is a warning about the potential of an IRA bombing campaign in England. As Barnes muses, the Irish in England are seen as a 'fifth column'.

> There were almost a million Irishmen living freely in England. From the Republic they shuttled back and forth to England every day of the week without passports, exempt from immigration controls. The Irish in England, Barnes reflected, represented a potentially terrifying fifth column.[35]

Shaun Herron, like Higgins, is another author who views the conflict in terms of its Manichean narrative possibilities. Herron was born in Carrickfergus, County Antrim in 1912 and died in Canada in 1989. He lived in Winnipeg and was an ordained minister in the Scottish Congregational Church. He was also a journalist and wrote three novels that deal with the Troubles. Two of them are discussed in this survey, both of which were first published in the United States: *Through the Dark and Hairy Wood* in 1972 (discussed in Chapter Three), and *The Whore-Mother* in 1973.[36]

According to Richard Deutsch, *The Whore-Mother*, which crudely and viciously demonises its IRA characters, was inspired by Herron's detestation of the Provos' bombing campaign.[37] A study of the psychology underlying unionism has, I feel, a particular bearing on Herron's almost pathological hatred of Irish republicanism as manifested in the novel.

> As ideologies and the interests which they construct and represent enter periods of crisis there is a tendency for them to take on regressive forms. At the extreme this may involve the dehumanisation of the threatening groups.[38]

The novel apparently won some critical attention and the author appeared on a number of television shows, where presumably he indulged his anti-Irish republican prejudices.[39] By comparison, *Through the Dark and Hairy Wood*, which focused on events 'from the Protestant side after August 1969… was a less polemical, less engagé' novel.[40]

The Whore-Mother is a novel of rage and of Ulster Protestant paranoia in which the Provos are shown to be 'psychotic scum' poisoned by a romanticised view of history administered by Catholic Church-run schools.[41] Johnny MacManus, a young middle-class Catholic, expects the approval of his former history master, Bull Bailie, when he announces his intention to join the Provos. Instead, Bailie is appalled and launches into a guilt-ridden tirade for his role in inculcating a warped sense of history and grievance.

> 'What makes you think any wrong we suffered was big enough to justify the killing of women and babies in furniture shops?' His anger was a confusion; it was against McManus and himself and the bombers and the Irish shroud.
>
> 'Christ, I'm guilty,' he said miserably, and sat down and forgot his drink.
>
> 'You pumped it into us about the raw deal we get in Ulster and now you're telling me we've suffered no wrongs?' McManus said, rebuilding his assurance.
>
> 'Oh Christ, boy, don't give me that stupid street-corner rhetoric – of course we suffered wrongs, but put today's nearly eight hundred deaths against the fact that some Catholics can't get work in the Civil Service having stood up and said we want to destroy the state. Is it human to kill eight hundred people for that? Is there no sense of proportion in us? Does mutilating babies equal gettin prestige jobs in a state we said we'd destroy? Ulster was not a Nazi state and there was no excuse for this wanton killin.'

The Provos are described as 'wanton killers'. Note too that the eight hundred deaths referred to are all attributed to those who 'want to destroy the state'. Of course, many people at the time believed, and many still do, that the Provos were engaged in a nakedly sectarian campaign in which 'women and babies in furniture shops' were purposively targeted. And, of course, many innocent people were killed in explosions caused by IRA bombs. However, it was never a policy of the IRA to deliberately kill civilians. The many unintended casualties and deaths that did result from the IRA's commercial bombing campaign and from attacks on

British Army and RUC targets were due to various factors, such as faulty timing mechanisms, and the lack of clear warnings or inadequate time given to vacate targeted premises. It is also the case that some bombings attributed to the Provos were in fact the work of British agents. The IRA as a matter of established policy admitted when it made mistakes that resulted in civilian casualties.

Herron, though, asserts in *The Whore-Mother* that the IRA were engaged in a campaign to foment sectarian war, as is described in the following exchange between two Provos, McCandless and Power.

> 'The purpose of the present policy of street assassinations,' he said in what to Powers was his pompous way, 'is to make the Loyalists attack the Catholic districts so that we can keep the loyalty of the Catholics and tighten our grip on them. I don't need to tell you that, Powers.'

> 'No.' Then why the fuckin hell tell me, you puffed-up windbag? 'We've got to make them fight. The more chaos – civil war at the least – the more chance we have of getting the British out and the United Nations in, and the Border cleared away.'[42]

Bull Bailie's abject admission of past hypocrisy for his role in warping the mind of his impressionable ex-pupil is melodrama worthy of a propaganda sketch at a Paisleyite rally, and contains a number of questionable assertions.

> 'And no jobs in the shipyards and no houses for Catholics who need them?' McManus said.

> 'A fact and a lie. All right, the shipyards are a Protestant preserve, but the houses – that's a civil rights lie and the IRA deeply influenced the civil rights movement. There's been no discrimination in housing since 1964 – five years before the trouble started, and everybody who wants to know the truth knows it. The truth was established by Coleraine University in an inquiry led by an American and staffed by a group of Catholic scholars. During the 'sixties, Ulster was puttin up more housin than any other country in Western Europe. We're lyin and we're killin and you believe every bloody lie you're told because people like me got at you in separate schools and filled you full of patriotic bullshit that gave us a lot of satisfaction and you a lot of illusions. By God, our priests and schoolteachers have a lot to answer for – first off, hundreds dead. We made people like you ready for the IRA not because we wanted you to kill but because we're emotional, self-indulgent bastards who never expect to have to answer for our self-indulgence and never expected you would do anythin but talk. You weren't ghetto Catholics. We could pour the stuff out on you without startin a fire. But there's damned little difference between the fools who got you ready and the IRA psychopaths who put you to work with a gun or a bomb when you're ready.'[43]

The reference to academic research purporting to disprove that Catholics were discriminated against in the allocation of housing misses the point. Allowing that more houses were built, the original Civil Rights protests were against the biased allocation of council housing.

The novel reads like a catalogue of stereotypes, like the Provos' supposedly petit-bourgeois support base implied in the nicknames of two republican leaders, 'Cullen the Garage and Heavey the Grocer'.[44] And the following excerpt, in which MacManus reveals the onset of his disillusion, could be found in an ABC of loyalist siege paranoia.

> [His] first disenchantment came with his first sight of how this universal loyalty was achieved. He had seen pregnant Mrs Nolan beaten on the belly, and her husband's shop wrecked, because he refused to pay the imposed weekly levy for Ireland One Nation. The whole street understood the word when it went out: Don't buy from Nolan. So Nolan went bankrupt, and because he was self-employed he couldn't draw the dole and had to go on relief. It was a lesson often repeated, and executed by little men who now ran a protection racket where formerly they had been despised petty thieves in the districts. The small-time criminals had become the enforcers of patriotic unity. Even here in the western Border backwoods, small Catholic farmers with cattle to be poisoned, or children to be maimed, kept check on the movement of Protestant neighbours to be shot or burned out.[45]

Herron apparently found it more comforting to live with the fantasy that the IRA could sustain the allegiance of nationalist communities through the vice-hold of racketeering and terror than face the reality that the ties between the movement and its supportive communities are complex and that the solidarity and support found in these communities is generated by common grievances and British state repression.[46]

Two prominent republicans of the period feature in the novel as subjects of Herron's spleen. One character, Clune, bears an uncanny similarity to Sean MacStiofáin.

> Clune was sittin there with an eye-patch over his left eye, tryin to look like that Jew-soldier from Israel! He tried to make a bomb last night, for Christ's sake, and it blew up on him and only made a wee poop that burned one of his eyes – singed his eyebrow, very likely, but he wants that patch for the telly – the wounded fuckin hero.[47]

In reality, MacStiofáin suffered an eye injury from a loyalist letter bomb. Herron names the second prominent republican, for MacManus

> wasn't like McGuinness, the Provos' military leader in the Bogside who was his age but not his kind. McGuinness would despise him and wouldn't understand him, anymore than he could understand McGuinness, now that he had met the kind.[48]

Any failure of understanding, of empathy, is Herron's. Incidentally, Gerald Seymour's *Harry's Game*, discussed below, also features a character seemingly modelled on Martin McGuinness.[49]

Charting an opposite ideological course is another novel first published in the United States. *World Without End, Amen* (1973) was written by the distinguished American reporter Jimmy Breslin, and displays some sympathy for the republican cause.[50] A comparison of Breslin's novel with the other novels discussed so far strikingly illustrates the range of responses that were still possible at the beginning of the period, before the bludgeoning effects of the Prevention of Terrorism Act, rushed through parliament in the wake of the Birmingham bombs, created a climate unfavourable to the expression of dissent. By the end of the period hostile representations became the norm.

The narrative period of *World Without End, Amen* is the summer of 1970. Following his suspension for beating up a black suspect, Dermot Davey, an American cop, takes a spot of leave in Ireland accompanied by his friend Johno. While in Ireland he meets Deirdre O'Doherty, a student radical who is later killed while electioneering for a candidate closely modelled on Bernadette Devlin. During his time in the North, Davey, the surrogate roving reporter's eye of Breslin, witnesses street disturbances and violence, noting all shades of opinion.

In contrast to the line adopted in novels such as Russell Braddon's *The Progress of Private Lilyworth* that the presence of the media actually foments street violence, the idea here is that the riots and shooting are a deterrent to the media, that if the violence stopped then the press and television would then concentrate on addressing the issue of nationalist grievances. Dermot is present when Deirdre puts the view to a group of traditional republicans while the district is under British Army siege, possibly based on the Falls Road curfew of July 1970.

> She stopped at O'Neill. She took out a box of cigarettes and offered them to the priest, who took one, and then to O'Neill and the two older men. She held out the box to Dermot. He took one. She did not look at him. She was looking straight at Joe O'Neill.
>
> 'We need the television to come here,' she said.
>
> 'That would be fine,' O'Neill said.
>
> 'If there were no shooting, then the BBC could come all through the area,' Liam said.
>
> 'Been shooting already,' O'Neill said.
>
> 'If it could end at that,' Deirdre said, turning to them.[51]

The scene illustrates the power interaction between Deirdre, a student radical, left-wing activist, feminist, opposed to violence, and O'Neill, the republican traditionalist, who it transpires is a Provo, and other older men. Deirdre continues:

> 'Can you not get the arms out of the area without using them?' Deirdre said to O'Neill.
>
> O'Neill grunted something.
>
> 'Then we could get the telly in. It would be extremely beneficial for us to have something on the telly showin' wee children with no food.'
>
> 'We all know there's no food,' O'Neill said.
>
> 'The people in London tonight and tomorrow would see hungry children,' she said.

'London? And what would we get from London. More bloody troops?'

'And who'd defend us today?' one of the men with O'Neill said.

'The telly would defend us,' Deirdre said. 'Soldiers are afraid of it.'

They laughed.[52]

Written with what one would imagine is appropriate post-Bloody Sunday irony, Breslin portrays Deirdre's incomprehension of the forces and interests that would collude to prevent media exposure of British Army brutality and murder.

Later, Dermot meets his friend Johno in a bar, who introduces him to the 'real thing', not a 'pinko hump'.

> Johno was in the smoke and the pale light with his arm around a guy in a neat brown suit. The guy had a thick neck and shoulders and he stood straight up. He had a face made of cut glass.

> 'Here,' Johno called out. 'Now we're finally gettin' with our own kind.'

> He put a hand on Dermot's shoulder to bring him close. He said in a low voice, 'This is Eddie Canavan. He's the real. He's not like that fuckin' Communist cunt you got up there. This is the real.'

> 'How are you?' Dermot said.

> The Canavan guy took his hand and looked Dermot in the eye. Canavan looked with narrowed eyes. He had high cheekbones that pushed the eyes together anyway. But narrowed into slits, as they were now, the eyes, blue eyes, looked particularly fierce. Canavan had short hair. As they shook hands, Dermot noticed how neat the suit was. Canavan was wearing a blue shirt and brown tie that went with the suit. He was the neatest person Dermot had seen since he came to Ireland. After a quick and hard pump of the hand, Canavan spun and faced the bar, snorting through a squat nose.

> 'He's in with Joe O'Neill,' Johno said.

> 'Joe O'Neill is in with me,' Canavan said. He said it without looking at them.

> Johno clapped Canavan on the shoulder. 'See? He's the real.'

> 'You up with that Deirdre O'Doherty, are you not?' Canavan said.

> Dermot didn't answer.

> 'That's a whore's get, the lot of them,' Canavan said.

> 'You see?' Johno said. 'Communist cocksuckers. I told you.'

> 'They say they're in the IRA,' Canavan said. 'They're IRA all right. The 'I Ran Away' brigade of the IRA.'

> 'He's in the Provos,' Johno said.

> 'We believe in getting the British out and fook the politics,' Canavan said.

'He's my kind,' Johno said. 'He's no pinko hump. Let's have a drink.'[53]

Canavan, the Provo, it seems, is an apolitical anti-socialist whom a racist bigot like Johno can readily identify with. Canavan's 'neatness' is accentuated to suggest, possibly, another media stereotype, to indicate the supposedly petit-bourgeois power base of the Provos (a stereotype also referred to in the discussion of *The Whore-Mother*), an accusation frequently levelled by left-wing critics of the movement then. The contrast between Canavan and the student activist Deirdre, who Canavan suggests is involved with the Officials (still active during the period covered in the narrative), couldn't be more striking.

The success of *World Without End, Amen* in the United States perhaps prompted Conor Cruise O'Brien to write his scathing review for the New York Review of Books entitled 'A Yankee at the Court of Queen Bernadette'.[54] The title indicates that the real target for Cruise O'Brien's spleen was Bernadette Devlin and the prospect that the novel would advance her cause among Americans. A more explicit objection of O'Brien's to the novel was that Dermot Davey, being a racist, should have gravitated towards the Provos, 'straightforward, no-nonsense patriotic Catholic killers', rather than the Officials, in the form of Deirdre.[55] That someone of Cruise O'Brien's clout – he was the twenty-six county Minister for Post and Telecommunications at the time – should have bothered to review a work of popular fiction, albeit a work from an influential journalist and purported to offer insights, says much for the sensitivities of those in power when the subject of 'Ireland' was invoked.

One political insider was motivated to do more than write a caustic critique. Some eight years before he became the Secretary of State for Northern Ireland, the Tory MP Douglas Hurd wrote a thriller about the Troubles. *Vote to Kill* was published in 1975, and possibly written during the actual lull in IRA activity occasioned by the run-up to the ceasefire of 1975.[56] The novel is dedicated: 'To Ted Heath from whom I have learned much'.

Perhaps to forestall any possible political embarrassment from commenting about incumbent political figures he set his narrative a few years into the future, to the period in fact when he was subsequently to hold political responsibility for British policy in the North, the early 1980s.

The novel opens with the election of a new Tory government. A major riot in Belfast is sparked by rumours that the incoming Tory administration will reintroduce internment. Internment ended some unspecified time before (in fact the last internees were released on 5 December 1975, presumably after publication of the novel). For some years now the 'Province' has experienced relative calm under Direct Rule. However, as the principal Private Secretary, William Pershore, reports, political tensions are simmering.

> In one sense direct rule has been a success for too long. The same moderate leaders, Catholic and Protestant, have been making the same speeches for five years now. They all say they want direct rule to end, but of course on their own terms. Since they know they can't get their own terms they

privately prefer direct rule by Britain to someone else's terms. But I'm afraid the extremists have been gaining ground again lately, partly for economic reasons, but partly in fear through sheer boredom.[57]

Into this relative calm strides an ambitious and charismatic Tory politician, Jeremy Cornwall, seeking power on the populist ticket of Troops Out. The novel is really Hurd's warning of what might happen should a future Tory government contemplate military withdrawal from the North. During a crucial speech opposing Cornwall's campaign for withdrawal the Prime Minister recites Philip Larkin's poem, 'Homage to a Government', epitomising Little England regret at loss of empire: 'Next year we are to bring the soldiers home/ For lack of money…' Hurd's authorial presence is sensed plaintively deploring the 'deep core of defeatism in the British nation which… [Cornwall] was tapping'.[58] Hurd, like his fictional Prime Minister, clearly regards withdrawal as a defeat.

Events in the North take a turn for the worse. Twenty members of the Greenjackets are killed in an IRA ambush on the Falls Road, signalling a return to the levels of violence of the past.

> Then there had been a lull, blessed at the time, but perhaps cruel in the end.
> For everyone seemed to have forgotten what they had learnt. Once again
> young men would blow themselves up with bombs, women curse and spit
> at their protectors, troops travel in vulnerable convoy, just as they had done
> when the last troubles started after 1969.[59]

The image of ungrateful spitting harridans is a stock characterisation, beloved of tabloid editors as much as thriller writers, and perhaps it isn't credible to expect that a Tory author might cause to wonder why ordinary people should be driven to displays of so much exasperated, inarticulate loathing of the British Army.[60] High body counts are another staple ingredient of the thriller, but Hurd may unwittingly be revealing that in government circles of the day there was an expectation that the IRA might become more sophisticated and successful in the scale and selection of its targeting. No IRA operation of this magnitude was undertaken until 1979 when eighteen British soldiers, most of them Paratroops, were killed in a landmine explosion at Narrow Water, on the same day that Lord Mountbatten was assassinated.

Hurd is not above suggesting a tenuous, even subliminal, linkage between the IRA and the criminal underworld. Clarissa Strong, a young English civil servant who is also an Irish republican, attempts to assassinate the Prime Minister with a crossbow. Apparently, the idea 'was a crib from the Kray brothers… They had a crossbow like that in the 'sixties. In a suitcase'.[61] The Provos and a London gangster, we are given to accept, are cut from the same cloth. Hurd neglects to mention that the Krays had served in the British Army.

The novel's central thrust, then, is a rehearsal of the arguments to counter calls for withdrawal. Paradoxically, throughout the novel Ireland is talked about as if it is still a colony – surprisingly, if this is a valid reflection of the thinking within the

Westminster power elite and surrounding political culture. It is commonplace, additionally, within establishment circles portrayed in the novel to refer to 'Ireland' when meaning 'Northern Ireland'.

Political intrigue also features in Gerald Seymour's *Harry's Game* (1975).[62] Seymour, who covered the North as a journalist, tries to anticipate the likely response by the British government to the killing of a leading politician. The story is set some thirty months after an actual incident alluded to, the IRA's uncovery of British Intelligence's *Four Square Laundry* surveillance sting, which would place narrative time at April 1975. In the novel, this is when Henry Danby, the Secretary of State for Social Services, and an ex-NIO minister, is assassinated outside his Belgravia home by a lone IRA volunteer. the British Prime Minister sanctions that in response an SAS man be sent to the North to kill the assassin. In his tenure at the NIO Danby had been responsible for regime policy at Long Kesh and had been repeatedly warned by the IRA to improve conditions there.[63]

Similarly to the last novel discussed, prior to the publication of *Harry's Game* there had not been a successful IRA operation of this magnitude carried out against a top establishment figure in Britain since the early 1920s. In this one respect the novel also bears comparison to Broderick's *The Fugitives* which, set during the Border Campaign, also involves an IRA assassination of a prominent politician in London. perhaps the actual level of violence and prominence of targets in the early to mid-1970s were considered by authors to be insufficient for narrative emulation, for thrillers are necessarily to do with spectacular events.

There can be little doubt that the IRA was doing its best during the relevant period to come up with suitably hard-hitting targets, what have since become known as 'spectaculars'. However, Seymour posits that at a meeting of the IRA Army Council in a chip shop (perhaps recalling O'Flaherty's *The Informer*) in Monaghan town, at which possible repercussions of the Danby killing are discussed, the mood is against future similar operations.

> 'But what's the reaction? If we did it again, they'd tear the bloody place apart. We'd not survive it. They'd be all over us. Down here as much as in the North.'

> 'That's what we have to weigh. What would happen to the whole structure? They'd go mad, knock bloody shit out of us. [...] Our need at this moment is not to go killing Cabinet Ministers from Westminster, but winning back what we lost at Motorman when the army came into Bogside and Creggan. We have to play on the tiredness of those people across the water. There's no stomach there for this war. They're soft there, no guts. They'll get weary of hearing of another soldier, another policeman, another bomb, another tout. It's the repetition that hurts them. Not another big killing. All that does is get them going. It affronts their bloody dignity. Unites them against us. We have to bore them.'[64]

This supposedly sage counsel is refuted by one of the men present whose opinion carries the day and whom Seymour bathes in a menacing, melodramatic light:

'The bigger man you get the better.' It was a Belfast man. He was of the
new school, and had come a long way since Long Kesh opened. He had
pitiless eyes, wide apart above his ferret nose, and a thin, bloodless
mouth.'[65]

The two central characters – the eponymous Harry Brown, SAS assassin, and
his prey, the IRA assassin Billy Downs – are both loners. In terms of their actions
there is an amoral equivalence between them, though Harry is depicted as
physically superior to his IRA counterpart.

Billy, tired of his life, contemplates life on the run with some relish.

'One more day, one more job. Then out. Leave it to the cowboys. The
heroes who didn't hold their fire, who shot wee kids. Squeeze the trigger
right through the scream of a five-year-old. Was that Pearse's revolution,
or Connolly's or Plunkett's? Was it, hell. Leave it to the cowboys after one
more day.'[66]

A distinction exists in Billy's mind between himself and his more reckless
comrades. But, of course, the distinction is in Seymour's mind. Billy is favoured
in terms of comparison with other IRA characters, so that in the end even his few
redeeming graces are proved insufficient beside the better British specimen.
Seymour, perhaps to avoid the charge of applying a crude nationalist stereotyping,
casts Harry as a Catholic, originally from Portadown. Nationality isn't therefore
the primary distinguishing characteristic of either; instead, it is the value system
that each man adheres to if only by dint of membership of a particular society or
organisation. The bottom line is that the Brits represent a physically and morally
superior, more efficient adversary, one not to be messed with, as exemplified in
Harry's attitude.

To the others they were the enemy, to Harry they were the opposition. They
didn't have to be the enemy to make them worth killing.

They're not heroes. Bloody lunatics, he said to himself as he pulled his sweater
over his head. They rejected all the ordinary things that ordinary people search for,
and chose to go on against these massive odds. It didn't involve Harry. The man
he was searching for was quite straightforward. He was a killer, he was a
challenge. Simple and clean. Harry could focus on that.[67]

Billy Downs, ultimately the victim, as scripted by the author, recognises the
superiority of his enemy, and thus is made to discursively connive in his own
subjugation as a stereotype.

He was formidable, this Englishman, in his old jeans and dark anorak, with
the clear-cut face, softer than those fashioned in the bitterness of Belfast. He
had not been reared through the anguish of the troubles, and it showed in the
freshness of his features. But he was hard, Downs had no doubt on that.[68]

Bill Rolston makes the point that novels when dealing with the North usually
feature two viewpoints represented in the characters, who are outsiders from their

respective social orders – the Brit agent who is a loner and disaffected with the system; likewise, the republican activist who is a renegade.[69] They are offered par excellence in *Harry's Game*. Contradictions are exposed in the bourgeois novel, because its condensation into characterisation reveals to the reader the clash of discourses, whether the author intends the effect or otherwise; more so in the popular thriller, in which stereotypes must carry the burden of signification. Given the absurd reductionism involved in these types it is not surprising that contradictions are more blatant. Only complexity of characterisation, range of character types, and an authentically represented narrative world can offset the worst aspects of reductionism; but there is no avoiding compression – selection is inherent to the process of writing fiction, therefore, contradictions will inevitably follow. The representation of the conflict in terms of a struggle between apolitical mavericks contradicts the motivations, interests, grievances, and ideological premises underlying each side.

Seymour has received praise for the authenticity of his descriptional detail of the North. Much is made of the time he spent as a journalist covering the conflict. He is good when he takes the trouble. For example, he doesn't miss that the Tartan gangs (Protestant/loyalist football supporters) regularly harassed nationalist shoppers in the centre of Belfast during the mid 1970s.[70] But there are several annoying notes, grating to a Northern ear. For example, he refers to barracks as 'police stations';[71] and Broadway is erroneously given a definite article, much as it is customary to refer to 'the Bone'.[72] More ludicrously, Josephine dabs her nose with a Long Kesh handkerchief, its crossed Thompsons' motif seen by Harry.[73] Long Kesh hankies were intended for decorative, not practical use (for it is likely that Josephine's nose would have been garishly smeared from the painted motif's running colours).

The novel is preoccupied with the in-fighting and lack of co-ordination between the British army, the RUC, the various British Intelligence agencies, and of the political interference in 'operational' intelligence matters. While hopelessly awry in its understanding of the culture of republicanism, Seymour's fiction nevertheless occasionally offers insights into the thinking in 'security' circles. Howard Rennie, for example,

> could remember the courses he'd been on in the early days before it all went haywire, and the troops arrived, when he'd been told across in England by dour-faced men with biscuit tans from long service in the Far East and Africa that the inside work by the police was the only hope of breaking a terrorist movement in its infancy. 'When you get the army in, lording it over your heads, telling you what to do, knowing it all, then it's too late. It's out of your hands by that time. The military on the streets means the enemy are winning, and that you are no longer a force for the opposition to reckon with.[74]

In contrast to the above point, also conveyed is the mood expressed earlier that during the mid-1970s the British state believed it had the upper hand in its war against the IRA. This mood is illustrated in the comments made by the wife of an RUC man. Downs has been chosen to assassinate an RUC Special Branch officer, Howard Rennie. He holds Rennie's wife, Janet, hostage in her own home while waiting for her husband to return. She tries to persuade him to go.

> 'If you go through with this they'll get you. They always get them now. It's a fact. You'll be in the Kesh for the rest of your life. Is that what you want?'

> [...] She persisted. 'It'll get you nowhere. It's the Provisionals, isn't it? You're beaten. One more cruel killing, senseless. It won't do any good.'

> [...] With growing desperation she took up the same theme.

> 'But you're beaten now. It'll soon be all over. All your big men are gone. There'll have to be a cease-fire soon, then talking. More killing won't help anything.'[75]

Harry's Game may be regarded as what was to become the quintessential Troubles thriller: a novel feigning amoral equivalence that in the denouement reveals the purported necessity of Britain's role in Ireland.

The mid-1970s saw the British government turn to repression in a twin-pronged attack on the republican movement, drawing the movement into a premature ceasefire while preparing a counter-insurgency onslaught backed up by all the power of the state. Because of miscalculation and attrition the republican response was tardy, creating an illusion of at best stasis or at worst a prolonged struggle with little to show for the sacrifice and pain. The British perhaps felt they had the war all but won. Certainly, many novelists were deluded into accepting the inevitability of another defeat for republicanism no matter how long it might take. Nothing, beyond the IRA's own agenda, analysis and conviction, seemed likely to upset or disprove the narrative drift of the novels to be published at this time. The enemy was laid bare. Republicanism in the form of Seymour's characters was a bitter twisted apolitical affair, and while those engaged on the Brit side in the dirty war might stoop to some low tricks they were in the final analysis on the side of the angels.

Bruce Merry quotes Jerry Palmer to suggest 'that the agent exists primarily to punish deviants who go against the consensus as to how all individuals should behave: in other words, to restore the reader's sense of security in his own world order'.[76]

In another quite common twist, some authors create a worthy enemy for the British army and intelligence agencies. After all, what kudos is there in tackling an opponent who doesn't present a testing challenge? At times the capacity of the Provos was deliberately inflated in order to exaggerate the dangers and thus lend justificatory exemplification to whatever 'security' actions were deemed necessary for the greater good. This may explain some plots in which the Provos execute operations of a magnitude beyond their actual proven capabilities and known resources in terms of actual and narrative time.

Losers are vulnerable to misrepresentation. History, as is oft repeated, is written by the victors. Republicans are by and large characterised in fiction by authors who accept as inevitable a British victory. Reading Troubles fiction as a contemporary chronicle, it is clear that the republican struggle was perceived to be ineluctably doomed in the face of superior force. With, at this stage, five years of Troubles fiction to base an opinion on, we can compare earlier representations of republicans. In Peter Leslie's 1970 novel, *The Extremist*, republicans are accredited with intelligence; loyalists, by contrast, are depicted as vicious atavistic, anachronistic, stupid.

But Higgins's *The Savage Day* and Herron's *The Whore-Mother* mark a change, explicable to a point by the deep antipathy towards the Provos because of the bombing campaign in the North. It is also a result, I would suggest, of an unquestioning absorption by certain writers of the dehumanisation of republicans, and of nationalists, personified at times in a tabloid outrage which wouldn't have gone amiss, for example, in the *Loyalist News*. So deep and widespread was the hostility shared by many people towards the Provos from 1972 onwards in particular that it became easier to take on wholesale the dehumanising mindset of loyalism and to echo its most morbid and pathological excesses rather than probe deeper for explanations to the conflict.

What evidence is there, then, about those who join the Provos? Despite the wealth of research that has been conducted on every aspect of the situation pertaining in the North since the inception of the conflict, published data on the social backgrounds of republican activists is a scarce commodity. Republicans are understandably reluctant to participate in any research project that might be used unwittingly or otherwise to inform their enemies. And until quite recently, contemporary republicans neither wrote their personal accounts nor assisted others in doing so.[77] Despite this reticence, the irony is that the IRA, and indeed the entire nationalist population in the North on which it depends for support, has been systematically screened and monitored by the British army for three decades, down to the colour of their bedroom wallpaper. None of this information is available to the general public.

This leaves a mere three surveys, relating to the social backgrounds of those, both republicans and loyalists, who appeared before the Diplock courts on scheduled offences in 1975, 1979 and in 1989/90, upon which to make a judgement. The first two surveys form the basis of a discussion of 'the paramilitaries' in *Ten Years on in Northern Ireland* (1980) by Kevin Boyle, Tom Hadden and Paddy Hillyard.[78] The third survey was conducted on behalf of Kevin Boyle and Tom Hadden, and is discussed in *Northern Ireland: The Choice* (1994).[79] The three surveys appear to largely refute both media and fictional stereotypes.

On the basis of the first two surveys, the authors were

> satisfied that the data establishes beyond reasonable doubt that the bulk of Republican offenders are young men and women without criminal records in the ordinary sense, though some have been involved in public disorders of the kind which frequently take place in the areas in which they live.[80]

The authors' conclusion was that

> both the IRA and its counterparts are rooted in their respective communities. Both are more permanent than their membership at any given time, in the sense that new leaders and recruits are always coming forward to carry on the traditions that have been established over more than 50 years. Both are concrete expressions of the shared aspirations and concerns of those communities; on the Catholic side aspirations for unification of Ireland and fears of continued oppression and deprivation.[81]

When the third survey was taken into account, the findings were similarly favourable, though some of the conclusions are questionable.

> Those involved are not, as is sometimes implied by government ministers or the press, habitual criminals or in some way psychologically disturbed. Most are broadly representative of the communities from which they come. They are more like young soldiers who have joined an army, partly because they believe in the cause they are fighting for, partly in search of prestige and excitement and partly because it provides employment in areas where jobs are hard to come by. In some respects they are not unlike those who join the British Army and who are deployed against them.[82]

Their conclusion ignores the very real distinction between republican and British army recruits: the former are volunteers, while the latter are professional, that is, paid. Further, it is a matter of IRA policy to deter recruitment from those who might seek to join for thrills, and to that end it is made clear that a commitment will involve sacrifices, imprisonment, possibly death.

In an assessment of the surveys, and in contradiction to the IRA's 'grocer' and 'chip shop' background alluded to in at least three of the novels covered in this period, Louise Shara notes that the figures suggest that the 'vast majority' of young people before the courts in both periods were working-class.[83]

In Chapter Five I will discuss how the republican movement survived the machinations of the British which led to the 1975 ceasefire and, in tandem with the ending of internment, the building of the H-Blocks, heralding the criminalisation front, and of how the conflict as it panned out between the years 1976 to 1981 continued to suffer fictional misrepresentation.

5.

Definitional Misrule: 1976-81

In Chapter Four I noted how the cease-fire of 1975 almost spelled disaster for the republican movement. The British military establishment was said to be furious at the Labour government for secretly negotiating the cease-fire. Their argument was that the IRA could have been defeated at the time. after all, the internment and special category cages were full, and IRA operations were greatly reduced from their 1972 and 1973 peaks. From this angle, the phased release of internees may have seemed a reckless and needless political gamble, a snatching of defeat from the jaws of victory. However, the achievement of an 'acceptable level of violence' had pertained only through the use of unparalleled repression, by the standards of western democracies, in republican areas throughout the North, and at an incalculable political cost to Britain's international reputation. 1976 in particular heralded a return to a level of IRA operations not witnessed since 1972.

In fact the British state had chillingly calculated its interests. Bringing Sinn Féin in from the cold was calculated to support the ceasefire, facilitate entrance into constitutional politics and draw republicans away from armed struggle. When Merlyn Rees, the new Northern Ireland Secretary of State, legalised Sinn Féin in 1974, paranoia increased among the 'securocrats'[1] of the day about a sell-out, even though legalisation was the intention of the previous Tory administration.[2] The ending of internment reduced if not entirely removed international opprobrium at Britain's role. But to those of us in Long Kesh who witnessed the construction of the perimeter wall of the H-Blocks at the very same time as internees were being released in dribs and drabs, it seemed that Britain had merely changed tack. To republicans, every British political initiative had its hidden military agenda. That agenda was soon made clear.

The British state embarked on a policy to impose its 'definitional authority' in a strategy designed to politically isolate Irish republicanism.[3] It had at its disposal the resources and the power to define the conflict. The means entailed a propaganda offensive which republicans identified as the three-pronged strategy of Criminalisation, Ulsterisation and Normalisation. Ulsterisation referred to the strategy of giving primacy to the indigenous police force for the battle against 'terrorism', a policy completed by 1977.[4] Normalisation referred to 'the overall strategy of downgrading the status of the violence... from that of a 'war' to mere criminal activity'.[5]   In tandem with the strategy, the 'conveyor-belt' justice of Castlereagh and the Diplock Courts ensured that the H-Blocks were full within two years. All those sentenced after the 31 March 1976 would be treated as criminals. The policy was ferociously pursued under Roy Mason, the Labour government's new Secretary of State who had replaced Merlyn Rees. Liz Curtis claims that the use of the term 'Godfather' to describe IRA leaders first came to prominence during Mason's term of office.[6]

The republican movement responded to this offensive by putting into effect a major rethink in strategy. The impetus for the new strategy came from within the internment and special category cages of Long Kesh. 1976 had followed 1975, as '74 followed '73, as 'the year of victory'. But no longer. This unrealistic shibboleth was a legacy of the British agenda to side-track republicans into the belief that British military withdrawal was on the cards. Not until Jimmy Drumm gave his Bodenstown address in June 1977 did talk of imminent victory subside. 'The Long War' was the new cry and voiced the realisation that the British would only move if they understood that the movement was in for 'the long haul' requiring a long-term commitment of republicans in pursuit of their goals. Only when the British understood that their military and political presence would always be resisted would they begin the process of withdrawal.

After some seven years of armed struggle, cruel lessons had been learned: firstly, that the movement couldn't fight the British state on military terms alone; and secondly, that a revolutionary strategy required not only an effective military arm but political representation. It wasn't a matter of a belated realisation by the movement about what had to be done but of putting this into effect against the attritional backdrop of counterinsurgency. An intense period of reorganisation ensued. The IRA reorganised from a brigade, battalion and company model based at a local level to a vastly more secure cell structure. Sinn Féin, too, would reorganise, and its policy formulations made more relevant to social issues, a development deemed particularly necessary if the party was to increase support and relevance in the South. A further stage in the development was inaugurated in early 1979 when *An Phoblacht* and the *Republican News* were amalgamated. A strategy was in place and in the process of being implemented that would build Sinn Féin throughout the country.

None of this occurred in isolation from other developments, some of which looked to have the potential to hinder the movement's further political progress, not least the emergence of the Peace People in 1976, who provided yet another arena for Britain's propaganda war. Their discourse of 'peace now' was translated by the republican grass-roots, who had suffered and witnessed years of repression, to mean 'peace at any price', and was answered by the republican demand for 'peace with justice'.

At a time when the focus should have been on pursuing to the fullest the potential of the new strategy, prison issues increasingly stretched the movement's scarce organisational resources and these proved ineffective in countering

Britain's criminalisation policy. As part of the criminalisation drive the British in effect had opened up another front in the prisons. The prisoners were left with no other choice than for themselves to take the initiative. The dirty protest (and by the end of the period under discussion, the hunger strikes) took up much of Sinn Féin's energies because of the need to publicise the ill-treatment of prisoners and the denial of political status.

After a reduction in operations during 1977 the IRA returned to the offensive, mounting a renewed and extremely effective commercial bombing campaign, targeting hotels and businesses throughout the North, and undermining Britain's normalisation policy. The La Mon tragedy was a major set back to this resurgence, and in its aftermath there was a renewed emphasis by the IRA on avoiding civilian casualties. Perhaps, too, it increased the hand of those republicans arguing for more effort and resources to be channelled into a campaign in England, where it was believed the war could be prosecuted to greatest political affect.

Within two years the cracks in the criminalisation strategy started to give. In late 1978 General Sir James Glover, the former Commander in Chief of UK Land Forces who had served as an Intelligence Officer in the North, compiled a secret intelligence report titled 'Northern Ireland: Future Terrorist Trends' which gave his assessment of the IRA's calibre and capabilities five years hence, that is, to 1983.[7] Glover's report, which was intercepted by the IRA and then released by them, much to the government's embarrassment, testified that the British admitted privately that they couldn't defeat the IRA.

Glover's assessment of the character of republicans contradicts the crudely sculptured popular image of IRA gunmen and mad bombers promulgated in the broadcasting and print media and also found in Troubles fiction.

> Our evidence of the calibre of rank and file terrorists does not support the view that they are merely mindless hooligans drawn from the unemployed and unemployable.[8]

And on the qualities of the 'leadership':

> PIRA is essentially a working class organisation based in the ghetto areas of the cities and in the poorer rural areas. Thus if members of the middle-class and graduates become more deeply involved they have to forfeit their lifestyle. Many are also deterred by the Provisionals' muddled political thinking. Nevertheless there is a strata of intelligent, astute and experienced terrorists who provide the backbone of the organisation.[9]

Leaving aside the General's jaundiced opinion of the movement's 'muddled political thinking', the report, emanating from such an expert quarter, had to be taken seriously. And yet his realistic appraisal that the IRA wouldn't be defeated was apparently dismissed in certain quarters. Margaret Thatcher, who had been elected leader of the Conservative Party on 11 February 1975, became Prime Minister in 1979. It was widely believed that she would reward Airey Neave, who was reputed to favour a military hard-line, with the position of Secretary of State for Northern Ireland. The intention signalled increased repression at a time when the thrust of Glover's report should have generated fresh thinking and a conciliatory political initiative. Neave was killed by an INLA bomb before he could take up the post and implement the crack-down. Nevertheless, some ten years after the arrival of the British Army, another opportunity to arrive at a settlement was squandered.

Another significant factor militating against a peaceful resolution was Ronald Reagan's crusade against 'international terrorism', begun in 1980,[10] which effectively acted to impede the development of and support for the Irish republican analysis in the USA.

Something had to give, but the movement was resolute. The deaths of ten hunger strikers changed everything, internationalising the struggle around the issue of political status and shattering the British line, heavily promoted through its embassies, that the prisoners were criminals. Sinn Féin's prospects soared as the benefits of electoral intervention became increasingly evident to old and new activists. Political effort was to be the most effective strategic direction for the movement in the coming years.

In the battle of discourses during the course of the 1970s the dominance of Britain's view of the conflict began slowly to be challenged. One facet of this discursive exchange was the increasing academic and journalistic interest, from the mid-1970s, directed to fiction dealing with or touching on the conflict. When was it first appreciated, however, that Troubles fiction as a body had become a publishing and cultural phenomenon, in terms of commercial and authorial interest? And further, and perhaps more significantly, when was it recognised that the genre overwhelmingly carried the British political establishment's line about Ireland?

Prior to 1976, the critical attention of academics and commentators had focused on Irish fiction published before 1970, ignoring novels written by non-Irish authors and popular fiction in general. For example, John Wilson Foster, author of *Forces and Themes in Ulster Fiction*, whose jacket blurb describes it as 'the first full-length critical study of Ulster fiction to appear', was dismissive of what he described as the spate of 'often contemptible and pseudonymous efforts that have cynically flooded the paperback shops since 1969'.[11]

When in 1976 Richard Deutsch produced an update on Irish Troubles fiction titled '"Within Two Shadows": The Troubles in Northern Ireland', covering novels published from 1969 to 1974, his focus, too, was on fiction by Irish writers dealing with the conflict.[12] The incorporation by Deutsch of the title of John Wilson Haire's 1972 play, which dramatised 'the mounting tensions and growing hatred of one another within families', signalled a view that the conflict was in essence a civil war.[13] His concentration on how Irish authors tackled the conflict, again, rather dismissively left 'aside the rest of the voluminous English-speaking production'.[14] He concluded with the startling (and, some might add, in view of the genre's by now starkly delineated discursive limitations, appalling) claim, from an unattributed source, that a Belfast publisher had received 'more than a hundred novels on the North'.[15]

Still, a fresh appraisal is discernible. Compare Deutsch's lavish, and I think justifiable, praise below of Martin Waddell's *A Little Bit British*[16] with the grudging response of John Cronin and, apparently, of local critics. Cronin had alleged that Waddell had 'lost his cool' in writing the novel, a 'serious [but failed, he implied] attempt at social satire' about Protestant fundamentalist bigotry.[17] For Deutsch, however, it

> transcends a novel on the North and its troubles to reach the level of brilliant satire... undoubtedly one of the masterpieces of Northern Irish literature of this period. Critics in the Province gave it the cold shoulder for it does not mince words regarding stupidity, bigotry and sectarianism wrapped up in sheer hypocrisy.[18]

The comment was made with the benefit of six years hindsight, and perhaps too much significance shouldn't be attached to a difference of opinion in regard to one novel, but I suspect that a reappraisal or alternative, more oppositional view was now emerging.

Two American (or American-based) academics, James MacKillop and Joseph Browne, were the first to deal with Troubles novels by non-Irish authors. Their contributions appeared in *Conflict in Ireland*, published in the USA in 1976. MacKillop, whose line in the article is sympathetic to the plight of Irish nationalists, looked at ten novels written since 1969. He also alluded to a further six, and commented that 'sixteen titles is an indicative investment by British and American publishers', given the convention at the time that the novel was in a 'state of atrophy').[19] In fact, some fifty two relevant novels were published during the time covered by their research.

MacKillop's essay shows an understanding of what Garret Fitzgerald would later dub 'the nationalist nightmare'. MacKillop also demonstrates a certain quizzical irony towards the widespread view of the conflict in Ireland as primarily tribal or sectarian.

> No popular literature incorporated anything of the institutionalized violence of the Six Counties, a story found only in narratives of emigrants. Nevertheless, the motif of Ulster's poisonous hatreds was a recognizable one in the English-speaking world...[20]

Joseph Browne's essay in *Conflict in Ireland* took an opposing and, indeed, rather pessimistic view of the likelihood of a future re-unification of Ireland.

> After eight more years of the imperturbable violence in Northern Ireland... a United Ireland is more cryingly absurd now than ever before... [E]veryone who writes of the hatred and violence... has certainly implied that the jeremiad will go terrifyingly on and on.[21]

Critics shared almost complete unanimity about a lack of literary merit in the bulk of these works. The attitude is caught well in a spoof interview in *Fortnight*.

Recently there has been a rash of novels on the theme of Irish conflict. Following the publications of Leon Uris and Naomi May, Sarah Nelson talks to world-famous American writer ART KRAPP about his forthcoming trilogy, 'Oceans of Blood'.[22]

The novel being so savagely traduced, is the best-selling *Trinity* (1976) by the popular American author Leon Uris, the publication of which coincided with this recent academic interest stemming from the USA. Krapp, unmistakably the lampooned Uris, describes his research for his latest blockbuster.

My wife and I came over for a week and took a whole lot of pictures… Plus I read the Irish papers back home and talk a lot with Ted Kennedy'.[23]

The novel, though dealing with events prior to the Easter Rising, 1916, came under sustained criticism for its pro-republican line, which to many people in the pro-union camp confirmed their view of the ignorance of Americans about Ireland.[24] *Trinity* concludes with the observation that

when all of this was done, a republic eventually came to pass but the sorrows and the troubles have never left that tragic, lovely land. For you see, in Ireland there is no future, only the past happening over and over.[25]

Three years were to elapse before an article appeared that argued against the pro-British line evident in the majority of instances of the genre. Again, the criticism came from outside. In 'The Troubles as Trash: Shadows of the Irish Gunman on an American Curtain', J. Bowyer Bell was the first to question the anti-republican bias of Troubles fiction generally.[26] As the title suggests, his focus was on novels published in the USA. He noted that:

With the rise of the present troubles in Ulster, a new interest has been shown in the contemporary IRA gunmen. It was not necessary to understand very much about Ireland or Ulster in order to insert the gunman into the plot; but like all crafts, time, loving care, and focus on detail ultimately produces a finer product. And those who construct thrillers have their aspirations as well. Thus, with varying degrees of success, authors have attempted to flesh out their gunmen. In so doing they reveal something about the laic perceptions of the Irish troubles…[27]

Any fleshing out of the stereotypes is due, Bowyer Bell suggests, to the aspirations of authors competing for their readers' growing need for ever more intricate plotting and depth of character, of what from a structuralist analysis would be termed transformations within the genre. As for what these thrillers reveal about 'laic perceptions', presumably such perceptions are already fed, or rather, undernourished, on ill-intentioned and disinformative media coverage, and therefore insufficiently informed to question shallow characterisations. He takes the point further:

A composite picture of the Irish Troubles can be gleaned by these thrillers, written by both the innocent and informed. It is hardly profound but may represent the wisdom of the common reader.[28]

The 'wisdom of the common reader' is in the sense employed by Bowyer Bell close to Gramscian 'common sense'.

Bowyer Bell identifies three types of IRA gunmen encountered in thrillers (such as those of Robert Charles).[29]

> First is the hard-man, the gunman of limited ideas and often malice, basic IRA, a killer doomed to die who often barely has a speaking part. Second is the soft-man, the idealist whose political background is drawn in a paragraph or two who gradually realizes the futility of violence, and thus may be ultimately saved. And third, the good-girl who like the soft-man joined the movement for decent purpose in the civil rights days and sickened by terror seeks to convert the soft-man.[30]

The imbalance discerned by Bowyer Bell of ascribing hardness only to men was subsequently corrected by authors who introduced the ice-maiden gunwoman, a type heavily indebted to tabloid distortions. I will say more in Chapter Six on the portrayal of republican women. In the article he goes on to count Frederick Forsyth as one of 'the classic practitioners... [who] made do without Irish gunmen'. This was true in 1978, though in Forsyth's 1991 novel, *The Deceiver*, an example of the species, Kevin Mahoney, is included. Unfortunately Mahoney's characterisation lacks the generic development of the type that we might hope for given the by then more than twenty years' hindsight at Forsyth's disposal.[31]

Bowyer Bell noted a change in American public perceptions which was attributable in part to the influence of stereotypical fictional representations. He described the changing attitudes as follows:

> gradually the IRA extremists took over and their use of violence has contaminated a just cause. The IRA, the odd misguided idealist aside, is a collection of mindless bombers and gunmen whose operations are counter-productive. The Irish rebel has become a terrorist. The British army and security forces are simply trying to maintain order.[32]

His argument was that the world-wide publicity accruing to IRA outrages was not to its political advantage. It was losing the propaganda war. The disadvantage to the IRA he attributed in part to 'a visibility made possible by the technological elegance of the communication industry – *including thriller production* [my emphasis]'.[33] This is a large assertion about the efficacy of fiction to impact politically in the shaping of public opinion. Regrettably, Bowyer Bell did not elaborate, or indicate the factors which he believed influenced 'thriller production'. He reinforced the assertion, however, in a surround of qualifiers:

> in some strange small way the thrillers on Irish matters may have played a part in the British campaign to restore order, if not justice, to Ulster... Surely, the British could ask for no more.[34]

It is perhaps surprising that the first critique of bias within the genre towards the republican position should have emanated from a non-Irish observer, albeit one so well-versed in Irish matters as Bowyer Bell, even if published in the Irish radical paper *Hibernia*. From a Northern nationalist viewpoint, for example, the allegation of bias was merely to assert the patently obvious. In effect, if not in intent, the genre seemed to many of its readers to perform as an adjunct of Britain's propaganda war, so far removed was the portrayal from the experience of people living in areas under British occupation. While one might imagine that republicans would have been at the forefront in highlighting fictional misrepresentations, more pressing instances of opinion-management or manipulation vied for attention, not least the attempts by the British authorities at this time to suppress *Republican News* in Belfast. Therefore, against this background, it is more understandable that the first contribution to correcting the misrepresentation should have come from outside.

As mentioned, the amalgamation of the northern-based *Republican News* with its southern counterpart *An Phoblacht* took place in 1979.[35] The first scrutiny of the genre from a republican appeared in the new format of *AP/RN* (the abbreviated title of the now combined papers) in February 1980. In a centrespread article, Una O'Neill began by commenting that events in 1979 'put the war in the North back on the map for British and Free State media'. Perhaps she had in mind a number of 'spectacular' IRA and INLA operations during the year: the IRA's Mountbatten and Narrow Water operations; the INLA's killing of Airey Neave. As a consequence, she argues,

> publishers, always looking out for fashionable and profitable topics, seem to have placed it [the conflict] back on the list of marketable products. Out-of-print books were re-printed in paper-back, unpublished manuscripts of dubious value were given a chance, and some journalists decided to start their careers as writers by having a go at 'the troubles'.[36]

The latter point was also picked up by academics, one of whom, Joseph McMinn, noted that 'a remarkable proportion of these novels ha[d] been written by journalists who have spent years covering the North'.[37] He mentions Kevin Dowling, Gerald Seymour, Des Hamill and Jimmy Breslin. McMinn also concurs to a degree with Bowyer Bell's view of the stereotypical distortions the genre is prone to propagate:

> the collective imaginative distortion, so close to those values associated with a media busily creating a new monster in our civilised midst, reveals a basic conservatism of form as well as feeling.[38]

In some of the fiction, particularly from the middle years of the 1970s, the expression of contempt for the IRA closely marked time with extremely hostile British tabloid-fed attitudes. In many instances, it has to be said, these attitudes were generated by civilian deaths and casualties from some of the IRA's worst operational blunders. What is most lacking in the fiction was any attempt to objectify the political and historical context. Instead, readers were presented with a bewildering litany of uncontextualised outrages, and every permutation of the mindless terrorists thug. As Una O'Neill observed:

They all cover [up] the same truth: that Ireland today is still colonised and people are struggling against foreign invasion... Brit oppression, for these writers, just does not exist any more. There might be the odd reference to past excesses, but now things have changed. Armed resistance, which was legitimate in previous times is now vile useless bloodletting.[39]

Her review concludes with an appeal for a less biased fictional treatment, from authors and the book-publishing world that largely failed to be heeded in the ensuing years.

Where are the writers who will speak the truth in the present tense? And since censorship in the publishing world is as harsh as in the press, where are the publishers who will have the courage to print their stories?[40]

The most thorough critical analysis of the genre to date, in which thirty four out of a relevant total at the time of 124 novels were surveyed, was also published in 1980. In 'Rough Rug-headed Kerns: The Irish Gunman in the Popular Novel', Alan Titley, teacher, broadcaster, an acclaimed writer in Irish and in English, argued that Ireland's experience of colonialism has meant that the received view of the Irish has been constructed from outside.

Shakespeare's one Irishman, Captain Macmorris, speaks slovenly and acts deplorably, while Richard II refers to 'those rough rug-headed kerns/ which live like venom where no venom else/ but only they have privilege to live'.[41]

Historically, these hostile constructions have been updated and modified in ideological service to an imperialist or colonial agenda, and have been resisted by the Irish. Contemporary fictional typologies, Titley argues, have their genesis in that historical context, and demonstrate the persistency of stock prejudicial images:

the Irishman as a nasty brutish creature of dim wits, uncouth appearance and, more dangerously, of inexplicable mind is alive and not so well and usually dying in the modern popular thriller thrown up, in the last ten years, by the Northern Ireland conflict.[42]

Fifty-two category (a) novels appeared between 1970 and 1975 inclusive. At least thirteen of the examples from this output are by Irish authors. One hundred and two Troubles novels were published between 1976 and 1981, representing a two-fold increase. This figure breaks down yearly as follows: in 1976, twenty category (a) novels; in 1977, twenty; fourteen in 1978; eighteen in 1979; sixteen in 1980; and in 1981, fourteen. The record of sixteen titles in 1973 was either exceeded or equalled in all but two of the latter six years. At first glance it may appear surprising that in 1980 the tally still amounted to seventeen. The assassination of Lord Mountbatten and the killing of eighteen British soldiers at Narrow Water, near Warrenpoint, on the same day in 1979, events that shocked the British establishment to its core, do not appear to have impacted on the popularity of the genre. But then few of the novels broke with what had by now been well-established as the genre's definitional parameters.

In the previous six-year period, nineteen of this grouping of novels are by Irish authors. Given that the period 1982 to 1987 saw a two-fold increase in titles published, the relatively fewer number of novels from Irish writers (twenty five) requires an explanation. One possible factor is that the latter period coincides with a reduction in topical, journalistic fiction (which, as I discussed in Chapter Three, particularly characterised the output during the early 1970s) and a rise in sensationalist, stereotypical renderings. That is not to argue that Irish authors are always better informed, displaying a more searching attitude towards Britain's role in the North. In fact some of the more anti-republican narratives came from Irish writers; for example, John Morrow, and Benedict Kiely.[43] Although singling out Brian Moore and Maurice Leitch for exception (because both had tried in their fiction to explain the underlying sectarian dynamic of the period before 1969 from the perspective of the Catholic/nationalist and Protestant/unionist communities respectively), in 1974 Seamus Deane remarked:

> Looking at our present writers, we could perhaps agree that the North has so far distinguished itself most in drama and in poetry and least in fiction.[44]

Endorsing this opinion, in 1976 Deutsch listed the Irish writers whom he felt should tackle 'the present Ulster Question'.

> One still waits for a novel from Brian Moore, Maurice Leitch, James Plunkett, Brian Cleeve, J.P. Dunleavy, Edna O'Brien and John MacGahern.[45]

Of these, only Moore and Leitch wrote novels during the period under focus that touched even tangentially on the conflict.[46] The poet Gerald Dawe cites a 1976 interview Moore gave to the *Irish Times* in which he opined that Northern writers were reluctant, given their proximity, to tackle the conflict.[47] Although somewhat equivocal about his own stance, Dawe did raise the same issue a year later, at a time when few critics, artists or commentators seemed prepared to 'take up the cudgel'. This time he cited an *Irish Times* article in which the journalist 'Jack Holland called for Irish writers to concern themselves with the Border Question'.[48] Holland went on to write two novels addressing aspects of 'the Border Question', the first being his 1981 novel, *The Prisoner's Wife*, first published in the United States.[49]

Moore's novel *The Doctor's Wife* (1976, Booker Prize shortlisted) is written from an expatriate, middle-class perspective. Mrs Redden, the titular Doctor's wife, easily unnerved since witnessing the Abercorn bomb in 1971 (an allusion to an actual bomb incident), is taking a break in France. Notre Dame, as seen from Mrs Redden's hotel window, is compared unfavourably with her more usual view of Napoleon's Nose, the hill overlooking north Belfast (where the United Irish leaders swore, as Tone put it, to 'break the connection with England'). Notre Dame, it is implied, is a place steeped in a universalised history while to her mind,

Belfast represents a local, parochial squabble, ignoring the fact of the shared historical and political motivations that had underpinned the upheavals in both countries.[50] Whether Paris or Belfast, Redden's perspective is too comfortably remote to apprehend ghetto realities. From her narrow perception, conflictual extremes are conflated: 'Paisley and the Provos' are tarred with the same alliterative brush.[51]

She encounters an American tourist, apparently misguided and underinformed about the reality of events in Ireland.

'It must be rough, right? Are they ever going to settle that mess?'

Mrs. Redden smiled what she hoped was a friendly smile. Yanks. [...]

'I guess you've just got to get the British out of there,' the girl said. Mrs. Redden did not honour this with an answer.[52]

Two notable treatments of the Troubles theme were published the following year from Irish novelists: Jennifer Johnston's *Shadows on our Skin* (1977) and Francis Stuart's *A Hole in the Head* (1977).[53] As for non-Irish writers, the conflict attracted the blackish imaginative engagement of the American travel writer Paul Theroux, whose 1976 novel *The Family Arsenal* seems to draw on a patchwork of contemporary sources to convey the redolence of a nation in surreal meltdown: the Beit art theft; Annie Maguire's 'bomb factory'; the Angry Brigade.[54]

Western capitalist society is rotten, he seems to suggest, but those who oppose it with a socialist or anarchist vision are also the soiled products of that system. The resulting concoction pokes at the supposed psychology and inner workings of an IRA Active Service Unit that resembles a cross between a makeshift anarchist cell and the Manson Family.

Murf, ex-Penge boot-boy, now a teenage Provo bomber, is summoned to a meeting by Sweeney, who is leader of the 'High Command', to whom he presents a new recruit, the American Hood, who works for the US State Department and who has forged passports for the Provos.

'This organization attracts a lot of funny boyos. I mean, unstable, people – mental cases.' He pronounced the word in the Ulster way, muntal. 'They belong in hospitals or with kind families, but they come to us and say they want to help.' He smiled. 'All they really want to do is plant a bomb somewhere – they don't care why. They're looking for victims.' He nudged his empty glass. 'It's made us a little suspicious of volunteers.'[55]

Earlier in the narrative, Hood enters the room of Murf and his girlfriend, the ex-groupie, Brodie. The couple are depicted as childlike, possibly with the intention of deprecating the types who Theroux surmises might get involved in radical politics or who are attracted to violence.

'Rise and shine,'

Brodie turned, smacked a toffee in her mouth and said, 'What do you want?'

'I've got a surprise for you. Today, you're going to leg a bomb in Trafalgar Square. This is big stuff, right? Get Lord Nelson flat on his back and fry those lions. All you do is stick some jelly in the column and you're laughing. What do you say?'

Murf said, 'He's garrity.'

'Shut up, bat-face and get your clocks out.'[56]

Hood is having an affair with Mayo, Sweeney's wife. She confides to Hood that there is going to be a bombing campaign in England: 'In terms of headlines, one bomb in Oxford Street is worth ten in Belfast.'[57]

For all his imaginative power Theroux doesn't always transcend the hoarier tropes seemingly so indispensable to the task of falsification.

Listen here. No one quits the Provos. You join for life. That's what I did – that's what everyone does, including you. I said, including you. It's like a family, see. No one quits a family.[58]

Quite apart from that fact that members volunteer and, therefore, are unlikely to do so without a 'get-out clause', the IRA would be an impossibly unwieldy organisation if it had retained the services of, and responsibilities for, a membership recruited during thirty years of struggle. One estimate puts a figure of 15,000 members who were imprisoned over that time span. If such an exaggerated membership were all to draw even basic living expenses from the movement, an elaborate fund-raising mechanism would be needed to service such requirements, equivalent to a corporation of possibly Rupert Murdoch proportions. At the very least, we might expect considerably more instances of fund-raising to pay for the burden. The membership estimate stands ludicrously beside the best-informed British Intelligence estimates of 300 operators at any one time. The IRA's General Army Orders stipulate clearly that '[m]embership of the Army is only possible through being an active member'.[59] Any failure to so be, he or she 'automatically ceases' to belong. Further, applications to rejoin by those who are dismissed or who resign have to be submitted to the Army Council. The very fact that the orders make such a provision for members who have resigned rubbishes the 'once in, always in' propaganda line.[60] The 'once in, never out' theme possibly originates in pulpit-condemnations of secret societies going back to the Defenders. The notion persists because it strengthens the lie of an oath-bound romantic nationalism, and of a movement which is arcane, self-serving, reliant on internal threats of force rather than the commitment of its members, and which exercises a parasitic hold on the communities it purports to defend, much like the Mafia.

Hood is curious as to why Murf is given to writing 'Arsenal Rule' on walls. Murf explains:

You started calling the flipping house an arsenal – remember? When you saw me clocks? [...] You write down Arsenal and everyone thinks it's the team. Right? It's our secret family, like, and no one has a fucking clue.' He chuckled. 'Right on,' they're saying, 'Up Arsenal' and they don't even know they're supporting us.[61]

The above episode, and indeed the whole novel, may work as a metaphor for what the author sees as the putative relationship between the IRA, the working class, and, to resort to Glover's tendentious phrase, its allegedly 'muddled politics'. Instead of promulgating the republican message and converting the people to the movement's aims, Theroux seems to imply, like Murf, that keeping people in the dark is necessary and, rather than open political activity, that clandestine and furtive manoeuvrings are a preferable means to an end. Another flaw underlying the novel is Theroux's apparent belief that the impulse to violence is explainable in terms of individual psychology rather than the social injustices at the root of the historical divisions within Ireland and between Ireland and Britain. Theroux appears to view 'terrorism' as a kind of dysfunction, but less of society than of the individual. It is hardly surprising, according to an interview Theroux is quoted as having given to *Publishers' Weekly*, that the novel 'was approved by most English critics'.[62] For all its flaws in terms of the wholesale incorporation of tabloid demonisation of Irish republicans and their alleged supporters among the British left, the novel remains a powerfully symptomatic description of English political anxieties in the mid-Seventies.

The mid-Seventies marked the appearance of some of the most vicious anti-republican and anti-Irish novels to appear during the last thirty years. To single out two, 1976 saw the publication of Chapman Pincher's *The Eye of the Tornado* and Robin Moore's *The Kaufman Snatch*, both of which excelled in racist barrel-scraping.[63]

Chapman Pincher is a writer and journalist specialising in security and defence issues. One would expect, therefore, that when turning his hand to fiction he would have drawn on his contacts and expertise in this area. And, indeed, in his foreword he lavishes credit on some high-powered sources.

> In making this work of fiction as true to life as possible the author is greatly indebted to senior officials, present and past, in the Defence Ministry, the Royal Navy, the Secret Intelligence Service, Scotland Yard, the Atomic Energy Authority, the U.S. Central Intelligence Agency and the Pentagon.

Very sadly, the paltry pay-off from this lofty insider access was a plot in which the IRA – with KGB help – hijack a shipload of nuclear weapons in an otherwise laudable intent, from a republican perspective, to destabilise the UK. The IRA threaten to detonate this cargo unless their as yet unrevealed demands are met. The fall-out of such a detonation would affect a broad swathe of southern England and Wales. Truly wacko ravings! We are in the loonscape of global communist threat and international terrorist conspiracy.

Alongside, it seems, the Irish, Pincher's other bête noire was the English working class, and the novel reads in large chunks like a catalogue of right-wing obsessions, contriving also to link organised labour with the then Soviet Union. Hence, in an explanation of the title, Pincher writes:

> Britain was not just a prime KGB target but the prime target, with certain trade unions serving as 'the eye of the tornado'... a CIA expression for any vortex round which a major KGB operation involving violence was planned.[64]

It transpires without due delay that the operation is led by Kevin 'Machine-gun' McNally of Kilkenny, 'one of the hardest and most fanatically anti-British of all the IRA hardliners'.[65] Absurd Oirish dialogue soon follows.

> 'Mebbe yer've never heard of me,' he announced to Sexton and those of the crew who were with him. 'Me name's Kevin McNally. I'm an officer of the Irish Republican Army – senior to all of you.'

The scene is so fatuously rendered that it seems disproportionate to mention again that no such importance is ever attached to rank by republicans, for whom the principle 'first among equals' more fittingly is applied to those with the responsibility of leadership. The bumptious McNally is also given to 'loose talk'.

> He turned to his second-in-command, a much shorter ferret-faced man, with a nose that made him look as though he had caught a chill when the priest christened him and had never shaken it off.

> 'This is Patrick Delaney, an explosives expert. You don't need me to be tellin' yer we're experienced in the explosives business. And Pat's the best. Remember Bloody Friday? Well, that was Pat.'[66]

And it may seem crassly pedantic to mention the obvious breaches in security in the voluntary confession to 'Bloody Friday' and the use of the perpetrator's name. The alleged bomber, Patrick Delaney, 'took off his jacket, rolled up his sleeves – revealing a red tattoo of the Sacred Heart on his left arm'.[67] After explaining McNally's troubled motivations in terms of revenge to those on board the hi-jacked vessel, Delaney's cloying piety is further revealed.

> Delaney laughed, displaying several decaying teeth. 'If these are foired, it'll be in anger all right. The big feller hates you English. His father was killed by the English and his da' before him. Or so he keeps tellin' us.'

> He produced a pocket-book and pencil and began making rough sketches and notes, humming as he did so snatches from the Catholic hymn 'Sweet Sacrament Divine'.[68]

With some foresight on Pincher's part, in the novel the Prime Minister of the day is a woman, who comes to power after a snap election: Margaret Fletcher – a thinly-veiled Margaret Thatcher.[69] Thatcher, as mentioned above, became leader of the Conservative Party in February 1975, some short time before publication of the novel, becoming Prime Minister four years later. With equal prescience, he also has a woman in the role of Secretary of State for Northern Ireland. He is far less astute in ascribing the attitudes of Irish republicans to women in power roles. Later, after a spate of bombings in London, the IRA's Army Council releases a statement:

> it was beneath their dignity to negotiate with a government headed by a woman who had appointed another woman to deal with Irish affairs.[70]

Even during the period covered in the novel, women, if not numerous, were in evidence at every level of command in the movement; and by the end of the decade this was even more the case.

Fletcher's War Cabinet assumes the worst of their ancient foe,

> that the IRA men might be desperate enough to sacrifice their own lives as well as those of their hostages if an assault by surface ship was attempted. They had been bloodily involved in Northern Ireland long enough to appreciate that to the irrational, near-mystical IRA mind, glorious failure appealed almost as much as success.[71]

Pincher's authorial voice is later heard bewailing the American response to the crisis.

> The reactions of Washington's State Department to the IRA outrage were inhibited as usual, because so many American voters had irish forbears forced to emigrate from the 'old sod' by the British.[72]

Irish America may predictably have been anti-British in sentiment, but Pincher ignores to mention, and in so doing reduces his narrative to crude disinformation, that the State Department has traditionally been pro-British.

The whole sad unintentional farce rolls on to a predictably bad ending, when the plainly unhinged McNally refuses to comply with orders from Moscow to defuse the nuclear devices. The American President, Lord, 'though deeply perturbed... was not really surprised. Nobody had ever controlled the Irish'.[73]

It is hard to conceive that *The Eye of the Tornado* could have been surpassed in awfulness, but the literary low-point of the last three decades quite possibly belongs instead to *The Kaufman Snatch* (1976), by the American popular writer Robin Moore. Moore, famously the author of *The Green Berets* (1965), was a Harvard classmate of Robert Kennedy Jr and used that connection, it is said, to gain access to an American special forces training course in preparation for that novel. Moore also researched extensively for his next major success, *The French Connection* (1969). He may have got too near the product during that project; otherwise why would an author who had established a reputation for a meticulous concern for authenticity have also written *The Kaufman Snatch*, probably the most execrable instance of misrepresentation to date about the Troubles?

The Thriller-speak of the cover blurb, back and front, leads the reader to expect that the plot of *The Kaufman Snatch* is based on an actual incident; and the allusion to *The French Connection* is designed to capitalise on the highly successful film released the year before based on the novel.

THE BIG IRA PAYOFF

Terrorism was the action!

But it takes millions.

Only Robin Moore could go behind the headlines to tell the story of the liquor dynasty heir and his hippy girlfriend, snatched for $2,200,000 to support the outlawed terrorist IRA.

Only Robin Moore could identify the homosexuals, CIA renegades, gun runners and revolutionaries who plotted the most gruesome bloodbath in western history.

Only Robin Moore could know about the lone black FBI agent who would stand between the assassins and their objective.
Only the author of *The Green Berets* & *The French Connection* could tell it the way it really was...

This plot summation might have been expressly designed to illustrate the following explanation of how popular fiction often sensationalises in order to mystify:

> What is, in 'real life', typically a terrorist strike becomes in popular fiction a 'caper', a 'heist'. This simplification of aims brings with it a reduction of incomprehensible political motivation (incomprehensible, that is, in terms of the ideology of best-selling fiction) to comprehensible human motives. These motives can be categorized as: money, criminality, grudge and madness.[74]

And in the 'author's acknowledgement' at the end of the novel, Moore reveals that

> the guiding genius behind this novel is my Irish colleague, Stan Gebler Davies. Stan was the architect of the various drafts through which the book progressed. It was he who saw the heavy if clumsy hand of the IRA behind a recent real life kidnapping and came to me with the concept of this story. And it was Stan who supplied the inside IRA information which make *The Kaufman Snatch* authentic.[75]

The role of the novel's 'guiding genius', the journalist Stan Gebler Davies, isn't entirely clear from the acknowledgement. However, the description 'architect of the various drafts' tends to suggest collaborator rather than commissioner, though as Jerry Palmer (citing John Sutherland) has written:

> [a]nother feature of the potential bestseller is that it may well be subject to commercial calculation before it is written: for example, the outline of a book... may be developed by someone who then commissions the actual writing by someone else.[76]

Moore's already bankable name could have attracted such a commission. Unfortunately, his reputation for painstaking research has saddled the venture with an ill-deserved authenticity. 'Only the author' could 'identify', and 'know', could ascertain the credibility of 'the inside IRA information' from an 'Irish colleague' of their involvement in a 'real life kidnapping'. Allowing for the hyperbole of the packaging of fiction, the author clearly wants the reader to buy the notion that the plot approximates reality. True, the narrative does fictionalise real characters and events. But verisimilitude is lost in Moore's desire, it seems, to dehumanise certain well-known republicans in the crudest of propaganda terms. For example,

> Sean Mac Stiofain, born John Stevenson… had been deposed after losing face after an unquenchable desire for a cup of tea had led him to forget that he was supposed to be fasting to death.[77]

In reality, Mac Stiofáin had fasted for fifty seven days and had been in considerable pain when ordered off the strike by the Army Council. Tim Pat Coogan implies that the strike was abandoned because if he were to die the result would be civil war.[78]

'Mac Stoifain' comes in for scurrilous abuse from his fictional successor as Chief of Staff. O'Rourke, 'The Provo High Command', who has just been released from Portlaoise prison, blames his caricatured predecessor for informing on him to the Special Branch in order to avail of the affections of Moira O'Grady, now under sentence of death for selling her story to the *Observer*: "'It was only Mac Stiofain was pantin' to get his dirty prick up O'Grady himself," muttered O'Rourke'.[79] Moira O'Grady appears to have been modelled on Maria McGuire, who in 1972 was arrested in the Netherlands, as she claims in her autobiography, while on a mission to buy weapons with Daithi O'Connell, then the IRA's Chief of Staff.[80] Moore's intention in this and subsequent vilifications may possibly have been to combat Irish republican support in the USA. He in fact devotes much of the novel's second chapter to lampooning Irish Americans. In a review of *The Sparrowhook Curse*, a more recent example from Moore's canon, fortunately not relevant to this survey, the author was similarly criticised for targeting Native Americans, who 'appear as alcoholics or shamans, [while] the one black man is a shifty villain'.[81]

The excerpts cited above could be excused for their risible scurrility; but in a fetid 'finale', dated 1977 (though the novel was published in 1976), Moore refers to the fate of Mrs McLaughlin. The reader is left in no doubt that she is modelled on Máire Drumm, the Sinn Féin vice-president who in October 1976 was murdered in circumstances similar to those described in contrived hindsight: 'In mid October last Mrs. McLaughlin was liberally sprayed with presumably prod bullets while lying in a Belfast hospital bed recovering from a stomach operation'.[82]

Mercifully, few novels dealing with the Troubles are as irredeemably dreadful. However, allowing that an essential reader response to escapist fiction is the suspension of disbelief, can the reader – not in this instance the Everyman on a Clapham Common omnibus but a typically observant traveller in a Falls Road taxi – can the reader remain detached from what he or she knows to be a flagrant distortion? The answer, I would suggest, is a qualified yes, but probably only when the novel compensates with exceptionally redeeming figurative or narrative qualities. An engaging literary style or ingenious plot construction may also cover a multitude of contextual false notes, allowing the reader to still acknowledge the skill of the author. But the reader who is far removed from the actuality or lived experience of the conflict, devoid of first-hand knowledge and thus possessing a reduced ability to discriminate between narratives that question and challenge political norms and those which function to perpetuate distortion and bias, is far less inclined to read against the narrative grain. There are few passive consumers of Troubles fiction in nationalist West Belfast, for whom the disparities between lived reality and its melodramatic depiction are positively Brechtian in their capacity to alienate.

Another novel to fictionalise Máire Drumm's killing is Christopher Hawke's 1979 novel *For Campaign Service*. According to the blurb, the author, an ex-Royal Marine, based this, his first 'full length' novel 'on his own experiences on active service'. If you leave to one side an aversion to yet another plot alleging IRA links to Libyan-financed international terrorist conspiracies, the novel has some quite good technical and locational detail. Although Máire Drumm was a hate figure to the British media Hawke shows some restraint in his fictional portrayal of the character based on her. He is also mercifully free of Moore's mordant glee when announcing that Mollie Fegan

> suddenly developed a painless lump in her breast which began to increase in size. Although reluctant to cancel any part of her busy round of Provisional Sinn Fein Executive commitments, she eventually underwent surgery. Malignancy was confirmed and the breast had to be removed. All was well until the sixth post-operative day when two masked gunmen burst into the hospital side-ward, and murdered the helpless woman as she lay on her bed.

One of the illegal Protestant organisations later 'claimed responsibility'.[83]

Palma Harcourt, the author of the thriller *A Sleep of Spies* (1979), worked for British intelligence.[84] Because of her intelligence background, which she draws on in her writing, her novel is a revealing guide to attitudes within the British political and security establishments. The novel is also useful in its perception of the official discourse of Irish governments during the 1970s.

Philip Camplin is a senior civil servant at the Ministry of Defence whose brief is the North. He is a candidate for promotion to the post of scientific advisor to the Ambassador. He is sent to Washington to brief the Ambassador about a recent incident which was proving extremely embarrassing to Britain's interests and image. The IRA, it was alleged, had phoned in bomb warnings during a 'March for Peace' in Belfast. When the British Army lieutenant in charge of the security operation tried to divert the marches away from the area of the bomb threat part of the crowd surged forward. The lieutenant ordered that tear gas grenades be fired to prevent the marchers breaking through. Fifty-five people, including ten soldiers, were killed by the gas, which was later discovered to have been part of a batch of experimental grenades developed by the same firm who made the tear gas.[85]

The plot rests upon the incident, which in Harcourt's narrative discourse we understand to have been a tragic but unfortunate 'accident': not because the deaths were unintended, but because the deliberate disruption of the peace march renders the IRA ultimately culpable for all that ensued. In true Widgery fashion Harcourt contrives a plot that exonerates Britain of responsibility and blame.

However, the American President is under pressure from the Irish-American lobby to intervene because of 'Massacre Day'. The British Ambassador wants to prevent this.

> I'm pretty sure the President won't take positive action unless his immediate advisers urge it, and they're not rash men. Of course, there's a lot of pressure on him – from the Irish Americans, from Congress, from well-meaning people shocked at what happened, from public opinion generally. They all want him to use his influence, to intervene, to 'help' the Irish. But he knows that active intervention would at best do irreparable damage to US-UK relations, which would please our mutual enemies, and at worst might turn Ireland – the whole of Ireland – into a battlefield like Vietnam.[86]

The body count is significantly larger than actual atrocities allegedly committed by the British or their agents – Bloody Sunday; Dublin and Monaghan bombings – though not large enough to convince Pamela Harcourt that a change in Anglo-American 'special relations' would ever have been seriously contemplated had an incident on this scale really occurred. After all, Britain had weathered international opprobrium over Bloody Sunday and the use of torture.

The novel displays a certain complacency about the continued sway of the British discourse in Washington. Within two years, however, the consequences of the hunger strike for Britain's carefully groomed image of neutrality created the climate for a shift in world opinion. In terms of American perceptions, as Holland argues, by the early 1980s

> the old consensus was broken; the idea that Britain was partly responsible for the Northern Ireland mess had taken hold.[87]

Another excerpt from the novel also illustrates the extent of the discursive shift that would occur within a short period. Mat Harworth, Camplin's boss at the Ministry of Defence, is sure that the IRA weren't the masterminds behind the tragedy: 'They've nothing to gain by bringing in the Americans and making Ireland a free-for-all'.[88]

> The Russians, fully aware that we would use our veto, had tabled a motion in the Security Council condemning our behaviour in Northern Ireland and demanding the immediate withdrawal of all British troops. This was an obvious ploy. More important was the fact that the Americans had also

voted against the motion, thereby creating more dissension in their own country. But the President had been firm, and it was mainly thanks to him that at least our allies were no longer crying for our blood. Eire's official restraint had also helped. The Irish Republic didn't want a free for all in the North, probably spilling over the border, any more than we did. And they certainly didn't want any foreign interference, in whatever guise.

Nevertheless, the situation was still bad. Tension was high and there was a great deal of bitter feeling on all sides. The suicide of the unfortunate lieutenant who had ordered the use of the killing gas grenades, his mother's subsequent nervous breakdown...had combined to create a considerable anti-Irish backlash throughout the UK, and to a lesser degree in the States and Canada. I was horrified by the hatred and vituperation shown everywhere by supposedly responsible people. Cynically I wondered how much of it was communist-inspired.[89]

The Russian motion though a ploy is in itself nevertheless a serious embarrassment, surely. The anti-Irish backlash seems disproportionate to the scale of Massacre Day, and suggests a double-standard of grievance, British lives being more valued than Irish lives. The fear of communist-inspired conspiracies is central to the narrative. The major shift that was to occur, however, concerned the official Irish and British governments' policies of 'containment' in regard to the North. As Joe Cleary writes, both governments have sought 'to represent themselves as more or less neutral 'external' brokers, disinterestedly working to help Northern Ireland overcome its lamentable 'internal' sectarian bigotry'.[90] But containment also meant ensuring that the problem was never internationalised (despite Taoiseach Jack Lynch's call in 1969 for UN intervention). Mat Haworth's certainty that neither government wanted 'any foreign interference, in whatever guise' may have been the official line in 1979, the narrative year, but within a few years the involvement of the international community, particularly the role of the Clinton administration, would be crucial to the peace process by exerting political pressure on Britain to reach an accommodation in the North. Certainly, at no point in the narrative is a rationale given for why Britain should remain, other than the spectre of chaos in the event of a withdrawal.

In the finale it emerges that Camplin's brother Patrick, an eminent psychologist, is a communist 'Co-ordinator' briefed to convert Ireland to communism.[91] He plans the mass poisoning of all Irish political prisoners in the North so that the British are blamed.[92]

Kevin Dowling's *Interface: Ireland* (1979) is a novel concerned with the manipulation of journalists in the North by the British military.[93] Dowling was a journalist who reported the North from 1970 to 1974. The hero of this first novel, Pascal Canning, has reported the North since August 1969 for the *Standard*. When he was a child in Manchester, his mother helped to shelter an IRA man on the run from Pentonville.

Pascal is fed a story about IRA racketeering. The source is a British Army Major based at Thiepval Barracks, Lisburn (which is in fact the headquarters of the British Army in the North). The novel explains, or excuses, the practice of an over-reliance on army contacts for news releases.

> Whenever anything controversial happened, the 'facts' could vary from minute to minute. Five, six or even a dozen versions of a major incident were commonly relayed to newsmen in the form of up-daters and corrections. An important by-product of this was the virtual internment of the city's newsmen in their offices. If they went out to see what had happened they risked missing the single constant of all objective reporting; which was the Army's perception of truth.[94]

When Pascal attends a party at Thiepval, Major Jack Loftus, head of PR for 39 Brigade, declares:

> 'Background intelligence,' he said, nodding towards the Brigadier. 'That's the way to win.' He nodded again, beaming. His face was a florid sculpture. 'We must try to know everything. Use a computer to remember it. The Intelligence census, and the good old computer, what? We'll beat the bombers. Soon restore peace.'

> Pascal returned his smile.

> 'You newspaper johnnies,' Major Loftus said, 'too pessimistic by half. We keep saying we're winning, but you won't believe us.'

> 'The bombing does go on.'

> 'Last gasp, old boy. We're making it hot for them now, eh, Colonel?'

> 'Certainly are,' said Colonel Ferguson.

> 'More than a third of the population literally taped!' exclaimed Major Loftus. 'Even know the colour of their wallpaper, Pascal. When they redecorate – tap on the walls.' He frowned, 'Secret caches of guns, what?'

> 'Yes,' said Pascal.

> 'How many pints of milk do they order? Need extra supplies when you shelter a terrorist gunman...'

> 'It's remarkably ingenious,' said Colonel Fergusson.

> 'This computer we have in London,' said Major Loftus eagerly, 'any soldier can talk to it now. Fearfully expensive installation. But your squaddie's in touch, by radio. Relay his questions from base.'

> 'Ministry of Defence,' said Colonel Fergusson.

> 'And damn useful if we get any trouble at home,' said Major Loftus. 'All these Trotskyists and Commies'.[95]

The passage is enlightening for its description of how in practice the British army makes use of low grade intelligence gathered as advocated by Brigadier Frank Kitson in *Low Intensity Operations*.[96]

It is claimed that in fact both Dowling and Chapman Pincher were used as conduits for questionable information in similar circumstances to those described above. In their capacity as journalists, both were fed stories by Colin Wallace, the former chief press officer at Thiepval Barracks. The investigative journalist Paul Foot reports that in 1970 the Ministry of Defence ordered the reorganisation of the Army's information department. 'Information Liaison' was set up, later to be known as 'Information Policy'. Its function, distinct from normal public relations work, was 'to use information and disinformation from Intelligence as one of the many weapons in the war with the IRA'.[97] As Foot explains, 'Information Policy was a separate unit working for the intelligence services but expected to operate under the cover of public relations. Its function was psychological warfare'.[98] One of the new unit's tasks was to brief visiting journalists. Colin Wallace claims that the unit fed a story to Pincher about American Vietnam veterans working as mercenaries for the IRA which duly appeared in the *Daily Express* (30 March 1972).[99] Wallace further revealed that in order to counter the effectiveness of the IRA using women to plant bombs, he supplied a story to Kevin Dowling which duly appeared in the *Sunday Mirror* (19 August 1973) claiming that static electricity generated by 'Frilly nylon undies worn by IRA girls may have helped to kill three of them'.[100]

Many of the cosy certainties expressed in the fiction of the period were about to be challenged by the international impact of the ten hunger strike deaths and the intransigence of the British government. Padraig O'Malley cites Des Wilson's opinion, which was a widely held view among nationalists, that the deaths marked 'the end of British rule in Ireland'.[101] Thousands of nationalists actively supported the prisoners' demands in demonstrations, attendance at the funerals, and in electoral support for hunger strike candidates and later for Sinn Féin. The journalist Peter Taylor argues that the support accruing over the hunger strikes 'was the first indication that the broad political base that Gerry Adams was looking for was potentially there'.[102] In fact the potential was clearly evident before then in the protests over conditions and in past examples of mass support and mobilisation over issues such as Bloody Sunday, and internment. But the forces necessary to achieve that end had still to be effectively mobilised. The next period saw the beginning of that process.

6.
Shifting Discourses

The last chapter covered the years 1976 to 1981, surveying fiction written during a period which heralded the implementation of Britain's military and propaganda offensive to criminalise Irish republicanism, up to the traumatic outcome of that policy in the H-Block struggle for political status, culminating in the hunger strikes of 1980 and 1981.

The long-term cultural and political effects of the hunger strike period are complex and uneven.

What is certain, however, is that the period covered in the present chapter, 1982 to 1987, coincides with a profound set back for, if not the demise of, the core component of Britain's criminalisation drive. The claim that republicans were merely criminals, with no support in their own communities or within nationalist Ireland, was a charge that proved increasingly difficult to sustain before the court of international public opinion, especially in the aftermath of the mass mobilisations in support of political status for republican prisoners, the national mourning at the deaths of ten hunger strikers, and the very visible legitimacy given to Sinn Féin by its electoral successes and growing organisational strength.

The changing perceptions marked the beginnings of a discursive shift that cannot be explained away in terms of Sinn Féin's supposed mastery of propaganda. Against enormous odds, rather, the movement had survived all attempts to silence it, and during the course of the 1980s met with increasing success in getting across its point of view to an international audience. However, the discursive breakthrough occurred only after years spent in the wilderness and through sheer doggedness in the face of the massive resources Britain pumps into the promulgation of its own spin through its embassies abroad, its huge diplomatic mission to create an image of the conflict in the North of Ireland favourable to its interests. As an illustration of the extent of Britain's efforts to counter the damage to its international reputation during the hunger strike, the author and journalist Roger Faligot quotes a *Sunday Times* report of the 21 June 1981.

> The Foreign Office sent 15 Psyops specialists to the British Information Service in the United States, who, in June 1981 received help of 'two senior government officials... [who]... left for the US yesterday in a new attempt to halt the flow of IRA propaganda'.[1]

And more recently, revelations about the role of MI6 in combating Irish American support for the McBride principles were aired on the internet, allegedly by a disgruntled former British spook.[2] In fact, Sinn Féin could never match Britain in terms of the financial, technical and organisational resources and influence needed to bear on perceptions internationally.

It was a time of searing political drama and quite momentous revolutionary change that impacted both politically and culturally. The realisation grew among activists that a seismic shift had occurred in the political landscape which had for so long disadvantaged republicans. Electoral politics were now seen to provide hitherto unrealisable opportunities for the movement to thwart British policy, and in addition would be instrumental in furthering its own organisational development, policies and strategies.

Although great strides were being made on the political front, the IRA too demonstrated its continuing ingenuity and determination to pursue the armed struggle. 1984 marked the fifteenth anniversary of the introduction of British troops. The bombing campaign in England had resumed after a lull, the new campaign resulting in the attack on the Grand Hotel, Brighton in October 1984 while the Tories were celebrating the end of their annual conference.

It is emblematic that Brighton should occur at the midway point of a struggle that has, at the time of writing, endured for thirty years. Republicanism was on the ascendant. Nationalism found a new confidence and voice, but such was the climate of hostility towards any advancement of the nationalist position that the revisionist big guns were not slow in assuming their attack formation. Desperate to counter Sinn Féin's success in election after election, the Southern political establishment launched the New Ireland Forum to shore up the fortunes of the SDLP by demonstrating a constitutional alternative to the republican strategy. The Forum proposed three options: a unitary state, a federal state, or joint authority. After the hunger strike deaths and the resultant success of Sinn Féin as an electoral force, public sentiments North and South simply would not tolerate anything less; but Thatcher curtly dismissed the proposals with 'Out, out, out'. With hindsight it can be seen that the British had overplayed their hand. International opinion was against them; constitutional nationalism was affronted. Pressures for a rethink mounted from the US Congress, from the Irish American lobby, from constitutional nationalist parties, and from civil rights and judicial bodies. This anger fed into the mainstream culture, and artists and intellectuals began to debate more openly Britain's role. A year later the Anglo-Irish Agreement was delivered, giving the Irish government a say in the administration of the North.

Unionists were apoplectic at the signing of the Anglo-Irish Agreement, but the failure of their often strident opposition to it was a crucial psychological turning point. Nationalist Ireland was quick to recognise that unionism and loyalism no longer had the clout they had demonstrated so brutally at the time of the Ulster Workers' Council strike in 1974. The unimaginable had occurred: unionism was seen to be defeatable if nationalists worked together.

The Agreement failed in its objective of weakening Sinn Féin vis-à-vis the SDLP; and Sinn Féin recognised there was a limitation on its growth potential in the South. These two factors necessitated a rethink from both parties. The result was a new imperative towards a broadfront nationalist approach that went beyond Sinn Féin's earlier policy of inclusiveness based on an anti-imperialist stand. Resistance to broad-front politics, previously scorned, now evaporated. These developments underlined the logic of Sinn Féin's strategy to internationalise the issue of the failure of partition and, in pursuance of that objective, to adopt a broad-front strategy, or as unionists were quick to term it, a 'pan-nationalist conspiracy'.

Sinn Féin's development continued apace. At the party's 1985 Ard Fheis, Gerry Adams emphasised the anti-imperialist outlook of the movement, for example citing fraternity with 'the Palestinians, the Chileans, Salvadorians, and Nicaraguans'.[3] And in 1987, conscious of the need to expand its support in the South, that year's Ard Fheis took the historic step of overturning its policy of abstentionism in regard to the Dáil. By May 1987 Sinn Féin had launched its peace drive with the publication of a major policy document, *A Scenario for Peace*.

While the discourse of criminalisation was being promoted, a counter-hegemonic ripple began to register that few could at the time recognise as being connected to the more open opposition of the day. The register was perhaps at its most subterranean in the work of the playwright Brian Friel. Friel was a co-founder, with the actor Stephen Rea, of the Field Day Theatre Company in 1980, staging Friel's *Translations* that year. The group set out to redefine Irish cultural identity. This cultural debate began earlier in *The Crane Bag* and *Innti*. Field Day's first stirrings were tentative, but it soon extended its remit into other cultural and intellectual projects. The backdrop to this development was the hunger strike, which transformed the wider cultural climate. Field Day came under revisionist attack in 1984 for being too nationalist and, from Edna Longley, for being patriarchal. Joseph McMinn answered the charge of nationalist bias made by Edna Longley, John Wilson Foster, *et al*.

> Attacks on Field Day for its politics are themselves concealed political objections. Those who throw up their hands in horror at the thought of bringing politics into art are never quite so innocent or disinterested as they would like to appear. What the begrudgers object to specifically is the dissemination of nationalist views of culture; views which they regard, like nationalist politics, as insanely irrational. Nationalism for them is a form of mental disorder and cultural backwardness. [...]
>
> Far from being a mystifying ideology, the language of contemporary Irish nationalism is critical and self-critical. Field Day is a cultural effect of that process of political self-examination, which is attributable to the 'Troubles'.[4]

Field Day published a set of pamphlets from leading cultural critics, such as Edward Said and Terry Eagleton, dealing with literary nationalism from a post-colonial perspective. Robert Johnstone wrote that 'the Field Day series of pamphlets has been a gale of fresh air in Irish intellectual life, and the pigeons have been fluttering about the dovecots since it started'.[5] Another development which in hindsight contributed to changing perceptions, both internationally and in Ireland, was the 'widespread growth in Irish Studies courses in the US, Canada, Australia, France, Britain... even Ireland'.[6]

Troubles fiction too continued to play, for the most part, its more shallow role, wittingly or otherwise, in the process of demonisation that helped to realise the propaganda aims of the British government. What impact, though, did these issues and developments have on fiction during this time?

Eighty-two category (a) novels were published during the period: twelve in 1982; eight in 1983; fifteen in 1984; twelve in 1985; fifteen in 1986; and twenty in 1987. In quantitative terms the figures indicate a reduction in the output of relevant novels; roughly an average of fourteen novels per year appeared compared with an average of seventeen during the preceding period. It isn't clear what significance, in terms of publishing and/or authorial interest in the events unfolding in Ireland and their wider impact, can be attached to this reduction. Nor is it clear what is the significance of the more noticeable dip in the figure for 1983, the second major slump in the genre's output. The last slump of similar magnitude was in 1974 when eight novels were published after the record sixteen novels published in the previous year. That fall, you may recall, was attributed by one commentator to a growing aversion to Troubles fiction due to IRA bombs in England. But perhaps a contributory factor for the 1983 reduction was the effect of economic recession of the early 1980s, although the genre had otherwise proven robust in the fiction market at times when other genres suffered.

A sizeable part of the explanation for the lower output of relevant fiction in the period under discussion, I would suggest, is that following the demolition of the criminalisation policy, for any narrative to be plausible to an informed or familiarised readership henceforth it would have to evince more understanding of the conflict and match the growing public awareness. Readers simply wouldn't be able so readily to suspend disbelief and to credit the narrative plausibility of novels that failed to square with the new, better informed perception arising from media coverage of the hunger strike period. After all, the British line had been that the IRA were criminals, but this didn't sit comfortably alongside the international perception that the hunger strikers were motivated by a selfless commitment to their common demand for political status. The market for popular fiction extended beyond the shores of Britain, to reach reading audiences less prone to accept unquestioningly the media spin on the topic of Northern Ireland. Perhaps this realisation of a shift in what the public would accept caused many authors to think twice before composing the usual, stereotypically-bound plot offerings. The lower number of novels produced may also indicate simply that it was no longer as commercially viable to market genre fiction which did not seriously address the new political climate. The realisation might be expected to influence publishers' choices in regard to new fiction and to editorial, marketing and promotional options. It is therefore plausible that the drop registered the onset of a discursive shift in a delayed response to the hunger strikes.

However, it is also likely, and not mutually exclusive of the above possibilities, that the publishing and marketing industries shied off from the genre because of public anger over the renewed bombing campaign in London in 1981 and 1982 following the end of the hunger strike. Many of the main publishers do show a hiatus in their output of category (a) fiction during the early 1980s which if viewed together indicates a quite significant reduction: Collins, none between 1983-85; Hamilton, none, 1978-82; Heinemann, none, 1971-84; Jonathan Cape, none, 1974-83; Michael Joseph, none, 1981-85.

One event that might explain the slight dip from fifteen to twelve relevant titles in 1985 was the Brighton bomb of October 1984. However, that year also saw a compensatory rise in the publication of relevant short stories and of category (d) novels. I would therefore tend to discount in this instance any significance to the low figure in terms of a public and/or commercial reaction to the bombing. Over all, the charts do suggest, as I argue, a correlation between low publishing figures and a rise in public dissatisfaction at the manner in which the conflict, particularly the handling and coverage of the hunger strike, was being addressed by government and in the media. These are all quantitative considerations, however, and it is necessary to ascertain whether developments and discursive shifts found expression in terms of narrative content.

A re-think is discernible in some of the novels to appear at this time, as the impact of events and issues such as the Anglo-Irish Agreement, the renewed bombing campaign in England, the supergrass trials of the mid-1980s, and the debate on abstentionism, leading to the historic decision of the 1986 Sinn Féin Ard Fheis to allow elected members of the party to take their seats in the Dáil, slowly began to be digested. In addition, a series of revelations about Britain's undercover war in Ireland gained considerable international attention: the Kincora scandal, the Stalker affair, shoot-to-kill, Gibraltar and the trauma surrounding the ensuing funerals. Slowly, public perceptions began to change, and the change in turn slowly began to be felt in the contents of novels issued in the following years.

Three developments in the genre are noteworthy besides the perceptible shift in its discursive content in many instances. Firstly, more women than ever before were writing fiction about the conflict. The reasons may have a commercial basis: women are reckoned to read more books than men;[7] and perhaps of more significance in terms of market pressures, from the 1980s, women were reckoned to buy more paperbacks than men.[8] It seems that publishers, the book trade, and women writers recognised a potential market opportunity. To meet this trend there was a corresponding though gradual increase in the numbers of women authors published generally, as women writers began to fill the gap in the market.

> Hardly more than a quarter of the authors are women – at least, for the first eight years it remained a steady 25% and only in the last years has it risen

a few points (to its new high of 39% in 1992). One should be asking if this figure corresponds to the percentages in publishing as a whole.[9]

Whatever the figures for fiction generally, in the period in question the ratio of women to men writing in the genre rose from the about 1:8 to about 1:5. And in some years the increased ratio overall was excelled. In 1983, for example, a year in which the reduction in new titles on the market equalled that of the previous low of 1974, two of the eight relevant novels were written by women.[10] And in 1984, the ratio rose from 1:3 to 1:2.5, with six out of the fifteen novels written by women.[11] However, with so few examples to deal with, caution is necessary in attributing statistical significance.

The second notable development in the genre, allied to the above, is that the input of many women writers invigorated the genre, setting a new standard of sensibility in the writing. In 1985 Joe McMinn had asked, 'what difference has the new women's writing made to contemporary Irish fiction?'[12] McMinn's concern extended beyond the genre and is limited to contemporary Irish fiction, but the fact of more women writing did make a perceptible difference. A year earlier, however, Fiona Barr, in an article marking the first Feminist Book Week, concluded that 'women have not yet found an authentic voice', though her concern was with the deficit of feminist as distinct from women's writing.[13] But from this period, women did begin to impact on the contents, and arguably, the 'voice' of Troubles fiction. Two examples stand out that were written within three years of Fiona Barr's comment: Frances Molloy's *No Mate for the Magpie* and Mary Beckett's *Give Them Stones* (the latter is discussed below).[14] Both were first novels by women from the North, published in England. With these and other examples, some of the slack was taken up in the publication of what by now had become the standard, often staid, thriller-format of the genre, by a new focus on women's direct experiences, in so doing filling a void in the fictional account. More consideration to the effects of violence on children is also evident, and some of the fiction was written for children and adolescents.

The increase of women writing about the conflict isn't to say, however, that the genre radically changed, or that as a consequence more of the same tired gamut of misrepresentations weren't reproduced, as the discussion below of individual texts will testify. The portrayal of female republicans for example, both in the media and in the genre, at times reached depths of prurience.[15] But then, stereotypes provide certainty in an uncertain world, and certainty is a main ingredient of this genre. More imaginative plotting and characterisation might undermine comforting and reassuring stereotypes. However, changes are discernible which arguably may have paved the way for some of the more imaginative, literate treatments of the conflict, by women and men, in the coming years.

The third noteworthy development was in the steady stream of novels about the conflict that were be dramatised either for television or the cinema.[16] Given the well-established evidence of the political sensitivity on the part of the broadcasting media towards the subject of Northern Ireland we might anticipate some selectivity as to what was and was not screened.[17] Liz Curtis argues that the 'reference upwards system', by which controversial programming decisions are invariably passed up the line of executive authority, thereby effectively ensuring censorship, is applied to more than news and current affairs programming. She quotes Richard Hoggart, who in *The Listener* (28 February 1980), details how drama

> on the troubles is very sensitive and involves reference upward, discussion, sometimes stalling: and so quite a number of plays have been delayed, denied repeats or relegated to late-night slots.

Hoggart further surmised that 'A play which viewed the struggle from the angle of the terrorists... would probably... have a pretty rough ride'.[18]

The sensitivity on the part of the powers-that-be in the broadcasting media towards programming about the conflict arises from the power of television to impact on the public consciousness in regard to sensitive or controversial political and social issues. Fiction generally is not judged to be as problematic to any comparable extent and much of the output is non-contentious, it is felt, leaving the reader safely secure in his or her prejudices. Perhaps, however, an exception can be argued in the case of popular thrillers in which the cumulative effects of narratives sympathetic to the IRA or critical of the government line on Ireland may cause anxiety in media and cultural decision-making circles. This consideration may arguably have had a spin off in self-censorship; authors aiming for the lucrative dramatisation of their work will be more wary of stepping outside the received viewpoint.

Perhaps the publication in 1987 of Hugo Meenan's *No Time for Love* might be considered as a fourth significant development, for it is the first example of a novel to be penned by a republican during the present conflict.[19] It was also the only novel from a republican to be written during the period under consideration. I will discuss this novel in due course. However, in 1985, *Iris* (an acronym for Irish Republican Information Service), a magazine produced by Sinn Féin's foreign affairs bureau, published the winners of a short story competition that 'illustrate very impressively three separate, but interwoven, aspects of political struggle in Ireland'.[20] Subsequent issues featured further short stories.

The survey will begin, however, with Jack Higgins's reassuringly quintessential contribution to the genre. His two novels written during this period might be described as freeze-framed, for he assembled the same range of formulaic devices and narrow perceptions as he deployed in the earlier novels, *The Violent Enemy* (1966), *The Savage Day* (1972), and *A Prayer for the Dying* (1973). With the publication of his 1982 thriller *Touch the Devil*[21] Higgins surpassed Joan Lingard's then record of five Troubles novels (her 'Kevin and Sadie' series). The novel marked his return to the Troubles theme after a gap of nine years, although he continued to be a prolific writer of thrillers throughout that time.[22]

The hero of *Touch the Devil* is Martin Brosnan, an IRA man of the old school who, as a former US Airborne Ranger and Vietnam veteran, a readership generally antagonistic to the mad gunmen and bombers of the new breed might tolerate as an interesting exception. His mixed lineage serves to underline the difference: 'The Brosnans came over [to the USA] during the famine a long time ago, all Protestants... My mother was born in Dublin. A good Catholic'.[23] Brosnan's intention when he leaves the army is to complete his studies at Trinity College, Dublin: 'Look up my roots. I speak a fair amount of Irish, something my mother drummed into me as a kid'.[24]

The novel is also interesting for the return of a hero from Higgins's first major success as a writer, Liam Devlin. Devlin first appeared in *The Eagle Has Landed* (1976) as the IRA man involved in a Nazi plot to abduct Winston Churchill. Perhaps Higgins was merely hoping to repeat the phenomenal commercial success of that novel, his first as a writer. It is also arguable that Devlin's reappearance in a 1982 novel wasn't entirely without guile, his return adding fuel to the media slur that the modern-day IRA are 'Green Fascists'.[25] Whatever Devlin's apparent integrity and individual courage, the reader is never allowed to forget that the character is fatally flawed by this collusive association with Nazi Germany, as alluded to in all his subsequent appearances in Higgins's corpus.

Nearly forty years later, and now 'one of the original architects of the Provisional IRA... [who] never approved of the bombing campaign',[26] Devlin comes out of retirement, deeply disillusioned.

> Oh, I'm still one hundred per cent for a United Ireland, but ten years is enough as far as I'm concerned. Too many dead...
>
> A bloody charnel house and what have we got to show for it?[27]

As ever, Higgins had a 'straw man' of Irish romantic nationalism in his sights, a reformulation of 'the Patriot Game' motif. The game, however, has spiralled out of Devlin's control: 'We're not playing the game any more. The game's playing us'.[28]

With Brosnan and Devlin on the side of goodness and light, generic bias requires a republican antithesis and this is supplied in the unlikely form of Frank Barry: a Protestant Ulsterman; ex-officer in the Ulster Rifles who served in Korea. Barry's uncle is an Irish peer and Orange politician. Motivated by a desire for money and kicks, he joined a violent republican faction, repudiated by the IRA, called Sons of Erin. The characterisation, this far, isn't so incredible when one recalls that Ronnie Bunting, the son of a prominent unionist politician, had joined People's Democracy, a Marxist organisation, at Queen's University Belfast and later was a founder member of the INLA. Ronnie Bunting was shot dead by loyalists in October 1980.

On the British side, that is, on the side of morality and fair play, are Brigadier Ferguson, in charge of Group Four, a section of DI5 charged with handling all cases of terrorism and subversion and answerable directly to the Prime Minister (very much in the mould of Margaret Thatcher) and his assistant, Harry Fox, a former Guards captain.

During a briefing about the renegade republican, Barry, Ferguson reprises a distinction invariably found in Higgins's plots about Ireland:

Oh, the IRA has its fair share of thugs and mad bombers and too many men like Frank Barry, perhaps, but it also has its Liam Devlins and its Martin Brosnans. Genuine idealists in the Pearse and Connolly and Michael Collins tradition. Whether you agree with them or not, men who believe passionately that they're engaged in a struggle for which the stake is nothing less than the freedom of their country.[29]

Even when allowing for the existence of principled republicans, the distinction serves to reinforce the notion of British tolerance. There is a willingness here to accept patriotism, however misguided the particular nationalist cause is regarded as a motivation. This is something that ultra-patriots like the character Ferguson can relate to. Fox, however, having recent experience of active service in the North, is more cynical: 'Sorry, sir, but I've seen women and kids run screaming from a bombing too many times to believe that any more'.

Ferguson too is Irish by descent: 'My grandmother was born in Cork'. Higgins seems to stress that anti-Irishness is not a part of the equation, suggesting that the key-players and decision-makers are a fairly tolerant, high-minded bunch, certainly above the narrow-mindedness and bigotry that by extension informs, we are led to assume, the 'thugs and mad bombers'. No realisation here that sectarianism was generated as a tactic by Britain historically as a means of 'divide and rule'. Higgins, himself of Irish and English stock, through his characterisations defends and promotes what he sees as the cultural legacy of the links between Ireland and Britain. In his books we are given to understand that the Provos stand opposed to that inheritance, besmirching its values.

Perhaps the novel's biggest distortion of the reality of the conflict in the North is the idea of KGB involvement in IRA operations. Barry, we are told, carried out an assassination abroad at the behest of the KGB.[30] Here we have one of the abiding themes of the genre: that spectacular acts of terror attributable to the Basques, IRA, and other terrorist organisations, are part of Soviet-inspired global terrorism designed to destabilise the West. The subtext is that on their own the IRA and its counterparts would not have the capacity to take on the British state. Barry is also tenuously linked to the assassination of Lord Mountbatten.[31] Colonel Nikolai Belov, of the KGB's 'Disinformation Department': '...we need to create as much [chaos] as possible in the Western World... chaos, disorder, fear and uncertainty'.[32]

Aside from the close resemblance of Margaret Thatcher to the novel's British Prime Minister of the day, the only concession to topicality is the theme of extradition, which in 1980-1 had again created a strain in Anglo-Irish relations, the South being seen as a safe haven for 'terrorists': 'In Ireland, you see, I'll be safe. Neither the British nor the French nor anyone else can extradite me. I'm a political offender'.[33]

Devlin crops up again to offer his assistance and advice to thwart a KGB plot in Higgins's 1985 offering, *Confessional*.[34] The KGB, it appears, predicted in 1959 that the IRA Border Campaign would peter out but that 'a conflict will break out in Ireland of a far more serious nature than anything that has gone before'.[35] In preparation for that eventual day, an agent is sent in 'deep and waiting'.

The opening pages read like a B-movie scenario. In a school for spies, the KGB's 'Department 13', 'responsible for murder, assassination and sabotage in foreign countries', enacts a supposedly typical IRA operation. The scene is an interesting device, revealing a number of stock assumptions and attributes which a prospective soviet agent provocateur is expected to assimilate: romantic nationalism; Yeatsian whimsy; Catholic devotion; hatred of informers; the trenchcoat supposedly de rigeur among IRA gunmen; and the putative ability to distinguish by appearance Protestants from Catholics.[36]

The novel is memorable for its depiction of a character bearing a close resemblance to a prominent republican: the IRA, it transpires, has reorganised its command structure under McGuiness (spelt with one 'n'):

> Anger showed in McGuiness's blue eyes for a moment.
>
> 'Ireland free and Ireland for the Irish. We don't want any Marxist pap here'.[37]

One of Higgins's recurring devices is to construct an episode or scene in which a verbal exchange occurs between a representative republican and someone from the British Intelligence establishment. Two aims are achieved in these set-piece exchanges: firstly, the British protagonist is shown to be morally superior; [s]he never relinquishes the high ground; and secondly, in some detail or other the British 'agent' somehow gets the better of the exchange – witness the following supposedly clinching rebuttal of the claim that the English don't understand the Irish.

> Billy [White, an IRA courier] lit a cigarette. 'The trouble with you Brits is that you never face up to the fact that Ireland's a foreign country. Just because we speak English...'
>
> 'As a matter of interest, my mother's name was Fitzgerald and she came from County Mayo,' Fox told him. 'She worked for the Gaelic League, was a lifelong friend of de Valera and spoke excellent Irish, a rather difficult language I found when she insisted on teaching it to me when I was a boy'.[38]

Higgins also establishes that Ferguson (representing all that is British) has more than just the business in Ireland to contend with: the Falklands; the Pope's visit; Argentinean attempts to procure Exocets,[39] and indeed there is a running commentary on the progress of the Falklands' War.[40] The subtext is plain enough: Ferguson's range of competency and responsibility, and by extension the higher interests and role of Britain on the world stage, diminishes 'Ireland', which by comparison is seen as a parochial squabble. The issue of Ireland as a distraction from the more pressing pursuit of Britain's global responsibilities is a theme encountered also in Douglas Hurd's two ventures into the genre to date.

I turn now to what must be the most studied and written-about novel of the Troubles, Bernard MacLaverty's *Cal*.[41] The novel was also made into a film of the same name (directed by Pat O'Connor, and starring John Lynch as the eponymous guilt-ridden hero, and Helen Mirren as police widow, Marcella Morton) in 1984, a year after its publication.

Cal McCrystal, aged nineteen, and his father Shamie were the only two Catholics living in a Protestant estate near Magherafelt, Derry. Cal, now unemployed, had worked with Shamie in the local abattoir but 'hadn't a strong enough stomach'.[42] Neither has he the stomach for violence. He has assisted the local IRA and now wants to sever links.

The narrative period is December, 1975 (see below), though there are flashbacks to his childhood and to the previous year when he drove the car used in an IRA assassination of an RUC Reservist. He is wracked with guilt and self-loathing over his role in the killing.

He learns that the local librarian, Marcella Morton, is the widow. He becomes infatuated and obsessed, and contrives to see more of her, taking a job as a labourer at her in-laws' farm to be close to her. Eventually they have a sexual relationship.

Cal's two republican associates are base metal stereotypes: Crilly is a thick psycho; Finbar Skeffington, a Pádraig Pearse clone. Crilly was a bully at school, and now works at the local abattoir. He got the job when Cal left.

> It was wise to be on the right side of him because he could be nasty when he wanted, even then. He was a big lad for his age [when in the third form with Cal] with large ears that stuck out at right angles from the side of his head. Somebody had once said that Crilly had ears like taxi doors and it had got back to him. Even though the boy was much smaller than him, Crilly had no compunction about breaking two of his teeth.[43]

Skeffington, a teacher, lives alone with his father, like Cal. Cal meets Skeffington at Crilly's home: 'Finbar Skeffington sat in an armchair beside the fireplace with his short legs straight out in front of him, looking at the high polish on his shoes'.[44] He greets Cal in Gaelic.

> Skeffington was small and round-faced with glasses – about thirty. He wore a sports jacket and a tie. On his lapel was a Pioneer Total Abstinence pin. His teeth reminded Cal of a rabbit's, an impression which was intensified by his habit of wrinkling his face to adjust minutely the glasses on the bridge of his nose.[45]

Bull Bailie, Herron's teacher in *The Whore-mother*, comes to mind. In both instances, we recall that Pádraig Pearse too was a teacher.

> 'The call has come for money,' said Skeffington, knitting his fingers together. 'American money is tailing off. Internment is losing the edge it had for producing the dollars. Now we need to gather some of our own'.[46]

The reference to internment, and a subsequent reference to the rent strike, suggests that it is the early 1970s, sometime between 1972 and 1974. However, from a diary entry made by Marcella around the time of her husband's killing, one can determine the narrative period as being December 1975.

When Cal expresses his lack of commitment, Skeffington's response reveals a clear dichotomy in his (Skeffington's) mindset between politics and action, and between the movement and the people.

> Others can ride on our coat-tails. The Gerry Fitts and the Humes. It's like a union. Some guys do all the work, others collect the pay rises without so much as a thank you. You have to steel yourself, Cahal. Think of the issues, not the people. Think of an Ireland free of the Brits. Would we ever achieve it through the politicians?[47]

Cal fails to avoid meeting Skeffington at a Gaelic Football match at Clones across the border. Skeffington mentions Crilly.

> 'There are not many aspects of our culture which interest Mr Crilly. But he's a useful man.'

> Cal looked at him.

> 'Come now, Cahal. Practical things have to be done. If you've a burst pipe you send for a plumber. If you have a war on your hands you send for the Mr Crillys of this world. The hard men and the bandits are the real revolutionaries, if you see what I mean. They get things done, they punch the hole for us to get through later.'

> 'What do you want me for then?'

> 'A movement like ours needs all sorts. Crilly, you, me even.'

> 'I still want out.'

> Skeffington put his hand on Cal's sleeve.

> 'That creates a big problem, Cahal. It would be out of my hands. I wouldn't like to see you hurt.'[48]

Once in, always in. Later Cal ponders: 'They shoot deserters – even deserters who protested that they had never joined in the first place'.[49] The trope is discussed in Chapter Five in regard to its use in Paul Theroux's *The Family Arsenal*.

Cyril Dunlop, Cal's foreman, who is an Orangeman, thinks that the IRA should be eradicated.

> 'Do you know what I'd do if I was in charge?' said Dunlop. He waited until Cal was forced to say no. 'Long Kesh is full of known I.R.A. prisoners, isn't it?' Again he waited until Cal replied, to give the appearance of logical steps in his argument. 'Well, every time a policeman or a soldier is shot I would put two of those bastards up against the wall and blow their brains out.

> 'That's nice.'

> 'This is war, son. I don't think you understand that. Sometimes I think Hitler had the right idea. He had the wrong cause, mind you, but he knew how to fight a war'.[50]

Cal drives the getaway car after Crilly robs a Magherafelt off-licence. Back at Skeffington's, where they take the proceeds of the robbery, Cal still maintains that he no longer wants to help: 'But it all seems so pointless'.[51] Skeffington, to refute Cal's assertion that he lacks feelings, quotes (and seems poised ever-ready to quote) Pearse's poem 'The Mother'.

My sons were faithful and they fought.

'Unlike you, Cahal.'

'But it is not like 1916.'

'It wasn't like 1916 in 1916'.[52]

In the local library Cal flicks through a history book:

There were pictures of Sir Edward Carson, Sir James Craig and the Reverend Ian Paisley, all on the one page. For sheer physical ugliness they were hard to beat. Three men with battering-ram blunt faces whose political fighting had left them looking like old boxers. There was a picture of Padric Pearse in profile. He had heard somewhere that Pearse never looked directly at the camera because he had the most God-awful squint. Cal read on the opposite page what Pearse had said, that the heart of Ireland would be refreshed by the red wine of the battlefields, that Ireland needed its bloody sacrifice. He closed the book and slid it back among the others.[53]

A potent figure of what might be termed traditional nationalism is replaced on the shelf to gather obscurity. The gesture is symbolic, though in fact reinforcing a skewed understanding of Pearse's historical role. Stephen Watt argues that MacLaverty demythologises or de-romanticises the myths of Irish nationalism. I would suggest, instead, that in *Cal* he draws too liberally on stock imagery and modes of representation.[54] Skeffington, for example, differs little essentially from Hugh Ward in Broderick's *The Fugitives*.

Later, a depressed Cal ruminates in the Mortons' empty cottage.

He thought of himself as a monk in his cell not only deprived of light and comfort but, in the mood he was in, deprived of God. He had ceased to believe in the one thing that dignified his suffering. Matt Talbot lived with chains embedded in him for the love of God. What if he had not believed in God and yet had continued with his pain? What if he had suffered for another person? To suffer for something which didn't exist, that was like Ireland. People were dying every day, men and women were being crippled and turned into vegetables in the name of Ireland. An Ireland which never was and never would be. It was the people of Ulster who were heroic, caught between the jaws of two opposing ideals trying to grind each other out of existence.[55]

In a flashback it is recounted how in the previous year Cal drove the getaway car for the attack on Marcella's husband. Before setting off on the operation Crilly had reassured Cal:

'Don't worry, Cal. This guy is the greatest bastard unhung, Skeffington says that we've got to squeeze the Police Reserve and the U.D.R. Maybe put people off joining them. So he picked this guy, this real turd who lives outside Magherafelt. And tonight we do him.' Cal said nothing. He cleaned the condensation from the outside of his pint with one finger. 'He planted a gun on two totally innocent guys about a month ago,' Crilly went on. 'They are up in Crumlin Road jail now. Not only that, but he had his mates give them a kicking to end all kickings and said that they had resisted arrest. He knew them too – two Catholic lads from the town – the big fucker'.[56]

Catholic morality, imagery and allusions pervade the novel in a sort of projection of Cal's guilt.

Although she was light years away from him he felt the enormous pull of her. And yet, like the moon and the earth, he knew that, because of what he had done, they could never come together. His sin kept them apart as surely as cold space. All that was left to him was to watch her. He had heard Father Brolley say once that sin was outlawing yourself from God. After death God did not point the finger and say, 'Depart from me, ye accursed'. You realised your sinfulness and remained outside. A man damned himself.[57]

The message at the heart of the novel is that Cal's role in the murder has put him beyond the moral pale – but not only in regard to Marcella.

He was in love with the one woman in the world who was forbidden him. He was suffering for something which could not exist. Apart from her age – what widow would look at a long-haired boy ten years younger than herself – by his action he had outlawed himself from her.[58]

Cal conflates the taboo nature of his love for Marcella with the love of Ireland, echoing a sentiment he earlier expressed: 'To suffer for something which didn't exist, that was like Ireland'.[59]

The Irish writer M.S. Power, a former television producer, is another writer whose work was later to be dramatised for television. His trilogy of novels *The Children of the North* was published between 1985 and 1987.[60] The trilogy was made into a major BBC four-part drama series, scheduled to be shown in February 1991 but rescheduled for the autumn because of sensitivity over the Troubles theme at a time when the British Army were in action in the Gulf.[61]

In the first of the trilogy, *The Killing of Yesterday's Children* (1985), Power pinpoints what he sees as the cultural and psychological differences between the indigenous and British security forces. Amoral or immoral equivalence is a running theme, though the British somehow salvage honour before the conclusion.[62]

Mr Asher, a ruthless and unscrupulous high-ranking RUC officer for whom the ends justify the means, is contrasted with Colonel Maddox, who is in the North to defeat the terrorists, and who believes in commitment, duty and patrician honour. Maddox later recognises the distinction between his role and Asher's.

> Then, suddenly, at last, though the feeling had been nurtured within him for longer than he would ever care to admit, he was humiliatingly aware of what should have been obvious a long time ago, that he, for all his rank and military power, was there to be manipulated, to put a respectable face on things, to demonstrate to a world for the most part bored with the violence and disinterested in the outcome that something was being done. And being done it certainly was, but by others, sinister men who wheeled and dealed in the business of death while he looked on.[63]

The contrast in the two men's characters and the differences in their approaches to their responsibilities may be read as a metaphor for differences in outlook and motivation between unionism and British metropolitan interests. The effect in the novel of these divergent perspectives tends to mitigate the role and culpability of Britain. When Maddox later lapses from his hitherto high standards of service, the implication is that he has been corrupted by proximity to the double-dealing and duplicitous Asher.

The republican protagonists are equally devious. Seamus Reilly, is a stage-godfather in clerical drag:

> in his black overcoat and black hat, carrying his large black missal with its embossed gold crucifix, gave a distinct impression of something clerical, though one could have been forgiven for imagining there was something more of the undertaker about him.[64]

A Provo 'Committee' member, Reilly orders Martin Deeley, experienced sniper ('for more than three years... their most successful assassin'),[65] to act as an assistant to Mr Arthur Apple who is to run a bookmaker's in Lepper Street, in the New Lodge, North Belfast. The business is a money-laundering operation for the Provos and Deeley is required to keep an eye on Apple. Apple (Prufrock-like, and similar perhaps to Maurice Leitch's creation Yarr[66] in his alienation) is a former minor British diplomat who has undergone some sort of a mental breakdown after service in Mexico. Deeley receives his instructions, the author specifies, on 31 January 1979. Deeley is subsequently ordered to assassinate Maddox while he is home in Berkshire.

Deeley is twenty-six. His father and older brother were shot dead and their bodies dumped in a waterlogged ditch. His mother wants him to avenge their deaths. He was fourteen at the time, although, inconsistently, on page 113 it is stated that he was barely sixteen then, which would make it either 1967 or 1969 – though such killings were unlikely to happen before the early 1970s. Elsewhere in the novel there is a reference to the hunger strikers – another detail which places narrative time out of sync with historical time.

The description of Deeley suggests immaturity (which thematically may be in keeping with the title).

His rare laughter revealed very white but incredibly small teeth, as though nature had made a hash of things or decided, for unkind reasons, that his puppy-teeth would be quite adequate.[67]

The theme is further suggested when later Reilly describes Deeley to Maddox.

Deeley is nothing. A thug. A little killer. A good one... but we have so many young men only too anxious to prove they can kill. The Deeleys of this land grow in every dung-heap in the city. Look in any house and you'll find one waiting to be discovered.[68]

The inferred identification of Deeley's childlike nature is an inversion of the romantic ideal of the child. Children appeared in romantic poetry, for example, as 'truly uncorrupted and as closer to nature'.[69] For Reilly, however, 'the Deeleys of this land grow in every dung-heap in the city'. The portrayal of the Irish as 'only too anxious to kill' comes from the mouth of an Irishman; therefore, the racist slur of the inherently violent Irish carries additional potency. One of Reilly's men, McIlliver, is described as having a 'pallid, stoat-like face' (and accordingly related in descriptional venom to the more usually ascribed ferret-like propensities of republicans in the genre).[70]

Apple, who is understandable as a sort of Old Testament retributive force, is later to accuse Reilly.

People like you always come out of things nicely. Somehow you manage to exploit the weaknesses and distress of others. You treat people like pawns. You shift their souls about in an evil game, crying brotherhood and patriotism and freedom and every other mindless cliché that fanatics have cried for centuries. And all the time you know what you are doing? I'll tell you what you are doing *Mister* Reilly: you are committing fratricide, you are crippling your country, you are chaining your people to the skeleton of horror and terror and hatred.[71]

Colonel Maddox is depicted at a dinner party at his Berkshire home.

Once he had dreamed of military greatness, of dying at the front, of leading his men over the top with astounding bravery and scant regard for his own safety, of wielding considerable power in Whitehall; but he had long since forsworn such chimeras. His tired, sagging eyes gave the impression of a once great man resigned to mediocrity, and he carried with him the furtive, nervous shadows and tics that service in Northern Ireland seemed to settle upon anyone assigned there.[72]

He stands as an emblem for duty, for the imperial mentality. This is in contrast to his wife's middle-class guests, who are ignorant of what is happening in Ireland. To his wife's question as to why he keeps going back there, he replies 'Duty'.

'Duty, indeed,' Nancy snapped scornfully. 'Let someone else have the duty. That's what I say. We should pull out and let those savages kill each other off. Like we did in India and places.'

He is drawn into an explanation for the conflict.

> He searched about for the words that would explain the tragedy of Ulster
> to the greedy, vacuous faces that stared at him, searched also for something
> that would orientate his thoughts. He felt himself drowning in the
> confusion of hopes and distortions, fears, truths, half-truths and lies,
> political wheelings and religious dealings that created the turmoil of
> Ireland, and the more his mind thrashed about the more he realized he was
> sinking.[73]

For Asher,

> terrorists appeared in an unending stream, generation upon generation, cut one
> in half and instead of one dead body you ended up with, it seemed, two live
> ones – both more dedicated and intense than the one you thought you had
> destroyed. And they blended into the community to such effect that one never
> knew who was who, the most innocent-looking often the most guilty, and if
> Asher had learned one thing through the years he had learned that nobody
> would ever penetrate the complex, unyielding Irish nationalist mind.[74]

When Reilly orders Deeley to kill Maddox at his Berkshire home, the
impression is given of a vast clandestine network of well-placed informants,
spiriting high-level and even seemingly superfluous data on important targets.

> 'They don't seem to see Berkshire as a likely place for us to strike. He will
> have a driver, of course. His wife is there. One house guest who might have
> left by Wednesday. A publisher of romantic novels, I hear.' Reilly grimaced
> widely, as if he found romance hugely amusing. 'There's a maid – a
> *domestic*, we were told'.[75]

Reilly is even able to answer Deeley's query whether Maddox has dogs: 'Two.
A retriever. Old, deaf and friendly. A pug. Hers'.[76] The impression gathers of an
omniscient IRA, with loyal insiders everywhere.

Maddox is an important target, Reilly tells Deeley, because it is necessary to
'Let the Brits know we are still in business'.[77] Apparently, the IRA, as represented
in the novel, judged their campaign to be ineffective thus necessitating an
attention-grabbing initiative.

Reilly objects when Deeley implies that Reilly enjoys the power to order people
to be killed.

> 'You imagine I *like* having people killed? Do you? Only shitty little thugs
> like you enjoy death. Yes, you *do*. You revel in it. It makes you feel
> important, gives your grotty little life some meaning. Jesus! You are
> fucking pathetic. You're as bad as those smug-faced bastards who portray
> us all as psychopathic murderers who wallow in blood and death. I can tell
> you this: I hate it. I loathe it.'
>
> [...] 'And another thing,' Reilly went on, 'you think it's easy for me to go
> about ordering punishments, don't you? Just a name on a piece of paper to

be struck off. Very clever. You stupid bastard. I *believe* in what we are
trying to do, but I am sickened to my stomach at the way we are forced to
achieve it. I ordered my own brother killed because he turned informer. I
suppose I enjoyed that? I cried for a week. And I still cry when I think of
his great pleading eyes. He shouted at me 'Not me, Seamus, not your own
brother' when they came and took him from the house. Dragged him
whimpering and screaming down the garden. But yes, him, my own
brother.' Seamus Reilly paused as if again watching his brother being taken
from his home. 'And you say I like it'.[78]

Larry Corrigan, whom the IRA knows to be an informer, is fed information by
Deeley about his role in the Berkshire shooting. Corrigan haggles with Asher for
a ticket to Australia in exchange for the information. Asher reveals to Maddox that
it is common practice for the IRA to use touts in this way, and that to the British
the touts are also expendable.

'...They hand over Deeley to us in the hope that we keep the heat off, in
case we turn up something more important while we search for your -'

'You mean Corrigan was actually ordered in here to -'

'- to give us the information we want and make a deal for himself? Yes.
That's exactly what I mean.'

'Good God.'

'It happens all the time. They're lovely people.'

'How many others have you sent to – Australia?'

Asher laughed, truly amused at the Colonel's naïveté. 'None. And, of
course, Corrigan won't be going either.'

'-?'

'He'll be killed.'

'And you'll allow that, after making an agreement with him?'

'Allow it? Colonel, we'll arrange it. Of course we'll make it look like a
punishment for informing, but we'll do it'.[79]

Daphne Cope, Deeley's girlfriend, (whose father is in Long Kesh, and who
works as a prostitute to support her mother)[80] is able to bring him up-to-date over
the phone.

'They say you tried to kill that Colonel in England – you didn't, though,
did you?'

'What else?'

'Oh. Larry Corrigan was sent to grass on you, to make a deal of some sort'.[81]

The hapless Corrigan, however, is seemingly bereft of insight into these
machinations, though we are led to believe they are common knowledge in the
ghettos, or at least among Daphne's clientele.

A conversation between Asher and Maddox takes place at the novel's despairing conclusion, revealing the pointless and selfish machinations of all involved.

'[Asher] I spend my life tidying up.'

'That's what Seamus Reilly told me. Cleaning up *he* called it, though.'

'Indeed?'

'Yes. You two seem to have something in common.'

'We do, don't we?'

'Yes, you do.'

Asher gave a short, sharp laugh that was really a snort. 'That's quite amusing when you think of it,' he said.

Maddox looked up at him with a long, mournful gaze. 'That must be what's wrong with me, John. I can see nothing remotely amusing about it. The two of you revel in deceit and corruption. I have never held either in very high regard.'

'Only because you've never before had to resort to them, Colonel,' Asher told him. 'Your nice, comfortable, Berkshire lifestyle doesn't lend itself to devious ways. We, however, have extraordinary lifestyles that demand extraordinary measures. You call it corruption and deceit, we call it merely wheeling and dealing. Wheels within wheels and deals within deals. It leads to only one thing – survival. Survival, if you want, of the fittest. The fittest in this case being the one who can deal the better hand, deal himself the aces. Seamus Reilly is now one ace in *my* hand, and I would be fool if I failed to use it,' Asher concluded.

Maddox closed his eyes and sighed, hoping that when he opened them again Asher might have gone. But: 'In a sense we play games,' Asher continued. 'Rather vicious, dangerous games, I agree, but games nonetheless. Games,' he added, 'that we know we really cannot win. That nobody can win'.[82]

Reilly gets his come-uppance at the very start of the third novel in M.S. Power's *Children of the North* trilogy, *A Darkness in the Eye* (1987).[83] The novel opens with the morning headline that the body has been found of Seamus Reilly, 'self-styled Godfather of the Provisional IRA'.[84] A tabloid slur, godfather, is thus projected as a personal epithet, as if any member of a group or class that considers itself exploited and demonised would so deprecatingly assume its enemies' abusive definitions. Later it is revealed that he was killed because of his apparent conversion from hard-liner to advocate of the nascent peace process.

Years ago I swore I would do everything in my power to see to it that Ireland was united. And, from time to time, violence was the only option.

[...] things have now changed. There is just a glimmer of hope that we can achieve our ends by political means so the violence has to stop.

Unfortunately, there are some, even within our ranks, who disagree with this policy. They see negotiations as weakness, terror as strength. Some of our most loyal followers have broken away from us and have sworn to continue the killings and bombings. Someone – finally – has sworn to take a stand against violence.[85]

The novel goes on to chart the preparations, execution and aftermath of the Brighton Bomb. The narrative proffers the simplistic evaluation that the bombing strengthened the hands of the 'hawks' at a crucial time when 'doves' within the movement were gaining the upper hand in redirecting policy towards politics.[86] Politics and violence are narrowly defined as mutually exclusive options, when it is clear that at the time the 'Armalite and ballot box' strategy prevailed. The reason is also clear: the British were not at this stage remotely interested in an inclusive settlement. Sinn Féin's electoral successes, its expanding political base and organisational development, were perceived as a serious threat to the SDLP. Far from encouraging any support within the republican movement for the 'constitutional' path, the British and Irish governments agreed on a strategy to undermine such a threatening development. The Anglo-Irish Agreement, signed just over a year after the Brighton bomb, was the British and Irish political establishments' vain attempt to curb the rise of Sinn Féin in the hope of bolstering the position of the constitutional-nationalist SDLP.

A.F.N. Clarke, as a former professional soldier who served in the North, writes authoritatively. *Contact* (1983), which traverses the borderline between fiction and autobiography, is an account of the author's 'own emotions, thoughts and reactions during two tours' of duty as a Paratrooper lieutenant in Belfast, 1973, and in Crossmaglen, 1976.[87] Clarke also wrote the screenplay for a BBC *Screen Two* production of the same name broadcast in January 1985.

The style is no-holds-barred observations of the daily grind of soldiering in what Clarke terms a 'corporals' war'. He makes many interesting observations; after a young boy dies during a gun battle between the IRA and the Paras, responsibility for who fired the fatal shot is contested.

Nobody gave a shit about the poor little bastard. Propaganda, that's what it's all about, and we play the game as viciously as everybody else. Human life becomes graded by the ability to be used for maximum publicity. Propaganda and publicity, the weapons of twentieth-century society.[88]

Clarke attests to the practice of doctoring plastic baton rounds and to the use of buckshee rounds during 'contacts', that is, engagements with the enemy. He also relates his brief encounter with Robert Nairac in Ardoyne, 1973. Nairac, in his subsequent role as a British army undercover agent in the south Armagh area, was later abducted and executed by the IRA.

Gerald Seymour, who as a former ITN reporter covered the North in the Seventies, might also be supposed to speak with some authority about the subject. *In Field of Blood* (1985) he seems good at detailing the routines and operational procedures of the British Army and the Intelligence community, almost in a fly-on-the-wall manner, and this aspect of his skill as a writer is quite credible.[89] He is less assured when describing the culture and environment of West Belfast and of its republican activists and support base.

Inane dialogue and inaccurate locational detail is rife. For example, a republican character refers to the RUC Special Branch as follows:

> No one ever informed in my day. You could beat the shit out of a man, and he never told. Whatever the 'tecs did in Castlereagh and Gough and Strand.[90]

Among republicans, the RUC Special Branch are rarely referred to as other than 'the Branch', and never as 'the tecs', an epithet owing more, I think, to the patois of the English crime thriller. And the idea that informers are a modern phenomenon, and that earlier republicans were a hardier breed, really doesn't merit a serious rebuttal. Another character, meanwhile, supposedly a Provo Battalion Commander, utters the sort of line that might be expected of a Cockney gangster, jealous of encroachments into his patch or manor: 'That's my place up there, Turf Lodge, that's my swim'.[91] Another example comes from a republican veteran ('a man listened to').

> 'You've gone for a big crack, Frankie. You've come in and you've chucked your weight all over. Your crack'll have to hurt, Frankie' [...]
>
> 'My crack'll hurt,' Frankie said.[92]

The above is a lame, even absurd attempt to mimic the Northern idiom. To 'have a crack at' something is popularly to have 'a go'; and the term had an additional, onomatopoeic resonance in so far as having a go might involve firing a rifle. However, here 'crack' is semantically extended beyond any usage to be found in Belfast. There may also be a confusion with the Gaelic word 'craic', meaning 'chat', which is common parlance in Ireland, perhaps particularly in the North, where 'What's your craic?' translates loosely as 'What news have you?'

Early in the narrative Seymour establishes that the central republican character, Sean Pious McAnally, is oath-bound to remain a Provo for life.

> 'You took an oath, you swore your oath,' the taller man said.
>
> Eleven years before Sean Pius McAnally had made his oath to the Organization. He had made it in his own home. They couldn't use the front room because his Da was watching telly, couldn't use the kitchen because his Ma was dishing the supper. He had made his oath on the upstairs landing, and they'd all had to whisper because his sister was trying to get his oath, he had offered his allegiance to the Provisional wing of the Irish Republican Army.
>
> 'An oath's an oath. An oath's a lifetime,' the smaller man said.
>
> 'An oath doesn't get torn up just because a boy wants to sit on his arse in the south...and let others do what the boy swore to do himself,' the taller man sad, and McAnally had to lean forward and strain to hear the words.

> An oath whispered on the landing of a three-bedroomed Housing
> Executive semi-detached. An oath made while a sister crooned to a baby
> while the telly blared a comedy, while Ma crashed the saucepans.
>
> [...] 'You're being told to obey an order from Belfast Brigade'.[93]

As in the example in Maclaverty's *Cal*, mentioned above, the implication that a
republican, 'once in' is 'always in' is a recurring nonsense in the genre.

McAnally's wife, meanwhile, is depicted as a sort of naive drudge, ever loyal in
a mindless manner, for Seymour allows no credence or weight to her for
supporting her partner's involvement. Instead, she is shown to rationalise her
support, excusing him anything.

> She blamed him for nothing. If the house leaked then that was the fault of
> the Brits who refused to come and repair it. If her man hadn't work then
> that was the fault of the Brits who wouldn't provide employment for the
> work force in the Nationalist housing estates. If Sean Pius McAnally was
> in the Provos then that was the fault of the Brits for putting their fucking
> soldiers on the streets of Turf Lodge and the 'Murph and Andy'town, and
> Whiterock. She would have thought the less of her man if he had not been
> in the Organization. She had nagged him once into going for a job at the
> De Lorean, and he'd been taken on, just after coming out of the Kesh, and
> the day he should have started he'd chucked it and gone with the ASU –
> that was somebody's fault, not her man's fault.[94]

Underlying the sarcasm Seymour suggests that there is no justification for
violence. However, whether unconsciously or not, Seymour gives her a positive,
supportive role: 'She would have thought the less of her man if he had not been in
the Organization' – the genre more usually portrays the opposition of wives to
their husbands' political commitment.

The depiction of Belfast Brigade's Officer Commanding is Faganesque, a
Dickensian parody.

> A cold, hard fucker, those that knew him well said he was. They'd met in
> the bars after McAnally had come out of the Kesh. They'd known each
> other when McAnally was a big man who was on the RPG-7 ASU. This
> was the Chief. There were three men behind him. None of them kids, none
> of them the prison fodder that were the Volunteers. Brigade men. Men that
> the Mirror called the Godfathers. The Chief wore a black donkey jacket
> with the collar up and round his cheeks, and he had a flat cap down over
> his eyes. His fingers were fidgeting, couldn't help himself. McAnally
> smiled. He had on the end of his tongue the name that the Chief was called.
> He was called 'Windsy'. Not to his face, but behind his back. It was said
> that he lived off Chinese takeaway, noodles and rice and spare ribs, and that
> was why 'Windsy'. Be a brave bugger, or a daft bugger, who would call
> him that to his face. A fierce face, power and authority jutting from the
> little that McAnally could see of it.[95]

Slurs are piled up high: armchair generals counterposed with 'prison fodder' volunteers; Godfathers; a view that fear is the basis of command. Without exception in the novel the IRA characters are portrayed as loathsome, grotesque, as sexual predators, and their wives, as sluts.

Notwithstanding these deficiencies, Seymour does appear to give a nod of appreciation towards the sort of dichotomy of attitude prevalent among British soldiers; the souped-up aggression towards the civilian population, resides uneasily, and inconsistently, with an empathy with that population's grievances – attitudes largely substantiated from a reading of A.F.N. Clarke's *Contact*, and from Antony Beevor's *Inside the British Army*.[96] Seymour illustrates the contradictory sensibilities in the following exchange.

> 'Once you feel sorry for them, then the next step is saying that if you'd been brought up in Turf Lodge that you'd be a terrorist, that sort of drivel.'
>
> 'I don't have to take that.'
>
> 'What I'm telling you is this, you muttering about known terrorists looking pathetic doesn't exactly move along our war effort. They're vicious psychopaths, and recognizing that is the first step towards grinding them down.'
>
> 'You know what...?' Ferris flared. 'That's precisely the attitude that has kept us here fifteen years, not winning...'
>
> 'They're vermin.'
>
> 'They're human beings, and when we start realizing that we might stop losing.'
>
> 'What utter shit...If you weren't a damned good officer I'd see this conversation went further'.[97]

But the briefest flicker of enlightenment is soon overcast by graphically dehumanising depictions of republican violence, and in a way that sets that violence apart from violence perpetrated in the name of British interests.

> The Chief had a way with touts. Cigarettes on the balls and the stomach, for the confession. Then the hooding. Then the noisy cocking of the pistol against the ear of the tout. Then the shot into the ground beside the tout's foot, so that he pissed himself and messed himself. Then the barrel against the back of the neck. Then the killing.[98]

In another example, Ferris, a young British Army officer, representing all that is worthy and humane, is appalled at the extent of the injuries to a young victim of an IRA punishment shooting.

> The corporal's masked torch shone down into a small white face. Ferris saw the terrified, staring eyes and the blood-drained cheeks that were smeared with tears.

Ferris's thoughts were racing. Bloody hit and run driver, no bloody lights in the street... But the corporal's torch was moving down the short length of the boy's jersey... Ferris saw the hole at the elbow, worn through...and the torch moved on down the boy's thigh. He saw the blood-soaked knee of the boy, and the dark bullet hole set in the spread of crimson.

'But it's a bloody child...'

'It's a child, Mr Ferris, and he's been knee-capped,' the corporal said grimly.

'God Almighty... I don't believe it...'

'He's Liam Blaney, he's thirteen years old. Father's in the Kesh...Want to see his stomach?'

The corporal didn't wait for Ferris's reply. He pulled back the boy's shirt, lifted his jersey. Ferris saw the burns and the bruises.

'Must reckon him an informer, sir,' the corporal said.[99]

McAnally, who turns supergrass, gives information that leads to the identification of a leading bomb maker based in Monaghan, in the South. Later, an SAS squad crosses the border and incinerates the man, a scene contrived to pander to the rawest lynch-mob mentality, and one can almost hear the whoop of approval Seymour expects of his readership. Seymour's tendentious handling of descriptions of violence illustrates Jerry Palmer's contention that in the thriller descriptions of the hero's violence are intended to exhilarate; while, on the other hand, the villain's violence is depicted in a cold-blooded light and is intended to nauseate.[100] In the battle of stereotypes good/hot is waged against bad/cold.

In the morality of the typical thriller, ends justify means. The hero is identified as righteous, implying, therefore, that the means s/he employs are justified. In essence, because in this case, and in the majority of instances of the genre, the hero represents British interests, his ends are assumed to be morally laudable. Wolfgang Iser distinguishes between the 'real' and 'implied reader', the latter incorporating

all those dispositions necessary for a literary work to exercise its effect – predispositions laid down not by an empirical outside reality, but by the text itself. Consequently, the implied reader as a concept has his roots firmly implanted in the structure of the text.[101]

The morality of Troubles fiction often corresponds to the values of collective emotion, of mob anger, meeting the vicarious desire for revenge of its implied readers, for whose assumed prejudices all too many writers pander. The implied reader, in other words, is therefore a project of the author's own mental outlook, through which, in the process of interpellation, the reader may identify subjectively.

As for the charge, illustrated in the above knee-capping episode, that the IRA victimises its own communities, no civilian casualties should be acceptable and every precaution necessary taken to avoid the occurrence. But, equally, and the point isn't made lightly, no conflict is without suffering inflicted on the innocent. Republicans, in my experience, do not sink to the cynical calculation of collateral damage. The following statistics, awful as they are, might go some way to supply a contextual rebuttal or at least bring some sense of proportion to the scale of violence as perpetrated by the respective protagonists. David Miller reports that 37.4% of IRA victims are civilians, while 54.4% of British Army victims are civilians.[102] And the ratios do not include numbers of innocent nationalists killed or injured due to collusion between loyalists and British forces.

Martin Waddell is an example of an author who doesn't sensationalise violence for effect, and indeed who shows considerable restraint when describing violence. Instead, he is concerned to express the effects of the conflict on children. In a series of novels for adolescents published between 1983 and 1989, Waddell, under the pen name of Catherine Sefton, explored the dark experience of sectarianism so rooted in the Northern psyche. The author has consistently aimed to address and explicate the nature of difference in the context of Northern Ireland. He is very conscious in his writing of the susceptibility of children to the fear of difference, of strangers and of outsiders. He posits that the attitude is learned by children in the home and at school, and fashions, and may even distort, their social development. In this view the perpetuation of bigotry and sectarianism results from the political socialisation of children.

The first of the series, *Island of the Strangers* (1983), was subsequently televised by ITV. In the novel, a young girl, Nora-No-Guts, asserts her independence of spirit and mind when her school friends gang up (the Defence Force) against a Belfast school party (the Gobbers) camping on the adjacent island of Inishnagal.

> 'They've no right coming here and fighting us.' Orla said. 'Nobody would ever fight here if it wasn't for people coming in from outside.'
>
> I didn't argue about it at the time, but the more I thought about it, the surer I was that Orla was wrong, the trouble was in us to begin with. If it hadn't been the Gobbers, it would have been somebody else, somebody who was the least bit different from the rest of us, so that we could pick them out.[103]

Nora reasons that the intolerance is due to a human fear, a matter of individual as well as group psychology, rather than having any objective basis in threat from outside. This theme recurs in the second novel in the series.

As I mentioned in Chapter Three, in early September 1996 Martin Waddell visited the H-Blocks to give a lecture on writing for children. This is a field he has excelled at, winning many prestigious awards: the Smarties Prize; the Kurt Maschler Award; runner-up for the Guardian Children's Fiction Prize; and also including the Other Award for *Starry Night* (1986).[104] In conversation with the author, he revealed that he was moved to write *Starry Night* by the Kerry Babies controversy.

Starry Night is set in an imaginary seaside town in the North of Ireland, Kiltarragh. The title, according to the author, echoes the image of the Starry Plough.

There was a fish tank behind the bar, with a green fish and a blue fish in it, and a plastic diver in a diver's suit, helmet and all. Above it there was the Starry Plough, that Mike told me was our real Flag, the Flag of Ireland, Protestant and Catholic together.[105]

The fish tank prefigures Glenn Patterson's similar use of a goldfish bowl as a metaphor for entrapment within a mode of thinking, used in his 1992 novel *Fatlad*.[106] The radical tradition of republicanism signalled by the Starry Plough is part of the background experience of a young Catholic, Kathleen Fay. When Kathleen discovers that her sister, Rose, is really her mother, the revelation coincides with the whole questioning of her received notions – as to the way her sister-in-law is treated by the family, for example, and her attitude to the Troubles. Kathleen's community is hostile to the presence of British soldiers. So is she, but her friend Ann from Belfast doesn't share her views.

'If we had our United Ireland, there'd be no soldiers,' I said. 'Why don't they just go home? There's no sense in them running round here waiting to get shot at.'

'Och, I don't know,' Ann said.

'What don't you know?' I said. 'The Brits caused the whole bother. If they would just clear out of Ireland we'd have North and South together in one country and it would be fine.'

Ann made a face.

'Everybody knows that!' I said.

'Everybody round here,' Ann said. 'That's not everybody. There's a lot of people where I come from who want to stay British.'

'Then they've no sense,' I said.

'How do you know?' she said.

'Sure everybody knows it,' I said. 'You ask anybody round here and you'll get the same answer. If we get the British out and have a United Ireland then we'll all be happy.'

'It's not as easy as that, Kathleen,' she said. 'If you took a vote on it, you'd lose.'

'If we can't vote them out, we'll blow them out!' I said. 'Everybody knows Northern Ireland was set up that way at the beginning, so there would be more Protestants in it than us. That's why their Ulster is just six counties, and not the nine counties it used to be. If it was nine counties we'd outvote them. That's the Brits' democracy for you!'[107]

Despite her espousal of the supposedly simplistic defence of armed struggle, which recalls an old tabloid slur attributed to republicans ('You can't bomb a million Protestants into a United Ireland, but you can bomb them out of it'), Kathleen is able to reason politically and to speak her own mind. But Waddell contrives the dialogue so that Kathleen's vocal outburst sounds immature and naive beside her friend Ann's more 'mature' and reasonably expressed opinion. The assumption underlying the exchange, and indeed the whole novel, is that the community's hostility towards the British Army is unthinking and reactionary. There is little appreciation of a causal relation between the sullenness of the local men and their perhaps justified resentment at the experience of a repressive military presence. You are left to wonder why the conflict began. Hostility to the British military presence, although raised as an issue, goes unexplained and therefore may appear irrational. In the republican analysis it is the oppressive nature of that presence which is at the root of the conflict. Would a military campaign against the British Army presence be sustainable if that presence was widely held by the communities in question to be benign or beneficial? It should be remembered that the British Army was initially welcomed in nationalist areas in August 1969. Despite the novel's failings, as seen from a republican perspective, or rather, this republican's viewpoint, Waddell consistently attempts in all his Troubles fiction to empathise with and to reach out to the 'other'.

A number of other novels written for children or adolescents appeared during this period. Despite their varied treatment of the conflict, they share the common theme of personal disaster due to republican violence. In Lynn Reid Banks's *Maura's Angel* (1984), for example, Maura Cuddy, whose father is absent on active service with the IRA, and whose oldest brother, Kieran, is a political prisoner, is helped to cope by an angel who fell to earth 'amid a bomb blast'.[108] And in Mary Ann Sullivan's *Child of War* (1984), thirteen-year-old Maeve is egged on to exact revenge by her school mates when her little brother becomes a victim of the violence.[109]

Stories written for children and adolescents are problematic in terms of their capacity to foster dominant values. There is a possibility that an equation might be drawn between the developing views and attitudes of the young characters depicted and the moral centre provided by the adult world, as characterised and mediated through the author's voice. The adult voice would be taken as authoritative and one representative of an established order or viewpoint. Therefore, the authorial line or discursive parameters of what the adult characters say and do may have a crucial didactic affect, especially on young receptive, even susceptible minds.

It is worth reflecting on why this concern with the trauma of children caught up in the violence should have become now so marked a feature in the fiction of this period. The novels cited do not belong to the thriller genre and are often quite serious attempts to address the issues surrounding victimhood. A review of a number of contemporary factors and concerns may provide a possible explanation.

The prior period is notable for the widespread media coverage given to street demonstrations in support of the hunger strikers. Images went around the world of children rioting, and reports of deaths and serious injuries of children caused by the use and, as many nationalists and republicans would claim, the indiscriminate misuse of British Army and RUC plastic bullets. The suffering of the hunger strikers' families, which received widespread media coverage (designed, it seemed at the time, to pressurise the families to intervene to halt the hunger strike on behalf of their respective sons and husbands), provided a powerfully emotive backdrop. In addition, the Kincora scandal surfaced in 1982, in an atmosphere already primed by an upsurge in reported cases of sexual and physical abuse of children. It was an especially worrying time to be a parent, and it is possible that all this anxiety fed into the consciousness of writers, and as I have indicated, especially women writers. Many of the women writers discussed could be said to have responded to relieve these 'national phobic pressure points', to use Stephen King's telling phrase.[110] But of course, from the outset of the Troubles the media 'homed in' on images reflecting how children were affected, between 1969 and 1970 particularly, on poignant images of little white coffins, of street burnings, of fleeing families, of children caught up in the early riots, rioting. As Des Wilson argues, some of the reportage was contrived.

> Sometimes pictures were composed to make a useful television or newspaper scene. One of the frequently appearing pictures in newspaper reports of troubled areas is that of children holding guns. The message is that evil people are encouraging this among children while they skulk in the background themselves. Many trouble spots are reported to the accompaniment of such child pictures. In Belfast they were set up by photographers. Sometimes local residents stopped them.[111]

There was considerable academic and professional interest too, as the number of studies on the impact of violence on children attests.[112]

During the 1970s only a few women writers centred their fictional narratives in a Troubles context: Menna Gallie, Joan Lingard, Elizabeth Boyle, June Drummond, Edith Morrison, Naomi May, Jennifer Johnston, Lucille Redmond, Fiona Barr, Palma Harcourt. And yet in the period under discussion eighteen category (a) novels by women were published (compared to ten in the previous period). And this figure excludes the number of women who had short stories published. For example, in *The Female Line: Northern Irish Women Writers* (1985), there appeared the following relevant contributions: Shirley Bork, 'The Palm House'; Anne Devlin, 'Five Notes After a Visit'; Polly Devlin, 'Dora'; Anne Noble, 'A Riot'; Anne-Marie Reilly, 'Leaving'; Jill McKenna, 'The Reprisal'.[113]

The effects of violence on the relatives of victims wasn't only a theme in children's fiction at this time, as Jennifer Johnston's *The Railway Station Man* (1984) attests; the novel's heroine is Helen, whose husband, a school teacher, is accidentally killed by IRA gunmen.[114] And in Deirdre Madden's *Hidden Symptoms* (1986), a student at Queen's has to deal with the impact of the murder of her twin brother.[115] One of the shaping events of the central character Martha Murtagh in Mary Beckett's *Give Them Stones* (1987) is the killing of her brother Danny by the British Army.[116]

Mary Beckett was born in Belfast, and taught in Ardoyne until her marriage in 1956. Her first novel, *Give Them Stones*, a 'feminine-first-person-narrative', concerns the struggle of Martha Murtagh to gain a limited sense of autonomy while rearing a family in Belfast during the Stormont years and the present Troubles up until the mid-1980s.

Beckett charts the history of grievance of a Catholic nationalist. One of the core themes is the generational transmission of values and beliefs. Martha remembers that as a child her grandmother's repeated message that only the younger generation could set things right, and by that she meant the task of improving conditions for Catholic communities. I am reminded of the claim in Douglas Hurd's 1975 novel *Vote to Kill* that nationalist hatred was bred by grandmothers. Martha is vehement in later years in wanting a United Ireland, and the narrative explores where this allegiance came from. Real grievances underlay the bitterness carried down.

> When the explosions began I took them as my protest. They happened at night. Nobody was hurt. They showed we were disgusted at the way things were turning out. They were shops and factories that were nothing to do with us. Broken glass all over the down-town pavements having to be cleared up every morning didn't worry me. It cost the English exchequer. They'd soon get fed up I'd thought. I didn't say this to anybody. When people said, 'Terrible, isn't it – all these places getting blew up,' I just said, 'Oh indeed,' and changed the subject.[117]

Martha's whole cultural environment was one of victimhood – being poor, from a nationalist community; as a Catholic (from bigotry and from the consequences of Catholic moral teaching); and as a woman. Even the killing of the three Scottish soldiers (an actual event referred to again and again in the genre)[118] cannot shake her conviction in the necessity of the IRA.

> When the three Scottish soldiers were shot up in the hills I didn't believe the IRA had done it. First of all I said it was the UVF or the military themselves in a private quarrel. Then I said it was done in self-defence and the bodies had been re-arranged. I never would let anybody say that the IRA had killed them after drinking with them in supposed friendliness.[119]

The novel is painfully, painstakingly accurate in its depiction of the qualms many nationalists feel when IRA actions go terribly wrong.

> Then I saw on the television girls running away from the Europa Hotel because there was a bomb warning. They were hotel workers. They were wearing mini-skirts because that was the fashion. and they were terrified, hysterical. In broad daylight in the sight of the whole country they lost their dignity the way I lost mine secretly in my bed in the dark worrying about my sons. And I knew it wasn't right to do such things to people. It wasn't right to risk killing them or hurting them, and it wan't right to frighten them. I said so to everyone from then on who mentioned the explosions.

> When women said, 'Isn't it terrible?', looking at me to see how I'd take it,
> I left them in no doubt.[120]

But she recognises the pressures on her community from without, from the actions of the British Army, and from the depth of grievance generated by such actions and the sense of powerlessness of those same communities in the face of daily humiliation and repression from the state.

> But the soldiers kept on doing terrible things, ending up on Bloody Sunday
> in Derry, and we had no one to look to, no one who cared about us, no one
> to protect us. After Bloody Sunday we were sure they were going to do for
> every Catholic district, pick out boys between seventeen and twenty-five
> and shoot them to show who was in charge. They did it in Derry, thirteen
> of them, and in the Widgery tribunal we never found out who told them to.
> It must have been somebody fairly high up, I always thought, not an army
> man. Armies aren't allowed to take decisions like that, except in Africa
> maybe. I often wonder is he sorry, that minister, or does he sleep sound at
> nights, happy that he was never found out, wasn't tried for war crimes or
> just for conspiracy to murder and put in Long Kesh. The world was
> shocked and that's what saved us, I'm certain sure, and Stormont was
> blamed and abolished. We were too far down to rejoice and the IRA said
> they wouldn't stop their campaign so there was going to be no peace.[121]

When, however, Martha witnesses the aftermath of an IRA kneecapping, which she believes was carried out to intimidate her for her failure to contribute to a collection for prisoners' welfare, she voices her opposition.

> So the Provos chose to knee-cap that boy at the wall of my shop where the
> sun had shone on me in the mornings. When they called the next Friday for
> my weekly contribution to their fund for the relatives, I said, 'No, you're
> getting no more.' We all gave money. Mostly I didn't mind because I knew
> some of it did go to the wives or mothers of prisoners. I didn't think the
> pittance they got from me would buy bombs or guns and although I didn't
> approve of anything they did they were the only people I could hear of that
> the English paid any heed to.[122]

The reader is in no doubt from reading *Give Them Stones* that Mary Beckett is writing from within the lived experience of a nationalist community, of rounded, flesh-and-bone individuals with their cares and dreams, courage and failings, keeping faith with an historical sense of outrage learned on granny's lap, and driven to build a better future – all in all, a welcome antidote to the walk-on proles and grocers-cum-godfathers usually served up for the undiscerning. Part of her underlying purpose in this novel, it appears, is the attempt to show why the republican movement maintains a considerable measure of support even when at times IRA actions may have offended people in nationalist areas. For although Martha may not 'approve of anything they did they were the only people… [she] could hear of that the English paid any heed to'.

Some other novels of the period seem merely to be justifications for a hard response to republican violence, and if anything, offer an even cruder incitement to vicarious desire for revenge than Seymour's *Field of Blood*. P.A. Foxall's The *Face of Fury* (1982), for example, features an avenging SAS man after a series of murders in London are linked to 'Ulster'.[123] Even more bizarrely, in the celebrated Science Fiction writer Frank Herbert's *The White Plague* (1982), John Roe O'Neill, while in Dublin researching Catholic attitudes to molecular biology, witnesses the slaughter of his wife and children in an IRA bomb.[124] His rage triggers a 'psychic split' into multiple personalities, among them 'the Madman' seeking revenge through the unleashing of a plague.

However, in the same year Father Des Wilson's *The Demonstration* was published.[125] I believe it to be the first novel(la) written from a position both sympathetic to nationalist communities and openly critical of the abuses of British government power. Other novels had dealt with the impact of state violence.[126] However, the emphasis in these novels is on how an individual, a main character, is radicalised, and much less, if at all, on the wider impact of such abuse of power on the entire community. The community's response is of secondary importance in these novels. *The Demonstration* is, I believe, the first attempt to correct the deficit, and is consciously, unabashedly polemical.

Des Wilson is, and was then, a prominent community worker in West Belfast. He served as a Catholic priest there from 1966 to 1975 when he resigned his clerical positions following a falling out with the Catholic hierarchy over church policy. As a pacifist he is a long-established critic of British government policies in the North, accusing them of destroying all peaceful solutions to the problem.[127]

The Demonstration is a novel without ego; that is, the novel isn't centred on or centrally concerned about the development or perspective of a central character or about how that character is changed (which would exclude it on certain definitions of the novel). Instead, although the narrator, Jack Irwin, a community worker at a Resource Centre-cum-advice centre in West Belfast, is an eye witness to events as they unfold, it is the tribulations of his community under occupation that is the novel's heart and soul. The subject of the novel is the community itself. Irwin, like the author, is uncompromisingly on the side of the poor and disadvantaged.

When the Resource Centre receives an influx of complaints from local people who have been refused benefits, Irwin contacts Matt Shevlin, a radical full time trade union organiser, whom 'the people knew... was on their side'.[128]

The Northern Ireland Office has announced that they are stopping all welfare payments pending reassessment because of alleged benefit fraud. Community groups and individuals protest but the media won't carry their protests.[129] West Belfast has the highest unemployment levels in the city and will therefore suffer most from the measure. Local people well versed in the machinations of the government see through the charade and recognise the move as part of a counterinsurgency strategy. Their suspicions gain credence when the area is flooded with British soldiers and armoured cars. The military presence is depicted throughout as unwelcome, ongoing, and relentlessly intrusive.

At a hastily convened meeting it is decided to organise a demonstration to the city hall. The idea is for Catholics and Protestants to combine, merging into a united front to converge on the city centre. John McIntyre and Sam Crossan are there representing working class Protestant East Belfast. However, the suspicion is raised by some trade unionists from a unionist background that the republican movement is orchestrating matters. This sectarian mindset is thwarting effective joint action. It is revealed that, in a classic divide and rule manoeuvre, the government has asked the UDA to help process social welfare claims by manning their offices, centres and clubs.[130] This leads to further squabbles. Women take the initiative and decide then and there to begin a march. A republican veteran intervenes.

> Frank Cowan is a small man, a middle aged republican whom I had met for the first time in 1969 when the smell of burning was in our noses. Parts of the city were in flames that day and he came to me in a little motor van with a few bits of furniture belonging to some family in transit from an abandoned home to a hastily created refugee centre in one of the local schools.
>
> He seemed to know so much about what was happening, to be so quietly decisive in what he said should be done, so calmly efficient in doing it. Since then he had turned up at every crisis, saving his words for the moment when they would do most good, laughing sometimes, alert always, knowing more than anyone else and forecasting accurately the course of events before the rest of us had even thought such things possible.
>
> If anyone could stabilise the meeting he could.[131]

The decision to march on Friday is taken. After the meeting, while giving a lift to two trade unionists back to East Belfast, Jack Irwin witnesses the murder of the occupants of a car who had been at the meeting.[132] It later transpires that the intended target was a republican who had also attended the meeting but who had left in a different car.

As an initial response to the withholding of benefits, republicans commandeer food delivery vehicles and distribute the contents to the people.

As the day of the demonstration draws near, the full scale of the British propaganda offensive against the communities of West Belfast   is revealed. Irwin learns while phoning Italy that the Italian media is reporting that the British government is cracking down on fraudulent claims because the money is going to the IRA. According to the report, extra troops have been flown in from Germany to meet anticipated trouble.

The march goes ahead. Instead of depictions of an amorphous mass of people we understand the organic genius of organisation behind the protest, entirely the product of the direct experience of grievance suffered by the communities concerned. The scene is set for the British Army to take on the demonstration. However, when a contingent from East Belfast, organised by John McIntyre and

Sam Crossan, join the march, the British relent. We see the coming together in common struggle of erstwhile opposing communities. Suddenly, an unidentified sniper shoots a British soldier dead. Despite efforts to conceal the body from his colleagues, upon its discovery they take immediate revenge by opening fire killing thirteen demonstrators.[133]

The novel ends with the narrator in editorial mode, drawing lessons from the thirteen deaths.

> The reality of the situation was... that the government had the means to starve the poorest of its citizens to death.

> Over and over I heard it said in those disastrous days that modern governments would not act in this way. But what if they did? What moral sanctions, what public opinion, would inhibit them if they did make such a decision? For all their dead and injured their experiment had been a success.

> They knew better now how to organise poverty, they knew who would object and who would not, they knew how to deal with the people on the streets who did.

> They had tested their belief that political movements could be crippled by forcing them to provide bread for children instead of guns for men.[134]

This is the author's thesis. It rises from the actual experience of siege and occupation felt by nationalist communities, and the belief that the North is a kind of laboratory of repression. Des Wilson is one of the very few experienced voices from a nationalist perspective to attempt a faithful rendering of that perspective in fiction. He succeeds in conveying something of the 'petri dish' realities of nationalist communities that are unwilling participants in an experiment in social engineering. One could argue, however, that the cross-community, trade union-organised support for the demonstration is unrealistic. Such unity of purpose must be, however, precisely part of any just solution.

The 'secret state' theme is also explored in G.F. Newman's 1987 novel, *The Testing Ground*.[135] Here, though, the inspiration for the narrative isn't an hypothesis but stems from well-documented abuses of power. The plot is centred upon an investigation of an alleged RUC 'shoot-to-kill' policy and the role of Sir Michael Newfield, Ulster Security Co-ordinator 'at the request of the PM'.[136] Newfield, dying of AIDS, has no compunction about having unprotected sex with boys procured for the purpose from the 'Kings House Community Home'.

Liz Curtis charts the problems Newman had in getting a screenplay of the novel, and of another play, televised. Curtis quotes a *Guardian* report (3 March 1989) in which it is revealed that a section of 'Here is the News', a thriller Newman wrote for the BBC, was cut because of

> a fragment of conversation between the attorney-general and a journalist which suggested that the prime minister knew the truth about the SAS killing of three members of the IRA in Gibraltar.[137]

And Newman's screenplay of his novel also ran into trouble.

> The BBC insisted that G.F. Newman rewrite a play loosely based on the
> Stalker investigation of the RUC's 'shoot-to-kill' policy and the Kincora
> boys' home scandal. He had to change the setting from Ireland in the past
> to Wales in the future. The original version, a three-part series, was based
> on his book *The Testing Ground* and was titled *Bentham* after the central
> character. The new version, shown on 17 September 1989, was a single
> play titled *1996*.[138]

Tom Clancy's bestselling novel *Patriot Games* (1987) met with no such
problems, and became a huge box-office success when translated for the big
screen. The novel's hero is Jack Ryan, an Irish American.[139] Ryan is a former
lieutenant in the US Marine Corps. Now an historian, he is in London to give a
lecture. While sightseeing with his wife Cathy and four-year-old daughter Sally he
witnesses an attempted kidnapping. Ryan is in no doubt who the culprits are: 'It's
the goddamned IRA';[140] 'Just like some Chicago gangster movie';[141] or
'something right out of a Dodge City movie'[142] – comments establishing the link
in his mind between physical force republicanism and gangsterism. However, the
perpetrators are not the IRA but a breakaway group of Clancy's creation, the ULA:
'Ulster Liberation Army, a Maoist offshoot of the Provos. Nasty buggers'.[143] Ryan
intervenes, disabling one of the assailants and killing another. The targets were the
Prince and Princess of Wales and their new baby, four months old.

The Queen visits Ryan in hospital, and she wonders why an Irish-American
would risk his life to save members of the British royal family. Ryan's reply
perhaps reveals that Clancy's underlying thematic target is Irish-American support
for the Irish republican struggle, which he equates with a criminal conspiracy –
the Mafia.

> Your Majesty, I cannot speak to your Irish problem. I'm an American
> citizen, and my country has enough problems of its own without having to
> delve into someone else's. Where I come from we – that is, Irish-
> Americans – have made out pretty well. We're in all the professions,
> business, and politics, but your prototypical Irish-American is still a basic
> police officer or firefighter. The cavalry that won the West was a third Irish,
> and there are still plenty of us in uniform – especially the Marine Corps, as
> a matter of fact. Half of the local FBI office lived in my old neighbourhood.
> They had names like Tully, Sullivan, O'Connor, and Murphy. My dad was
> a police officer for half his life, and the priests and nuns who educated me
> were mostly Irish, probably.
>
> Do you see what I mean, Your Majesty? In America we are the forces of
> order, the glue that holds society together – so what happens?
>
> Today, the most famous Irishmen in the world are the maniacs who leave
> bombs in parked cars, or assassins who kill people to make some sort of
> political point. I don't like that, and I know my dad wouldn't like it. He
> spent his whole working life taking animals like that off the street and

putting them in cages where they belong. We've worked pretty hard to get where we are – too hard to be happy about being thought of as the relatives of terrorists.' Jack smiled. 'I guess I understand how Italians feel about the Mafia.'[144]

Clancy was criticised by Irish Americans for his portrayal of the conflict in the novel. He responded to the criticism in an article entitled 'My Views on Unity'.[145] He revealed that in researching the novel, in 1987 he travelled to England where he met Metropolitan police officers and 'good friends' in the Royal Navy. Unsurprisingly, he came away with the opinion that the IRA was a Marxist-Leninist organisation intent on establishing a 'Cuba' off the coast of Britain, a charge first gaining provenance, you may recall, in a Monday Club pamphlet. Opposed to republican violence (though apparently not a pacifist, as a photograph of him posing beside his own Sherman tank would attest),[146] he claimed, however, that the 'only possible solution to the Troubles is political... and that solution is the peaceful reunification of Ireland'.[147] 'Stormont', he asserted, 'should never have existed'.[148]

In *Patriot Games* Clancy wrongly attributes the killing of Lord Mountbatten to the Irish National Liberation Army, and in the interview he claims that this was the novel's 'only factual error'.[149]

The period ended with the publication of the first novel from a former republican activist, Hugo Meenan's *No Time for Love* (1987).[150] Meenan, who in his career to date has served in the British Army, later joined the Officials and then the IRSP (Irish Republican Socialist Party), was released from prison in 1982. The novel's location is centred in Derry but moves to the South and to Germany. Hugh O'Donnell (O'D), a former British paratrooper, is the officer commanding a Trotskyist splinter group of the IRA called Saor Éire. There is some confusion about the narrative year, the cover blurb claiming it is the early 1970s. Bloody Sunday is in the recent past. However, there are references to seven-day detention orders. These were only introduced following the Birmingham pub bombing of October 1974. The Official IRA is referred to as if they are still at war then when in fact they had declared a ceasefire in May 1972.

Meenan, perhaps in response to the propaganda line that republicans control their districts through fear, seems moved to set the record straight about the motivations of those who gave succour and support to the movement. This is illustrated by the excerpt in which Frank Maguire, a pensioner, allows his council house to be used for a Battalion Staff meeting.

> His family had grown up and left home years earlier: three sons worked in England and the other two along with two daughters were dispersed through America. Since his wife died he had lived alone and took every opportunity to assist the IRA and its support groups. From the inception of the Northern Ireland state in 1921 Frank had been aware of the indifference, bigotry, hatred and conniving brutality of the various

institutions of government towards the Catholic minority. He had been on the dole for over thirty years and blamed the English, Irish and Northern Ireland governments for his plight. His feelings about America were ambiguous: he loved that country for its opportunities and he hated it bitterly for attracting his children away from home.[151]

Meenan deals with another preoccupation of many republicans: the contending pulls of the personal and the political. Brenda McGlinchey, Hugh's girlfriend, and their five-year-old son Philip, are to move to London, where Brenda has got a job with the BBC. Hugh sees them before they go, and reveals his optimism about the struggle.

'...you're not opposed to the struggle yourself, are you?'

'You know I'm not. I just don't think it can be successful.'

'Well, you're wrong: it can be successful and we can have victory within a year.'

'You know that for a fact, do you?' She was self-consciously sarcastic as she stood facing him, her arms folded across her breasts.

'Don't be so sarcastic. I spend most of my waking hours thinking and working to make it come about. Before now it was only a dream of wrecking the state and attempting to create some worthwhile kind of life. But the movement has grown so much in the past year I can hardly believe it. We have the means now – or will have soon – to create a situation that can't help but lead us to victory. All we have to do is get the factors together in the right way. That will happen this year. If it doesn't I will hang up my hat because it's now or never'.[152]

The passage reveals Hugh's naivety for believing in an imminent military victory. But then it has to be said that in the early 1970s many republicans still clung to such illusions. Hugh is arrested leaving Brenda's. Much of the second chapter (pages 29-52) deals with his brutal interrogation by the RUC Special Branch in Ballykelly interrogation centre.

Later, at Saor Éire's GHQ staff meeting in Leitrim, in a large, isolated farmhouse on the shores of the Shannon, Hugh outlines a somewhat grandiose plan which he had been formulating for months.

'What have you got in mind?' asked the Chief of Staff, 'another South Armagh situation?'

'Something like that,' answered O'D, 'only I was thinking more in terms of a city this time. The Brits aren't worried about the country areas – we control plenty of them as it is. But if we take over and control a built-up area it will give them an entirely different type of problem. An election under those circumstances would be an ideal situation for us to step into the political arena. We would become the main election issue, not to mention an international issue. And Christ knows that could bring the Brits to their knees permanently. Under the right circumstances we could see it becoming a United Nations issue. And that, of course, would be ideal'.[153]

He proposes that Saor Éire change their strategy of a military campaign of attack on the British army throughout the North and instead concentrate their resources by taking control of Derry: 'We would run it like an independent state and set up a revolutionary council to control it, like the Soviet in Limerick in the Twenties'.[154]

In a touch of wish-fulfilment for workers' solidarity, Meenan depicts O'D's return to Cork, where he receives a comradely welcome from the dockers, all apparently in the know, following a successful arms raid on a British army base in Germany.

'Finbar [Barry], I thought my arrival would have been a close secret?'

'Twas, boy, 'twas. Sure only the dockers knew of it,' came the reply.

There was no answer to that. 'Only two hundred dockers on the Cork docks,' thought O'D. 'Then all the pubs in Cork tonight – and tomorrow the world. Great ways we have of keeping secrets in Ireland.' It would have been futile to say anything to Finbar who would immediately have launched into the family background of every docker to prove their pedigree.[155]

In another episode, Meenan illustrates where he stands on the class issue. Clive Sebastian Hanley, a British spy, lives in a Georgian mansion near Greysteel, Derry. He is to be executed and his property destroyed.

'Good God, man! Are you mad? Do you realise what this house is worth? It's one of the most valuable houses in Northern Ireland and of enormous historical interest. You will be wiping out a valuable part of your own culture if you raze it.'

'Correction, Mister Hanley,' said the gunman, 'we will be wiping out a part of your culture, which is a lot different from mine.'

'At least let us save some of the paintings – there is a wealth of art here which will never be replaced if you destroy it.'

'You must be joking,' said the man derisively. 'Let you save an art treasure that is the exclusive possession of the upper class? An art treasure that me and my class would never set eyes on? Don't make me laugh – that's the first bloody thing that's going up!'[156]

The episode may be based on the actual killing by the IRA of Sir Norman Stronge (aged 86), a former speaker of the Stormont parliament, and his son James (aged 48), a former Ulster Unionist MP for Armagh (1969-72). They were assassinated, and then their home, the 500-acre Tynan Abbey, was bombed, on 21 January 1981. The IRA issued a statement claiming that the operation was a reprisal for sectarian murders in the mid-Ulster area perpetrated by loyalists.

Bernadette McAliskey and her husband survived a shooting by loyalists shortly before the killing of the Stronges.

In regard to the attitude expressed in the novel about art treasures being the exclusive property of the upper class, when threats were made to destroy the ransomed Beit collection the Price sisters (recently transferred from imprisonment in England to Armagh prison after a protracted hunger strike during which they were force-fed), had a letter published condemning the threat, and pointing out that as former art students they recognised the collection was part of a shared heritage.

On the Brandon edition cover, *The Sunday Times* journalist Liam Clarke is cited. He describes *No Time for Love* as dealing with 'Red Hugh' O'Donnell's 'fatal devotion to war' and the effects on his family and his humanity. The epithet '*Red* Hugh' is not used in the novel, and is Clarke's tendentious addition. Despite Clarke's spurious implication of a link between O'D's plans and Easter Week, O'D isn't an adherent of blood sacrifice, à la Padraig Pearse and romantic nationalism. In the novel's conclusion, O'D seems chastened by the failure of his tactics and has come to realise that 'victory in a year or two' is beyond the organisation's capacities.[157] However, Meenan offers no hard evidence in the novel of an appreciation of the necessity for political organisation, and the military path seems the only option. The nearest he gets to hinting that more is required than a sole reliance on armed struggle is when O'D responds to Brenda, who is about to depart for good with their son.

> ...there is more than one way to fight our struggle. Our organisation may be smashed in Derry for now, but while the same conditions exist we will always be able to rebuild our organisation.[158]

In his review of the novel for *Iris*, Frank Whitney commented on the novelty of a positive fictional portrayal of a republican:

> a typical thriller hero [...] on the other hand, it is nice to see a larger than life republican hero for a change. In a genre where republicans are depicted as psychopaths, Mafia-type gangsters or misled idealists, it is a tremendous relief to come across a novel about the North in which there is such a positive republican hero.[159]

In the remaining years of the decade other novels by republicans were to appear, acting as a corrective to the previous years of neglect of the republican viewpoint. In the next chapter I will chart this and other developments in the genre, to bring the account up to the end of 1993 and the Downing Street Declaration.

7.
A Scenario for Peace: 1988-93

This chapter covers the period 1988 to the end of 1993, with the Downing Street declaration of 15 December. The period saw the steady application and development of Sinn Féin's strategy for peace. At the same time, the IRA intensified its campaign to a level not seen since the early 1970s, thereby defeating Britain's strategy of containment.

All the reorganisation, growth and development of Sinn Féin in previous years had been in preparation for its peace strategy. Designed to lead to a just settlement, the strategy was launched, as already mentioned, with the publication in May 1987 of the document *A Scenario for Peace*. To recap briefly, the genesis of the peace strategy owed much to the debates and rethinking that had taken place in the prisons prior to and during the truce of 1975. One of the great ironies of the last thirty years is that the reorganisation and building of Sinn Féin had been initially delayed while valuable human and material resources were directed into the battle for political status centred on the H-Blocks. This delay was partially due to the British game plan to defeat Irish republicanism by criminalising the independence struggle, and one component of this strategy, arguably, was to lock the movement into the distraction of prison-centred struggle. The movement was slow in recognising that the British government had opened up a new offensive front in the H-Blocks. However, of necessity the movement responded vigorously to a timetable not of its making. The H-Block campaign proved to be a catalyst and by the mid-1980s Sinn Féin had overcome many of the obstacles to its development and was perched to effectively alter the prevailing zero-sum discourse of war to one offering a settlement based on equality and compromise and of negotiation for peace.

However, before Sinn Féin was able to make further progress it had first to win the debate with other nationalist parties, and particularly convince Fianna Fail and the SDLP of the correctness of its analysis. Only when this vital discursive preparation began to change the nature of the debate from a security to a peace strategy could an effective counter to Britain be mounted in Washington and within Europe. Only then was Sinn Féin able to impact internationally. Republicans accused the Southern political establishment of a 'dereliction of its duty and proclaimed, de jure, mandate to reunification', arguing that this failure necessitated the armed struggle. Republicans put constitutional nationalists on the spot by asking what was the alternative to armed struggle. Gerry Adams, addressing Southern political leaders in an *Irish Times* article (13 June 1988), called for 'a consensus of the clear national majority on Irish reunification as a policy objective and an international and diplomatic offensive'.[1]

In 1988 Hume talked with Adams for some months and there was an exchange of lengthy documents. Adams claimed in an interview for *Magill* (August 1988) that the SDLP moved away from support for an internal settlement; therefore a key aspect of Sinn Féin's analysis was now taken up by the SDLP.[2] These talks reached agreement in September 1993 when a joint proposal was written, what was to become known as the Hume/Adams proposal. Meanwhile, there was a protracted, secret contact between the movement and the British government.

The success of this broad-front approach between Sinn Féin and constitutional nationalism North and South was realised in the promotion of the peace process, a process pursued by a united Irish nationalism in opposition to those forces within the British establishment whose goal was the military defeat of Irish republicanism.

There were set backs and successes. In October 1988, in response to the Ballygawley bus bombing two months previously, the British Home Secretary, Douglas Hurd, banned Sinn Féin from speaking on the airwaves.[3] Despite this propaganda advantage and in apparently open contravention of its overarching military strategy since the mid-1970s, the Secretary of State Peter Brooke indicated in a speech tailored to Sinn Féin's peace overtures, that Britain had no selfish strategic or economic interest in remaining in the North. However, there was a suspicion that the speech was designed to open up a rift between 'hawks and doves' within the movement. Martin McGuinness refuted the 'hawks and doves' line as pursued by Brooke and also by John Hume.[4]

Henry Patterson, in outlining these developments, depicts a contestation during the 1980s between militants and politicos, with the former winning the argument at the end of the decade – hence the intensified bombing campaign in England. Ongoing internal debate is in the nature of any successful political movement, but the IRA never relented from its commitment and determination to prosecute the war; only the logistics had altered, coupled with a deliberation over what was most effective in the changing circumstances. Perceptible lulls in the intensity of the armed struggle are therefore explainable in those terms and by attritional factors rather than from a 'primacy of politics' logic. Although he alludes to several major IRA operations, Patterson downplays the significance of the IRA's increased military effectiveness from 1989 onwards. Consider the impact alone of the following IRA operations in England, for the purpose overlooking the human costs and solely in terms of their effect on the British policy of containment: September 1989, ten Royal Marine bandsmen were killed; July 1990, the bomb at the Stock Exchange, London; February 1991, the mortar attack on Downing Street at the height of Desert Storm; April 1992, Baltic Exchange; February 1993, Warrington Gasworks; March 1993, Warrington; and in April 1993, the bombing of the Nat West tower. It can be argued (as do some unionists in the 'No' camp, for example) that the IRA's actions created the necessary conditions for the peace strategy, ensuring that the movement bargained from a position of strength.

Against the backdrop of these developments, another dimension to what might be termed the ascendancy of nationalism and republicanism was being created in nationalist areas. Many of the areas that bore the brunt of repression and disadvantage in the North experienced a cultural resurgence. In West Belfast, for example, this was manifested in a range of cultural activities: writing clubs; the growth of the Irish language; the establishment and increasing prestige of the West Belfast Festival. One factor underlying the thinking behind the establishment of the Festival was the need felt throughout nationalist areas to provide a more positive and constructive focus, particularly for youth, during the annual internment commemoration, which it was felt had in recent years often descended into an annual vandalfest involving disruption to local communities and destruction of local property. To that end the organisers of the Festival aspired 'to channel the energies of the youth into constructive activity, and to present a positive and creative side'.

Ronan Bennett attributes the cultural renaissance in West Belfast in the 1990s to a reaction to the British media's vicious portrayal of the entire people of the locality after the killing of two British soldiers.[5] Following the incident, Britain had regained some lost ground in its policy of isolating the republican message. The whole of nationalist West Belfast was demonised by sections of the British media. And not only the British media. It should be remembered that a funeral cortege with good reason thought it was under loyalist attack, but the incident is also slanted in Dean R. Koontz's *Midnight* (1989). In the novel, a woman journalist remembers covering a funeral in the North when 'the mourners had metamorphosed into a pack of savages,' killing 'two British plain-clothes army officers patrolling the area in an unmarked car'.[6] According to Danny Morrison, echoing Bennett, the idea of a festival was

> given flesh by Gerry Adams' and community activists after the demonisation of the local community – following the killing of two corporals at the funeral of Kevin Brady in Andersonstown – the festival has grown exponentially from its relatively humble first outing.[7]

The end of the Eighties provided another breakthrough in the battle of discourses. The period marked the first serious academic opposition to revisionism (meant in the sense of an understanding of the past in accordance with a unionist agenda) with the publication of Brendan Bradshaw's seminal critique, 'Nationalism and historical scholarship in modern Ireland'.[8] The revisionist project can be distilled down to one discursive imperative, Liam O'Dowd argues: to reinforce the view that the twenty-six counties are 'co-terminous' with the Irish Republic, thus excluding the North.[9]

And in 1990, for the first time, Troubles fiction was subjected to critical discussion in the form of a seminar organised as part of the West Belfast Festival, though one critic who attended and who found redeeming features in the genre bemoaned the apparent unanimity of view that disparaged it.

> Gerry Adams... was there and a few other people, most looking like students. I felt out of place, even though, having studied literature in the States, seminars on books came as second nature. What also set this occasion off was that there was no debate. Everyone in the room was deeply scornful of 'troubles' fiction, and none disagreed one iota that all of them might best be shredded up for cat litter.[10]

The end of the decade also heralded profound changes globally that ten years later are still being worked through. 1989 marked the collapse of the USSR and its empire, effectively bringing to an end the Cold War and marshalling in an era concerned with defining the New World Order. The United States, as the only remaining superpower, sought to champion its political hegemony. The reverberations of the new political dispensation were felt in a new focus on resolving some of the most intractable national conflicts: in the Middle East, South Africa, and 'Northern Ireland'.

1989 had also marked the twentieth anniversary of the introduction of British troops onto the streets of the North. It was a time for recommitment, and it was a time for reflection. The Time to Go group in Britain organised a charter to garner renewed public support for a British army withdrawal. The omens were propitious for the further political advancement of Sinn Féin and for progress towards a political settlement. And in 1991 another important landmark, the seventy-fifth anniversary of Easter Week, nearly passed without a fitting commemoration had the Reclaim the Spirit of 1916 Committee not organised throughout Ireland. The campaign forced a rethink on the part of John Bruton's Fine Gael government who would rather that the lesson of how the state was formed through violence be quietly forgotten.[11]

Some quite major form of shift or turning point in relation to people's consciousness or awareness about the conflict had occurred during the 1980s, finding fruition in the 1990s. Undoubtedly, the hunger strike was the catalyst. Its effects, however, were complex and nurtured or reinforced other cultural developments, the manner of the resulting discursive shift perhaps conforming to a 'gestalt switch'.[12] This chapter will be concerned with the extent to which these momentous changes were reflected in the fiction of the period.

Eight category (a) novels appeared in 1988; eighteen in 1989; twenty-one in 1990; twenty-two in 1991; twenty in 1992; and sixteen in 1993. Save for the 1988 low, the figures display a reasonable consistency of interest, which exceeded that of the previous period, discussed in Chapter Six. The noticeable dip in titles published in 1988 is most probably attributable to the perception of market-sensitivity arising from the Remembrance Day bomb in Enniskillen on 8 November 1987. Ordinarily, one would have thought that the prospect of public interest generated by the upcoming twentieth anniversary of the arrival of British troops might have caused writers and publishers to seek to mark the occasion, and to that end, perhaps hold over publication from 1988 till the following year. However, as far as I have been able to determine, rather than an event to be capitalised upon, the anniversary saw only one work of fiction written and published specifically to coincide with it, Aly Renwick's *...last night another soldier...*[13] Renwick was a founder member of Troops Out, and the novel, discussed below, is written from a republican, anti-imperialist perspective.

Surprisingly, it seems that the anniversary elicited no other direct reflection in fiction. Danny Morrison's first novel, *West Belfast*, also discussed below, although published in the same year, was not written with the intention to mark the anniversary.[14] The novel's appearance at this time was fortuitous. Morrison, Sinn Féin's Assembly member for Mid-Ulster, 1982-86, turned to writing fiction only after the Assembly was dissolved in 1986. He completed the novel in May 1988. It was eventually published in November 1989.[15]

The output of fiction during the period is distinctive on three accounts: firstly, as mentioned, republicans began to appear in print; secondly, there was an increase in the number of Irish writers in the genre, an increase that corresponded to the upsurge in popularity of new Irish fiction generally, particularly from the late 1980s, and notably from Ronan Bennett, Robert McLiam Wilson, and Glenn Patterson;[16] thirdly, and related to the last point, some prominent Irish authors dealt with the conflict for the first time. The reader may recall, as I mention in Chapter Five that as far back as 1976 Richard Deutsch had implied criticism of Irish writers of wide repute for failing to deal with the conflict.[17] Rather belatedly, for example, Brian Moore was to contribute to the genre.[18] All the authors cited are discussed below.

The whole of the 1970s saw only twenty-five works of category (a) fiction by Irish authors out of a relevant total of 124. During the 1980s forty-three out of one hundred and forty relevant titles published were by Irish authors. The increase stabilised during the period 1984 to 1993 at about five titles (apart from the 1991 figure of nine) per year until a surge in titles that has continued to the present. During the 1990s as a whole, eighty titles by Irish authors appeared out of a total of 210 to date. The rise in this output therefore is measurable in real terms and as a percentage of the overall output.

Irish authors were also more likely to return in their fiction to the subject of the Troubles. Of the fourteen most prolific writers in the genre, that is, authors who have written four or more relevant works, nine are Irish-born.[19] The increase in Irish authors published at this time speaks of the comparatively healthy state of Irish fiction. Irish publishing was also in a healthy state, though as few as thirty of the aforementioned texts were novels first published in Ireland. London continued as the Mecca for the Irish creative diaspora.

In common with the previous periods discussed, the fiction of the years 1988 to 1993 shows a diversity of perspectives, themes and genres. Among the range of themes discernible, the following seem to have particularly excited the imagination of thriller writers: drugs; international terrorist links; prison escapes; IRA spectaculars; the 'secret war'; and 'hawks versus doves', especially when progress towards dialogue appeared closer. However, it should be noted from the outset that the presence in print of so many Irish authors did not in itself radically alter the perspective. Irish authors brought to the genre a wide divergence of outlooks and experience that matched the general play of understanding of the conflict that pertained in Ireland; various shades of nationalism jostled and jarred with a panoply of views broadly pro-British, or at least anti-republican, in sympathy. In fact, most of the Irish authors mentioned had London publishers. As a rule British publishers had seemed generally less willing to risk contentious fictional treatment of the conflict and yet now it appeared to be the case that novels more questioning of and sceptical towards Britain's role in the North could be countenanced as commercially viable.

This more open attitude also allowed some imaginatively critical fictional examinations of the conflict from British thriller writers with a media or journalism background. To give three superior examples: Gavin Esler's *Loyalties*, Graham Hurley's *Reaper*, and Gordon Stevens's *Provo*.[20] Despite these quite laudable if flawed attempts to achieve balance or moral equivalence, many of the same old stereotypes were churned out during the period, for example, in Frederick Forsyth's *The Deceiver*.[21] But the prevalence hitherto of the pro-British discourse was now more readily questioned and in some instances challenged. And the challenge came from American writers, too, as evidenced in Hanna Wakefield's *A February Mourning*.[22]

We have seen how developments within the H-Blocks dominated the early 1980s and how the prison struggle shaped events on the outside. That process of struggle continued throughout the decade but on a more subdued note, apart from the escape of thirty-eight republicans in 1983. The British were still determined to criminalise Irish republicanism and the prisons remained a hotly contested front in that struggle. Republican prisoners had to resist and finally overcome the forced integration of republican and loyalist prisoners. Finally during the mid-1980s republican prisoners gained a measure of self-determination within their wings, achieving the space and freedom to organise their own cultural and educational programmes. The wings became republican communities in which a 'culture of criticism' was promoted that challenged traditional values. Influenced by the Brazilian educationalist Paulo Freire's *Pedagogy of the Oppressed*,[23] republican prisoners implemented a structured education programme 'rooted in the student's own experience of the world'.[24] This enterprise resulted in the successful completion of several artistic and cultural ventures. A drama group staged *The Crime of Castlereagh*, based on the prison writings of Bobby Sands. Poetry workshops were organised, and a poetry magazine, *Scairt Amach*, was published periodically. In addition, the work of seven republicans was published by South Yorkshire Writers: *H-Block: a selection of poetry* (1992); and *Voices of Oppression*, an anthology of poetry written by republican women held in

Maghaberry Prison, was published in the same year. History workshops organised in the H-Blocks had previously led to the collaborative writing of *Questions of History*, published in 1987.

In 1989, 'in conjunction with Republican POWs in other jails throughout the world', republicans in the H-Blocks also produced a new quarterly magazine, *An Glór Gafa/The Captive Voice*.[25]

The first issue appeared in autumn 1989. The last issue of the magazine (Vol.10, No.1) was published in August 1999, one month after the release of the last Provisional POWs from the H-Blocks under the provisions of the Good Friday Agreement. The first edition's editorial summed up the prisoners' commitment and purpose.

> The state is not sustained by force alone. Those who claim to rule over us constantly reinforce and update their message – a message which says that they are right and that the status quo is the only correct way to order society. The media, the education system, and churchmen and politicians all play their part in guarding against the dissemination of revolutionary ideas.
>
> Overt censorship is also employed to ensure that people are not contaminated by those who call for them to reject a system which forces half of our young people to emigrate, which allows a third of Irish people to live in poverty, which is unable to provide meaningful work for a fifth of the workers, and which requires thousands of armed troops to suppress those who call for human dignity and national rights. It is surely a measure of the strength of Republicans that they are barred from the broadcasting media.
>
> Thus, the gaols have been the arena for a different struggle – the struggle through education. Time and a common purpose have enabled us to study the nature of the world in which we live and to educate ourselves to become better able to bring about change in the Ireland of today.
>
> We are political prisoners in every sense of the term. In gaol we continue as political activists determined to do all in our power to bring about the day when British troops no longer walk our streets and imperialism's writ no longer runs in our country. *An Glór Gafa* will reflect this by presenting our views on those issues which affect the daily lives of people throughout Ireland and by suggesting our ideas for a way forward. It will also bring to life our feelings and experiences through poetry and short stories. We hope our Captive Voice will be heard by all those who share our vision of freedom in a socialist Republic.

Most issues included a short story. The preponderance of short stories concern social issues such as violence in the home; environmental issues – for example, the destruction of trees; some reminiscences about childhood; personal experiences of prison life; the hardships faced by prisoners' relatives. The range of concerns and issues raised in these stories is testimony to the humanity of the writers and an eloquent rebuttal of the stereotypical representations of republicans.

Few of the short stories appear to mention the Troubles. Why? A possible explanation is that first attempts at creative writing are often autobiographical, while many republican prisoners attempting to write for the first time may fear committing to paper something that could be considered 'loose talk' or might assist their enemies. Therefore, this consideration represents a formidable psychological blockage to overcome for republicans in prison who wish to write. As to why it took so long for republicans to turn to fiction, I think the task of writing requires a certain space and distance, and both are scarce commodities in the middle of a war. And for many years, as I've indicated, because of the battle over conditions, even imprisonment failed to provide that notional space to write.

Among the contributors of relevant short stories to *An Glór Gafa/The Captive Voice* were Laurence McKeown, Felim O'Hagan, Brian Campbell, Jim McVeigh, Pádraig Wilson and Paddy O'Dowd.

Laurence McKeown's 'Very Important Person', relates the infamous incident in which Labour MP Don Concannon told a dying hunger striker that the British Labour Party, then in opposition, fully supported the Tory government's line on refusing to recognise political status. In the story, Francy, a hunger striker, is reading a letter when he is informed that a Labour MP is due to visit him. Soon after, Don Concannon, accompanied by prison and NIO officials, enters his cell. But to Francy, the contents of his letter from an old friend are more important.[26] Felim O'Hagan's 'The second last time he cried' depicts Micky, eighteen and on the run three months, in tears as he recalls his stupidity in forgetting to remove ammunition from the family house, in consequence of which his mother and his brother, Sean, were imprisoned.[27] In 'The Rosary' Jim McVeigh describes how a disparate group of women from a nationalist district are united in prayer, finding common cause through having loved ones engaged in the blanket protest in the H-Blocks.[28] Pádraig Wilson's 'The Buffer Zone' recounts a humorous moment in a Sinn Féin advice centre.[29] And Paddy O'Dowd's 'Two Wheels from Amsterdam' is a part-autobiographical childhood reminiscence of Stigsy, a local country postman who was interned and who died six months after being released.[30]

Aly Renwick's novel *...last night another soldier...* (1989) is unapologetically a counter to the British view of the conflict, intended to capitalise on a presumed heightened public interest due to the twentieth anniversary of the introduction of British troops. Renwick, a Scot, is a former British soldier, although he didn't serve in Ireland. The two central characters of the novel are Sorcha, a young Catholic girl from the Clonard area of West Belfast, and a young Scottish soldier, Billy Johnstone.

The novel opens in the summer of 1966. The previous year's meeting in Belfast between Terence O'Neill and Sean Lemass angered many unionists. This anger found its most vehement expression in the rise of Paisleyism. Tensions had risen. Sorcha recalls nationalists' hopes of reform despite the tensions caused by the death of a local man in hospital following a sectarian shooting.

The narrative shows what it was like for a nationalist under Stormont rule. In an exemplary incident, based on an actual event, Sorcha's father loses his job when a brick is thrown from his building site at the Queen's car during a royal visit, even though he had nothing to do with the incident.

> 'The peelers came for your da again, took him into the Springfield Road barracks for a couple of hours. They asked him about the brick thrown at the queen again, kept on about your granda, him having been a IRA man and that.'
>
> Sorcha's da looked up at her. 'They showed me to the B-men,' he said.
>
> 'There were some B-Specials there, said they wanted to see your da,' her ma explained.
>
> 'Said I was a troublemaker, needed to be taught a lesson,' her da cut in again.[31]

The incident illustrates the bigotry and ignorance of the RUC. One of the reasons later often cited for the failure of internment was the use of out-dated intelligence files on nationalists which resulted in innocent people being arrested merely because of the past involvement of relatives.

The history of the civil rights movement is charted, through Sorcha's early involvement, and of how she later joins the Provos. Many of the incidents and significant developments of the next twenty years are seen through her eyes. She witnesses how ordinary people defend their areas, first from sectarian attack and then from incursion by British soldiers. Aly Renwick also chronicles their fierce pride in the history of communal resistance.

After Sorcha's home is raided, she is near to tears as she explains what has happened to her grandmother.

> As she blurted out about the damage the old lady looked up. Sorcha's voice dried up and she nearly choked: her gran was smiling fit to bust.
>
> Grandma saw the look of horror on Sorcha's face, 'Five years, five years dead and gone, and the bastards are still chasing him,' she said chuckling away.[32]

The novel's other central character, the squaddie Billy Johnstone, has his first glimmerings of class consciousness when he witnesses young recruits being ordered to act as servants for officers.[33] Later, Billy's squad is briefed by the CO to patrol an IRA funeral. The orders were to ensure that no IRA colour party was allowed to fire a volley over the coffins.

> 'The Protestants won't like it,' he had said. 'And I want the hides of anyone who tries.'
>
> The CO had accepted an invitation to visit a well-to-do unionist family at the weekend and didn't want them making any sarcastic remarks about his men's ability to deal with the 'taigs', which was how his boss usually referred to the people of the Falls Road.[34]

Tragically, Billy is killed by an IRA sniper. Prior to his posting to Belfast, Billy had met Neil McKinnon, another Scotsman, older than Billy and more politically aware, while on a training exercise in Kenya. Neil bought his release from the army shortly after, and is subsequently invited to speak at a Troops Out meeting in London. Beforehand, Neil had heard of Billy's death: 'Last night another soldier was shot dead in West Belfast'.[35] Neil reveals that during his service in Aden, Officers divided squaddie against squaddie to see who could get the best kill rate.

At the novel's end, Sorcha recalls reading an article by Eileen, a comrade who was killed in a premature explosion.

> It was in Eileen's handwriting and was about the people of Ireland at the time of the first world war. Almost half a million Irish people had fought on Britain's side and almost a sixth of these did not return. The loyalists signed up and went on to make their blood sacrifice on the Somme because they were told it could help stop home rule. Three hundred thousand from the south also joined the British because they thought it would help bring home rule after the war had ended. George Gilmore, a republican and socialist, had told how he saw a recruitment poster in Belfast saying 'Fight Catholic Austria'. Taking it down he then went to Dublin and stuck it up again next to another recruitment poster which said 'Save Catholic Belgium'.[36]

At heart the novel is anti-imperialist, not anti-war. Aly Renwick finds common cause between 'the Levellers who refused to fight in Cromwell's army in Ireland in 1649', to whom the book is dedicated, and those in Britain who question contemporary British policy towards the North. The author was himself a founder member and, for a number of years, a national organiser of the Troops Out Movement. He isn't a pacifist but fiercely critical of the underlying political ideology motivating the history of British interference, not only of its involvement in Ireland but its whole imperial past. The power of this novel resides in the fact for this reader that he was left to wonder where Billy's growing political consciousness might have led him had he not been killed. In contrast to the motives and purpose giving an underlying dignity to the deaths of the republicans in the novel, Billy's death is seen as a terrible squandering of unfulfilled potential. By extension, the wastefulness of imperialism is laid bare.

Published in the same year, Danny Morrison's *West Belfast* opens in an idyllic though poor childhood of that locale's past. We are therefore privy to the childhood reminiscences, innocence, dreams and frustrations of young nationalists as they grow, reaching early adolescence on the eve of the Troubles.

The lives of the two main characters, John O'Neill and Angela McCann, are interwoven in the narrative with the story of Jimmy, John's youngest brother. They act as witness to the unfolding of events: the Divis Street riots of October 1964; the riots of August 1969 that culminated in the introduction of the British Army; the Falls curfew; and internment. John and Angela become teenage lovers then grow apart; John becomes a merchant seaman; Angela ends up in a London squat, on drugs. The book offers many insights into the feeling of nationalists during these seminal moments, in many instances recounting actual incidents.

'Good for youse, son?' an old woman shouted to the young soldiers who had bewildered looks on their faces as they took up positions on the Falls Road, though it was made clear by the men that they weren't getting behind the barricades. For behind the barricades a new IRA was being built to ensure that Nationalists were never left defenceless again.[37]

John, now an IRA volunteer though still in the merchant navy, notices a change while home on leave.

The most changed feature about life in West Belfast, noticed John, was the high level of troop activity and the coldness of the people towards them. They were no longer the British army but were now called the 'Brits'. Confrontations were regular occurrences and John couldn't believe the turn-around in attitudes. People were now complaining that they were seeing the British soldiers ten times more often than they had ever seen the RUC. They had merely swapped oppressors: nothing had altered.[38]

The novel also provides an explanation of why the IRA resorted to its commercial bombing campaign.

The Belfast Brigade during the 1970 curfew had set off bombs outside banks in Andersonstown in an attempt to overstretch the British army and RUC and lure them away from the Falls. It had also planted incendiary devices in city centre shops to create a similar diversion. As units proliferated a very low level campaign of bombing commercial and business premises in the centre of Belfast was begun. It took the war out of the Nationalist ghettoes and forced the extra deployment of soldiers in city centre checkpoints who would otherwise be engaged against the IRA in its bases.[39]

And later we are offered an insight into what in the early days may have been considered likely recruit material to the Provos.

In a two month period, over forty youths had applied to join the Battalion's companies – units based in, and drawing their membership from, specific districts.

John and Stevie [Donnelly] interviewed some of these recruits.

'Why do you want to join the IRA?'

'Gabh mo leithscéal. Abair sin ar's, le do thoil,' [Pardon me, Could you repeat what you said please?]

'Oh, a gaeilgeoir! Certainly, I'll repeat it,' John was pleasantly surprised.

'Speak in English. I don't understand.' Stevie insisted, sounding irritated.

'I've always believed that Ireland was a nation long before England. I believe that we're entitled to our own heritage and to freedom. I'm a great admirer of Pádraig Mac Piarais and have read all his poems...'

His starched white shirt annoyed Stevie.

'Could you throw a nail bomb? If I told you to shoot somebody could you do it?'

'Well, if I was trained properly I could throw a nail bomb but I wouldn't shoot anyone unless I was absolutely convinced that it was the right thing to do...'

'Could you take being hated?'

'What do you mean?'

'If an operation goes wrong your ma or girlfriend could be calling the IRA 'bastards' and it might have been you who was responsible. You'll hear it from the priests during Mass. You'll read it in the papers that we're wrong. When you're arrested the Brits and cops will hate you with a venom you've never seen before. The screws in the jail will detest you. So could you take being hated?'

'Umm, I'll have to think about that.'

A second potential recruit is interviewed.

'Why do you want to joint the IRA?'

'The Brits won't leave us alone when we're standing at the corner. They're always fuckin' us about.'

'Why do you want a united Ireland?'

'I'm not that fussed. Haven't thought about it much.' He shrugged his shoulders to show that he had no burning enthusiasm for political rearrangements.

'Everytime you stand at the corner they come along and tell you to move off. I'm fed up with it and just want to have a blarge at them.'

'What do you think?' John later said to his comrade.

'You know me. I'm not into the language thing, the culture. We'll make a fighter out of the last one, and his politics can come later, but I wouldn't be for the first one.' [40]

The most poignant testimony to the calibre of an IRA recruit is in the diaries of Jimmy O'Neill, killed while on active service. The diaries form the epistolary conclusion to the novel and show the typical range of interests of a young adolescent, and of his growing political consciousness as the crisis in the North increases. Absent are the stereotypes and prejudices that proliferate in the genre.

Gerry Adams, besides his anecdotal pre-Troubles and prison recollections *Falls Memories* (1982) and *Cage Eleven* (1990), has also had a collection of short stories published, *The Street and Other Stories* (1992).[41] Most of the stories are set in West Belfast and give 'an insight into the psyche of the ordinary people... who have so gallantly endured and adapted to the military occupation of a foreign power'. Interviewed by Mairtín Crawford for *Fortnight*, Adams has said that he 'enjoyed writing most... *The Street* [and that he doesn't] enjoy the polemical or political side of [his] writing which [he] regard[s] as a duty, a responsibility'. The collection ran foul of the broadcasting authorities in the South, who banned a promotional advertisement featuring Adams's voice.

Published in 1991, the focus of Ronan Bennett's first novel, *The Second Prison*, is narrower than Aly Renwick's or Danny Morrison's.[42] Instead of the historical sweep of their respective first novels, Bennett's deals primarily with the impact of the conflict on the central character, a recently released republican prisoner, Augustine Kane. Bennett is himself a former republican prisoner.

Kane goes to London to kill Declan (Dec) Mulholland whom he suspects of being a tout. It is 1988. Kane was the OC of an unspecified republican unit – I assume related to the IRSP and INLA. Five years previously, the unit, based in West Belfast, was so successful that a specialist detective from London was sent over to smash them. When an operation is foiled and one member of the unit, Hughie, is shot dead, Maxie Maxwell is suspected of touting. He is killed. It later transpires that two other members of the unit had been recruited by the specialist. Kane was imprisoned. Now he is out and seeking Dec.

Kane owes his commitment to an unquestioning admiration for Seanie, a ruthlessly efficient operator. There is little evidence that his motivation stems from any deeper ideological understanding. In London, before he can carry out his plan to kill Dec, Kane is arrested. He is interrogated by Tempest, a detective who he later discovers was the specialist sent to Belfast five years earlier to smash Kane's unit. Kane is charged with conspiracy to murder. Ten months later, in April 1989, he is acquitted of the charge and walks free.

The title, *The Second Prison*, is a metaphor for the difficulties of life after prison, of how the experience of release after incarceration can in itself be a constraint, and of how former operators may feel trapped, imprisoned both by history and their past commitment.

The novel deals with a common range of concerns of many republicans: feelings before going on an operation; anxieties about interrogation; imprisonment, and the relationship between political prisoners and ODCs; and the toll on personal relationships from the demands of political involvement. In that respect it is similar to many of the concerns given expression in Meenan's *No Time for Love* and Morrison's *West Belfast* .

The core theme of Ronan Bennett's second novel, *Overthrown by Strangers* (1992), like the first, is the nature of commitment and what motivates the individual to become politically involved. The theme is established when Sean Quinn, a newly-released republican prisoner, has the following conversation in the back of a car with an old comrade who wants to know why he is tardy about reporting back for active service.

> 'I ask you to come to see me. You say, tomorrow. You're just out of jail. You need time. But I know if I had asked you to come now, you would have said yes. Why?'

> Quinn shrugged. 'I don't know what to tell you. There is nothing else.'

Seamus gazed directly at him and did not speak for some moments. 'Well,' he said at last, and with a certain disappointment in his voice, 'it's always harder to put these things into words. It's easier just to do, though there are those who would say that's an excuse not to think.'

'You don't have to think when there's nothing else: no options, no dilemmas.'

Seamus said, 'Tell me, what's the main thing that makes Denis different from you and me, and the people we work with?'

Quinn shrugged.

'It's this. He is an individual. He does not understand – he can't grasp – what it means to be part of something, thinks it's absurd, thinks it restricts him. Now where does that take you, if you're like Denis? It means you will do whatever you have to get what you want. The individual is greedy, cowardly, mean. The individual has nothing behind him, no strength, no direction'.[43]

Sean is subsequently shot by a former comrade, his wife's lover. Sean leaves Belfast while still not fully recovered from his wounds, deeply disillusioned at the treachery of his former comrade and at his wife's infidelity. The rest of the narrative tracks his travels in the States, where he gets involved with a group searching for a missing political activist in Guatemala.

Sean's experiences prove the necessity for collective action if meaningful change is to be accomplished; the role of the individual is downplayed: 'the act of one person, alone, changes nothing, satisfies no one, only deludes you into thinking you can do something'.[44]

The novels discussed this far were all written by republicans, from perspectives unashamedly sympathetic to the republican struggle. I will now discuss some examples from Irish writers, none of whom are republican in terms of affiliation, and some of whom are hostile to the republican movement.

Eve Patten, commenting on the work of a new generation of novelists from the North, suggests that their use of such postmodernist devices as 'perspectivism, ambiguity and displacement' is evidence of 'a sustained constitutional and psychological identity crisis germane to any representations of a contemporary Northern Irish self-image'.[45] She dubbed Robert McLiam Wilson, and his contemporary Glenn Patterson, 'prodigal novelists', both having moved to England, and each returning in their work to the site of the past, seeking to comprehend and give fresh expression to the cultural plurality lost sight of in the battle for discursive supremacy.

Robert McLiam Wilson's debut novel, *Ripley Bogle* (1989), is ambitious in scope and form.[46] Seemingly a Bildungsroman, charting the eponymous Bogle's first-person narrative account of his prodigious childhood to what appears by his prodigal early twenties to be a proclivity for expatriate mind games, by the end of the novel amounts to a confessional tale. Wilson's 'use of an overweening alienated soliloquist'[47] throughout facilitates the dissimulation. Bogle, in the London passages, bears some resemblance to Knut Hamsun's mendacious character Andreas Tangen in *Hunger* (1890).

Born in 1964, Wilson lived in Turf Lodge until he was twelve, when his mother, brothers and sisters moved to Antrim. Antrim was then a small predominantly Protestant town, and far removed from what McLiam Wilson may have considered the stifling nationalist culture of West Belfast as it is possible to get, unless you add his time as an undergraduate at Cambridge. He was only seven when internment was introduced. His mother was anti-republican. In an interview to promote his later novel, *Eureka Street* (1996), discussed in Chapter Eight, he cited this move as one of the reasons he escaped the communal pressures to become involved and to join the IRA, what he termed the

> necrophiliac tradition of Irish republicanism in which death is so honoured and definitive of the movement. Young men wanting to make their mark have corrosive fantasies about heroism and self-immolation. Certainly in the Seventies a lot of men went to prison at 17 when they mightn't have done two or three years later. They might've become moderate, had less testosterone, and a girlfriend, a child even.[48]

The motivations underlying commitment to any cause, any thing, are complex, but are here reduced to teenage angst. There are individuals to whom this description may well apply, but they are untypical and are soon weeded out by the harsh material realities of the conflict.

Ripley Bogle, a semi-autobiographical creation, doesn't belong. He is a conscientious rejecter of the definitional authority of his cultural background, of its values and strictures. Internalising estrangement from the 'Irishness' expected of him, and after a sojourn at Cambridge University, Bogle ends up on the streets of London, a tripolar exile from home, ambition and society. Beneath his rambling, dissembling identity crisis he is slowly tallying what Gramsci termed an 'inventory of traces', the myriad unrealised sources that socialise the individual.[49]

Bogle reflects on the social environment of his childhood and of the response of nationalists to the conflict.

> There aren't actually very many bombs and guns around as yet – just a lot of jobless Catholics getting the shit kicked out of them and having their homes burnt down on Protestant feast days, adding to their well-stocked catalogue of hatred and injustice.
>
> Soon, however, will come the Civil Rights marches. The Protestant lot will get annoyed. They (reasonably, I feel) would rather like their civil rights to remain exclusively Protestant. Soon the British Army will be drafted in to protect the Catholic minority from the brutality of their Proddie countrymen. Maladroitly enough, the British Army will then shoot a little bunch of unarmed Catholic civilians, clerics and toddlers on Bloody Sunday. In their turn, the Catholics grow rather peeved and start

exterminating a whole plethora of soldiers, policemen, prison officers, UDR men, Protestants, Catholics, English shoppers, Birmingham pubgoers and men who make the mistake of editing the Guinness Book of Records.

Tsk, tsk, tsk! What chance did we ever have? For a piece of normality? Not much.

You see, they made a very big mistake with the Catholics. They really shouldn't have pushed them around like that. It was bound to break sometime. And break it did. The Catholics of Ulster may well have been a dreadful collection of drunken, wifebeating, educationally disadvantaged, bastardguttersnipes but it was soon discovered that they had another talent to add to their knack of repeatedly impregnating their foul hagwomen beyond the bounds of obstetric probability and their bewildering capacity for talking shite. That third talent was, of course, killing people. Damn right. Few do it better.[50]

The trope of the violent Irish – or here, the violent Catholic northern Irish – has a long and ill-reputable lineage in service to a narrow expansionist British nationalism. Even when nationalist hurt is foregrounded (a good example being his description of internment morning), Bogle's indiscriminate tongue lampoons away to Gothic effect, sparing no quarter or side, except perhaps the British, redeemed as somehow not all that bad when bathed in an ironic glow.

You know, I always felt rather sorry for the British in Ireland. They didn't want to be there. The Protestants had originally wanted them there but got browned off when their presence began to interfere with traditional Loyalist rites of Catholic killing. It wasn't strictly Britain's problem though to be fair, they had committed some worthy cock-ups in the preceding four hundred years or so and Bloody Sunday had been a little tactless. Still, it was no reason to have to keep dying all the time.

The British were onto a very bad thing in Ulster. They couldn't win: if they left there was civil war and if they stayed they got crapped on from all sides. It couldn't have been much fun.

They were always getting into this kind of trouble, the British. In India, those Indians and Pakistanis were always kicking the dung out of each other as the dear old Brits tried to pull out. They were asked to stay a little longer. They did and got crapped on some more and slagged well off for their trouble. It was the same with Palestine after the war. The Jews and the Arabs have never really been the best of buddies. So who suffers? Trying to keep the peace. Trying to play the game.

Let's face it. Most European countries have had their empire at some time or another. Eventually, they crumble and another one comes along. This is what interregnums are – brackets of history. The British got it wrong. They grew all philanthropic and noble. They were the only imperial power ever to try giving their empire back. That was their mistake. We wogs, us wogs, we didn't like that. Not at all.

Of course, little hiccoughs like Amritsar, Bloody Sunday and the Velt Camps didn't help. But nobody's perfect. It's hard to like the British but I try.[51]

The irony displayed throughout is revealed in the novel's closing pages to be a masquerade, an evasive strategy, a massive state of denial, and by the end of the novel, slowly stripped of pretensions, Bogle comes full circle back on the journey of self-recognition, of who he is and where he came from. Bogle is a cipher, rootless, unassimilated and habitually on the fringes. Instead, his moral universe is supplanted from without.

Wilson's narrative strategy is a response to a very postmodern anxiety, in which relativism reigns and all absolutes are rendered out of step with a sensibility that favours complexity and plurality, and in which the concept of utopian order and resolution is considered intellectually redundant. In *Ripley Bogle*, an empty or specious cosmopolitanism fills the void left by the rejection of a misapprehended Irish nationalism.

Like *Ripley Bogle*, Brian Moore's *Lies of Silence* (1990) lacks any sense of being written from within the shared experience of a community. Moore, who died in California in January 1999, although born in Belfast had lived outside Ireland since 1948. Set in an affluent North Belfast suburb, the overall sense conveyed by the novel is of remoteness from the Troubles even when the conflict directly impinges on the lives of the characters.

Michael Dillon, thirtyish, a hotel manager and poet manqué, and his Canadian lover, Andrea Baxter, a Queen's University Belfast graduate in her early twenties, are held hostage in their home. Dillon is forced to drive a proxy bomb to his hotel, where a reception for a Protestant firebrand politician is to be held that afternoon. The central theme is a questioning of the morality of individual responsibility for social conflict, and of how private morality and public morality may conflict.

Troubles fiction overall, as I am at pains to demonstrate, distorts the realities of the conflict. There isn't one reality, however, but contending perspectives that amount to significant differences in the ways the conflict is interpreted. I write from an Irish republican perspective. Very few authors write from that perspective or have succeeded satisfactorily to characterise that viewpoint. Moore, for all his imaginative power, has failed to give an account that a republican would recognise as an authentic representation. This is due, in my view, to the fact that he writes from a specific class outlook inimical to the ideas, values and objectives of the republican movement.

One of the novel's central premises is the supposed gulf between the affluent, and the ghettoised poor, a gulf that Moore seems to imply transcends atavistic tribal loyalties based on religion.

His house was in the north end of Belfast, part of that much larger city which surrounded the central ghettos, a quiet, unpublicised, middle-class

Belfast where Protestants and Catholics lived side by side, joined by class, by economic ties, even by intermarriage, in a way the poor could never be.[52]

There is some surface truth in this image, but it fails to recognise the extent to which sectarianism permeates *all* sectors in the North.

When an IRA unit takes over Dillon's home, their conduct appears efficient and, in the circumstances, courteous, although there is tension among them arising from a clash of wills and personalities. Moore may have been influenced by media accounts of the civility shown by IRA escapees towards the occupants of houses taken over and the later testimony of the escapees themselves.

Moore does attempt to go beyond the habitual stereotypes of republican gunmen. I have to say, though, that I do not recognise the 'types' he depicts. However, the representation is probably a valid reflection of how some middle-class Catholics would see the IRA, and to whom the repressive presence of British army and RUC patrols in areas like the New Lodge is an 'unknown'. Sharon Shervington, writing in the *New York Times* quotes Moore on the similarities in motivation for joining LA street gangs and the IRA.[53] By implication the typical IRA recruit is mere cannon fodder for the Godfathers.

In the excerpt in which Michael Dillon transports the bomb along the Antrim Road, Moore has 'tidied up' the route. I know that part of Belfast particularly well. Somebody making the journey from the upper, more affluent end of the Antrim Road to the city centre will perceive that journey differently than, say, an unemployed nationalist from the New Lodge Road (the large nationalist area Dillon has to pass on his journey to work). For Dillon, the existence of this nationalist/republican 'stronghold' is peripheral to his experience; he very nearly doesn't 'see' it. The IRA team described in the novel comes from that area or an area very similar.

Moore doesn't, however, absolve Britain of blame.

> Dillon felt anger rise within him, anger at the lies which had made this, his... birthplace, sick with a terminal illness of bigotry and injustice, lies told over the years to poor Protestant working people about the Catholics, lies told to poor Catholic working people about the Protestants, lies from parliaments and pulpits, lies at rallies and funeral orations, and, above all, the lies of silence from those in Westminster who did not want to face the injustices of Ulster's status quo. Angry, he stared across the room at the most dangerous victims of these lies, his youthful, ignorant, murderous captors. What are they planning to do today, what new atrocity will they work at to keep us mired in hate?[54]

Despite attributing blame to successive British governments for turning a blind eye to unionist misrule, at base *Lies of Silence* is deeply apolitical in that it fails to appreciate the root causes of the conflict and of the collective resistance of nationalists. Moore's target is the morality of the response to that misrule, and he avoids causal questions. Republicans have indeed perpetrated some terrible deeds.

Much suffering has been caused during the last thirty years. However, no side in the conflict has a monopoly on suffering, or of culpability. But blame, surely, is rightly due to the real power broker, the sovereign power, Britain. Equating the violence of the oppressed with that of the oppressor is a moral cop out. People living in nationalist communities responded to the situation that they found themselves, in a manner that demonstrated their relative weakness. No approaches other than armed conflict seemed capable of preventing a return to Orange supremacy, let alone the achievement of a united Ireland. Republican violence may be shown as an effect of that failure, but Moore accepts the lie that the IRA is motivated to breed hate and bigotry, and that the problem is intrinsically sectarian.

Perhaps significantly, the jacket and blurb in the original 1990 edition give no indication that this is a novel dealing with the conflict. Instead, the presentation and, presumably, the marketing strategy were designed to capitalise on Moore's reputation as a writer, and appeal to his established readership. The novel was marketed as 'literary' fiction, and to draw attention to the novel's Troubles theme might have undermined the strong and proven selling point of reliance on the author's literary fame. The novel was shortlisted for the 1990 Booker Prize.

Frederick Forsyth's *The Deceiver* (1991) is the only one of his considerable output of thrillers to deal directly, though only in one of the novel's four subplots, with the Troubles.[55] Sam McCready is a former Cold War hero who, since the collapse of the Soviet Empire, is bereft of an enemy on which to vent his now redundant skills. McCready, Desk Head of D[eception] D[isinformation] and Psy-ops, challenges his early retirement. In defence four cases are cited proving his worth, past and (so it is argued) future. In the third, A Casualty of War, he counters a Libyan-backed conspiracy to ship arms to the Provos in 1987. Gerry Adams gets a mention. In the novel's somewhat batty conspiracy thesis, nevertheless told with a straight face, not only the Provos are set to benefit from the arms consignment.

> It would be a multi-package shipment, when it came. Some weapons for the Spanish Basque separatists, the ETA. More for the French ultra-left group, the Action Directe. Another consignment for the small but lethal Belgian terrorists, the CCC. A large present for the German Red Army Faction, at least half no doubt to be used on bars frequented by US servicemen. More than half the shipment for the IRA.

> It was reported that one of the IRA's tasks would be the assassination of the American ambassador to London. McCready suspected that the IRA, mindful of their fund-raising operations in America, would farm that job out, probably to the Germans of the Faction, successors to the Baader-Meinhof gang, diminished in numbers but still deadly and prepared to take contract work in exchange for arms.[56]

Such an operation is hardly likely to endear the Provos to an American audience. I suspect that Forsyth's intention was precisely to undermine potential support in the States for the republican cause.

In another episode designed to extract maximum contempt for the Provos from the reader, Kevin Mahoney, a ruthless IRA 'gunman', hijacks a car while evading capture from a former SAS captain, Tom Rowse, and kills a child to save his own skin. Mahoney

> hauled the old man out by the jacket, clubbed him to the ground with the Colt, jumped into the driving seat and was off.

> There was a passenger in the car. The old man had been taking his granddaughter to the circus. Rowse stood in the road and watched as the passenger door flew open and the child was thrown out. He heard the thin scream from down the road, saw the small body hit the road, saw the body struck by the on-coming van.[57]

Rowse tells McCready that the child's death was no accident.

> 'Yes,' said McCready softly, 'we know it was him. Despite the eighteen witnesses who said he was at a bar in Dundalk at that hour.'

> 'I still write to her mother,' said Rowse.

> 'The Army Council wrote too,' said McCready. 'They expressed regret. Said she fell accidentally.'

> 'She was thrown,' said Rowse. 'I saw his arm.'[58]

In a metafictional moment, Forsyth has given the British agent Rowse an interesting background as a thriller writer.

> Even as a novel, his first book had caused outrage in the Curzon Street headquarters of MI5. The book was about Northern Ireland, seen from the point of view of an undercover soldier, and it had rubbished the counter-intelligence efforts of MI5.[59]

This consciousness of the Troubles genre is similar in ways to Robert McLiam Wilson's apparent parodying of a Troubles thriller in parts of *Ripley Bogle*, and Lionel Shriver's discussion of the genre in *Ordinary Decent Criminals* (see below), and it could be seen as a self-conscious device to add distance from the grosser examples typifying the genre.

The Deceiver merits a place beside Herron's *Whore-mother*, Pincher's *The Eye of the Storm*, Robin Moore's *The Kaufman Snatch*, and Eddy Shah's *Fallen Angels* (1994 – discussed in Chapter Eight), in a repository reserved for future academics seeking insights into the most scabrous excesses of anti-republican propaganda in fiction. However, if the old bigotry persisted, public attitudes towards Britain's role in Ireland were changing, and novelists were perhaps as likely, if not more likely now, to respond with more informed and informative narratives to meet the growing levels of awareness. This shift towards a more informed fiction at this point is partly explainable by a flurry of exposés and revelations about Britain's duplicitous role in Ireland that gained considerable attention in the late 1980s and early 1990s.[60] With this background, previous certainties and assumptions were no longer tenable if authors aimed for a credible fictional account of the conflict.

A number of superior Troubles thrillers written by accomplished journalists were published at the beginning of the 1990s that drew on their experiences of reporting the conflict. The main theme of Gavin Esler's first novel, *Loyalties* (1990), as suggested by the title, is the integrity of each side's commitment to its view and purpose.[61] Loyalties, of course, are often misplaced, questionable, divided or misguided, personal or political, and it is this problematic of loyalty that Esler addresses, for it is one given equal applicability to both 'sides' in the novel. An inherent theme here, interestingly (because it also features in the two following novels discussed), is that of moral equivalence.

A cynical television journalist, Tony Morgan, who has been reporting the conflict for twenty years, is commissioned by a satellite channel to film an interview with a recently escaped Provo, P.J. O'Neill, who is reputedly in charge of the bombing campaign in England. Through Morgan's narration, several presumptions, conventions and stereotypes usually in evidence in Troubles fiction are given a fresh examination. As such, this is in keeping with not only the author's informed status but also that of the more questioning attitudes of a reading public less inclined than ever to accept formulaic misinformation about what was happening in their name in Ireland. Morgan reluctantly admits to himself that 'senior Provisionals... tended to be intelligent rather than stupid, part of the society in which they operated rather than some kind of monster from the outside'.[62]

Morgan interviews O'Neill, who justifies the armed struggle in terms of 'the rights of any oppressed people to throw off the oppressor'.[63] Morgan responds in the habitual tones of middle England, or, in O'Neill's view, with 'a bit of typical British propaganda'.

> 'And don't you oppress?' Morgan asked. 'Isn't the IRA's boot on the neck of the civilian population in Northern Ireland from whom you extort money, upon whom you prey?'[64]

Disappointingly, O'Neill's arguments are dismissed, not with counter-arguments but by the unspoken and unspelled-out indictment of their supposed unreasonableness, and recourse to 'whataboutery'.

> O'Neill hit back with the usual litany of British wrongdoing, from Bloody Sunday to internment and the shooting of a twelve-year-old girl by paratroops in South Armagh. Why don't you condemn that? If murder is murder then why isn't it murder if the British forces do it? And so it went. Every time Morgan pushed him on terrorism he replied that it was a war of national liberation and if Morgan wanted to call it terrorism that was fine. But didn't the British now sit down with all sorts of people who were formerly regarded as terrorists? The Israeli government? The successors of the Mau Mau in Kenya? Wasn't George Washington regarded as little more than a terrorist when he freed America from British rule? Not quite. It was the 'whataboutery' Morgan knew he could expect. Every time he made a

point about what the IRA were responsible for, O'Neill would dodge the
question and say 'what about' something else which the British or the
Protestants had done. Round and round the Irish mulberry bush. But
whatabout...[65]

In an episode in which O'Neill is confronted by an elderly Dublin supporter and
asked what can be done about the problem of heroin addiction in her
neighbourhood, his response is authoritarian and paternalistic: first obtain power
then use it in the service of the people. He explains to her:

> if the modern Irish state with all its resources could not tackle the problem
> then there was no way the Republican movement could do so. She looked
> crestfallen.

> 'Until the creation of a socialist united Ireland,' he said, and she began to
> cheer up. 'Once the National Question is settled then we can begin to sort
> out other things. Until then, the struggle in the North has to be our one
> priority.'[66]

The stage-ist approach is thus epitomised: first get the Brits out, then the other
problems can be more effectively tackled. Arguably, this may have been a more
accurate description of republican thinking in the Seventies but was certainly
redundant in terms of narrative time. This is the IRA thought of as a vanguard,
acting for the people but detached and 'above' them, without the symbiotic
relationship that in fact exists and which a radical political movement must foster
if it is to secure the sufficient loyalty of its support base.

The various representative republican characters – besides O'Neill, there are
Billy McKeever (the Boxer), Brendan Kelly (the Skull) and Larry Kennedy (the
Thin Man) – do get to explain themselves and their respective loyalties, or are
seen and judged accordingly in the eyes of each other, but the result suggests a
confusion rather than cohesion of purpose.

> McKeever could not understand what a life might be like not being involved
> in the armed struggle against the British. It was all he had ever wanted to
> do, the thing which gave him respect in the New Lodge Road area where he
> had been raised, the thing which gave his life a sense of purpose. It was the
> kind of respect he thought O'Neill himself might have got in the priesthood,
> yet he chose a different way. They all knew about his background and his
> supposed vocation which he had abandoned for the armed struggle.
> McKeever never understood why such a choice, which had not been open
> to him, had been so easily rejected by O'Neill. Would he not have served
> Ireland just as well as part of its church? Whatever the reasons, there was in
> the man, McKeever now recognised, a strange sense of ambition which
> shone through everything he turned to. It was as if O'Neill was not content
> with doing what he did, but wanted to go down in the history books as the
> best ever, the man who really did change the world. It was the kind of naked
> ambition McKeever saw in Brendan Kelly, and did not like.[67]

It is debatable whether the mix of motives described in the above excerpt is Esler's deliberate narrational device to portray the republican movement as faction-ridden. However, given fiction's imperative to express action and motivation through characters, almost inevitably the genre formally demands a concentration on the deeds and loyalties of individuals. Contention is a structural necessity. Esler very possible based O'Neill partly on Brendan McFarland, who as the media reported following his escape with thirty-seven others from Long Kesh in September 1983, had attended a seminary before his republican involvement.

The novel worthily rehearses many of the arguments and concerns then current about the absurdity of the banning of Sinn Féin from the airwaves, imposed by the British Home Secretary, Douglas Hurd, in 1988 and only lifted in 1994, subsequent to the Downing Street Declaration.[68] In this regard, its focus on the processes of media-manipulation compares well beside Kevin Dowling's *Interface: Ireland* (1979).

Perhaps the novel's final message is that state violence is no solution to a political problem – after all, one of the terrorists survives to carry out, extra-narratively, a plan to bomb HMS Britannia.

The target of Graham Hurley's *Reaper* (Macmillan, 1991), meanwhile, is HMS Invincible as she prepares to sail for the Falklands.[69] Padraig Skullen, 'charged with running the Provo Away Teams, the handful of men and women whose job it was to re-export the iniquities of British rule back to the mainland,'[70] with remarkable prescience predicts how Thatcher might respond to an Argentinean invasion of the Falklands. The year is 1982 and the IRA is determined to avenge the hunger strikers.

Like Esler, Hurley gives a mix of republican types, some not entirely unfavourable. Tale the opinion of one character, Buddy: 'Provisional IRA, he thought, the lunatics in the black balaclavas, the monsters savaged by the tabloid press, so very different in the flesh.'[71] O'Mahoney, meanwhile, is 'a difficult character, independent, mulish, deeply unforgiving, but a man with a great deal of mainland experience, a man [Skullen] knew he could trust'. And like Esler's character O'Neill, who once intended to be a priest, Hurley's Skullen is

a religious man, [who] abhorred the waste of life. But his job was to make the occupation of the Six Counties intolerable for the Brits, to break the national will to stay, and that meant exporting violence on as grand a scale as high technology and clever targeting would permit. It was a war they were fighting, a just war, and there'd be no true peace without due sacrifice.

To date, he'd done well. But his particular brand of Republicanism – his reverence for the past, his respect for the old heroes, his rectitude, his insistence on strict discipline – was fast going out of fashion. The new breed of Volunteer, men like O'Mahoney, owed nothing to this world of his, and did little to hide their derision. In Belfast's phrase, his shelf life was strictly limited, and he knew it. But before the tide of history swept on, leaving him finally beached, he wanted to make one last mark on the movement, a contribution so unique that his name would never be forgotten. This yearning for a kind of immortality was, he accepted, a weakness. It smacked of vanity, of showmanship, but that didn't matter. History, after all, was his subject, and no one knew better than he did that history was written by the men who took the biggest risks.[72]

A conflation of tropes and ideas jostle for attention here: sacrifice – even though the intention is that it is the enemy who will sacrifice blood; personal glory; the great men theory of history. Sadly, there is in the novel scant understanding of how the movement's collective experience has hammered home the lesson that unity means strength, a lesson crucial to republican strategy.

The narrative closes in late October 1982 with a hint that the Grand Hotel, Brighton is the IRA's next target.

Gordon Stevens is a former investigative journalist who also, like Hurley, has a background as a television producer. Topicality is to the fore in his 1993 novel *Provo*.[73] Set in 1991/2, although touching on events in 1969 and 1980, there is a reference to the Brighton bomb and the Downing Street mortar attack in February 1991. The cover blurb of the Harper Collins 1994 paperback edition reads, 'Two women... one war... no rules'. Although there is more to *Provo* than this sensationalist tag line suggests, much of the drama does centre on the competition between two female protagonists: IRA volunteer Philippa Walker (Siobhan McCann) aka 'Sleeper' versus Cathy Nolan aka 'Catcher' who works for British Intelligence.

We learn what led Philippa Walker to join the IRA, but no such profiling is allowed for Cathy Nolan. Perhaps this is because Nolan (even though she's Irish – an Ulster Protestant) is working for British interests, and so her motivations are taken to be understood and, implicitly, worthy. The narrational pitch, therefore, isn't towards those of an Irish republican or nationalist persuasion.

Philippa isn't a reluctant terrorist, which is the way women have more often been characterised in this type of fiction. She is the obverse of that stereotypical coinage, the passive female whose role is ancillary to the male volunteer. Philippa is a highly motivated, even obsessively driven operator.

In an otherwise quite reasonably well-informed novel it was disappointing to encounter the old chestnut that 'once in, never out'.

'We're not doing the hit?' There was a flash of anger in Kincaid's question which he regretted immediately.

'I obey orders, Billy boy. You obey them as well.' Logan's look was withering. 'You don't want to, or you want out, that's fine with me.' And then you're finished. Then you're dead and buried, because even though you don't know half what you think you know, you know too much anyway.[74]

Stevens attempts to strike a balance. You see this in the moral equivalence drawn between the depiction of the British Intelligence establishment and the IRA's Army

Council – intrigue and empire building are common to both sides, is the message. Both sides are depicted as being equally determined, ruthless and perhaps principled. For example, Quin, a contender for the post of IRA Chief of Staff,

> was playing his own game within the Provisional IRA, just as Michaelmass was playing his own game within M15. Perhaps the Provos were playing their own game within Irish politics, just as M15 was playing its own game with the other arms of the security set-up on the mainland.[75]

In common with Esler and Hurley, Stevens's depiction of the corporate nature of the IRA is a trend which may amount to a transformation in the genre. Generally speaking, the IRA is seldom represented in Troubles fiction as a coherent, organic organisation, with chains of command and an internal dynamic. We recognise in the fiction that there is a hierarchical presence: the 'Organisation', but the focus all too often has been at a lower level of power, more often concerning stereotypicalised individuals. Esler, Hurley and Stevens in common represent the movement as a corporate structure, nearly on a par with a large multinational company. In a backhanded sort of fashion, the IRA as represented above has become an entity of power now worthy of its enemy.

The imperatives of the British discourse must prevail, however, and in the final moral tally it is the IRA which is represented torturing a British agent, the unfortunate Fairfax.[76] In contrast, British violence is shown within understandably appropriate rules of engagement, and clinically executed, even excusing a roadblock shooting – which may work subliminally to justify shoot-to-kill operations, and perhaps Gibraltar.

A more irreverent angle on the IRA's notional corporate outlook is contained in Lionel Shriver's *Ordinary Decent Criminals* (1992), in which an Army Council meeting could be, she implies, any other big company's drafting of its annual business plan.

> They were obligated to x number of routine bombings, y number of assassinations, and at least one high-profile, all-out Incident a year, just to keep up appearances. He sometimes pictured the Army Council mapping out the year's campaign much like any advertising firm with a job to do, having another coffee, letting the conversation wander; bearing down again, the foolscap black with crossed-out ideas: Anderson McAuley Primark: Crown court three judges (in rapid succession); drumming their fingers, trying to think of a new angle, combing the map for an RUC station they hadn't hit in a while, racking their brains for a catchy gimmick to sell the struggle like any other product whose billboards had gone stale.[77]

The novel was originally published in the USA as *The Bleeding Heart* (1990), the title suggesting a brand of Liberal, an icon of Catholic piety, and the hoary-old dig at the supposed nationalist culture of victimhood (ignoring the reality of the spirit of resistance shown by nationalist communities). The author, originally from South Carolina, is a Belfast-domiciled journalist, and the novel is a well informed, if jaundiced, commentary on the political scene. The narrative context is late 1988, and the American publication date was closer to the political climate following the Enniskillen bomb than that pertaining at the time of the novel's reincarnation.

As for the representation of republicans in the novel, who for the most part are depicted as grievance-wallowers, Shriver is wrong in at least one regard. The character Farrell O'Phelan, an independent nationalist politician and, incredibly, a freelance bomb disposal operative, winds up the local patrons of a republican social club in West Belfast who objected to his portrayal of them on *Panorama*.

> Nationalism and Unionism, emotionally, are forms of arrested adolescence. Pre-adolescence. Unionists are still clutching on to mother's skirt. Nationalists seem more traditionally rebellious, but the rebellion is traditional and therefore not rebellion at all. Foreigners [...] often see Republicanism as a radical ideology, and Sinn Féin invites this misperception with its latching on to the ANC, its quotes in An Phoblacht from Camilo Torres and Castro. However, handed from father to son, it is more accurately conservative, right-wing. Joining the Provisionals in West Belfast is the equivalent of working for Daddy's law firm in America. No one in Ireland gets away from his parents; no one grows up.[78]

Perhaps the point needn't be taken too seriously. In Chapter Four I mentioned the scarcity of social data on the backgrounds of IRA recruits. To my knowledge, there has been no research on the extent of IRA involvement as a 'tradition' within families. I can only offer an informed opinion from my own experiences of imprisonment from 1973 to 1975 and from 1985 to 1999. I would say that most of the generation of republicans who were interned or sentenced in the 1970s and early 1980s were not from what might be thought of as traditional republican families. My perception, based on my time in the H-Blocks between 1996 and 1999, is that neither is the present generation to any significantly different extent, that is, those who joined the IRA in the late 1980s and the 1990s, although I've been in prison with comrades whose fathers, for example, were interned with me. Having said that, I would surmise that there are few families from nationalist areas who don't have one member who has had or has a connection to the movement. This is precisely why prisoner issues are so strongly supported in nationalist areas. However, that is a different matter from suggesting that involvement in the movement is a sort of select club whose membership depends on familial ties. Shriver does, in the alter ego of her character Estrin Lancaster, an American writer resident in Belfast, evince some empathy towards young people from nationalist areas whose experience of state harassment may have led them to volunteer, but it is a highly partial understanding of their motives, seemingly lacking in cause other than revenge.

> Many of these men had been kicked and jeered at as scrotes by the British Army, searched and detained just for being Catholic, refused the right to take a leak or get a drink of water for hours, and while a lot of the abuse

was minor, it added up, and it was often the little things that got you; surely at one time or another they had all gone home red in the face from their spread-eagle in Castlereagh, vowing to get the bastards back. It was a big leap from there to the IRA and Estrin wouldn't make it in her most understanding of days, but she could see the jump was short on Whiterock Road.[79]

For O'Phelan, the ineptitude of government was a primary motivation.

The Provisionals had won a whole new flush of converts, thanks to the careful, perfectly alienating maneuverings of the British government; Farrell suggested that Britain's every move in the strikes had been so brilliantly calculated to recruit for the IRA that you had to suspect Margaret Thatcher of being an undercover Irish terrorist herself, and when she died they were sure to plant her in Milltown Cemetery right next to Bobby Sands.[80]

Estrin, gadfly in spirit, is in search of control over her own life, a quest more appealing to her than submission to convention. The novel questions the nature of national identity, and commitment, whether to a cause, a place, a person, or to a sense of self. The exploration of personal relations is analogous to the relationship between nationalism and unionism – only compromise will lead to a just outcome; submission to the 'other' will ensure an unequal result – there will be no partnership, nor union of spirits, but a state of dependency, for example, with nationalists reliant on unionist goodwill.

Two other noteworthy and thoughtful fictional treatments of the conflict should be mentioned. The first, by the playwright and novelist John Arden, defies categorisation. Arden's *Cogs Tyrannic* (1991) is structured in four sections, each deploring the misuse by humanity of its tool-making ability – which putatively sets us on a higher evolutionary plane than the rest of the animal kingdom.[81] In the relevant section, 'Like a Dream of a Gun', Arden deals with the misuse of technology, specifically news-manipulation by Psy-op operatives.

After lance corporal Alfred Truethought is killed by an IRA landmine in 1984, a poem is discovered in his locker. The poem is promoted as part of a British army public relations exercise, until the allegation is made that the poem was one of several stolen during a British Army raid, and is in fact the work of an IRA escapee, Tadhg Ó Cuinn, who was killed by the SAS across the border.

The second noteworthy novel, *A February Mourning* (1990), is a collaborative effort. Hannah Wakefield is the pen name adopted by two women, both American who settled in London in the early 1970s. One is a former editor, the other, a solicitor. In this, their second novel, the main character is the solicitor Dee Street, an American practising in London, who appeared in their first collaboration, the much acclaimed novel *The Price You Pay* (1987) which touched on the plight of Chilean exiles. In this outing Dee Street is at first reluctant to take on the case of Gerry Ryan, a senior Irish republican explosives expert. It is the time of the Anglo-Irish Agreement, 1986. Eight alleged members of two mainland IRA cells have been arrested. Dee is unhappy that Sue (Suze) Aspinall, one of six partners in her feminist law firm, has agreed, with another of their partners, Nicola Steyning, to take on the case of one of the IRA suspects, a woman who is pleading not guilty. Dee suspects that Steyning is driven to court controversial political cases for her own political ambitions. The chief suspect, Gerry Ryan is apparently about to turn supergrass.

> Our weekly office meeting was unusually heated that Monday morning. I wasn't the only one unhappy about the way Nicola had agreed to represent one of the IRA suspects betrayed by the informer Gerard Ryan without going through our procedure for accepting controversial cases. Simone resented being 'bounced', as she put it, because she thought the IRA were a load of thugs and hoodlums who were proof if any were needed that two wrongs don't make a right. Rita, declaring herself indifferent to the moral debate, was concerned simply that, because the IRA were perceived as terrorists, involvement in a case of this kind could damage our reputation with victims of violence. In Maggie's opinion the IRA were victims of violence themselves – 'freedom fighters engaged in a just war against colonial oppressors'.[82]

Sue Steyning supports Nicola: 'It's not as if there's a queue of solicitors eager for IRA cases. I'm willing to support her when I'm available'.[83]

When an anti-nuclear campaigner, Annie Murphy, is found murdered and Sue discovers a Bobby Sands' poem among the victim's property, suggesting a link with the IRA conspiracy trial, Dee is indignant.

> 'I know who Bobby Sands is,' I snapped. Outrage raced up my body, jerking it to its feet, filling in the pockets where energy used to be. 'And how dare you, how dare you. Annie Murphy gave up a lot for that peace camp. She may gave given up her life for it for all I know. The last thing she'd have died for was a violent group like the IRA. That is what you're implying, isn't it?... Well? Isn't it?'[84]

While involved in the women's Peace Camp at Moleham Heath, Murphy had taken photos inside the American missile base. The significance of the suggestion of an IRA link to her is that the Peace Camp had been infiltrated. It is suggested that Dee should go to the North to interview any possible defence witnesses and to investigate whether there is an Irish connection.

> '... talk to people – see what you can dig up face to face.'
>
> Images rose up – black hoods over heads, eyes and mouth, three gaping jack'o'lantern holes; cars burning in the streets; rifles pointing at the world.[85]

Dee is extremely reluctant to do so, but at a partners' meeting she is persuaded that she is the only one free to go.

As the narrative proceeds, Dee increasingly questions all her past assumptions about the Troubles and the media reportage of them. She meets relatives of

Theresa's clients who are living in Divis Flats. She is appalled by the poverty but touched also by small acts of generosity.

> As I accepted a mug of tea and passed along the plate of chocolate biscuits, I realised what must have been sacrificed for such an act of hospitality. This was a woman, after all, who was supporting three children on supplementary benefit while her husband was in gaol.

> Not that she seemed to feel any bitterness or shame or frustration; on the contrary. 'My Seamus,' she said to me, 'is not some kind of common criminal. The British Army is a foreign army of occupation and he was fighting against it. He's a political prisoner.' She was equally proud of her father, her elder brother, her father-in-law and her husband's younger brother, all of whom had also served time for the same reason – and now her niece Maire, too, the first woman in the family to be put behind bars.[86]

Theresa and Dee stop

> 'at the ramshackle gate of what looked to [Dee]... like a derelict house.

> This was headquarters of the group whose name the English media always referred to as 'Shin-Fane-the-political-wing-of-the-IRA'? How come such an empire of fiends to occupy such an impoverished dwelling?[87]

The manner in which Dee's views about the conflict have been transformed because of her trip to Belfast, illustrates how a changing subjectivity may occur through first hand experience. On her return she shares some of these experiences there with Sue.

> The words I hadn't been able to find earlier... now seemed to come effortlessly, fuelled by a sense of outrage I didn't know I'd acquired until I heard it in my voice. When I eventually began to wind down, Suze whistled as if to say well I'll be damned. 'Well I'll be damned,' she said, 'you've had your head turned around.'

> 'It was impossible not to. Being there, seeing how people are forced to live – I understood why the Catholics in the North were so inspired by the American black civil rights movement in the late sixties. The parallels are so clear – the racism in the North – but I've never really seen it that way before. The Anglo Saxon English ruling class has played divide and rule among two tribes, the Irish Celts – the natives – and the Scottish Celts, who they began to plant in Ulster in the seventeenth century. If the working-class Loyalists would only just realise how they've been used'.[88]

The above excerpt in effect is emblematic of the discursive shift occurring in Ireland during the whole period under discussion in this and in the previous chapter. Indeed, the later crop of fiction reflects in varying degrees the overhauling of previous certainties due to changing political tides, and the significance of which is understandable as part of that more profound cultural and political adjustment in progress from the Troubles' inception that I alluded to at the beginning of this chapter. On the evidence of changes within the genre, the reading public were increasingly disinclined to accept narratives and characterisations palpably out of step with the more informed public perception, and writers, who after all are also people, had to take cognisance of this growing awareness. It could be said that 'reality' and 'representation' were seriously out of alignment, but that from the late 1980s onwards there is some evidence of a convergence, however unevenly demonstrated throughout the period. The genre could be said to have acted like a seismograph in charting discursive change; but the metaphor ignores the active agency of literature in helping to shape the public morality and mood. In this light, Troubles fiction not only reflected, but also contributed to changing perceptions. The genre also contributed, therefore, in however limited an extent, to that wider spirit of opposition and of the emerging consensus necessary for the more direct challenge to the prevailing hegemony provided in the republican movement's peace initiative that led, in an attenuated form, to the Downing Street Declaration.

8.
Troubled Resolutions: 1994-99

The Downing Street Declaration, signed by the British Prime Minister John Major and the Irish Taoiseach Albert Reynolds on 15 December 1993, purported to offer a framework for a resolution of the conflict in accord with Sinn Féin's own peace proposals. It held that a renunciation of violence would gain an opportunity for the republican movement to advance its objective through dialogue and open, peaceful political means. The reverberations from the Declaration were soon felt in the New Year. Amid high drama and raised hopes, calls were made for the IRA to respond by calling a ceasefire. Sinn Féin's response was to seek clarification of key aspects of the document. For Sinn Féin, Britain's subsequent prevarication had totally vindicated the scepticism about the document expressed throughout the movement and wider nationalist constituency.

However, international pressure forced the British government to yield some ground. On 19 January the media ban on Sinn Féin was lifted. Then on 31 January, despite fierce criticism from unionists and apoplectic denunciations from the Tories, Gerry Adams was allowed into the USA for the first time after President Clinton personally intervened to grant his visa. The US State Department had refused previous visa applications by Adams and other prominent republicans on the grounds that to grant visas would offend Britain, an important ally. However, the 'special relationship' was not so important in the post-Cold War environment, therefore Clinton had more room to manoeuvre.[1] On 10/11 March the IRA carried out a mortar-bomb attack on Heathrow Airport. Although the bombs failed to detonate, it was nevertheless seen as an audacious operation, and established that the movement was acting from a position of strength. Then at Easter, the IRA called a three-day cessation of operations. The prospects for progress in the process appeared good.

August 14 1994 marked the 25th anniversary of the arrival of British troops. It is worth reflecting that at the time of their introduction there was no IRA threat, yet it would take a quarter of a century for Britain, with all its resources, to reach a military stalemate. The British had understood for a long time that levels of violence could only be managed; the IRA couldn't be defeated. Within weeks, on 31 August, the IRA declared a 'complete cessation of military operations', thus ending a campaign that had endured since the previous occasion of an IRA ceasefire in 1975, and prior to that, in 1972. The loyalists followed suit about six weeks later, on 13 October.

Adams said: 'I am satisfied that Irish nationalism, if properly mobilised and focused, at home and internationally, now has sufficient political confidence, weight and support to bring about the changes which are essential to a just and lasting peace'. However, the opportunities and heady optimism generated by the IRA cessation were soon dissipated as the Tories, with a reduced Westminster majority and now reliant on support from the unionists, stalled the peace process behind what republicans viewed as the trumped-up call for arms decommissioning. Neither Westminster nor the unionists had shown much understanding that progress required a conflict resolution scenario.

The IRA's cessation ended in February 1996 with the Canary Wharf bomb. London had broken its commitment to negotiation; Dublin had broken the nationalist consensus. Despite the opprobrium and denunciations, international interest was still at a premium. 'Northern Ireland' had become a symbol for how the most seemingly intractable conflict situation could be amenable to a solution if dialogue was facilitated. The perception among many republicans was that for the moment no progress could be made, and therefore that no renewal of the cessation would be declared while the Tories were still in office.

Not surprisingly, given the political uncertainties in Ireland and further afield characterising the final years of the 20th century, the fiction of the period reflected a lack of closure and of resolution.

In 1994 twenty seven Troubles' novels were published; in 1995, twenty six; and in 1996, thirty three. The figures represent a significant increase on the years covered in the last chapter. Apart from 1988, when only eight novels appeared, the other years saw an average of seventeen.

In 1997 only eighteen relevant novels were published. Why? Following the IRA's return to military operations, a drop in interest in Troubles fiction might have been expected for 1996, in the manner that previous 'security' low points impacted on publication, production and sales. However, as the figures indicate, 1996 was *the* record year. Despite a sharp frosting of the political climate, perhaps publishers and the booksellers and distributors were obligated to honour contracts and deadlines. Therefore, it is conceivable that the reduction in 1997 was the industry's delayed response. Even so, the fall was from a record high. The 1988 reduction, attributable to the Enniskillen bomb, was more severe. Now public, and indeed international, awareness and interest in events and developments, whether bad or positive, ensured a relatively buoyant market for the genre.

Tony Blair's Labour Party won a landslide victory in the 1997 General Election. The parliamentary arithmetic had changed: Labour didn't need the unionists. Gerry Adams and Martin McGuinness were both elected for Sinn Féin. Progress was again possible if the political will was there. The new political atmosphere helped produce the Good Friday Agreement which was soon followed by the renewal of the IRA's cessation.

These developments, as ever, had an effect on the contents and output of Troubles fiction. A continuing interest in the market for Troubles fiction was predictable, and in fact, 1998 saw the publication of twenty one relevant novels. However, the figure does not truly reflect the scale of narrative interest that year. In addition, a further fourteen titles were published which, though dealing only marginally or tangentially (or indeed containing the barest allusion) with the conflict nevertheless signalled the centrality now of the issue in the public domain.[2] Another factor to consider was the disrupture of previous certainties, which may have caused many writers to question the standard range of stereotypes. Never before had the British and unionist discourses been so subject to challenge at an international level. Sinn Féin, and therefore the republican analysis of the situation, now had a high media profile. The republican perspectives and arguments for the first time reached a wide audience; the narrow demand for decommissioning was countered by the analysis that a wider demilitarisation was required; opposition to supremacist Orange marches headed the demands for implementation of an equality agenda. Figures for 1999 are incomplete: I collected details on fourteen relevant novels but suspect that more were published.

One strategy for coping with current anxieties is to seek solace in the past. Many of the first crop of novels published during this period are based on or allude to past actual events, some casting a narrative net across previous decades. Jack Holland, for example, in his novel *Walking Corpses* (1994), deals with the supergrass trials of the early 1980s;[3] Patrick Quigley's *Borderland* (1994), set in his native Monaghan, refers to the 1950s Border Campaign and to the 1974 UVF bombing.[4] Though published in 1994, these novels were probably written in 1993, that is, amid the uncertainties and vacillations in the period prior to the signing of the Downing Street Declaration.

The trend of trawling the past for themes and narrative grist changed as confidence in the peace process percolated within the altering discourses, particularly under the impact of the IRA's cessation later that year. The Belfast-born author David Park, who has written several works of fiction inspired by the conflict,[5] observed that

> in the initial months of euphoria which followed the IRA's ceasefire there was much literary speculation in Ireland about how Northern Irish writers would reflect the new flood of optimism and, as in some political circles, much glib talk of drawing a line under the past.[6]

The result was a veritable Babel of novelistic responses wrought in the tumult of complex changes, broadly reflecting many of the political and social cross-currents, anxieties and agendas of the various interests affected by the new circumstances. The hegemony largely characteristic of the previous 25-year output had never been so challenged. A clear counter-hegemonic trend was the more likely inclusion of a sympathetic republican character, if only to knock him or her down as the sectarianism and criminality attributed to violent republicanism are emphasised in the end. This scenario is injected with additional topicality because of media allegations of hawks versus doves which had resurfaced in the wake of the Agreement, 'valuable propaganda for the British government but untrue'.[7] In some instances there was a feeling that potentially the new situation might impact on fiction in the manner feared by writers of spy novels at the conclusion of the Cold War.

Perhaps the first fictional trend discernible was the output's topicality; developments and incidents were hardly off the front pages and television screens when drawn on by thriller writers as a source of inspiration. The range of themes and subjects were now more directly related to ongoing events to an extent perhaps not seen since the beginning of the Troubles, when, as I argued in Chapter Three, topicality was a defining feature of the output. Previously the norm had often been to pillage the past as a source for narrative material. Unsurprisingly, the vacillations of the peace process and the resultant changes in the political culture were the core developments to engage the imaginations of fiction writers, particularly in the process's post-ceasefire manifestation. Now, the process loomed as an overarching narrative fixation, necessitating for many writers a more critical, analytical creative response, though traces of the old thematic imperatives were still evident. In many instances, the themes covered now mirrored the concerns, and in instances appearing to promote the agenda, of those hostile to perceived political gains made by Irish nationalism. Many novels promulgated the line of unionists and elements of the Tory party opposed to any gains made by republicans: that IRA 'hawks' were out to wreck the process; that republicans were milking a relaxation in security to extend their drug-dealing and criminal activities. The concerns of nationalists, predictably, were still under-represented in the fiction, particularly the destabilising role of the 'securocrats', to use Martin McGuinness's term.

Another interesting thematic innovation in the genre is the number of novels prompted, it seems, by American involvement in the peace process, particularly, by the visit of President Clinton in 1995. At least two novels appeared about threats to an American President during a visit to promote peace. In David M. Kiely's *The Angel Tapes* (1997), the Angel of the title plants a bomb in Dublin which kills five people, and then targets a US presidential visit;[8] and in James Kennedy's *Silent City* (1998), terrorists and right-wing religious fundamentalists link up to plot the assassination of the black American President who is flying into Dublin.[9]

Even when novels ranged further back, the concern was often with the moment. In some examples the recourse to a past context was effectively in service to thinly disguised attempts to counter the battering the British discourse was now routinely subjected to. For the journalist and author Martin Dillon, in his first novel, *The Serpent's Tail* (1995), this in effect entailed exploring the link, as understood in terms of an anti-republican discourse, between Sinn Féin and the IRA.[10]

Though set in the mid-1970s (a number of actual contemporary events are mentioned: the IRA's uncovering of British Intelligence's 'Four Square Laundry' operation in October 1972; the assassination of the leading Loyalist Tommy Herron; the 1974 Dublin bombing), the novel reads as if it is very much influenced by the political agendas of the 1990s, and as I've indicated, particularly the debate about the nature of the link between the IRA and Sinn Féin.

The novel also explores the thesis that the ballot box/Armalite strategy sprang fully-fledged from the military wing. This line is pursued in the narrative as if politics is conceivable as a set of ready-made policies and ideas which the movement was able to adopt, as if it suddenly dawned on the leadership that the IRA needed a political wing, and snapped the command: You, you and you: Form a political party. Instead, the development emerged from hard experience and a continual process of analysis and political engagement at leadership and grass-roots levels.

The plot, according to a cover blurb, is 'based on the true story', liberally adapted from Dillon's account in *The Dirty War*, about a British intelligence scam to discredit republican hawks, foment sectarian attacks by the use of Military Reaction Force (MRF) counter-terror gangs, and thereby influence a more dove-ish IRA leadership prior to the 1974/5 ceasefire. This counter-insurgency intent has the unforeseen consequence of occasioning a rethink leading to a struggle for the leadership of the movement, which leads to the promotion and implementation of the ballot box and Armalite strategy. SAS Major Tim Johnston briefs Richard Milner, MI5.

> 'It's like this. I set up the Military Reaction Force under classified orders using some of my own people and a mixture of agents we'd recruited from within the IRA and the loyalist paramilitaries. It was based very much on our operations in Cyprus and elsewhere. But it was a lot more sophisticated than previous campaigns.'
>
> 'Only the generals and military intelligence knew about this one. My task was to create counter-gangs, train people to behave like the IRA and carry out assassinations which we could blame on the enemy. My people operated with IRA weapons. The intention was to draw the Provisional IRA and the Official IRA into a feud, and carry out sectarian killings to encourage a war between the IRA and the loyalists.'
>
> Johnston drank some more wine. 'I thought this approach was too crude. So I decided to look for a more sophisticated way of getting at the Provisionals, because they were emerging as the greatest threat. Then some of our intelligence people suggested that we set up a bogus laundry service, to get us into the Andersonstown area, where we knew the Provisionals had their best men.'[11]

Dillon has claimed that 'the message [of the novel] is about the futility of violence and how young men are sacrificed as pawns, drawn into a situation they don't understand'.[12] This notion is given clearest expression in the novel in an excerpt describing the Republican Plot in Milltown cemetery, Belfast, which 'held the monuments to IRA dead, many of them young men who had given their lives to a conflict they scarcely understood'.[13] If such a comment were made in a general sense about the level of political awareness of combatants in all conflicts, then it would be valid, and would usually emanate as criticism of war. Conscripts in both World Wars may only have had the barest understanding of the issues involved in either conflict. Motivations for young men (and women – whose sacrifice and role is overlooked by the author) are varied and complex. Leaving aside the not inconsiderable distinction between conscript and volunteer, volunteering in some instances may have been not an entirely thought-through reaction to the presence and behaviour of British troops, but witness reaction of itself could not have sustained such a protracted campaign without the supportive analysis and framework which came from the pooled historical experiences of the people. There was a culture of resistance and a communal experience of repression from which to view events.

Dillon worked up the plot as a film script, and in 1993 a screenplay won a European Script Fund award. The novel's publication in 1995 was fortuitous in commercial terms because of the international focus now on the North following the IRA's August 1994 cessation. A Sunday tabloid reported as a news item that W.H. Smith intended to place the novel on its 'prestigious' summer list: 'A special deal has also been secured to place it on the shelves of supermarkets throughout Britain'.[14]

It is claimed that in the novel Dillon, a journalist much praised in certain quarters for his supposed contribution to public awareness and understanding of the intelligence war, was able to reveal more than he could in his factual accounts of Britain's undercover war against the IRA.[15] The cover blurb solicits a credential for the author's expertise from no less a figure than Conor Cruise O'Brien: 'Martin Dillon is the greatest living authority on Irish terrorism. He is our Virgil to that Inferno in all the varieties of its torments'. A disclaimer at the beginning of the novel states that though he 'occasionally used the names of real people [Gerry Adams, Martin McGuinness and Danny Morrison feature as a triumvirate of 'young Turks']... all the characters are completely imaginary and are not intended to resemble any actual individuals, whether living or dead'.

Danny Morrison has noted that Dillon's central republican character, Brendan McCann, bears an uncanny resemblance to the greatly respected republican, Brendan Hughes.[16] Brendan Hughes was OC of the IRA Blocks during the dirty protest period, and fasted for fifty three days during the 1980 hunger strike, only terminating the protest in the belief that the British had conceded to republican demands. Hughes wrote a highly cogent review of Dillons's *The Dirty War*, in which he argued that in a supposedly factual account of Britain's counter-insurgency war Dillon had mitigated the worst excesses of the British state to the actions of a few bad apples.[17] Like his fictional model, Hughes was lifted in the Malone Road in the mid-1970s.

Whether Hughes's subsequent imprisonment is accurately reflected in the following episode from the novel is quite another matter.

In the lecture-room thirty men sat on wooden benches [...]

'As some of you already know, I am your new OC.' [...]

'There is a war going on and we're part of it, though some volunteers in A Wing seem t'have forgotten that. The prison regime is designed to break us. That's why we must never forget that as prisoners of war we're still part of the struggle.'

Brendan surveyed the rows of men, most of them aged between eighteen and thirty-five. The majority hadn't known earlier IRA campaigns; they belonged to a new generation shaped by conflict. The Provisionals had won their hearts and minds from the day the barricades went up and the British Army defined its enemy as the Catholic population.

'You', he said, pointing at each row, 'are the vanguard of a new phase of the struggle, and that requires political re-education.'

From inside his jacket he produced a torn newspaper headline and held it in the air.

'This is not what we're about,' he shouted, his face contorted with rage. '"Two More Protestants Killed in Revenge Attacks by the Provos." Is that what we're about... killing our fellow countrymen? Have we forgotten that the enemy is the British presence?'

[...] 'The Brits use the loyalists to kill our people t' force us into a sectarian war. Why? It's simple! They want t' make this a tribal conflict. That way, it makes it easy t' criminalise us. Their tabloid newspapers tell the world we're not freedom fighters but mindless thugs killing innocent people. By doing that they gradually try t' steer us away from our real purpose... and that weakens us and traps us in a religious war. We have t' send a clear message to our leadership that we don't approve of sectarian revenge killings.'

As each man present rose to his feet to applaud, Brendan called Patrick Rodgers to the front of the room and told him to begin the first lecture.

'This is where it begins,' said Brendan quietly to him. 'Don't forget that many of these guys have families out there who are vulnerable t' loyalist attack and have been brought up to hate Prods. So, take it easy... Develop the argument gently'.[18]

The subtext is all too transparent: that the movement was inherently sectarian until Brendan McCann's stand. The import of what McCann is saying to those present is that the leadership is responsible for sanctioning sectarian revenge attacks and that the leadership should be notified of their disapproval. The new direction is spelled out.

In prison [McCann]... used the time to guide them politically, making sure they knew how to develop the strategy of the Armalite and the ballot box.

'The smoking gun is not enough to win a war,' he had stressed time and again. 'The odds are in favour of the Brits, and international opinion will support that. It's essential to develop a dual strategy and win the hearts and minds of the young and the next generation'.[19]

Dillon depicts Sinn Féin's political development and strategy as one engineered by forward-thinking militarists, like McCann. In other words, Gerry Adams, *et al*, are merely dancing to the IRA's tune. Therefore, the novel may provide ammo for those who would seek to highlight the alleged structural linkage of the two organisations. Dillon's journalistic reputation may gain the novel's thesis a wider acceptance than merited.

During the ceasefire, the aforementioned group of 'young Turks' around Brendan plan a bloodless coup.

> They planned a strategic takeover of the IRA, with the emphasis on transferring power from dublin to the North and getting rid of foley, Skillen and Mckee, the leaders of the Belfast Brigade. Every candidate earmarked for a role in the new, transformed organisation was a northerner.

> 'It's us who're fightin' the fuckin' war... it's our blood that's on the streets and in the ditches... so it's us who should make the decisions. We'll need young men like Gerry Adams, Danny Morrison and Martin McGuinness to help us give equal status to the Armalite and the ballot box. We have to win the hearts and minds of the young people to sustain a struggle'.[20]

Released from prison in late 1976, Brendan McCann encounters old comrades.

> he saw familiar faces in lines of men stretched along three walls. A tricolour was pinned to the back wall and under it stood four masked men in military fatigues, each carrying an automatic rifle held across the chest. in front of them was a long wooden table and seven chairs.[21]

'Seven chairs', we might suppose, would be the seating arrangement for the seven-man Army Council.

> Three young men broke ranks and warmly shook his hands.

> 'This is Gerry Adams,' said Rodgers, indicating a man in a tweed jacket and spectacles who looked like a schoolteacher. 'And this is Martin McGuinness... and Danny Morrison.'

> Brendan laughed. 'To hear him,' he said, playfully nudging rodgers, 'you'd think I'd never met you three.'

> Brendan took Adams aside and beckoned to Morrison and mcGuinness to follow.

> 'It's time for you guys to leave... Your job is politics... just make sure that Sinn fein develops a ballot box strategy which gives us the political cutting edge we need. I'll look after the rest'.[22]

The films *In the Name of the Father* and *Michael Collins* met with much criticism because they condensed incidents and the roles of several of the people involved for artistic reasons. Perhaps the author, if responding to the line that his novel contains several historical inaccuracies, would proffer a similar defence. But there is a convention that actual incidents referred to in historical romances, even in Troubles Fiction, are accurately detailed in terms of dating. In *The Serpent's Tail*, however, there are a number of historical inaccuracies; for example, the supposed likelihood in the narrative of a feud breaking out between the IRA and the INLA in early 1974, even though the IRSP, let alone the INLA, was formed later, in December of that year. In addition, there are some real howlers.

...he hurried to a washbasin and spat into it.

'Rather you than me,' remarked Rodgers with a grin, as Brendan filled his mouth with water and gargled.

'Here, you open it.' Brendan threw an object at him. 'Be careful... We may have t' use it again.'

Removing a razor blade from under his mattress, Rodgers went towards the basin and meticulously sliced open a tampon. With the precision of a watchmaker, he removed a tiny role [sic] of paper.[23]

As Danny Morrison queried in his review of the novel: 'Tampaxes? Why don't they just carry the messages wrapped in cling film?'[24]

If an unseemly haste to publish so as to milk a particular moment of heightened public interest might generously explain the deficiencies of the above example, more literary novels appeared than ever before despite commercial exigencies. Among the best are Dermot Healy's *A Goat's Song* (1994) and Patrick McCabe's *The Dead School* (1995), both of which are discussed below.

Also in that category are Seamus Deane's *Reading in the Dark* (1996), Ronan Bennett's *The Catastrophist* (1998) and Edna O'Brien's *House of Splendid Isolation* (1994).[25] The last of these probes the mix of attitudes about the North to be found in the twenty-six counties – ambivalence towards republican violence, and the cult of the gunman on the run. During the novel's promotion it was widely reported that O'Brien had researched the novel by visiting republican prisoners in Portlaoise. These included Dominic McGlinchey (the former INLA leader who, shortly before publication, was shot dead in Drogheda, allegedly by his former associates), though McGreevy represents a composite from all the prisoners she met. Deane's *Reading in the Dark* is, if anything, more 'writerly', to use Barthes' term, and is a wonderful evocation of the treachery of memory, and of the slow unteasing of the truth about the past from local processes of myth-making, denial and disempowerment. A comparison might be drawn with Bennett's *The Catastrophist*, for both novels close at the beginning of the Troubles, in Derry and Belfast respectively.[26] Each is also in part autobiographical, drawing on memories of childhood, teasing historic reality from communal myth, to locate the narrators' later consciousness and development. Although primarily dealing with events in the Belgian Congo, 1959, there are many allusions in *The Catastrophist* to Irish nationalism. As in his two previous novels, *The Second Prison* and *Overthrown by Strangers*, Bennett explores the nature of commitment to a political cause. Deane's novel was a Booker Prize finalist and Bennett's was nominated for the Whitbread.

The historical sweep back over old ground in these novels was in service, perhaps, to a self-conscious awareness of the regenerative capacity of fiction to re-appraise, revaluate past traumas. Fiction could contribute to the task of collective healing. Thus in one narrative strand of Dermot Healy's *A Goat's Song* (the title derives from the original Greek for tragedy), empathy is gradually awakened as we accompany the character Jonathan Adams, a former RUC officer, on an odyssey of cultural re-identification as he distances himself from a past mistake. In 1969 Adams was caught on camera batoning civil rights marchers, an iconic image of supremacist brutality. The fictionalised episode is based on the actual incident when an RUC inspector batoned demonstrators during a NICRA (Northern Ireland Civil Rights Association) march in Derry on the 5 October 1968. The newsreel of that incident did much to draw international attention for the first time to the nature of Stormont rule. The power of the narrative resides in the fact that a figure personifying the contempt of the Orange state for civil rights, which collective nationalist memory might have placed beyond the bounds of redemption, is shown to be all too humanly frail. Perhaps Healy's message is that if we can begin to forgive or understand the character, perhaps there is real hope for an inclusive society in the future.

Healy's depictions of the republicans encountered in the novel, and of the several other references to the conflict, are uniquely drawn, one feels, from his detached writerly intelligence based on first-hand observations and encounters. One chapter, 'Guilt-tripping', describes a conversation between the novel's central character, Jack Ferris, and a republican prison escapee, De Largey, on the run in the South. Healy is a master of the illusion of letting his characters speak for themselves, devoid of the constraints of stereotypical attitudinising and political correctness. The result is that sense of listening to a rounded human being, to dialogue encapsulating the sum total of all that character's strengths and weaknesses, and of not hearing a character burdened with some archetypal imperative.

> That's why they have jails. Jail makes all the difference. Prison can break ye, or ye can break out of prison. It depends on your experience of prison and on your experience of family life. I'd a wain but I'd no family life. But when I went inside I started guilt-tripping. From day one I was hung up on my son.
>
> [...] In the blanket protest you had four to five hundred men cocooned in the one place. They had nothing but themselves, so they had to rely on spiritual strength. Out here there are so many distractions. See here, where

I'm sitting, I can look out the window. I can go out and be a part of that –
of what's outside. But inside you get to know the value – not of what's out
there – but who's in there beside you. [27]

The novel stands as my personal favourite out of the more than 150 texts with
a Troubles' theme I've read in the course of this study. A close second is Patrick
McCabe's *The Dead School* (1995).

The Dead School is a metaphor for the stultifying hold on the potential of the
present of a misapprehended, mythologised understanding of the past, specifically
targeting the corrosive legacy of Irish nationalism as established by the War of
Independence and Civil War. The two central characters, Malachy Dudgeon, born
1956, and Raphael Bell, born 1913 are teachers. As a boy, Raphael witnessed his
father's murder by the Black and Tans. Hatred of British rule is instilled in the boy
by his Uncle Joe.

'For eight hundred years the likes of that animal that shot your father to
death have been trying to break us. They haven't managed it yet and they
never will. Not while we have young cubs like you coming up – am I right,
Raphael?' [28]

In small chapters, often of only one page, each a tableau, McCabe records
Raphael's growing disillusion with the past as the horror of the news from the North
mounts. One such chapter is called 'The Walton Programme'. Raphael listens every
Sunday to *The Walton Programme* on the radio, which featured rebel songs.

When they played the songs of old, it was hard not to think of the reaping
race and the day they carried his father shoulder high across the fields. It
was hard for him to stop his eyes misting over when he thought of all those
good times that were gone. But when they played 'The Boys of the Old
Brigade' and 'The Rifles of the IRA' he smiled again. Smiled because he
was proud. The Black and Tans had tried to make his father bend the knee
but he wouldn't and didn't because his name was Bell. A proud and noble
soldier who died a noble death in an Irish field beneath an Irish sky.[29]

In the next chapter, shorter still, Raphael refuses to accept the veracity of a
newspaper report about civilian casualties from an IRA action.

A young boy went into a shop, two years after Neil Armstrong came back
from his travels. 'I want two penny chews, a packet of wine gums and a
bottle of lemonade please,' he said and was blown to bits. Raphael read about
it in the paper. The shopkeeper got blown up too. There was a photograph of
them both with sheets over them. You could see the young fellow's shoes and
socks. Underneath the photo it said the IRA had done it. Raphael went crazy.
He said they couldn't have done it. He said to Nessa [his wife], 'They
couldn't have!' But when he mentioned it to Father Des, the priest replied,
'Oh, they did it all right. It was on the news. There's no question about it.'

After that, Raphael just stood there because he couldn't think of anything
to say. He just stood there scraping the top of his index finger with his
thumbnail.[30]

Raphael tells his pupils about how the 'Old' IRA abandoned a culvert bomb in order to protect civilians. He compares this action with the recklessness of the Provos.[31]

His wife dies. The day after she is buried the British ambassador is blown up (an actual incident, which occurred on 21 July 1976). He has some kind of a mental breakdown, staying indoors, drinking, under the delusion that he is back in his role as schoolteacher reading old school books and course work. He refers to his home now as the Dead School.

Raphael has a disturbing dream of horses being burned, their eyes melting in the heat and his Uncle Joe laughing at the spectacle.[32] The dream was brought on by the psychological impact of the changes to the certainties of his life: permissiveness and the rocking of old values; the IRA's bombing campaign, which he resents as a slur on his father's ideals. In another dream, he sees a Black and Tan castigating his father whom he holds responsible for murdering his mate. Through these dreams he begins to understand the Black and Tans' hatred of his father, which he had witnessed as a child. Subconsciously, he is now coming to terms with the possibility that his recall of his father's role is faulty and that perhaps there is another side to the stories he has been nurtured on. The underlying motif is that the older republican tradition is also culpable for the modern-day Troubles.

At the height of the bombing campaign during the early to mid-1970s, the Provos met with increasing criticism for supposedly dishonouring the patriotic legacy of the men of 1916. From a certain perspective in the South, a distinction was made between the old and contemporary IRA. A more recent revision had them equally culpable, for now Irish nationalism, the grand narrative of 1920, which viewed partition as unfinished business, was held to be the problem.

As well as revisiting and revising the past in the light of new evidence and perspectives, fictional narrative can also be utilised in the revisionist project. Sebastian Barry's *The Whereabouts of Eneas McNulty* (1998),[33] for example, 'depict[s] the Irish war of independence as a celebration of violence for its own ends by a bunch of psychopaths and similarly paints the troubles in the north in 1969 according to ethnocentric colonial analysis'.[34]

Robert McLiam Wilson's second Troubles novel, *Eureka Street* (1996), is another consciously well-crafted work, though one difficult to otherwise categorise.[35] Its concerns are contemporary and Wilson is an often brilliant writer. *Eureka Street* is self-confessedly an ambitious novel. Wilson claimed in an interview for *Time Out* that he was working on the 'Belfast Ulysses'.[36] The novel was work-in-progress at least as far back as 1992, under the working title of *OTG*.[37] The narrative was therefore taking shape before the IRA's August 1994 cessation, and perhaps the unforeseen turn of political fortunes favouring Irish nationalist discourse may have overtaken the author's original formal intention towards a biting satire, no doubt critical of Irish republicanism but also taking a a necessarily wider parodic sweep. Edna Longley described it as 'a novel of the 'peace process".[38] The result, unfortunately, often descends into low farce, which in later stages of the novel is more suggestive of John Morrow's *The Confessions of Proinsias O'Toole* (1977) in its leaden reliance on comic patter and enacted anecdote than the 'encyclopaedic realism' of James Joyce.[39] Chuckie Lurgan's character owes much to O'Toole, whom Edna Longley describes as a 'talented con-man, on the make from all sides'.[40] In an excerpt dealing with events after the cessation, Gerry Adams and Sinn Féin, in their roman à clef guise of Jimmy Eve and Just Us, are scurrilously targeted.

> Jimmy Eve and a coterie of Just Us celebs had flown to Washington immediately after the announcement of the first ceasefire. Despite having less than 12 per cent of the Northern Irish vote, they ambled into the White House and hung out with the President [...].

> The Americans loved Eve... He had a patchy beard which grew up to his eyes and a mouth like a guppy. There was no way around it, the man looked like a weasel [...].

> ...His hairy, carnivorous smile was everywhere.[41]

To Chuckie Lurgan, portrayed as both con artist and liberal-minded Protestant, all of whose friends are Catholic, Eve is a 'duplicitous Nazi'.[42]

It is as if at some point during the writing of the novel events wrong-footed Wilson's sensibilities and previously stated intention, leading him to abandon the Great Ulster Novel, which per se would require a nod to objectivity and inclusion, and instead to take sides, in effect interpolating a unionist discourse, or at least preferencing a highly partisan view.

> Jimmy Eve had known for some years that almost everything he said was untrue. Mostly, that had not mattered. After a decade of Margaret Thatcher, he had learnt to believe his own lies in some careless, auto-pilot way. The consciousness of deceit was one he found easy to repress, to tuck away somewhere dark in his unthinking mind. But the sensation of being a liar was ever present again. It was disturbing his equilibrium and ruining his peace. He had even begun to wonder guiltily whether other prominent members of Just Us were conscious of what liars they were. His own lies were talismanic, mathematical. When he said that he only wanted dialogue he meant that he only wanted total victory. When he told reporters that he respected the rights of the Protestant community he meant that soon they wouldn't have any. When he called publicly for international monitoring of human rights in Northern Ireland, he certainly didn't intend them to poke their noses into any of the naughtiness of his chums in the IRA.[43]

I am not saying that Wilson shouldn't promulgate a particular view. Far from it. I completely agree with the opinion he expressed in a promotional interview about the necessity for committed writing.

> 'Some people say that writers are observers but I think that's bullshit. Writers engage. You participate and if you don't intend to participate when

you write its pointless… Satirists would say that what they are for is to
correct folly or wickedness by mocking and ridiculing it.'[44]

I do feel, however, that Wilson did a disservice to his own project by the failure
to achieve a broader, more inclusive narrative. Healy's *A Goat's Tale* comes
closest to the ideal of that inclusivity. In *Eureka Street*, Republicans are depicted
in an external, parasitic relationship with the Catholic nationalist communities
they claim to defend. On the criterion of empathy the novel fails. It is also a failure
of political understanding, and surely the two are interwoven.

The savage lampooning of republicans in *Eureka Street* suggests that Wilson has
nurtured and honed partisan views inculcated and learned from an early age.
Perhaps his childhood in Turf Lodge was particularly formative in this regard. He
hasn't transcended or moved on from what appear to be early, festering prejudices
regarding republicans. He seems to have felt displaced from Belfast long before
he found himself in exile in London. The wonder is why a writer of his undoubted
gifts, clearly evident in *Eureka Street* as much as in *Ripley Bogle*, should so
cavalierly jettison critical detachment and discipline for burlesque. Travel and
distance do not appear to have broadened the mind. The authorial voice at times
typifies those who sit in cafes and bars, comfortably removed from and above the
realities of conflict, scoffing at the plebs in West Belfast .

Chapters ten and eleven are the novel's kernel (perhaps written prior to the
ceasefires), and together are a formalised disjuncture in the narrative. Ten is a
humanist paean to the city, formally differentiated from all preceding and
subsequent chapters by the resort to unjustified typeface; eleven details the
horrific impact of a bomb in Fountain Street.

> [Rosemary] turned into the small sandwich shop to which she always went.
> She stopped at the door to let a handsome, raffish young man in a green suit
> pass by. He, struck by the flush of her face and neck, smiled flirtatiously
> and held the door open with a vaguely gallant air. She smirked happily and
> stepped under his arm. She turned to murmur some thanks and stopped
> existing.[45]

Wilson proceeds to catalogue the names of the dead, dignifying each with a
thumbnail biography. The effect is deeply touching, realised in a kind of stunned
dispassion beyond anger. The intent in the juxtaposing of the two chapters is the
shock of juncture, but there is something austerely calculating in the closure of
this section, which foregrounds another formal contrivance, a Brechtian deceit to
alienate the reader out of the happy narrational delusion: '*The pages that follow
are light with their loss. The text is less dense, the city is smaller* [my emphasis]'.[46]
Wilson is perhaps saying that the obscenity of the human wastage is beyond
comprehension and the capacity of narrative to explicate. The account of the
atrocity cannot be assimilated into the narrative universe. If so, does this mean that
Wilson believes that realist fiction is redundant as a response or witness to
violence? Or can the deficiency of his attempt to express the hurt be, again, merely

a failure on the part of his imagination? Pat McCabe more successfully made the point without resort to formal trickery in *The Dead School* by allowing a small detail of the horror of a car bombing to speak for itself.

> A young boy went into a shop, two years after Neil Armstrong came back from his travels. 'I want two penny chews, a packet of wine gums and a bottle of lemonade, please,' he said and was blown to bits.[47]

A recurrent theme in Wilson's writing is that the conflict has insulated the North from an awareness of the more violent nature of conflict in the wider world. In 'Cities at War', an eloquent indictment of violence, he argues, referring to the Gulf War, that 'Belfast isn't special anymore'.[48] In *Eureka Street* the violence of Belfast is petty when compared to a Saturday night in New York[49] or San Diego.[50] This notion was similarly conveyed in Lionel Shriver's *Ordinary Decent Criminals* (1992 [published in the USA in 1990 as *The Bleeding Heart*]) in which Estrin Lancaster, who like the author is an American writer domiciled in the North, says that 'a walk through Hell's Kitchen made West Belfast seem cute'.[51] The portrayal of the conflict as squalid and not in any way comparable to real warfare, is a theme traceable back to Higgins's *The Savage Day*; the British Tommy knows what war is all about, unlike the romantics and/or psychopaths of Belfast. Wilson would reduce the republican struggle to psychopathology and traduce it as pathetic machismo.

In collaboration with Glenn Patterson and Carlo Gebler, Wilson subsequently made a documentary for Channel 4, a polemic against punishment beatings called *The Baseball Bat in Irish History*. David Trimble's 'irresponsible' and 'cynical' playing of the 'Drumcree card' spurred his much-publicised move to France, he says.[52] A comparison of these two polemical stands suggests a complex, maturing perspective that may yet produce significant further contributions to the genre.

In keeping with the new requirements of compromise and reconciliation demanded by the peace process, other narrational and formal strategies were also attempted. The reappraisal of past attitudes and certainties is also a theme of *Irish Times* journalist Eugene McEldowney's *A Kind of Homecoming* (1994).[53] In this, the first of four novels featuring RUC Superintendent Cecil Megarry, the reader comes to empathise with the character's present more pragmatic outlook, in which he no longer adopts an absolutist position in his attitude to republican violence, through a number of revelationary flashbacks. Megarry investigates a series of apparently sectarian murders that are being blamed on the IRA. But Megarry has his doubts.

He attends a regular Security Committee meeting. Among those present are the Secretary of State, the Commander of Land Forces, and the Chief Constable. He is reluctant to brief them fully. After the meeting a mysterious Major Prescott buttonholes Megarry.

> 'Did he have a point, do you think?'

> 'How do you mean?'

'What Fleming said. Maybe it is sectarian. That could be a serious development.'

Megarry was shaking his head. 'I don't think so.'

'But it's a possibility?'

'Everything's possible.'

'But it would make sense, wouldn't it? A round of sectarian killings would suit the IRA. Take the heat off them. Fleming was right about that.'

Megarry saw a small man in a black raincoat hovering in the background. He hadn't noticed him before. He had a resigned look as if he was used to waiting.

'I'm not convinced of that. I don't see what they have to gain. And where does McCarthy fit in? He was a Catholic.'

'But Stewart was a Protestant. And they've killed Protestant civilians before.'

'If they think they're involved with the security forces, yes. Or mixed up with Loyalist paramilitaries, or informing. But as a general rule, we're the enemy: you and me; the army; the RUC; the RIR.' He stopped. 'Anyway, how do we know it was the IRA? Nobody's claimed responsibility'.[54]

The scene counters the propaganda line of IRA sectarianism. The movement's opposition to sectarianism is absolute and is, in fact, founded on the principle of inclusivity. It is also pragmatically based on the historical and contemporary realisation that Britain has used sectarianism to further its interests by creating division among those whose combined opposition would pose a threat to those same interests.

Also sinisterly introduced in the above excerpt is 'a small man in a black raincoat', who next appears on the last page ('A small man in a black raincoat passed by and then turned for a moment and stared at them. Megarry met his gaze and the man lowered his eyes and walked quickly away'). Perhaps he symbolises all that is corrupt on the British side of the conflict; the suggestion is that he is a 'string-puller' at a higher level, and the antithesis of Megarry, who, for all his faults, is representative of an older, traditional style of 'beat'-policing.

Megarry expresses doubts about the efficacy of his counter-terrorist contribution in the past.

'…they're back. Stronger than ever. It's like sowing dragon's teeth.'

'We have to keep trying. We have right on our side.'

'No,' Megarry said. 'It's not a question of right and wrong. We, too, have people who would think nothing of putting a gun to a man's head and blowing his brains out.'

'But there has to be an authority. A moral centre. That's what we are.'

Megarry lifted his drink. 'I'm not sure any more. I think we're all bound up in this thing together, us and the terrorists. Like Siamese twins. As if it was preordained and we had no control over it. Sometimes I think that the course is already set and nothing we do can alter it. We just play our parts to the bitter end'.[55]

Another formal strategy much in evidence in relevant novels at this time is the location of narrative time some years into the future, its usage explainable perhaps by the flow and flux of events and the general uncertainty of future developments, as well as a growing millennial consciousness. The tendency closely paralleled a similar phenomenon in the early 1970s. Russell Braddon's 1970 novel, *The Progress of Private Lilyworth*, it may be recalled, was set two years in the future.[56] Few then could have predicted how the conflict would pan out during the immediate future. It is a risky business to base a thriller on contemporary events at a time when those events are heating up. The turn of events is apt to render such storylines redundant. Similarly in the present period, Shaun Clark's *Underworld* (1997) is moved a year on to Belfast of 1998 during the on-and-off 'peace'.[57] Other time-shifts are suitably vague: Colin Bateman's *Divorcing Jack* (1995)[58] and Daniel Easterman's *Day of Wrath* (1995)[59] are both set in the 'near future', while Rebecca Tinsley's *The Judas File* (1996), another shade of vague, is set in the 'not-too-distant future'.[60]

Douglas Hurd's location of his novel *The Shape of Ice* (1998) six years from Labour's landslide victory in the 1997 General Election is especially replete with hostages to fortune.[61] It is difficult to separate wishful thinking from dire prognostications: a new Tory administration has been one year in office after five years in opposition; the 'Breakaway faction of the IRA' resumes a violent campaign. The group had previously rejected the 'Blair Settlement', and had 'gone to ground after the assassination of Gerry Adams'.[62]

A bolder leap ahead is envisioned in Keith Baker's *Inheritance* (1996), which deals with post-Troubles Belfast in the year 2016, though flips back to events of October 1996.[63] The author is BBC Northern Ireland's Chief Editorial Advisor and their former Head of News and Current Affairs. In *Inheritance*, Jack McCallan, the son of a murdered RUC man, becomes embroiled in the uncovering of a till then successfully hidden conspiracy to kill IRA hawks to procure a peace settlement in the late 1990s. Republican hawks are seen in Baker's narrative retrospection to have posed the greatest single threat to the peace process. The reality of the present political difficulties, as understood by republicans, is that the influence and impact of 'dissident' republicans have been eclipsed by the threat from an alliance of right-wing Protestant fundamentalism, dissident loyalist factions, and securocratic elements from the British military and political establishment.

By setting the narrative twenty years hence, the author may have intended to forestall possible criticism and controversy over the portrayal of RUC and political establishment dirty tricks. Apart from the departure of Ian Paisley, a new King on the throne, and a revamped 'Police Service' under the leadership of a woman, the novel is recognisably of the present moment: no replacement has been invented for the Styrofoam cup; and the CD ROM has proved remarkably resilient against the tide of technological innovation.

Similarly, Peter Cunningham's *Tapes from the River Delta* (1995) is set 'in a post-ceasefire world that extends into the next millennium'.[64] There are even examples of incursions from the past into the present; for example, Ian Watson's *Oracle* (1997) in which a time travelling Roman centurion gets mixed up with the IRA in England.[65] And from the future to the present – in Ian McDonald's *Sacrifice of Fools* (1996), 'Northern Ireland is transformed by a "massive experiment in social engineering", when a community of aliens is introduced to "break the historic pattern of a bi-polarized society".'[66]

As indicated so far, the single greatest narrative preoccupation, whether given imaginative realisation in genre or literary fiction, was derived from the vacillations of the ongoing peace process. Many plots mirrored the constant media speculation of a struggle between hawks and doves. Titles began to appear giving immediate expression to the anxiety of the moment, such as Paul Anthony's *The Fragile Peace* (1996).[67]

Typical of this anxiety, and a high contender for the title of worst novel of the Troubles, is Eddy Shah's *Fallen Angels* (1994).[68] Shah's offering, published prior to the 1994 cessation, peddles the line that the IRA was undermining the efforts of London and Dublin to achieve a just settlement.

> Sinn Fein and the IRA had grasped the initiative from the British and, in spite of their recent bombing outrages in Belfast which had killed ten innocent passers-by, were now the peacemakers in the eyes of the gullible American public.[69]

The propaganda line is heavily applied: 'gullible' American support; '*their* recent bombing outrage', and for 'their' read 'Sinn Fein *and* the IRA'. And if that is an insufficient incitement to prejudice, republicans and their supporters are further branded by the company they keep: 'The IRA gets support from American nationals, Libya and probably Iraq'[70] – *probably* Iraq!

Topicality is again the benchmark, and Shah seems to have 'cut and pasted' a plot from a database of news headlines. As well as current events (such as the IRA's mortar attack on Heathrow, the 'Phantom Sniper', and the Chinook crash), he also contrives to include allusions to past incidents (the killing of Nairac and of Mountbatten) and snide targeting of right-wing bêtes noire (Dominic McGlinchey, the Ierland Komitee, Noraid), a veritable ABC of the author's prejudices. We are served up yet again the threadbare sectarian tagging: in Belfast 'manhood was bar-mitzvahed when you kicked your first Prod unconscious'.[71]

With all this spleen, something has to give, and a vicarious vigilantism is pandered to in a story of a group of SAS assassins, styling themselves 'Angels', who in revenge unofficially target IRA hawks in an attempt to coerce the IRA into supporting the 1993 peace process. The Angels leave a calling card (a similar warning and acknowledgement is given after each operation).

> 'The execution of the murderer Tim Flaherty was in accordance with the Rules of Engagement as laid down by the Irish Republican Army. In an attempt to fight fire with fire, as the only means now left open to resolve the question of Irish terrorism, Soldier Raphael, under orders of the Highest Command, carried out the execution of the criminal Tim Flaherty and his supporter Jed Geraghty. Should the acts of violence by the Republicans continue, then the Highest Command will have no alternative but to order quick and terrible retribution against those who are the enemies of a peaceful and just solution for the Irish situation'.[72]

Shah contrives to squeeze every fluid ounce of propaganda out of the plot. One theory advanced to explain the killings is that

> the PIRA hadn't paid the Colombians for the drugs they were selling on the street to boost their funds, and that's why they were being hit.[73]

The Angels are eventually destroyed by a joint initiative involving British, American and Irish security co-operation. But the novel's conclusion is clear: however unsavoury, because of the Angels,

> terrorist action ceased on the mainland and in Ulster. For that, the British and Irish populace were extremely grateful.

The public knew it might not last, but at least it could open the doors for the Provos and the IRA [sic] finally to come and join the peace talks.[74]

Post-ceasefires, wrangling began over who won the war, or whose contribution to peace really mattered. A novel spinning the line that the IRA was brought grudgingly to ending its campaign through SAS ruthlessness both exonerates all previous dirty tricks and provides a vicarious face-saver for those who cannot stomach the fact that the IRA remains undefeated.

Other examples of the current anxiety include James Kennedy's *Armed and Dangerous* (1996).[75] To the acute embarrassment of the British authorities, several republican prisoners nearly succeeded in escaping from Whitemoor prison in England within weeks of the IRA cessation. The incident inspired Kennedy's plot in which 'an IRA active service unit breaks out of prison intent on destroying the ceasefire... forcing the British and IRA to team up to stop them'. In Tom Foote's maritime thriller *Undertow* (1998), Jim Prendergast survives, though his wife and daughter drown, when his yacht is rammed by a merchant ship off the West Coast of Ireland.[76] MI6 suspect the ship was running guns for a maverick IRA unit intent on destabilising the peace process. And in Murray Davies' *The Drumbeat of Jimmy Sands* (1999), republican hard-liners are still out to try to wreck the peace process.[77] The role of opposition from securocrat elements is also dealt with, another testament to the slippage that the British discourse was increasingly more subject to. In Terence Strong's courtroom thriller, *Rogue Element* (1997), when Ulsterman Roddy Littlechild, an ex-MI5 agent, refuses one more assignment, the killing of an old schoolfriend who is opposed to the peace process, he is framed by his former employers for killing an IRA man, another old schoolfriend.[78]

Following the IRA's ending of its cessation in February 1996 with the bomb at Canary Wharf, London, a spate of novels appeared about IRA operations in England: Reg Gadney's *Just When We Are Safest* (1996), in which the IRA attempt to blow up MI6 headquarters at Thames House;[79] in Marian Urch's *Violent Shadows* (1996), Tara, of Irish extraction, joins the IRA after meeting Michael, a member from Belfast and becomes involved in the England bombing campaign in 1981;[80] in Patrick McCabe's *Breakfast on Pluto* (1998), located in the early 1970s, a transvestite, Patrick 'Pussy' Braden, is arrested after being innocently caught up in an explosion at a London bar;[81] Terence Strong's *The Tick Tock Man* (1994) is about an IRA bombing campaign in London.[82] The 'Tick Tock Man' is an expert from Northern Ireland brought in to deal with booby-trapped bombs. In Hugo Barnacle's *Day One* (1998), set in 1982, Gareth MacMichael, a British Intelligence officer, tries to convince 'a twitchy Belfast supergrass known as the Tambourine Man to finger the active-service unit holed up in Stoke Newington'.[83] Unknown to Gareth, he is their intended next target. Louise Doughty's *Crazy Paving* (1995), recounts the daily drudge of a group of London office workers, concluding with a bomb attack.[84] The following cutting from a post-ceasefire review would have been unthinkable after Canary Wharf.

> A perceptive tale of office life in the middle of the Irish bombing campaign on London. Fast, fun, astute and definitely one for young Londoners and office workers to identify with.[85]

The review's glib London Blitz stoicism indicates the rapid extent to which public perceptions can vary according to current perceptions of danger.

The propaganda line about the alleged involvement of the IRA in drug running and crime received a fresh airing. In Simon Weston and Patrick Hill's *Cause of Death* (1996) the message is clear enough: in the vacuum created by the ceasefire, republicans turn to crime.[86] Interviewed by Philippa Kennedy, Weston revealed that in researching the novel he and Hill visited the North 'twice with expert guidance from friends in the security forces who pin-pointed known haunts of para-militaries from both sides'.[87] He concluded that 'far from being political, the majority of stuff over there is criminal'. The review included a summary of the novel in a boxed inset, a device that makes it unclear whether the following crude propaganda was written by Philippa Kennedy or belonged to the narrative.

> In the mid-Eighties, the IRA had masterminded a world wide chain of drugs operations to help fund its activities. It had also claimed that it would defeat the British authorities by undermining the economy with cheap drugs which in turn would destroy society and cost millions of pounds to put right. The scheme had proved a dismal failure. But the use of drugs as a method of raising funds was here to stay.[88]

Recurrent media accusations linking the IRA with drug trafficking have to be seen in the context of the ongoing propaganda war. Drugs, accordingly, had now superseded the contribution of extortion and racketeering to republican coffers. As an article in *AP/RN* highlighted, allegations about IRA involvement in drugs first surfaced as a media concern in 1988, and were part of an anti-republican propaganda offensive in the South to prepare the public for the Dublin government's support for an internal settlement in the North.[89] Lurid accounts abounded of Mafia links, the trade in Angel Dust, and collaboration over drugs between republicans and loyalists, with the intention of softening public attitudes to the potential use of internment. None of these reports were ever substantiated, and when they resurfaced in 1991 were flatly denied by the republican movement. Rather inconsistently, *AP/RN* argued, reports of a drug-linkage were at odds with stories which appeared in the Southern media claiming the group Concerned Parents Against Drugs was a republican front. Interestingly, Ron McKay's *The Catalyst*[90] was published in the same year, and is perhaps the first novel with a drugs-for-guns plot.[91] An earlier novel, written in a different propaganda climate, Elliot Cannon's *Stand By To Shoot* (1973), has the IRA procuring arms from someone whose business also involves drug-pushing, though it is perhaps significant that the narrative eschews all suggestion that the IRA was interested in similarly diversifying its interests.[92] Some eighteen years later, however, the propagandists considered public opinion to have been suitably prepared for accusations linking the IRA with drugs.

Other writers were not slow in picking up the narrative potential of the drugs and racketeering themes. James Hawes' *A White Merc with Fins* (1996) is a caper novel with some IRA involvement in a money-laundering scheme.[93] Jack Higgins's *Drink with the Devil* (1996) relates how the Mafia and an IRA maverick target a gold bullion haul destined to fund loyalists.[94] Deirdre Purcell's *Sky* (1995) details an Irish nationalist 'conspiracy to ship drugs and guns into Eire and assassinate Prince Charles on a visit to Dublin'.[95] The drugs theme was perhaps given its crudest airing in Shaun Hutson's *White Ghost* (1994), published prior to the IRA cessation.[96]

In Hutson's novel Sean Doyle, 'the counter terrorist', working for the Counter Terror Unit, is given the job of infiltrating the IRA to recover British Army weapons taken during an IRA ambush. During his investigations he discovers that the IRA are in business with Hong Kong Triads.

> 'But you don't sell drugs on the streets. You're soldiers, not pushers.'

> 'We don't sell them, but there are plenty who are willing to do it for us, not just in Ireland either. Some of the drugs are shipped to Germany, France, even the States. The money that's collected from their sale comes back here to the organisation.'[97]

On hearing of the Triads' religious and patriotic pedigree, Doyle muses on the republicans' degeneration into drug trafficking.

'The Triads aren't bound by honour or family like the Mafia. With them it's a religious thing. That's why it's stronger,' the policeman continued. 'Years ago they were freedom fighters, patriots.'

Like the IRA, Doyle mused.[98]

There is an absurdly realised encounter between Doyle and Dermot Christie, an IRA prisoner in a Long Kesh cell during the blanket protest period when protesting republicans smeared their cells with their own excrement rather than endure the systematic brutality from prison wardens during the slop-out routine. Doyle tortures Christie, and succeeds in extracting the prisoner's brother's address in Andersonstown, though not without revealing his own (or is it the author's) scatological prurience.

> The counter terrorist glanced down at the slop bucket, saw that there was dark fluid in it and something solid floating there. He grabbed the handle and hurled the contents over Christie.

> A shower of excrement splattered the Irishman, some of it showering the bed, pieces of soft faeces dropping to the concrete floor with a soft splat...[99]

> The stench from his excreta-soaked clothes was appalling...[100]

> Doyle noticed that [Christie's]... face had squashed a lump of soft excrement beneath it.[101]

Innovatively for the genre, in this second post-cessation period not only republicans are open to accusations of drug running. In keeping with the greater scepticism about the role of the British forces because of the greater exposure of the 'dirty war', narratives become credible in which British army personnel are now more prone to similar accusations. In Simon Conway's *Damaged* (1998) an Army officer masterminds a drug-run from Afghanistan to the North during a post-ceasefire expansion in the market.[102]

Another strong feature to emerge during the latter part of the period was the number of novels dealing with the role of the SAS and British Intelligence agencies in undercover activities, some of them written by former SAS men, and others by SAS groupies. John Newsinger has attributed the apparent growth in interest and popularity for this type of novel to the rise in 'popular militarism', that is, the 'celebration of British military prowess' which marked post-Falklands War Britain.[103] Publishers such as 22 Books (the Little, Brown imprint) catered for the growth in interest, for example, by issuing a series of 'factoid' novels chronicling SAS exploits. The fifth of these, Shaun Clarke's *Soldier E: Sniper Fire in Belfast*, was published in 1993.[104]

A contributory factor to the rise in interest in this type of fiction was the jolt to the future credibility of the spy genre after the collapse of the Soviet empire and resulting end to the Cold War. Britain's 'dirty war' in Ireland was now available to take up the slack for thriller exploitation. The first manifestation of the trend, however, was not in fiction but in popular military memoirs. Following the failed efforts of the British government to prevent the publication of Peter Wright's memoirs, there was a relaxation in the application of the Official Secrets Act which until this time had acted to constrain former soldiers from recording their experiences. A flood of personal accounts from former SAS men subsequently appeared.[105] Some of the accounts were unscrupulous fabrications, 'widely dismissed as nonsense' – for example, the allegation in *Violent Delights*[106] that Mairead Farrell, one of three volunteers killed by the SAS in Gibraltar, had had a love affair with an SAS man.[107]

In some sense shadowing these accounts of personal involvement in the 'dirty war' was the publication in the pre-ceasefire period of a biography from a former republican who had severed his links while in prison, and in the post-ceasefire period, several accounts from republicans-turned-British agents, all providing new grist for the thriller mill.[108]

The spate of SAS, or 'dirty war' thrillers to emerge is divisible thematically along two streams: revenge and, in some instances allied to this, the tackling of crime, particularly involving drugs. They merely received a new lease of life by the relaxation alluded to above. However, as the discussion of Shah's *Fallen Angels* demonstrates, there was a long-established precedent for this type of thriller, though these earlier efforts were the product of journalists rather than of former soldiers. Seymour's 1975 thriller *Harry's Game*, in which the eponymous assassin is sent to Ireland on the orders of the British Prime Minister to revenge the killing of a government minister, is one of the earliest examples.[109] There is also Foxall's *Face of Fury* (1982), in which the SAS are sent to 'Ulster' following murders in London.[110] Perhaps this sub-genre's zenith was reached in Kevin Dowling's *Interface: Ireland* (1979),[111] which stands out for taking a more critical look at the role of British Intelligence agencies in the conflict.[112]

The narrow thematic and discursive parameters of many of the later breed of SAS-type thrillers is perhaps to be gleaned from the following review snippets. In Chris Ryan's *Stand By, Stand By* (1996), an SAS sergeant seeks revenge when the IRA kills his wife in Belfast.[113] The trail leads to Columbia and an IRA training camp set up in league with the cocaine barons. A *Guardian* critic described the novel as 'a thin post-colonial pamphlet of received right-wing views...plus rehashed anecdotes from the SAS Bumper Book for Boys.'[114] In Andy McNab's *Remote Control* (1997),[115] the hero is Nick Stone,

> [a] free-lance agent for British Intelligence having left the SAS after taking part in the shooting of IRA terrorists in Gibraltar in 1988. He is sent to Washington to tail two IRA men. Once there, he visits an old SAS colleague, only to find the man and his family brutally murdered. The sole survivor is seven-year-old Kelly. Stone and the traumatised girl flee and quickly realise they are being hunted by an unknown group of men and have stumbled on a conspiracy involving governments, terrorists and big business.[116]

In Shaun Clarke's *Underworld*, mentioned earlier, 'the on-and-off 'peace' in Northern Ireland leads to a massive crime wave. Former IRA paramilitaries, using the skills they've learned during the Troubles, turn to organised crime on a huge scale to create a massive criminal empire based on drugs, prostitution, bank robbery, protection, money laundering – and the illegal sale of arms'. SAS Sergeant Michael Burton is assigned to 'neutralize' the 'six major Belfast gangs'. In Chris Ryan's *Zero Option* (1997),[117] 'SAS sergeant Geordie Sharp arriv[es] back from an overseas mission to discover that his four-year-old son has been kidnapped by the IRA'.[118] At a time, then, when Troubles fiction was generally catering to a more informed readership, these dirty war novels pumped stale air into old stereotypes which for the most part had passed their sell-by dates.

In Chapter Seven I referred to the greater degree of nationalist communal pride and spirit, as evidenced in the growing popularity of the West Belfast Festival. John Gray, the Chief Librarian at the Linen Hall Library, Belfast, has judged the West Belfast Festival short story competition. One entry, he revealed, was

> [s]et in 1998, after the Northern Ireland political settlement. Gerry Adams has retired from politics and is Visiting Professor of Irish Literature at Boston College in the United States.

> Back in Belfast there is a mysterious series of murders. The victims are all former republican leaders who have become leading poets. The new cross-community Northern Ireland police service is unable to solve the crimes. Gerry Adams is called out of retirement to help. He, too, is immediately killed as a traitor to republicanism. It is fiction, but one that points out the risks that peacemakers have taken.[119]

The growth of Gaelic cultural activity in the 1990s, particularly in West Belfast, is also reflected in the publication of novels in Gaelic which tackle the Troubles. At least three have been published since 1996: Seamus Mac Annaidh's *An Deireadh* [The End], in which an Irish civil servant involved in the peace process is on his way to London to present a report, when it mysteriously disappears;[120] Mairtin Ó Muilleoir's *Ceap Cuddles* [Elect Cuddles], which deals with shenanigans at Belfast City Council;[121] and Aodh Ó Canainn's *Tearmann na gColær*, dealing with the impact on the Donegal Gaeltacht of the Derry civil rights movement of the late 1960s.[122] The publication of three novels in Gaelic since 1966 may not appear overly significant but I have found only three titles published during the preceding decades of the contemporary conflict, all from the latter half of the 1970s: Tarlach Ó hUid's *Adios*, Annraio Ó Liathain's *Nead na gCreabhar*, and Breandan Ó Doibhlin's *An Branar gan Cur*.[123] Although not dealing with the contemporary conflict, a novel written in Ulster-Scots, or Lallans, also appeared: Philip Robinson's *Wake the Tribe O'Dan*.[124]

For the first time many works appeared which concentrated on or featured loyalist violence. For example, Richard Crawford's *The Minstrel Boy* (1994),[125] James McKeon's *Operation Pontiff* (1994),[126] Eoin McNamee's *Resurrection*

Man (1994),[127] Glenn Patterson's *Black Night at Big Thunder Mountain* (1995),[128] Rebecca Tinsley's *The Judas File* (1996),[129] William Trevor's short story, 'Lost Ground', from his *After Rain* collection (1996),[130] Jo Bannister's *No Birds Sing* (1997),[131] Adrian McKinty's *Orange Rhymes with Everything* (1997),[132] Geoffrie Beattie's *The Corner Boys* (1998),[133] and Daniel Silva's *The Marching Season* (1999).[134] As Bill Rolston has tellingly observed, the role of loyalism is largely ignored in spite of the fact that the genre 'faithfully replicate[s] dominant British explanations of the aetiology of the Northern 'troubles''.[135] In fiction, almost apart from a few novels written in the early Seventies, loyalism was the dog that didn't bark until the 1990s, regardless of its status in the dominant discourse as the other main protagonist. I would proffer a number of factors to explain this 'silence'. In the early 1970s the British media were quite sympathetic to the plight of nationalists; in fiction this required some characterisation of the role of loyalists in fomenting the nascent violence. Their virtual 'absence' from the subsequent fictional account during the years up till the 1990s is in keeping with the unspoken understanding that the conflict, far from being sectarian in nature, was between Irish republicanism and the British state. This is a scenario, as I have indicated, in contradiction to the 'warring tribes' line that nevertheless informs the fiction. Loyalism's sudden emergence into the narrational limelight in the 1990s is explainable on two accounts. Firstly, that the role of collusion between loyalism and British Intelligence and security agencies increasingly entered the public domain (though republicans had always considered loyalist groups to be largely a paramilitary arm of the state). Secondly, from 1995, novelists caught up on the reading public's demand for informative fiction in the light of loyalism's emergent public face after the ceasefire declared in October 1994 and the emergence of the PUP and UDP as the political expression of loyalism.

More fiction from Irish republicans appeared: Sean P. Murphy's *Foreign Chains* (1996);[136] Danny Morrison's *The Wrong Man* (1997);[137] Gerry McGeough's *Defenders* (1998);[138] Ronan Bennett's *The Catastrophist*, mentioned above; and a short story by Declan Moen, 'Enclosure', included in *Racconti? Ireland '96* (1996).[139] Two of the four are debut novelists. Their novels are thematically similar. Republicans generally are perhaps still too close to events which for them represent an ongoing, continuous traumatic stream. This is reflected in the quite narrow concentration of issues and themes in the fiction written by republicans: security; the experience of interrogation, imprisonment, the dislocation of family and relationships. Another common factor is the focus on events from the earlier years of the contemporary conflict, partly explainable because some of the novels have an autobiographical dimension, being influenced by personal involvement and a continuing political commitment. Typically, the narratives are set in the 1970s or 1980s, when the authors were active and before imprisonment. The experience of conflict was still too raw for these authors who in common took part in the struggle.

The critical reception of work by republicans is also significant.[140] For example, when Danny Morrison's third novel *The Wrong Man* was released in early 1997, it initially excited as much extra-literary, news reportage as it did the attentions of the review pages and literary supplements.[141]

Liz MacPherson in her interview with Morrison for the *Irish News*,[142] and Mary Holland's for the *Observer*,[143] treated the publication of the new novel as a topical story rather than a literary event. The media-perception then current was of the likelihood of a full-scale return to violence and each wondered whether such a development might affect the author's reported determination to write full-time. Their comments on the quality of the novel were quite favourable. Danny Morrison's past as a leading republican strategist and spokesperson more usually guarantees a carping press.

The Wrong Man is an unsettling and thought-provoking read for a republican, marking the author's return after a lapse of more than a decade, much of it spent in prison, to the territory of his first novel, *West Belfast* . The conflict has ground on. Belfast has changed. Danny Morrison has changed. He exhibits less overt compassion in the third novel. The writing is more controlled, the tone, stark. A palpable sense is conveyed of the dark urgency of life under British occupation: the roadblocks, p[ersonal identity]-checks, dawn raids; the ubiquitous surveillance accompanied by the drone overhead of helicopters. Republicans know the costs of resistance to British rule: the graves, the prison cells, the disruptions to family, and wrecked personal relationships. For those familiar with that emotionally attritional terrain the novel may rouse the pain of loss. There is also the pain of survival and the responsibility to complete republican aspirations. Morrison faithfully depicts the micro-culture of secrecy and siege of active service volunteers and their taut circles of familial and communal support, vital to the furtherance of the struggle, but as is clearly demonstrated in the novel, always at a cost.

How, though, will readers unfamiliar with the collective trauma of republicans heed this novel? Robert McLiam Wilson has described the role of the writer and of character-creation as follows:

> In order to understand, to estimate the suffering of others we basically pretend that we are them. We put ourselves in their place. We swap shoes. (Perhaps fiction, that organised shoe swapper, has some point after all).[144]

However, Wilson's parenthesised doubts about the 'point' of fiction also surfaced, as I argued above, within the structure of *Eureka Street* where he appears to query the efficacy of realism to adequately express the horror of violence. To a readership unfamiliar with, and perhaps unlikely ever to get close enough to the actuality to judge, fiction has this empathetic potential, as Wilson concedes. The republican experience is rarely provided a fictional expression free of distortion. In *The Wrong Man* it has seldom been expressed better.

But what of the critics? As a backhanded compliment to Danny Morrison's republican curriculum vitae, great things were apparently expected of him. Kate

Fearon in *Fortnight* implied that Danny is a literary under-achiever because of his failure to produce the 'Northern Irish' equivalent of Jung Chang's *Wild Swans* (1991) or Vikram Seth's *A Suitable Boy* (1993).[145] Why did she imagine that he would aspire to a partitionist fiction as implicit in the use of the term 'Northern Irish'? Morrison stands accused in the review for not sufficiently exploring the pros and cons for the use of force against injustice. True – perhaps; but that would have made it a different novel, not necessarily a better novel, though the task is one for which the author is pre-eminently suited, given his background.

The author and *Irish Times* journalist Eugene McEldowney who condemned it as 'another turkey' delivered the most swingeingly caustic verdict on *The Wrong Man*.[146] Danny's crime of omission this time, it seems, was his failure to produce a novel comparable in stature to Alan Paton's *Cry the Beloved Country* (1948), often cited as an exemplar of engagé fiction. It seems to me that McEldowney evaluated the novel within an overly strict interpretation of where the parameters ought to be set for the conventions of a political novel. For McEldowney, Morrison has not transcended the recourse to stereotypes, which more than any other narrative ingredient defines Troubles fiction. The point is scathingly made and undeserved. There is a deft handling of the characters, a level of terse delineation appropriate to the pace and development of the plot. Indeed, Alannah Hopkins, in her review for the *Tribune*, praised his 'characterisation of the women'.[147] It struck me that the character of Roisin Massey, wife of ASU-leader Raymond, is especially well drawn. And Tina, the ASU member who ends up imprisoned, though sketchily rendered, remains a powerful presence (and as a survivor, redeems the novel's rather grim though realistic body-toll). But McEldowney's criticism of Morrison's characterisations is focused on the sparer definition afforded the RUC and British army characters compared to those of Roisin, Raymond, Tod Maloney, etc. He perceives the lack of a credible counter to the republican characters.

The criticism surprises me. In his first novel, *A Kind of Homecoming*, examined above, McEldowney to his credit steered clear of contrived balance, the imperative to present equally all shades and sides. The notion that narrational conflict requires a sort of 'level playing field' for heroes *and* villains is as old as the novel, even though the latter tend to lose. But as Arthur Koestler argued, invoking a more ancient aesthetic, 'a nonhuman agent or principle' may also serve as a protagonist – 'chaos, fate, God' – to which we may add the disruptive agency of state repression.[148] McEldowney intrinsically understands this, as his first novel demonstrates; the character of Megarry works so successfully because of the projection of a plausible surround of nationalist alienation and state skulduggery, furnishing tension and depth to the RUC man's individualistic outlook. Megarry is all the more sharply realised as a result.

Morrison similarly enfolds his characters within 'the nationalist nightmare'. This milieu is a tangible reality as well as a projection of their fears. The RUC, for example, are shadows, deliberately underdefined, an only partially-known, therefore more menacing enemy. Republicans rarely get closer to the RUC than in the involuntary exception of a Castlereagh or Gough Barracks 'interview'. The intense, often scary, kitchen-house back entry focus of republicans ever alert to betrayal, the potential for escape, and the clandestine presence of the enemy, is an authentic and brilliantly realised descriptive aspect of the novel. For a readership seeking to gain an understanding of the lived experience of a republican activist in Belfast during the relevant textual period, the novel is recommended.

If McEldowney's review is little better than a piece of hatchet-jobbery, other critics, even when positive about the novel's merits, betray a tendentious understanding. Alannah Hopkins, for example, talked of 'the effects of the sectarian struggle', and of 'the damage that sectarian violence brings to the lives of both men and women'. The term sectarian in regard to this novel is insidious and needs to be challenged. There is nothing in the novel to justify its use in this manner. When an off-duty UDR man, Joe Powderly is shot dead by Raymond it is made clear that he is not being singled out for his religious affiliation but because he revealed his membership of a state force loathed by nationalists. Before the slip-of-tongue that sealed his fate, the IRA team was on the point of leaving, quite aware that Joe Powderly was a Protestant. The former Presbyterian Moderator John Dunlop has written of the grief of Protestant communities, which perceive such attacks to be sectarian: 'the stark fact remains that most of [the victims] *were* Protestants'.[149] Another stark reality is that if the IRA had chosen to engage in the type of naked sectarianism often attributed to them, then car bombings in Protestant districts would have required far less expenditure of logistical resources than used in the effort to target specific members of the British military machine and political establishment. Allegations from some unionist politicians that the IRA was engaged in a policy of 'ethnic cleansing' in border areas do not stand up to serious scrutiny.[150] Daithi O'Connell observed that during the War of Independence an overwhelming number of RIC men killed were Catholic. Then, as now, religious affiliation was immaterial.[151]

To state the regrettably obvious, the republican movement's membership and base of support is overwhelmingly Catholic. However, fewer republicans these days, in my estimation, are practising Catholics. There are many exceptions; and this important component of the broad constituency of Irish republicanism is given expression in Gerry McGeough's first novel, *Defenders*.[152] The dedication on the novel's title page, 'In Honour of Our Lady', underlines the hold still, particularly I would hazard to say in rural areas, of Catholicism. The author, a leading republican, is a devout Catholic, and the novel explores the nature of political conviction, drawing an analogy between republican commitment and religious vocation. In the face of pulpit condemnations and the threat of excommunication, republicans who are Catholic have had to examine their consciences. For many of them, unable to reconcile their religious and political beliefs, this has led to a distancing from the church.

McGeough began the novel a few years previously. In 1996 his collection of prison writings, *The Ambush and other stories*, was published, the title story of which was adapted from the opening chapter of the then uncompleted novel.[153]

In *Defenders*, Father McCann explains to Brendan Doherty why vocations for the priesthood are falling off:

> 'I believe that many of those with vocations, who would otherwise be candidates for the priesthood, have dedicated themselves to the national struggle and have become deeply involved in the IRA instead.'[154]

Brendan, while a student at Trinity, tells Turlough that he intends to study for the priesthood. He believes that his life was spared by a miracle when he escaped the SAS ambush of his unit.

The title *Defenders* establishes a link in the reader's mind between the struggle of the contemporary republican movement and the long history of resistance by agrarian secret societies. The central character, Turlough Gallagher, is the OC of an IRA active service unit in Tyrone in 1980/1. McGeough gives a vivid account of the activities of Turlough's unit during the hunger strike period.

Numerous staple preoccupations of republican volunteers are addressed in the novel: interrogation; security; disillusion; Brit propaganda ('The British regarded…[the nationalist practice of leaving lights off to provide cover for the IRA] as passive support for terrorism. The locals knew it as sympathy for 'the boys' and the cause of Irish freedom');[155] the morality of violence; the hypocrisy of the British ('They call us violent, he thought, yet they've gone to the ends of the earth to pick fights with people in their own lands, and then steal those lands and their riches from them').[156] Many of the misconceptions about republicans are challenged. For example, in response to the frequently encountered lie that republicans are driven by a martyr complex, the members of Turlough's unit are shown to take elaborate precautions to ensure their own safety and that of civilians: 'they had no desire whatsoever to become three more martyrs for old Ireland'.[157]

The propaganda line that IRA attacks are largely mounted from the South suits the British, who wish to assert that there is a reduced 'internal' threat, and that the 'security forces' are on top of the situation; and it fuels unionist fears about incursions from the 'foreign' country across the border, and about external interference in 'the Province's' affairs, thus re-enforcing their siege mentality. At a NIO security meeting:

> 'If I may begin with you, Chief Superintendent Watson,' [Robin] Chandale [NIO official] went on. 'What can you tell us about last night's incident and this Cregroe place? Was it a cross-border attack as the media reported?'
>
> 'Well, of course,' Watson began dryly, 'the cross-border bit is utter rubbish, as you well know.'
>
> 'No, I don't bloody well know,' Chandale snapped.

'Then may I remind you,' Watson continued with a cold smile, 'that the report was in line with NIO disinformation guidelines. Our internal terrorist problem is all but under control, if you recall.'[158]

A British agent during an attempt on Turlough's life kills Turlough's fiancée, Cathy. At the novel's close, Turlough, now in the States, reflects that they were due to marry on the same day that Bobby Sands was to die. The moment allows him to at last grieve properly and he finds a renewed hope and purpose while at Our Lady's Chapel in St Patrick's Cathedral. Although we are not told his intention now, the author's own history suggests that Turlough's purpose was a rekindled political commitment.

David M. Thomas's debut novel, *Anger's Violin* (1998), contains that rarity outside of fiction written by former republican activists, a sympathetic characterisation of a republican.[159] A review in a British Sunday tabloid criticised the novel precisely for its favourable depiction: 'an IRA murderer makes a strange hero'.[160] Despite this welcome narrative quirk, the novel remains quite dismissive about republican politics.

Owen Morgan Parry, the hero of *Anger's Violin*, is a tour guide, the perfect cover, it seems, for an IRA courier. Armed with 'a few languages and a knowledge of Europe', the Welshman is a prized recruit entrusted with a package. Best-laid shenanigans start to unravel soon after Amsterdam. MI6? A tout?

The title, *Anger's Violin*, is a pun on 'Violon d'Ingres', which apparently translates as 'side-line' (Colin Bateman resorted to similar titular wordplay in *Divorcing Jack* to approximate Dvorak). The great French painter Ingres also played a mean fiddle. Now 'side-line' hardly conjures an image of dedicated zeal, and we learn early that Parry intends this to be his 'one last tour and one last mission. For the Cause'. Why then did the Welshman join the IRA?

> Who else [but the IRA] was there fighting that smug English ruling elite who, with all their forelock-tugging collaborators, had ground the miners into the dust and pissed and shat on the hopes of an entire generation, my generation?

Working class anger is a commendable inner resource. But ultra-left qualms about 'individualism and opportunism' assail Parry during the mission. What has carrying a packet across Europe got to do with the class struggle? Disappointingly, for a novel in which the nature of commitment, personal and political, is a running theme, the question goes unattended and the reader may therefore misconstrue that Irish republican politics and motivations are as muddled as Parry's.

Novels depicting the IRA on the side of the angels are rare. Thomas does improve on the stock thriller treatment of republicans. An exception is the characterisation of Ned Nolan, whom Parry likens to an SS guard: 'capable of the worst brutality by day and all Schubert by night'. The same Nolan 'went wobbly' after a Brit interrogation, and the IRA had to send him to the Caribbean for a spot of R&R. If one were to accept this as given then, evidently, welfare provisions

have vastly matured since the days when a weekend in Bundoran was the extent
of republican largesse.

Gramsci, according to Christopher Pawling, highlighted the 'dialectic between
ideology and utopia which is so crucial to the constitution of popular fiction'.[161] In
'normal times' the 'strangely composite' nature of what Gramsci identified as
'common sense' characterises formulaic fiction. The form of the novel requires
what Raymond Williams termed a 'magical resolution', that is, a favourable
outcome in personal terms but in political terms failure is encoded. This is because
a character may, for example, escape from a situation beyond the power of human
agency to change or determine. According to Pawling, however,

> at the moments of intensified political and cultural struggle the balance
> begins to tip the other way and common sense adopts a more Utopian
> outlook, so that there is an active popular demand for literature which
> embodies alternative values.[162]

'Utopian' here signifies an aspiration, and not the achievement of a perfect
resolution, be it social or narrational.

When this understanding is applied to the nigh on thirty-year production of
Troubles fiction, then a more questioning trend is discernible in many more of the
examples to appear from the late 1980s. The genre, of course, is defined by its
focus on a context that could hardly be called 'normal'. However, censorship,
black propaganda, and news management created a sense of normalcy reflected in
the hegemony of one ideological outlook, that of an anti-republican discourse.
Nevertheless, once the challenge to that hegemony, led by the republican analysis,
particularly in the post-hunger strike period, began to make inroads into the public
domain and popular consciousness, popular fiction demonstrated a more
questioning stance, giving expression in its range of characterisations to
previously excluded, or marginalised, oppositional voices, and 'alternative
values'. During the entirety of the peace process, which embraces properly the
period since Sinn Féin's own peace initiative launched in 1987, this trend is
illustrated in the gradual increase discernible in the incidence of empathetic
portrayals of republicans in fiction, if only to knock them down in the final count.
It is also to be found in the many examples of those Irish authors, north and south,
whose prose fiction embodied the search for a new more inclusive sense of
identity, and the reappraisal of past attitudes and roles which transcend the narrow,
partitionist discourses. This is an ongoing process and there is still far to go. The
unresolved nature of the political situation in the North must surely mean a
continuation of the generation of troubled resolutions in fiction. However, as I
have tried to stress at a number of points in this survey, it should be realised that
popular fiction has a role, for it is not a mere reflection of the state of discursive
or ideological play but '*intervenes* in the life of society' by contributing to the
creation of meaning.[163] Perhaps the new millennium will impact on the genre, as
perhaps it will on the political situation, in a conscious striving to express and
achieve inclusivity.

9.

Conclusion: the Uncreated Subject

To this point I have outlined a critical history of Troubles fiction, that body of prose fiction whose narrative field is the contemporary conflict since the late 1960s, a conflict arising from the abject failure, as republicans see it, of partition. This generic frame of reference covers about 480 novels in English dealing directly with the conflict. The primary concern has been to demonstrate that the bulk of the output promotes, conforms to, and is informed by, a view of the world in line with dominant political discourses.

My concern in this concluding chapter is to attempt to explain hows and whys. Initially, this entails a consideration of whether the genre's discursive bias is a product of political and commercial pressures and restraints. The focus now, in other words, is on the mechanics of a process to the extent that such a process is operative. Then, through the poststructuralist understanding that has underpinned this survey, I will summarise an explication of the role of popular fiction in the struggle for discursive hegemony.

How, then, is misrepresentation manifested at the level of individual texts and of the genre? What processes are involved? The extent, if any, of the role of censorship – a traditional recourse of governments, agencies or interested groups and individuals attempting to shape or constrain public perceptions – is an obvious first port of call for consideration.

The journalist and broadcaster John Pilger has written of how a culture of censorship works in Britain.

> The bias of the state operates through a 'consensus view' that is broadly acceptable to the established order. Perhaps in no other country has broadcasting held such a privileged position as an opinion leader. Possessing highly professional talent and the illusion of impartiality, as well as occasionally dissenting programmes, 'public service broadcasting' has become a finely crafted instrument of state propaganda.[1]

Certainly, there is a considerable body of opinion and research to support the contention that governments have sought to influence the debate about the nature of the conflict in terms of television documentaries and drama. In July 1985 Leon

Brittan, the then Home Secretary, came close to invoking the Broadcasting Act, Section 22, effectively banning an edition of BBC's *Real Lives* which included an interview with Martin McGuinness. The BBC withdrew the film.

Have there been any instances pointing to a similar pattern of official disfavour regarding Troubles fiction? Given media manipulation by governments, is it so unreasonable to ponder whether pressure is either exerted or executable on publishers, booksellers, or on writers regarding specific texts?

The exercise of such powers does not have to be targeted at specific disfavoured texts. The political ideas and position of an author may be sufficient to incur censorship even when these may not be controversially expressed in fiction. Ad hominem censure is exemplified by RTE's refusal in August 1992 to broadcast an advertisement submitted by Brandon Books promoting Gerry Adams's short story collection, *The Street*.[2] RTE explained that the advert was refused because Adams' voice was used, in breach of Section 31 of the South's legislation banning Sinn Féin from the airwaves. However, Adams was not speaking in his capacity as President of Sinn Féin, or indeed as a member, but simply to promote the sale of a work of fiction, and as such what he had to say should have fallen outside of the legislation's remit. It should also be remembered that since 1987 Sinn Féin had been promoting its peace strategy, and was at the time holding talks with the SDLP, of which the Irish government was fully briefed, and also secretly talking to British government representatives. The extent to which RTE was out of step with current developments was further demonstrated when an independent radio station, 98FM, interviewed Adams about the ban. However, a High Court decision upheld the ban. One year later, the Writers' International Festival in Dublin platformed Adams's fiction to protest against state censorship.[3] Similarly, PEN and Article 19 campaigned against the ban. All this was happening while the Hume/Adams initiative was being formulated which would find a limited expression in the Downing Street Declaration.

The intolerance still encountered in the media from politicians and social commentators at any suggestion of a point of view sympathetic to republicanism is well illustrated by the reception to the news that an American Congressman, Peter King, intended to publish a novel based on the Troubles. The Ulster Unionist councillor Nelson McCausland questioned King's motives.

> I am always concerned when people are trying to make money out of the troubles in our land and this is obviously an attempt to do that.
>
> Peter King's involvement politically in the past has not been helpful and I think that it's probably the case that his literary endeavours will be similarly unhelpful.[4]

When Peter King's *Terrible Beauty* was published nine months later, it met with a mixed critical reception.[5] Malachy McCourt's verdict was that King had performed 'an extraordinary literary feat' in entering the mind of the novel's IRA hero; and in the celebrated columnist Jimmy Breslin's opinion, the novel was 'a beautiful piece of writing'. Despite these laudatory reviews of a first novel, *Kirkus Reviews* described *Terrible Beauty* in the following terms: 'an unfortunate excursion into the politics of Ireland', and 'a piece of IRA agitprop that Brendan Behan himself wouldn't be able to read with a straight face'.[6] The review opined that 'if King is looking for a photo-op with Gerry Adams, he's earned it'.

Returning to the question of censorship, according to Harold Clarke, who for more than forty years was a leading figure in the Irish book trade, at least in regard to Ireland censorship is today less of a problem.

> The Censorship Board still exists, but there really is a change of climate. There is still an occasional book ban, just a token banning, perhaps half a dozen books in the past year.

But Clarke raises a connected concern.

> Now, however, that form of censorship has been replaced by the problem of defamation, in connection with the Northern Ireland troubles in particular, when they existed. When names were named we had to be terribly careful because if someone reckons they have been defamed they can take action against the author, the publisher, the printer, the distributor, any of those, as they can in Britain. And in a lot of cases, particularly with small Irish publishers, Easons would be a much better target than the publisher.[7]

In Chapter Four, you may recall, I mentioned how the Linen Hall Library, Belfast, had to restrict access to a novel, Peter Driscoll's *In Connection with Kilshaw*, due to an injunction taken out by a leading politician incensed at its supposedly libellous characterisation of himself.

And if Easons is susceptible to the type of pressures referred to by Clarke, then the larger British distributors like W.H. Smith and Menzies can also be expected to be wary of handling potentially litigious prose material regarding the conflict.

Broadly supportive of Clarke's opinion, in an interview about censorship in Ireland Edna O'Brien claims that today 'not as many books are now banned'.[8] However, O'Brien qualifies this: 'we have to take into account the prevailing social climate. Banning is only the tip of the iceberg. Keeping our psyches closed is the main bogey'.[9] Terry Eagleton would appear to concur with O'Brien's suggestion that self-censorship is insidious. Eagleton argues that 'to be an acceptable author at all in a certain society may mean writing from a certain "position"'.[10]

A culture of censorship? The wariness of publishers and distributors to fall foul of libel laws? Overt censorship seems a less likely resort when these other factors may so successfully manage or manufacture consent at the social level.

The author Salmon Rushdie argues that 'literature is the art least subject to external control, because it is made in private… The more money a piece of work costs, the easier it is to control it'.[11] He is employing a relativist argument: Hollywood, for example, clearly does impose a different order of creative straitjacketing, as evidenced in the multi-billion dollar film industry's often narrow imperatives. Rushdie's view, however, while expressing a truism is too complacent about the susceptibility of fiction to external pressure. The novel is also a product, after all, which is publishable, marketable, packageable, and distributable – a whole value-adding process prey to market forces and the pulls of a commercial environment. Once the personal hurdle of self-censorship has been negotiated, these later *public* stages may subject the product to manipulation, not only in the commercial aspects but also at the levels of fictional content and form. John Sutherland argues 'that the cost of producing a novel will ultimately condition the kind of fiction which is produced'.[12] Sutherland also writes of the commercial pressures on publishers.

> First novels are riskier than those by established, brand-name authors. Other 'rare events' cynics would say, are the selection of overtly high brow novels, novels with genuinely contentious political themes or any work which may be feared to disturb the somnambulistic reading preferences of the mass reading public.[13]

The evidence, as such, for direct interference in the realm of prose fiction is anecdotal, amounting to opinion and suspicion among a few writers and critics of a reluctance among publishers and the book trade to deal with works they might judge politically contentious.

Perhaps Sean P. Murphy's *Foreign Chains* might well be deemed politically contentious. Murphy, who died in 2000, was a former republican prisoner. He was quoted in the *Andersonstown News* as saying that he experienced difficulty in getting the novel published because of its republican line.

> 'I was determined to publish the book in Ireland where I would have maximum control over its content,' explained Sean. 'Sometimes when a book leaves your hand, it comes back somewhat different from when it left you. I didn't want that to happen to *Foreign Chains*' [...]a string of Northern printing houses found the material too hot to handle. 'No less than six firms in the North refused to publish the book but we finally found a publisher in Dublin,' explains Sean.[14]

In private correspondence the author claimed that initially December Press agreed to publish the novel but because of Canary Wharf 'publishing stopped... as the job was ready for the presses' – a clear illustration of how a particularly sensitive political moment can impact on publishing decisions. Aware of the importance of providing alternative perspectives on the conflict, Murphy finally had to resort to vanity publishing. He was put in touch with John Wood publishers, Tallaght, Dublin who agreed to publish 'though they made it known that their name should not appear on the book. Printed in Ireland had to suffice'.[15]

How though might a publisher be vulnerable to pressure? Through fear of losing a lucrative contract? Of market sensitivity to political developments? Financial restraints? Banks exerting pressure? Is it conceivable that other writers may be uncomfortable because of the association with a controversial author in the same publishing stable? Through pressure via old-boy cronyism on top management? All speculation, some of it pretty wild. Without the corroboration of people in the publishing industry, it is virtually impossible to substantiate claims of instances of pressure being exerted to prevent the publication or stymie the sales or impact of some fiction. Who is going to admit having succumbed to pressure?

The writer and journalist Peter Berresford Ellis can speak about these matters with considerable authority. Early in his career he worked on a weekly magazine dealing with book publishing, and has long taken an interest in popular fiction as a medium of propaganda. He has written over seventy books, the best known of which is perhaps *The History of the Irish Working Class*, although the majority of his works are popular fiction. Interviewed on my behalf, he gave personal testimony of the type of pressure alluded to above in regard to his historical novel *The Rising of the Moon*.[16]

> I had a very good editor at Methuen, who I told the story line of *The Rising of the Moon* to, who thought it was a good tale… But the fact was, it was an historical story based on the Irish Republican Brotherhood's attempted invasion of Canada in 1866, which resulted in the creation of the Dominion of Canada, because prior to that it was independent colonies. And the one factor that created a united Canada was in fact a reaction to the IRB's invasion. So, it was important from an American viewpoint because the IRB were all veterans of the American Civil War. There was an American Civil War input into this. It was important from a British viewpoint because it was the one act where the United States were able to put pressure on Britain to extract reparation for Britain's siding with the Confederacy during the Civil War. Had it not been for this action the government of President Johnson as it was then would not have been able to [have]applied blackmail. *They would have sat back and let the Fenian army cross into Canada and form their bases, and let Britain get on with it* [my italics]. As it was Britain paid the money to the US government. As soon as that was promised the American army stopped the main invasion. So, it was a very exciting and powerful story. It was commissioned by that editor. I duly delivered the book, and as I said, it was published.[17]

The contents described, particularly the claim of an initial American tolerance of the Fenian venture in Canada, might be judged embarrassing still to Britain's interests, and especially to its much vaunted 'special relationship' with the USA. Furthermore, the largely forgotten episode of Britain's 'siding with the Confederacy' may also have caused some discomfort should a wider knowledge of it penetrate the American public's consciousness.

Berresford Ellis recounts how soon after the novel's auspicious promotional start things began to go wrong.

> There were printing problems. There were distribution problems. There were promotional problems. I would arrive somewhere to give readings

from the book and the shop would not have got copies of the book for me to sign. And all this built up over quite a long period and it went on, carried on from the hardback into the paperback, and in the end I was resorting to actually taking books round physically myself to readings so that people wouldn't be disappointed. The Irish Book Fair here in London, where there was supposed to be a big launch when the hardback came out was sent three copies, and there were about 150/200 people listening to me reading and waiting to get copies for me to sign, and I didn't have any copies. This, obviously, reading between the lines, was a problem somewhere. To say that this was merely inefficiency on behalf of the publishers, who were one of the major publishers, is I think being a bit disingenuous about the situation. So, I think this is one example where a book that is not liked in certain quarters, and I think the quarters were within the distributors and the publishers themselves, because what the commissioning editor likes the directors will throw out the next day. But they'd spent a bit of money on this book so probably they didn't like to do it that way. They liked to get their money back [and]… fulfil the sales potential that there obviously was there. Certainly, it disappeared quite rapidly. It did go on the Irish bestseller list for six weeks or more, whereupon it went out of print. And I would have thought because it was on the bestseller list there would have been a demand for a reprint. At least that's what I thought but I was told that no, there would be no reprint. So, maybe that is an example, but I can't give that as evidence that would stand up in a court of law. But it's just one of the things I've encountered in my career.[18]

Derek Parker, editor of *The Author*, published quarterly by The Society of Authors, concedes that it 'is of course possible' that there may be a reluctance among publishers and the book trade to deal with novels that are judged politically contentious. However, he finds 'it difficult to suppose that any publisher receiving the MS of a really brilliant republican or pro-IRA novel… would hesitate for a moment to publish it – they are far too eager to make money for that!'[19]

Parker makes a compelling point, though he does concede the possibility that such reluctance exists on the part of the industry. Berresford Ellis recounts Alan Titley's experience in this regard. Titley, a broadcaster and critic, is regarded as one of Ireland's finest writers, in English and Gaelic. Berresford Ellis relates that Titley sent him a copy of an unpublished novel, *The Scarlet Mushroom*.

I thought it was extremely good. It pursued a line which I had argued for quite a while, that in the early part of the Troubles there would not have been a problem in disengagement from the six counties by certain elements of the British political establishment had the Republic signed up to NATO. And this was one of the bases of Titley's theme. In fact, I've been aware of this idea in mainstream British political thinking way back. If you go back to 1969 when the Monday Club published a pamphlet which was headed – the title was *Ireland: Britain's Cuba*. And in fact as late as 1974 I had a radio debate with a guy called Utley who'd stood as a unionist prospective parliamentary candidate in Down. He was then Deputy Editor of the *Daily Telegraph* and, of course, he was a member of the Monday Club, and he wrote all the *Telegraph* leaders on Ireland and Irish politics, you see. And in the hospitality room after toe to toe ding-dong debate, etc, he actually confirmed this attitude to me that that was still going on in '84. Of course, this was, what, five, six years before the Cold War ceased to be, and the Soviet Union started to crumble. But these people really did think of Ireland strategically, and Utley said to me that there was no way […]the British political establishment could allow a neutral country on the western flank of this country in those circumstances. Titley took this up, but of course it was not a popular line and certain people would have tore their hair out rather than admit it. *The Scarlet Mushroom* was a very well written thriller. […]So despite the merits of the book as I said, I think British publishers immediately had their hackles up, that this novel was proposing this idea, and in the end of the novel a withdrawal is negotiated based on this fact.[20]

Berresford Ellis showed Titley's manuscript to 'one or two' editors who confirmed that its contents were problematic. Publishers

are not happy in taking on board thrillers set against the current conflict in the North that take lines opposed to the popular British political notion of what is going on, or was going on, maybe I should say, in the North.[21]

Berresford Ellis's testimony in relation to *The Rising of the Moon* and Alan Titley's unpublished novel may concern exceptional instances of pressure. In both cases, a respected author has written a novel whose subject might be construed as potentially embarrassing to a section of the British establishment. The literary quality of each would seem beyond doubt. But what of those more mundane, less than brilliant manuscripts that land unsolicited in the fiction editor's in-tray? This is a consideration that hardly seems to have put in doubt the prospects of publication of some of the worst anti-republican novels, many of which appear devoid of literary merit. It is difficult to imagine that worse than Chapman Pincher's *The Eye of the Tornado* was ever more deserving of a rejection slip.

On balance, it seems that the pressures on writers, publishers and booksellers are far subtler than any semblance of external interference can explain and are a matter of cultural and political environment rather than process. This is a view shared by the Irish publisher Steve MacDonogh, who does not see direct censorship as the problem.

In general, I would say that the greatest difficulties tend not to be associated with acts of censorship or prohibition but to do with the context of the ownership and character of publishing companies and the book trade, which have tended to regard oppositional voices as lying outside the pale.[22]

MacDonogh's view tallies with Peter Berresford Ellis's that the core of the problem lies with the book industry. Berresford Ellis points to the near-monopolistic sway of the big distributors, W.H. Smith in England, Menzies in Scotland, and Easons, an offshoot of W.H. Smith, in Ireland.

> Unless you can get a book accepted by the central book buyers of those three firms you do not get a good distribution. There were attempts in the late 1960s/1970s to set up an alternative mass distribution, which didn't last long. There was one particular firm that lasted for several years but then were taken over by W.H. Smith.[23]

He argues that this commercial advantage has an effect on what is published; and to add to an already complex picture, the powerful role of the book distributors is power that may only appear or be presented as the play of mere commercial forces.

> So distribution was were you had your immediate hang-up... publishers realised that unless they could convince W.H. Smith, John Menzies, Easons, they were not going to really get a distribution within – I'll use the geographic term – the British Isles. So, you didn't have to rely on centralised censorship, you had to rely on the fact that publishers were aware of that distribution problem, and they knew that if they couldn't get the book bought by those central book buyers then it was commercially unviable and the commercial unviability of the book just led to a commercial decision. So it was not as straightforward as publishers dealing with contentious political matter. [...]The thing about the UK generally is that heaven forbid you don't have censorship overtly but there are all these minor cogs and wheels going on, where you have a covert censorship which is far more insidious and you can't put your finger on and say this is happening because so much of it is by attitude rather than a written censorship set of rules.[24]

Berresford Ellis also points to the educationally and culturally privileged backgrounds of many people in the publishing and book-marketing world.

> There is no banned list. It just depends on people from the same cultural background, the same educational background. You find still in this so-called egalitarian society that everyone who has a say came in the Fifties. You still find the major jobs taken by people from English public schools, and they share political, cultural attitudes, where anything radical, certainly in Irish terms, would never surface through the system of checks and balances that have been put in place through, not just publishing but as I say, the distribution world, because anyone can set up a publishing company. The problem is how do you then distribute it.[25]

It is arguable that a similar exclusivity in the shared cultural background and common assumptions of many of the authors of Troubles fiction may provide at least a partial explanation for some of the biases to be found. Authors, by and large, are middle-class and share an individualistic outlook, and are therefore relatively disinclined to empathise with political movements or any collective actions. Inherently, collective actions demand a group commitment and the subsuming of ego for the common cause. Ronan Bennett, referring specifically to Irish writers, has commented that 'art, if it is to be worth anything, should be in tension with norms and given wisdom… Writers, by and large, do not get involved'.[26] This is a view endorsed by Dermot Healy.

> 'Novelists are hugely traditional and conservative,' he continues. 'They may fight against what other writers are doing and against stylistic limitations, but they are rarely revolutionary in a social or political sense. The novelist is removed from the world because of the amount of time spent in the construction of the work. You rely on books to pick up on the contemporary world.'[27]

Both authors have produced novels that have dealt earnestly with Troubles' themes, challenging received views. Artistic detachment versus political engagement is the dilemma at the heart of Ronan Bennett's novel *The Catastrophist* (1998), the former expressed by James Gillespie, the novel's hero.

> I was always too much the watcher, too much l'homme-plume; I was divided, unbelieving. My preference is the writer's preference, for the margins, for the avoidance of agglomerations and ranks.[28]

Gillespie's lover, Ines Sabiani, a political activist and idealist, upbraids him for his comfortable, middle class background and outlook.

> Few people have this privilege. When you are on history's losing side, when you are poor and cursed to eat bread, to accept your enemy's point of view is to accept starvation and slavery.[29]

To judge by the numbers of journalists and teachers who have written Troubles fiction (and indeed most fiction generally), writing is a largely middle class pursuit. The Troubles are rarely experienced directly by these writers. The commitment required for membership of the republican movement is foreign to their experience. The movement is comprised overwhelmingly of working class volunteers. Writers often tend to take the stance that volunteers are misguided in a similar way that young men are often portrayed as the cannon fodder of history, a theme, it may be recalled, in Martin Dillon's *The Serpent's Tail*. The republican experience is somehow a devalued, inauthentic experience to which the condescending attitudes of many writers can never fully relate to or empathise with. This is perhaps to be understood as more of a cultural failure than any shortcoming of the imagination. And the greatest shortcoming is the omission of the authentic experience of Irish republicanism. The critic Hugh Kenner has remarked that 'Joyce obeyed a principle Hemingway later enunciated, that a writer's omissions will show only when he omits things because he doesn't know them'.

However, the problem with this approach to an understanding of the marked bias of the genre is that it doesn't account for those authors from a similarly middle class background whose work does in fact attempt inclusion – work that does not exclude, whether wittingly or through ignorance, the republican perspective.

Healy, above, referred to the writer's reliance 'on books to pick up on the contemporary world'. The potential limitations of this reliance are more insidiously harmful than a merely solipsistic removal from events. In the planning stage of a work of fiction the points of reference consulted by the novelist will contribute to the shape of the outcome. An author may, for example, research a novel via the cuttings' files of national and daily newspapers. Bearing in mind the wide perception of media bias, in this way an earlier distortion of events may be further filtered through a jaundiced lens. What appears in print is filed and collated, and to the unwary and partisan writer alike gains the status of documentary evidence or historical source material, no matter how remote the veracity of that material might be from the events reported.

All of the above arguments and approaches fall short of producing a singularly coherent and comprehensive explanation of the hows and whys of the extensive misrepresentation of Irish republicanism evident in much of the relevant fictional output. Empirical evidence there is, offering circumstantial testimony but not of sufficient force to seal a debate or reach a sustainable verdict. If factors such as censorship in its various guises, or the class alignment and disposition typical of many if not the majority of authors, amount to insufficient proof, then from what approach or basis do we assemble a case to either explain the bias or make comprehensible the gathered evidence?

As I have argued from the outset, the demonstrable bias of the genre towards the British discourse on the conflict is best explainable by current poststructuralist literary criticism. The ideas of Gramsci and later interpretations and applications of these are formative. From this body of thought, Troubles fiction demonstrates the paramountcy of one discursive position. Other discourses are at play, and the dominant one has been increasingly under challenge since the early 1980s.

Edna O'Brien, you will recall, suggested that the 'prevailing social climate' rather than direct censorship, was responsible for the insidious pressures upon authors to conform in their writing to the dominant discourse.[30] The process of the play of power at the level of discourse is where the bias of a given discursive position becomes clearer. To paraphrase Marx, the ideas of the ruling classes are also the dominant ideas in society. Gramsci, taking this idea further, understood that the complex social, political, economic and cultural organisation definitive of modern society, the myriad social exchanges necessary for its functioning, requires the consent of its citizens, not their coercion. Consent is manufactured. Every discourse has its agenda. Discourses are in contention: the goal is hegemony.

I also discussed in Chapter One how ideology, that is, 'meaning in the service of power', is an accumulative effect within discourses and how fiction, through the process of interpellation, reinforces dominant values and meanings to achieve a wider societal acceptance. Fiction is a secondary means of achieving hegemony, secondary or supportive to those other hegemonic apparatuses such as the education system, the church, the family, etc. However, fiction shouldn't be underestimated for its power to further the acceptance of a particular point of view as natural or commonsensical. While one text is hardly likely to irrevocably affix its authority and convert the reader to its common sense, certain novels have been powerful in shaping public perceptions about republicans: for example, Seymour's *Harry's Game* or Clancy's *Patriot Games*. Of more significance, though, is the extent that a genre as a whole can contribute to the wider diffusion of its underlying dominant discourse, and thus help to reinforce or promote a tendentious and, in many instances, perhaps erroneous view of political realities.

I am not arguing that a text or even a corpus of works will determine what a reader thinks in some crude brainwashing process. Again, the effect of ideology is accumulative, and we should never lose sight of the human agency factor. I am saying that the preponderance of one discursive position illustrates the social, cultural, economic, commercial and political power behind that position. There is a battle of discourses being waged: the prize is the subjectivity of the individual. Wider cultural imperatives are acting independently and collusively to shape perceptions. We should also recognise the role of the reader, what the reader as an interpreting agent brings to the reading because of his or her discursive engagement with the text. It is precisely because the reader brings his/her own agency to the reading experience that the interpellant power of the text (therefore bias) can be withstood.

I referred also in Chapter One to how subjectivity is 'neither unified or fixed' and of how in moments of heightened social tension conflicts of interest are exposed. This incurs a process of questioning that produces 'conflicting subject positions for the individuals involved'.[31] This understanding again foregrounds the role of human agency. A crisis of hegemony, when the reigning discourse comes under increasing and effective cultural attack, is manifested in more adventurous, radical, questioning Troubles fiction. The weakening of the hitherto dominant discourse is reflected in a more questioning readership which in turn loops causatively back into the publishing and distributive fields where largely commercial concerns and decisions can be expected to correspond to changing public perceptions. This situation pertained after the hunger strike when the previous dominance of the British position that republicans were criminals came under increasing challenge; by the late 1980s Britain began to be seen for the first time internationally as a protagonist and not a neutral party as promulgated in the official discourse.

Throughout this survey I have eschewed consideration of the literary worth or otherwise of the genre. However, I would say that the significance of popular, as opposed to literary fiction (or between 'readerly' and 'writerly' texts in Barthes' distinction) is that because the former reaches a larger readership, potentially it is more important in the role of interpellation. There is a greater tendency for popular fiction to reflect and promote dominant values. Literary fiction, on the other hand, displays more evidence of counter-hegemonic questioning of those values. Quite why this should be so is open to question, but I would hazard two factors that are worth further consideration. Firstly, a writer who bothers to explore new language, new forms and modes, and to explain some aspect of the world through their use, is more likely to be conscious of the need to challenge received ways of understanding. Secondly, by defamiliarising some aspect of reality, it can bring it into sharper focus or reveal hitherto hidden aspects. These are especially pertinent considerations in regard to the increase in literary Troubles fiction since the late 1980, an output that marks an increased discursive tension, although this isn't to claim that formally radical fiction is also politically radical.

However, Francis Stuart seems to discount the effectiveness of consciously literary fiction to impact politically. He suggests in his novel *Memorial* that there is a correspondence between 'mediocre' writing and an asphyxiating imperative to uphold societal norms.

> On this island we have a host of writers, good, bad and mediocre. The few good ones and the large number of bad ones have their uselessness to a utilitarian, consumer society in common. It's the middle lot, the medium number, who compromise with this society by writing commentaries on it, creating people who fit its ideas of what fictional characters should be: close relations of those in works already safely established as literature.[32]

Stuart implies that 'good' novels, that is, from those writers who do not compromise in their scrutiny of received values, are less of a threat to society than 'the medium number' because the latter are more prone to be consumed by the broad reading mass. And 'bad' novels are open to ridicule and easily dismissible, countering their 'propaganda' value. Society, it is suggested, can tolerate dissent so long as it is contained within set limits, that is, largely confined to an educated, mostly professional and highbrow readership. In this reckoning, a radical, questioning, subversive popular fiction would soon fall subject to pressure. There is evidence of this in regard to the banning of playing certain pop records by the BBC. The banning of a song as seemingly innocuous as Lennon and MacCartney's 'Give Ireland Back to the Irish' is one example, perhaps only explicable because of the fear engendered within the broadcasting establishment that such an idea might take hold among the hundreds of thousands of young people who not only buy records but tune in to Radio One and watch 'Top of the Pops'. By extrapolation, overt censorship of fiction might only arise as an option to counter the popularisation of subversive, counter-hegemonic ideas. Imagine the reception of a Jack Higgins novel that popularised in no uncertain terms the demand for British withdrawal.

While not wishing to overstate the case, I think Stuart actually underestimates the power of popular fiction to influence popular perceptions. The battle of discourses that has been waged within the genre, which is in turn a facet of the bigger discursive struggle for hearts and minds being fought out at the media front, has been ongoing for thirty years. Only as the republican movement successfully challenged containment and exclusion, and in so doing brought its discourse of inclusion and peace with justice to the fore, did the genre open up to oppositional discourses. It is extremely difficult to gauge what effect this bourgeoning discursive glasnost, particularly evident since the late-1980s, has had on the bigger sociocultural sphere.

There is also an increase in references to the Troubles in mainstream fiction – not the thriller genre per se – which is perhaps symptomatic of two trends. Firstly, because of the peace process, the issue has been projected to the foreground of public consciousness; a climate exists for a more informative narrative treatment. Much of the taboo of the genre as slight or shallow has evaporated. The theme is more likely to be touched upon in mainstream fiction, perhaps as a subplot or even as a bare reference. This development is particularly evident in the figures for 1998, when some fourteen category (d) novels were published, a record figure. Secondly, the changing context has undermined many of the presumptions and conventions on which the genre was previously predicated. What is marked by the study is that reality and representation are mostly out of alignment until the late 1980s and early 1990s, when there is an evident convergence in many examples.

The last thirty years of struggle cannot be ignored. A long period of reflection is perhaps needed in which some sense of that period gains ground in our collective sense of who we are. Fiction can facilitate this process of reaching a mental accommodation with our recent history. Equally, the struggle should not be avoided as a subject of literary attention and engagement. Within the varied contents of the genre are many painful reminders of what we have come through to date. Also there is a massive lacuna of representation, an indefensible failure to give expression to the collective voice of grievance of Irish republicanism and of those communities disparaged and discriminated against who regard the IRA as a people's army. But the task of understanding the past is ongoing, and fiction will play its explanatory, retrospective, cathartic, healing role, hopefully with less recourse to pallid, anaemic representation and instead a resort to an accelerated stress on the integrity of each other's story.

Troubles fiction won't end with the closure of the armed struggle. The spy novel, after all, is still with us post-Cold War, though the genre has had to take on board, for the sake of credibility, the emerging New World Order. I am sure that future novels written on the Troubles theme will have to accordingly respond to the changing circumstances.[33] And these changing circumstances may demonstrate as never before the dialectical play of discourses. Joseph McMinn has speculated that 'if and when an outstanding novel does emerge, it will achieve a presently unrealized distance from the values of the media and the reductionist psychologizing of the thriller'.[34] Healy's *A Goat's Song*, written some fourteen years after McMinn's comment, is one of a number of likely contenders, and encouraging for the future of the genre. The narrative context is no longer ghettoised in Troubles fiction. Perhaps the genre in a transformed mode will contribute to the creation of a fresh, more tolerant and inclusive subjectivity. Stephen Dedalus in *Portrait of the Artist as a Young Man* declared his intention to forge in the smithy of his soul the 'uncreated conscience' of his race. Few would doubt that the task lies beyond the capacity of any single writer, any privileged discourse, any individual subject; but perhaps the first inklings, the initial resonances, will find a register in fictive form in a vanguard subjectivity, uncreated at this present interpellant juncture.

Notes

Chapter 1 – Introduction: Misrepresentation and Reality

1. Mark Lieberman, in a nevertheless favourable review of Danny Morrison's *West Belfast*, strongly advising against an extensive reading of the genre: *Fortnight*, January, 1990, p. 23.
2. Jack Higgins, *The Savage Day* (London: Collins, 1972).
3. Oscar Wilde, *The Picture of Dorian Grey*, Preface.
4. Liz Curtis, *Nothing but the same old story: The roots of anti-Irish racism* (London: Information on Ireland, 1985), p. 62.
5. Michael Foley, *The Road to Notown* (Belfast: Blackstaff, 1996), p. 26.
6. Lionel Shriver implies in her novel *Ordinary Decent Criminals* (Harper Collins, 1992) that the term originates with the Linen Hall Library's stock of fiction dealing with the conflict, part of its 'Northern Ireland Political Collection': a 'rather cheerless genre' [p. 175]. The novel also relates a bar game in which the participants give examples of locational inaccuracies in the geography of Belfast in Troubles fiction, which illustrates the cultural impact of the genre.
7. *The Oxford Companion to Irish Literature*, ed. by Robert Welch (Oxford: Clarendon Press, 1996), p. 571.
8. Frank Ormsby, 'John Morrow', *Fortnight*, 5 February 1971, p. 20.
9. D.E.S. Maxwell, '*Imagining the North: Violence and the writers*', *Eire-Ireland*, Vol. 8, No. 2 (Summer, 1973), pp. 91-107 (p. 91).
10. John Wilson Foster, *Forces and Themes in Ulster Fiction* (Dublin: Gill and Macmillan, 1974), p. 257.
11. Jerry Palmer, *Thrillers: Genesis and Structure of a Popular Genre* (London: Edward Arnold, 1978), p. 137. Palmer is critical of this definition.
12. Eve Patten, 'Fiction in conflict: Northern Ireland's prodigal novelists', in *Peripheral Visions: Images of Nationhood in Contemporary British Fiction*, ed. by I.A. Bell (Cardiff: University of Wales Press, 1995), pp. 128-148 (p. 128).
13. Deirdre Molloy, *Fortnight*, March 1996, p. 33.
14. Seymour Chatman, *Story and Discourse* (London: Cornell Univ. Press, 1978), p. 18.
15. Tom Clancy, *Patriot Games* (London: Collins, 1987).
16. Martin Waddell, *A Little Bit British* (London: Tom Stacey, 1970).
17. Dermot Healy, *A Goat's Song* (London: Harvill, 1994).
18. Edna O'Brien, *House of Splendid Isolation* (London: Weidenfeld and Nicolson, 1994).
19. Patrick McCabe, *The Dead School* (London: Picador: 1995).
20. Seamus Deane, *Reading in the Dark* (London: Jonathan Cape, 1996).
21. Shaun Hutson, *Renegades* (London: Macdonald, 1990); *White Ghost and Knife Edge* (London: Little, Brown, 1994 and 1998 respectively).
22. Frank Herbert, *The White Plague* (New York: Putnam, 1982).
23. Douglas Hurd, *Vote to Kill* (London: Collins, 1975); *The Shape of Ice* (Little, Brown, 1998).
24. Roy Bradford, *The Last Ditch* (Belfast: Blackstaff, 1981).
25. Danny Morrison, *West Belfast* (Dublin: Mercier, 1989); *The Wrong Man* (Dublin: Mercier, 1997).
26. Malcolm Bradbury, *The History Man* (London: Secker and Warburg, 1975).
27. John Montague, 'The Cry', in *Death of a Chieftain and Other Stories* (Dublin: Poolbeg, 1978, MacGibbon and Kee, 1964).
28. Anne Devlin, 'Naming the Names', in *The Way-paver* (London: Faber and Faber, 1986).
29. Gerry Adams, *The Street and Other Stories* (Dingle: Brandon, 1992).
30. For example: W.A. Ballinger, *The Green Grassy Slopes* (London: Corgi, 1969); J.G. Farrell, Troubles (London: Jonathan Cape, 1970); Thomas Kilroy, *The Big Chapel* (London: Faber and Faber, 1971); Leon Uris, *Trinity* (London: Andre Deutsch, 1976), and *Redemption* (London: Harper Collins, 1995); David Marcus, *A Land Not Theirs* (London: Bantam, 1986); Peter Berresford Ellis, *The Rising of the Moon* (London: Methuen, 1987); Thomas Flanagan, *The End of the Hunt* (London: Mandarin, 1996).
31. A copy of my doctoral thesis, entitled *'Troubles Fiction: a critical history of prose fiction dealing with the conflict in the North of Ireland since the late 1960s'*, contains a bibliography of all relevant fiction, and is obtainable from the library of the University of Ulster, Coleraine.
32. Bill Rolston and Robert Bell, *'Literature of the 'Troubles'*, is available from the Linen Hall Library, Belfast. An updated compilation is available on the internet as part of the CAIN project.

33. Collins/Harper Collins, 41; Heinemann, 20; Hamish Hamilton, 20; Robert Hale, 20; Coronet, 18; Michael Joseph, 17; Hodder & Stoughton, 18; Sphere, 16; Pan, 15; Blackstaff, 14; Fontana, 14; Secker and Warburg, 14; New English Library, 12; Jonathan Cape, 11: 250 out of a total of 480 relevant novels.

34. Joseph McMinn, 'Contemporary Novels on the 'Troubles', *Études Irlandaises*, No. 5 (December, 1980), pp. 113-21 (p. 114).

35. Tom Bradby, *Shadow Dancer* (London: Bantam Press, 1998).

36. Gavin Esler, *Loyalties* (London, Headline, 1990).

37. Among the journals examined are *The Honest Ulsterman* and *Fortnight*. I also consulted early editions of *Hibernia*. In addition, the following bibliographies were consulted: *A Biographical Dictionary of Irish Writers*, ed. by Anne Brady and Brian Cleeve, (Lilliput Press, 1985); *The Macmillan Dictionary of Irish Literature*, ed. by Robert Hogan (1980); *The Mercier Companion to Irish Literature*, ed. by Sean McMahon and Jo O'Donoghue (Mercier Press, 1998); *The Oxford Companion to Irish Literature*, ed. by Robert Welch (Oxford: Clarendon Press, 1996).

38. *States and Societies*, ed. by David Helm, *et al* (Oxford: Basil Blackwell, 1983), p. 87.

39. A Sinn Féin Education Department video, *Republican Ideology*, which emphasises the pragmatism of the movement's beliefs, lists them under the headings separatism, anti-sectarianism, secularism, feminism, and nationalism. The video stresses that sectarianism, which it is Britain's strategy to encourage, undermines the struggle; and it is mentioned that the prominence of feminism encoded in the Easter Proclamation was due to the importance of the issue and of the involvement of women in the struggle at the time.

40. *The Green Book* is reproduced in Martin Dillon's *25 Years of Terror* (London: Bantam, 1996), pp. 353-84.

41. Constitution and Rules (Sinn Féin, 1983).

42. *Ibid*.

43. Jack Holland, 'A Northern View', *Irish Echo*, 20-26 May 1998.

44. Eamon Phoenix, *Northern Nationalism: Nationalist Politics, Partition and the Catholic Minority in Northern Ireland 1890-1940* (Belfast: Ulster Historical Foundation, 1994).

45. Eamon Delaney, *The Casting of Mr O'Shaughnessy* (London: Bloomsbury, 1995), p. 4.

46. The IRA's Constitution stipulates that '[T]he Army shall be known as Óglaigh na hÉireann'.

47. 'The Provos', though originally pejoratively applied by its enemies to denote the provisional nature of the establishment of the organisation's first Executive, is my preferred term because of its subsequent widespread usage even among its own support base. 'Provies' is also a popular variant. However, I use the terms Provos, IRA and Óglaigh na hÉireann interchangeably. Many republicans, it should be noted, object to the term.

48. Tony Bennett, 'Marxism and Popular Fiction', in *The Study of Popular Fiction: A Source Book*, ed. by Bob Ashley (London: Pinter Publishers, 1989), pp. 173-83 (p. 180).

49. Quoted in Elizabeth Bouché, 'No Big Thrill', *Fortnight*, No. 312, December 1992, p.46.

50. I use the term 'transformation' in the structuralist sense of changes in the basic narrative elements within a genre, such as character types, localities, gadgetry, as discussed by Stuart Sim, 'Structuralism and post-structuralism', in *Philosophical Aesthetics: an introduction, ed. by Oswald Hanflung* (Oxford: Blackwell in association with the Open University, 1992), pp. 405-39: 'the tracing of transformations in a genre over time can be very revealing about literary and cultural development' (p. 414).

51.John B. Thompson, *Ideology and Modern Culture: Critical Social Theory in the Era of Mass Communication* (Oxford: Polity, 1990), p. 7.

52. Claud Cockburn, *Bestseller: The Books that Everyone Read* (London: Sidgwick and Jackson,1972), p. 13.

53. John Sutherland, *Bestsellers: Popular fiction of the 1970s* (London: Routledge and Kegan Paul, 1981).

54. Bruce Merry, *Anatomy of the Spy Thriller* (Dublin: Gill and Macmillan, 1977).

55. Christopher Pawling, 'Introduction', *Popular Fiction and Social Change*, ed. by Christopher Pawling (London: Macmillan Press, 1984), p. 4.

56. For an interesting new approach to the field, evident from the title, see Fay Geary and John Morison, 'An illustration of the literary approach to the study of law: the 'mysteries' novels of the nineteenth century and the 'Troubles thriller'', in *One Hundred and Fifty Years of Irish Law*, ed. by N. Dawson, D. Greer and P. Ingram (1996), 105-123.

57. Foley, p. 284.

58. Alan Titley, 'Rough Rug-headed Kerns: The Irish Gunman in the Popular Novel', *Eire-Ireland*, Vol. 15, No. 4 (Winter, 1980), pp. 15-38 (p. 18).

59. J. Bowyer Bell, 'The Troubles as Trash: Shadows of the Irish gunman on an American curtain', *Hibernia*, 22 January, 1978, p. 22.

60. Pawling (1984): in his 'Introduction', Pawling uses the term 'paraliterature' to mean that popular fiction is the 'other' by which the canon, the proper concern of scholarly attention, is evaluated.

61. Kevin Boyle, Tom Hadden and Paddy Hillyard, *Ten Years On in Northern Ireland* (London: The Cobden Trust, 1980).

62. Tim Pat Coogan, *The Troubles* (London: Arrow Books, 1996), p. 248.

63. J. Bowyer Bell (1978).

64. Henry Nash Smith, *Virgin Land: The American West in Symbol and Myth* (Harvard University Press, 1971), chapters 9 and 10.

65. John Sutherland, 'Bounty Hunter', *London Review of Books*, 17 July 1997, pp. 26-7 (p. 27).

66. *'I' is not for Indian: The portrayal of Native Americans in books for young people* (Program of the ALA/OLOS Subcommittee for Library Services to American Indian People, American Indian Library Association, Atlanta, 29 June 1991), compiled by Naomi Caldwell-Wood and Lisa A. Mitten, p. 9.

67. Jerome Rothenberg, 'American Indian Poetry and the 'Other Traditions', in *The New Pelican Guide to English Literature: Vol.9: American Literature* (Penguin, 1988), pp. 583-94 (pp. 584-85).

68. Noam Chomsky relates that of an estimated original population of 12 to 15 million at the time of Columbus's arrival, only 200,000 Native [North] Americans were left by the mid-19th century: 'The Manufacture of Consent', in *The Chomsky Reader*, ed. by James Peck (London: Serpent's Tail, 1988), pp. 121-2.

69. Fanon, p. 93.
70. John B. Thompson (1990), p. 7.
71. Sutherland (1981), p. 34.
72. Stephen King, *Danse Macabre* (London: Macdonald, 1981), p. 18.
73. Scott McCracken, *Pulp: Reading Popular Fiction* (Manchester University Press, 1998), p. 164.
74. Raymond Williams first used the term 'cultural materialism' in the 1980s to mean the analysis of culture as, to quote Terry Eagleton, 'a material formation, complete with its own modes of production, power-effects, social relations, identifiable audiences, historically conditioned thought-forms': *Literary Theory: An Introduction, 2nd edn* (Oxford: Blackwell, 1996), p. 198.
75. Terry Eagleton, *Ideology: An Introduction* (London and New York: Verso, 1991), p. 194.
76. Ferdinand de Saussure, 'Course in general linguistics', reproduced in *Art: Context and Value* (Open University, 1992), ed. by Stuart Sim, pp. 366-377.
77. Chris Weedon, *Feminist Practice and Poststructuralist Theory* (Oxford: Blackwell, 1987), p. 30.
78. Ashley, p. 137.
79. *Ibid.*, p. 137.
80. English Studies Group, University of Birmingham, 'Recent Developments in English Studies at the Centre', in *The Study of Popular Fiction: A Source Book*, ed. by Bob Ashley (London: Pinter Publishers, 1989), pp. 145-47 (p. 145).
81. Bob Ashley, in *The Study of Popular Fiction: A Source Book*, ed. by Bob Ashley (London: Pinter Publishers, 1989), p. 138.
82. Gramsci defined 'common sense' in these terms: 'Stone Age elements and principles of a more advanced science, prejudices from all past phases of history at the local level and intuitions of a future philosophy which will be that of a human race united the world over': *Selections from the Prison Notebooks of Antonio Gramsci*, ed. by Quintin Hoare and Geoffrey Nowell-Smith (London: Lawrence and Wishart, 1971), p. 324.
83. Weedon, p. 23.
84. *Ibid.*, p. 41.
85. Seamus Deane, 'The Writer and the Troubles', *Threshold*, No. 25, Summer, 1974, pp. 13-17 (p. 13).
86. Eagleton, p. 196.
87. Lionel Shriver, *Ordinary Decent Criminals* (London: Harper Collins, 1992; originally published as *The Bleeding Heart*, New York: Strauss & Giroux, 1990), p.98.
88. Joe Cleary, ' "Fork-Tongued on the Border Bit": Partition and the Politics of Form in Contemporary Narratives of the Northern Irish Conflict', *South Atlantic Quarterly*, Vol. 95, No.1 (Winter 1996), pp. 227-276 (pp. 231-2).
89. In the 1950s, Daniel Bell used the term 'end of ideology' to mean the exhaustion of political ideas; the term was reminted post-1989 to assert that the collapse of the Soviet Union and the emergence of the New World Order signal that liberal democracy has won the battle of political discourses and that there are no longer any other contending big ideas.
90. Eagleton, p. 112.
91. Michael Farrell, *Northern Ireland: The Orange State* (London: Pluto Press, 1976), pp. 94/5.
92. Jack Holland, *The American Connection* (Dublin: Poolbeg, 1987), p. 230.
93. T.W. Crusias, *Discourse: a critique and synthesis of major theories* (New York: Modern Language Association, 1992), p. 121.
94. Tony Bennett, 'Marxism and Popular Fiction', in *The Study of Popular Fiction: A Source Book*, ed. by Bob Ashley (London: Pinter Publishers, 1989), pp. 173-183 (p. 179).
95. Weedon, p. 21.
96. Whelan, Kevin, *The Tree of Liberty* (Cork University Press, 1996), p. 133.

Chapter 2 - A Morbid State: 1960-69

1. Eamon Phoenix, *Northern Nationalism: Nationalist Politics, Partition and the Catholic Minority in Northern Ireland, 1890-1940* (Belfast: Ulster Historical Foundation, 1994), pp. 5-6.
2. Michael Farrell, *Northern Ireland: The Orange State* (London: Pluto, 1980), pp. 85/6.
3. Tim Pat Coogan, *The IRA* (Glasgow: Fontana, 1980), p. 420.
4. Bob Purdie, 'Was the Civil Rights Movement a Republican/Communist Conspiracy?', *Irish Political Studies* 3 (1988), pp. 33-41 (p. 33).
5. Eamon McCann, 'The British press and Northern Ireland', in *The manufacture of news*, ed. by Stanley Cohen and Jock Young (London: Constable, 1973), pp. 242-61 (p. 242).
6. *Ibid.*, pp. 242-3.
7. John Cronin, 'Ulster's Alarming Novels', in *Eire-Ireland*, Vol. 4, No. 4 (1969), pp. 27-34 (p. 27).
8. Michael Longley, 'Introduction', *Causeway: The Arts in Ulster*, ed. by Michael Longley (Gill and Macmillan, 1971), pp. 7-9 (pp. 8-9).
9. John Sutherland, *Fiction and the Fiction Industry* (Athlone Press, 1978), p. 208.
10. Among the relevant titles not surveyed are Janet McNeill's *As Strangers Here* (1960), about a Presbyterian clergyman's refusal to indulge his congregation's wish for ritual denunciations after a terrorist bombing during the Border Campaign; Brian Cleeve's *Vote X for Treason* (1964) and *Dark Blood, Dark Terror* (1966), both featuring Sean Ryan, former IRA man turned British agent; Terence De Vere White's *Tara*, (1967); W.A. Ballinger's *The Green Grassy Slopes* (1969), which tracks the rise during the 1930s of a Protestant zealot, a proto-Paisley; and Brian Friel's short story, 'Johnny and Mick' (1962), described as a 'pertinent short story' by James MacKillop in his essay 'Ulster Violence in Fiction' in *Conflict in Ireland*, ed. by E. Sullivan and others (Gainesville: Florida University Press, 1976), pp. 130-52 (p. 133).
11. David Lodge, *The British Museum is Falling Down* (Penguin, 1983 (1965)).
12. Liam O'Flaherty, *The Informer* (Sceptre), p. 73.
13. *Ibid.*, p. 99.

14. *Ibid.*, p. 8.
15. Peter Berresford Ellis, 'Shamrock in the Sky', *The Irish Democrat*, November 1987, p. 2.
16. Harry Patterson, *Cry of the Hunter* (London: Arrow, 1979 (1960)).
17. John Sutherland, *Bestsellers: Popular fiction of the 1970s* (Routledge and Kegan Paul, 1981), p. 147. Also see Mandy Hicken and Ray Prytherch, *Now Read on... a guide to contemporary popular fiction* (Gower, 1990), p. 7.
18. Ciaran Carty, 'Poor wee boy, indeed', *Sunday Tribune*, 11 June 1995.
19. Sutherland (1981), p. 16.
20. Sutherland (1978), p. 97.
21. *Ibid.*, p. 16.
22. Patterson, p. 12.
23. *Ibid.*, p. 16.
24. *Ibid.*, p. 19.
25. *Ibid.*, p. 19.
26. Jack Higgins, *A Prayer for the Dying* (London, Collins, 1973).
27. John Broderick, *The Fugitives* (London: Weidenfeld and Nicolson, 1962).
28. Is it coincidental that the leading character in both novels discussed is called Fallon? In *A Prayer for the Dying*, Jack Higgins reveals that Fallon means 'stranger from outside the campfire' in Irish, [p. 40].
29. Broderick, pp. 194-5.
30. *Ibid.*, p. 198.
31. The manner of the representation of Ward's sexuality in the novel contradicts Broderick's own homosexuality. Brighid McLaughlin writes that Broderick, 'despite writing about sodomy in his fiction [though not in The Fugitives], ... had never articulated his own sexuality': 'The lonely torment of John Broderick', in the 'Sunday Life' supplement, *Sunday Independent*, 29 March 1998, p. 6.
32. John Montague, *Death of a Chieftain and Other Stories* (Dublin: Poolbeg Press, 1978 (1964)).
33. *Ibid.*, p. 58.
34. *Ibid.*, p. 64.
35. *Ibid.*, p. 82.
36. *Ibid.*, p. 83.
37. Maurice Leitch, *The Liberty Lad* (Belfast: Blackstaff, 1985 (1965)).
38. *Ibid.*, p. 50.
39. *Ibid.*, p. 135.
40. *Ibid.*, p. 136.
41. The same fate befell Leitch's second novel *Poor Lazarus* (London: MacGibbon and Kee, 1969): *Banned in Ireland: Censorship and the Irish Writer*, ed. for Article 19 by Julia Carson (Routledge, 1990), p. 97.
42. Leitch (1965), p. 112.
43. John Wilson Foster, *Forces and Themes in Ulster Fiction* (Dublin: Gill and Macmillan, 1974).
44. Julia Carson (1990), p. 105.
45. *Ibid.*, p. 106.
46. John Cronin (1971), p. 78.
47. David Lodge, *The British Museum is Falling Down* , p. 29.
48. Jack Higgins, *The Violent Enemy* (London, Collins, 1981).
49. Carty, *op.cit.*
50. Higgins, p. 8.
51. *Ibid.*, p. 9.
52. *Ibid.*, p. 18.
53. *Ibid.*, pp. 83/4.
54. Maurice Leitch, *Poor Lazarus* (Belfast: Blackstaff, 1985 (1969)).
55. *Ibid.*, p. 10.
56. *Ibid.*, p. 55.
57. *Ibid.*, p. 188.
58. *The Concise Oxford Companion to English Literature*, ed. by Margaret Drabble and Jenny Stringer (Oxford: OUP, 1990), p. 339.
59. David Lloyd, *Anomalous States: Irish Writing and the Post-Colonial Moment* (Lilliput, 1993), p. 89.

Chapter 3 - Old Men's Lies: 1970 - 72

1. Quoted by Martin Fallon, a disgruntled former IRA man in Jack Higgins's *A Prayer for the Dying* (1973), p. 132.
2. Michael Longley, 'Introduction', *Causeway: The Arts in Ulster*, ed. by Michael Longley (Dublin: Gill and Macmillan), pp. 7-9 (p. 9).
3. John Cronin, 'Prose', *Causeway: The Arts in Ulster*, ed. by Michael Longley (Dublin: Gill and Macmillan, 1971), pp. 71-82 (p. 82).
4. Eavan Boland, 'The Northern writers' crisis of conscience. 3: Creativity', *Irish Times*, 14 August 1970.
5. Longley (1971), p. 8.
6. Michael Farrell, *Northern Ireland: The Orange State* (London: Pluto, 1980), p. 263.
7. May McCann, a Queen's University Belfast lecturer who has written extensively about folk music and politics, gave a series of lectures in the H-Blocks between 10-12 September 1996 on republican ballads.
8. What Raymond Williams, in *The Long Revolution* (1961), termed the 'structure of feeling'. According to Stuart Hall, Williams argued that 'only literature... could faithfully reproduce what it felt like to live in a certain

period': 'A Critical Survey of the Theoretical and Practical Achievements of the Past Ten Years', in *The Study of Popular Fiction: A Source Book*, ed. by Bob Ashley (London: Pinter Publishers, 1989), pp. 164-172 (p. 166).

9. Gabriel Garcia Marquez, interviewed in *Writers at Work* (1984).
10. Peter Leslie, *The Extremist* (London: New English Library, 1970).
11. Martin Waddell, *A Little Bit British* (London: Tom Stacey Ltd, 1970).
12. Menna Gallie, *You're Welcome to Ulster* (London: Victor Gollancz, 1970).
13. David Brewster, *The Heart's Grown Brutal* (Angus and Robertson, 1972).
14. James Carrick, *With O'Leary in the Grave* (London: Heinemann, 1971).
15. Edna Longley, *The Living Stream: Literature and Revisionism in Ireland* (Bloodaxe, 1994), p. 151.
16. W.A. Ballinger, *The Green Grassy Slopes* (London: Corgi, 1969), J.G. Farrell, *Troubles* (Jonathan Cape, 1970), and Thomas Kilroy, *The Big Chapel* (London: Faber, 1971).
17. Geoffrey Bell, 'Without bitterness: an interview with Edna O'Brien', *Fortnight*, No. 47 (5 October 1972), pp. 19-20.
18. Richard Deutsch, ''Within Two Shadows': The Troubles in Northern Ireland', in *The Irish Novel in Our Time*, ed. by Patrick Rafroidi and Maurice Harmon (PUL, 1976), pp. 131-54 (p. 151).
19. James MacKillop, 'Ulster Violence in Fiction', in *Conflict in Ireland*, ed. by E. Sullivan and others (Gainesville: Florida University Press, 1976), pp. 131-150 (p. 135).
20. Of the remaining six novels not discussed, at least four were written by authors born in, or with a close connection to Ireland. Joan Lingard, for example, was born in Edinburgh, though raised in Ireland, and wrote three of the six, but still leaving half of the total of sixteen penned by non-Irish writers: Joan Lingard, *The Lord on Our Side* (1970), and *The Twelfth Day of July* (1970); Lee MacKenzie, *Hadleigh* (1970); Tom McIntyre, *Through the Bridewell Gate* (1971); Robert Crawford, *Whip Hand* (1972; Hugh C Rae, 1974); and Joan Lingard, *Across the Barricades* (1972).
21. Gallie, p. 9.
22. Gallie, p. 127.
23. Eavan Boland, 'The Northern writers' crisis of conscience. 1: Community', *Irish Times*, 12 August 1970, p.12.
24. Gallie, p. 30.
25. *Ibid.*, p. 94.
26. *Ibid.*, p. 96.
27. *Ibid.*, p. 96.
28. Michael Farrell, 'Long March to Freedom', *Twenty Years On*, ed. by Michael Farrell (Dingle: Brandon, 1988), pp. 54-74 (pp. 56-7).
29. Gerry Adams, 'A Republican in the Civil Rights Campaign', in *Twenty Years On*, ed. by Michael Farrell (Dingle: Brandon, 1988), pp. 39-53 (p. 47).
30. Gallie, pp. 209-210.
31. Michael Farrell (1980), p. 267.
32. Waddell (1970).
33. *Ibid.*, pp. 42-3.
34. *Ibid.*, p. 9.
35. Michael Farrell (1980), p. 262.
36. Leslie, p. 98.
37. *Ibid.*, p.5.
38. *Ibid.*, p. 64.
39. *Ibid.*, p. 64.
40. *Ibid.*, p. 2.
41. *Ibid.*, p. 27.
42. Shaun Herron, *Through the Dark and Hairy Wood; The Whore-mother* (London: Jonathan Cape, 1972 and 1973 respectively).
43. Leslie, p. 49.
44. *Ibid.*, p. 11.
45. Gerry Adams, 'Republicanism and Socialism', *Fortnight*, September, 1983.
46. Leslie, p. 16.
47. Gallie, p.11.
48. Lloyd, David, *Anomalous States: Irish Writing and the Post-Colonial Moment* (Lilliput Press, 1993), p. 125.
49. *Ibid.*, p. 125.
50. Conor Cruise O'Brien, 'A Global Letter [February 1972]', *Herod: Reflections on Political Violence* (London: Hutchinson, 1978).
51. *Ibid.*, p. 20.
52. *Ibid.*, p. 23.
53. James Barlow, *Both Your Houses* (London: Hamish Hamilton, 1971), p. 5.
54. *Ibid.*, p. 6.
55. *Ibid.*, pp. 12-3.
56. *Ibid.*, p. 17.
57. *Ibid.*, p. 178.
58. *Ibid.*, pp. 178-9.
59. *Ibid.*, p. 186.
60. Jeremy Harwood, Jonathan Guinness, John Biggs-Davison, MP, *Ireland – Our Cuba?* (London: Monday Club, 1970).
61. Leslie, p. 250.
62. Joan Lingard, *The Twelfth Day of July* (1970); *Across the Barricades* (1972); *Into Exile* (1973); *A Proper Place* (1975); and *Hostages to Fortune* (1976).

63. Russell Braddon, *The Progress of Private Lilyworth* (Michael Joseph, 1971), p. 134.
64. *Ibid.*, p. 47.
65. *Ibid.*, p. 52.
66. *Ibid.*, p. 78.
67. *Ibid.*, pp. 5-6.
68. *Ibid.*, p. 116.
69. John Banville, *Hibernia*, 14 May 1971, p. 17.
70. Braddon, pp. 43-4.
71. *Ibid.*, pp. 135-6.
72. Carrick, *With O'Leary in the Grave*, Forward.
73. *Ibid.*, p. 66.
74. *Ibid.*, p. 61.
75. Eamonn McCann, *War and an Irish Town* (London: Pluto, 1980), p. 60.
76. James Wood, *Road to Canossa* (London, Hutchinson, 1971), p. 25.
77. *Ibid.*, p. 130.
78. *Ibid.*, pp. 105-6.
79. *Ibid.*, pp. 134-5.
80. Unionists refer to 'the province' to denote 'Ulster' partitioned from the historic nine-county province which included Monaghan, Cavan and Donegal, a usage Irish nationalists would eschew.
81. Shaun Herron, *Through the Dark and Hairy Wood* (London: Jonathan Cape, 1973 [1972]), p. 22.
82. *Ibid.*, p. 24.
83. *Ibid.*, p. 42.
84. *Ibid.*, p. 43.
85. Brewster, *The Heart's Grown Brutal*.
86. Other examples of titles drawn from *Yeats's poetry*: David Martin, *The Ceremony of Innocence*, 1977; Mildred Downey Broxon, *Too Long a Sacrifice*, 1981; John Brady, *A Stone of the Heart*, 1988; Eugene McEldowney, *Stone of the Heart*, 1995.
87. Brewster, p. 24.
88. *Ibid.*, p. 3.
89. McCann (1980), p. 90.
90. Brewster, p. 80.
91. *Ibid.*, p. 144.
92. *Ibid.*, p. 200.
93. *Ibid.*, pp. 212-13.
94. Jack Higgins, *The Savage Day* (London: Collins, 1972).
95. Higgins, pp. 54-5.
96. Carty, Ciaran, 'Poor wee boy, indeed', *Sunday Tribune* (11 June 1995).

Chapter 4 - A Publishing Phenomenon: 1973 - 75

1. *Setting the Record Straight* (Sinn Féin).
2. Henry Kelly, 'Northern Ireland: Beginning or End', *Éire-Ireland*, Vol.7, No.1 (1972).
3. The two remaining titles were a novel in Dutch, Wim Hornman's *Kinderen van het Geweld* (Haarlem: Gottmer, 1973), and a short story collection by the TV broadcaster Charles Witherspoon, *A Sea of Troubles* (Belfast: Blackstaff, 1973).
4. As quoted in Gerry Smyth, *The Novel and the Nation: Studies in the New Irish Fiction* (London: Pluto Press, 1997), p. 114.
5. John Kirkaldy, 'English Cartoonists: Ulster Realities', *Éire-Ireland* (Fall, 1981), pp. 27-42 (p. 36).
6. Des Wilson, *Democracy Denied* (Cork: Mercier Press, 1997), p. 153.
7. *Ibid.*, p. 153.
8. Richard Deutsch, ''Within Two Shadows': The Troubles in Northern Ireland', in *The Irish Novel in Our Time*, edited by Patrick Rafroidi and Maurice Harmon (PUL, 1976), pp. 131-154 (p. 150).
9. *Ibid.*, p. 150.
10. *Ibid.*, p. 150.
11. J.A. Sutherland, *Fiction and the Fiction Industry* (Athlone Press, 1978), p.166.
12. Deutsch., p. 152.
13. Richard Hoggart, 'Ulster: a switch-off TV subject?', *The Listener*, 28 February, 1980, pp. 261-62. Hoggart, concerned at the dearth of informative drama, queried whether in fact 'Ulster' was a 'turn-off TV subject'. He noted a 'wariness' among heads of television drama rather than any weariness among the viewing public, citing the fact that the highest ever figures for the BBC's *Play for Today* was for a play concerning the death of a British soldier in the North.
14. Anthony Smith, 'Television Coverage of Northern Ireland', in *War and Words: The Northern Ireland Media Reader*, ed. by Bill Rolston and David Miller (Belfast: Beyond the Pale Publications, 1996), pp. 22-37 (pp. 30-1).
15. Roger Faligot, *Britain's Military Strategy in Ireland: The Kitson Experiment* (Brandon/Zed, 1983), p. 80.
16. Peter Driscoll, *In Connection with Kilshaw* (London: Macdonald, 1974).
17. In addition to Wim Hornman's *Kinderen van het Geweld* [see footnote 1], four novels in French appeared in 1974: Jean-Loup *Coudent's Mefiez-vous de l'Irlande* (Paris, Fayard); Gerard De Villiers' *SAS: Furie a Belfast* (Paris, Plon); Jean-Gerard Imbar's *Ah, ca IRA!* (Paris, Gallimard); and Gilles Rosset's *Le Point d'Irlande* (Paris, Denoel).
18. Giles Clark, *Inside Book Publishing* (London, Routledge, 1994).
19. John Sutherland, *Bestsellers: Popular fiction of the 1970s* (London, Routledge and Kegan Paul, 1981), p. 21.

20. *Ibid.*, p. 24.
21. *Ibid.*, p. 31.
22. In private correspondence with Steve McDonogh.
23. Jack Higgins, *A Prayer for the Dying* (London, Collins, 1973), p. 132.
24. *Ibid.*, p. 12.
25. *Ibid.*, p. 63.
26. Janet Coleman, 'St Augustine: Christian political thought at the end of the Roman Empire, in *Plato to NATO: Studies in Political Thought* (Penguin Books/BBC Books, 1984), p.52.
27. John De St Jorre and Brian Shakespeare, *The Patriot Game* (Coronet, 1974 [1973]).
28. J. Bowyer Bell, 'The Troubles as Trash: Shadows of the Irish gunman on an American curtain', *Hibernia*, 22 January, 1978, p. 22.
29. De St Jorre and Shakespeare, p. 32.
30. *Ibid.*, p. 33.
31. *Ibid.*, p. 42.
32. *Ibid.*, p. 49.
33. *Ibid.*, p. 49.
34. *Ibid.*, p. 49.
35. *Ibid.*, p. 229.
36. Shaun Herron, *Through the Dark and Hairy Wood* (New York: Random House, 1972), and *The Whore-Mother* (New York: Random House, 1973).
37. Deutsch, pp. 142/43.
38. John D. Cash, *Identity, Ideology and Conflict: the Structuration of Politics in Northern Ireland* (Cambridge University Press, 1996), p. 72.
39. James MacKillop, 'Ulster Violence in Fiction', in *Conflict in Ireland*, ed. by E. Sullivan and others (Gainesville: Florida University Press, 1976), pp. 131-150 (p.146).
40. Deutsch, p. 144.
41. Herron (1973), p. 37.
42. *Ibid.*, p. 27.
43. *Ibid.*, pp. 45-6.
44. *Ibid.*, p. 169.
45. *Ibid.*, p. 85.
46. The complexity is particularly well-illustrated in a novel by Mary Beckett published much later: *Give Them Stones* (1987).
47. Herron (1973), p. 87.
48. *Ibid.*, p. 208.
49. See also Jack Higgins's *Confessional* (London, Collins, 1985), p. 57, which is discussed in Chapter Six.
50. Jimmy Breslin, *World Without End, Amen* (New York: Viking, 1973).
51. *Ibid.*, p. 154.
52. *Ibid.*, p. 155.
53. *Ibid.*, pp. 217-18
54. Reproduced in Conor Cruise O'Brien, *Herod: Reflections on Political Violence* (London, Hutchinson and Co., 1978), pp. 104-109.
55. *Ibid.*, p.109.
56. Douglas Hurd, *Vote to Kill* (London: Collins, 1975).
57. *Ibid.*, p. 16.
58. *Ibid.*, p. 54.
59. *Ibid.*, p. 28.
60. Another example: 'the monstrous rhythm of clanging dustbin lids, that curiously offensive hymn of hate of the Catholic women of Belfast', in the thriller by John De St Jorre and Brian Shakespeare, *The Patriot Game* (Boston: Houghton Miffiln, 1973), pp. 34-5.
61. Hurd., p.214.
62. Gerald Seymour, *Harry's Game* (London: Diamond Books Omnibus Edition, 1993[1975]).
63. *Ibid.*, p. 297.
64. *Ibid.*, p. 401.
65. *Ibid.*, p. 402.
66. *Ibid.*, p. 453.
67. *Ibid.*, p. 457.
68. *Ibid.*, p. 481.
69. Bill Rolston, 'Mothers, whore and villains: images of women in novels of the Northern Ireland conflict', *Race & Class*, 31, 1 (1989), pp. 41-57 (p. 42).
70. Seymour, p. 346.
71. *Ibid.*, p. 297.
72. *Ibid.*, p. 314.
73. *Ibid.*, p. 346.
74. *Ibid.*, p. 301.
75. *Ibid.*, pp. 434-35.
76. Bruce Merry, *Anatomy of the Spy Thriller* (Dublin, Gill and Macmillan, 1977), p. 17.

77. The accounts of former and/or disaffected members are cited in Chapter Eight, to which might be added Maria McGuire's *To Take Arms: A Year in the Provisional IRA* (London: Macmillan, 1973) and Sean MacStiofain's *Memoirs of a Revolutionary* (Edinburgh: Gordon Cremonesi, 1975). More recent insights can be gleaned from the following: Brian Campbell (ed), *Nor Meekly Serve My Time* (Belfast: Beyond the Pale, 1994); Gerry Adams, *Before the Dawn* (Heinemann in association with Brandon, 1996). In addition, interviews with republicans are contained in Kevin Toolis's *Rebel Hearts* (Picador, 1995) and Jonathan Stevenson's *'We Wrecked the Place': Contemplating an end to the Northern Irish Troubles* (New York: The Free Press, 1996).
78. Kevin Boyle, Tom Hadden and Paddy Hillyard, 'Chapter 3: The Paramilitaries: Republican and Loyalist Groups', *Ten Years on in Northern Ireland* (London: The Cobden Trust, 1980).
79. Kevin Boyle and Tom Hadden, *Northern Ireland: The Choice* (London: Penguin, 1994).
80. Boyle, *et al* (1980), p. 19.
81. *Ibid.*, p. 23.
82. Boyle and Hadden (1994), p. 80.
83. Louise Shara, 'Thugs and hooligans', *Fortnight*, No. 325, February 1994, p. 18.

Chapter 5 - Definitional Misrule: 1976 - 81

1. Martin McGuinness's term, first used in the late 1990s, defining those who, despite the peace process, advocated repression of Irish republicanism.
2. Paul Foot, 'Colin Wallace and the Propaganda War', in *War and Words: The Northern Ireland Media Reader*, edited by Bill Rolston and David Miller (Belfast: Beyond the Pale Publications, 1996), pp. 158-90 (p. 172).
3. In *The Trouble With Reporting Northern Ireland: The British State, the Broadcast Media and Nonfictional Representation of the Conflict* (Avebury, 1995), David E. Butler uses the term definitional authority to mean 'the power to 'set limits' on everyday consciousness' (p. 141).
4. Antony Beevor, *Inside the British Army* (Corgi, 1991), p. 256.
5. Dermot P.J. Walsh, *The Use and Abuse of Emergency Legislation in Northern Ireland* (London, The Cobden Trust, 1983), p. 12.
6. Liz Curtis, 'Reporting Republican Violence, in *War and Words: The Northern Ireland Media Reader*, ed. by Bill Rolston and David Miller (Belfast: Beyond the Pale Publications, 1996), pp. 309-328 (p. 324).
7. Tim Pat Coogan, *The Troubles* (London: Arrow, 1996), p. 248.
8. *Ibid.*, p. 249.
9. *Ibid.*
10. Jack Holland, *The American Connection* (Dublin: Poolbeg, 1987), p. 173.
11. John Wilson Foster, *Forces and Themes in Ulster Fiction* (Dublin, Gill and Macmillan, 1974), p. 256.
12. Richard Deutsch, ''Within Two Shadows': The Troubles in Northern Ireland', in *The Irish Novel in our Time*, ed. by Patrick Rafroidi and Maurice Harmon (PUL, 1975), pp. 131-154.
13. *Ibid.*, p, 133.
14. *Ibid.*, p, 132.
15. *Ibid.*, p, 152.
16. Martin Waddell, *A Little Bit British* (London: Tom Stacey, 1970).
17. John Cronin, 'Prose', in *Causeway: The Arts in Ulster*, ed. by Michael Longley (Dublin, Gill and Macmillan, 1971), p. 82.
18. Deutsch, p, 136.
19. James MacKillop, 'Ulster Violence in Fiction', *Conflict in Ireland*, ed. by E. Sullivan *et al* [eds] (Gainesville: Florida University Press, 1976), pp. 131-150 (pp. 133-34).
20. *Ibid.*, p, 132.
21. Joseph Browne, 'The Literature of Violence: The Writer and Northern Ireland', *Conflict in Ireland*, ed. by E. Sullivan *et al* (Gainesville: Florida University Press, 1976), pp. 155-68 (p. 155).
22. Sarah Nelson, 'Oceans of Krapp', *Fortnight*, No. 136, 5 November 1976, p. 7. Naomi May's novel, incidentally, is titled *Troubles* (London: John Calder, 1976).
23. *Ibid.*, p. 7.
24. Leon Uris, *Trinity* (London: Corgi, 1977 [Andre Deutsch, 1976]). *Trinity* is estimated to have sold over eight million copies.
25. *Ibid.*, p. 890.
26. J Bowyer Bell, 'The Troubles as Trash: Shadows of the Irish Gunman on an American Curtain', *Hibernia*, 20 January 1978, p. 22.
27. *Ibid.*, p. 22.
28. *Ibid.*
29. Robert Charles, *The Hour of the Wolf* (1974); *The Flight of the Raven* (1975); *The Scream of the Dove* (1976); *The Prey of the Falcon* (1977) – all published by Robert Hale, London.
30. Bowyer Bell, p. 22.
31. Frederick Forsyth, *The Deceiver* (Transworld, 1991).
32. Bowyer Bell, p. 22.
33. *Ibid.*
34. *Ibid.*
35. Peter O'Rourke, 'Remembering the Past: Republican papers amalgamate', *AP/RN*, 19 January 1995.
36. Una O'Neill, '1979 Paperbacks: Flimsy covers for the same lie', *AP/RN*, February 1980.
37. Joseph McMinn, 'Contemporary Novels on the 'Troubles, *Études Irlandaises* (No. 5, Dec 1980), pp. 113-21 (p. 114).

38. *Ibid.*, p. 121.
39. Una O'Neill.
40. *Ibid.*
41. Alan Titley, 'Rough Rug-headed Kerns: The Irish Gunman in the Popular Novel', *Éire-Ireland* (Vol. 15, 4, Winter, 1980), pp. 15-38 (p. 16).
42. *Ibid.*, p. 17.
43. John Morrow, *The Confessions of Proinsias O'Toole* (Belfast: Blackstaff, 1977); and Benedict Kiely, *Proxopera* (London: Victor Gollancz, 1977).
44. Seamus Deane, 'The Writer and the Troubles', *Threshold* (No. 25, Summer, 1974), pp. 13-17. (p. 14).
45. Deutsch, p.151.
46. Brian Moore, *The Doctor's Wife* (Morrison and Gibb, 1976); and Maurice Leitch, *Silver's City* (London: Secker & Warburg, 1981).
47. Cited by Gerald Dawe in his review of *Trinity* by Leon Uris, *Fortnight*, 5 November 1976, p. 9.
48. Gerald Dawe, 'Old Bones of Contention', *Fortnight*, No. 151, July 1977, p. 13.
49. Jack Holland, *The Prisoner's Wife* (New York: Dodd, Mead & Co., 1981).
50. Moore, p. 14.
51. *Ibid.*, p. 24.
52. *Ibid.*, p. 15.
53. Jennifer Johnston, *Shadows on our Skin* (London: Hamish Hamilton, 1977); and Francis Stuart, *A Hole in the Head* (London: Martin Brian and O'Keefe, 1977).
54. Paul Theroux, *The Family Arsenal* (Penguin, 1977 [Hamish Hamilton, 1976]).
55. *Ibid.*, p. 201.
56. *Ibid.*, p. 64.
57. *Ibid.*, p. 97.
58. *Ibid.*, p. 274.
59. General Army Orders are contained in the IRA's *Green Book*, a recruitment manual, which is reproduced in Martin Dillon's *25 Years of Terror* (Bantam, 1996), pp. 353-84
60. Nevertheless, the 'once in, always in' trope is frequently met. To give some examples: Robin Moore's *The Kaufman Snatch* (NY: Manor Books, 1976), p. 10; Bernard MacLaverty's *Cal* (Belfast, Blackstaff, 1983), p. 103; Gerald Seymour's *Field of Blood* (London, Fontana, 1985, p.17; and Gordon Stevens' *Provo* (London, Harper Collins, 1993), p. 185. I haven't been able to check whether Dan Mahoney's *Once in, Never Out* (New York, St. Martin's Press, 1998) deals with the theme, as suggested by the title.
61. Theroux, pp. 194-5.
62. J.A. Sutherland, *Fiction and the Fiction Industry* (Athlone Press, 1978), p. 60.
63. Chapman Pincher, *The Eye of the Tornado* (London: Michael Joseph, 1976); and Robin Moore, *The Kaufman Snatch* (USA: Manor Books, 1976)..
64. Pincher, p. 54.
65. *Ibid.*, p. 35.
66. *Ibid.*, p. 10: Note Delaney's 'ferret-face'. In Chapter Four, in reference to Leslie's *The Extremists*, I mentioned the not infrequent resort by authors to attribute ferrety features to republicans. A reference to ferret-like features is also contained in Gerald Seymour's *Harry's Game*, discussed in Chapter Five.
67. *Ibid.*, p. 13.
68. *Ibid.*, p. 14.
69. In a review, Harry Barton, the author of two early comic novels about the Troubles, is less coy about who Fletcher was modelled on: 'the Head of MI6 tells himself that he admires Mrs Thatcher's legs. A rattling bad yarn, this. Biggles, you might call it, without the innocence': *Fortnight*, 10 September 1976, p. 15.
70. Pincher., p. 87.
71. *Ibid.*, p. 33.
72. *Ibid.*, p. 66.
73. *Ibid.*, p. 185.
74. John Sutherland, *Bestsellers: Popular fiction of the 1970s* (London, Routledge and Kegan Paul, 1981), p. 191.
75. Moore, p. 301.
76. Jerry Palmer, *Potboilers: Methods, Concepts and Case Studies in Popular Fiction* (London and New York: Routledge, 1991), p. 39.
77. Moore, pp. 19-20.
78. Tim Pat Coogan, *The IRA* (London, Fontana, 1980), p. 518.
79. Moore, p. 20.
80. Maria McGuire, *To Take Arms: A Year in the Provisional IRA* (London: Macmillan, 1973).
81. *Publishers' Weekly*, 'The Sparrowhook Curse' (5 August 1996).
82. *Ibid.*, p. 299.
83. Christopher Hawke, *For Campaign Service* (London: Corgi, 1979), p. 239.
84. Palma Harcourt, *A Sleep of Spies* (London, Collins, 1979).
85. *Ibid.*, p. 121.
86. *Ibid.*, p. 19.
87. Jack Holland, *The American Connection* (Dublin: Poolbeg, 1987), p. 231.
88. Harcourt, p. 33.
89. *Ibid.*, p. 115.
90. Joe Cleary, ''Fork-Tongued on the Border Bit': Partition and the Politics of Form in Contemporary Narratives of the Northern Irish Conflict', *South Atlantic Quarterly*, Vol. 95, No.1 (Winter 1996), pp. 227-276 (p. 232).

91. Harcourt, p. 199.
92. *Ibid.*, p. 200.
93. Kevin Dowling, *Interface Ireland* (London: Barrie and Jenkins, 1979).
94. *Ibid.*, p. 63.
95. *Ibid.*, pp. 72-3.
96. Frank Kitson, *Low Intensity Operations* (London: Faber, 1971).
97. Paul Foot, 'Colin Wallace and the Propaganda War', in *War and Words: The Northern Ireland Media Reader*, edited by Bill Rolston and David Miller (Belfast: Beyond the Pale Publications, 1996), pp. 158-90 (p. 162).
98. *Ibid.*, p. 161.
99. *Ibid.*, p. 170.
100. *Ibid.*, p. 169.
101. Padraig O'Malley, *The Uncivil Wars* (Belfast: Blackstaff, 1983), p. 268.
102. Peter Taylor, *Provos: Part 2*.

Chapter 6 - Shifting Discourses

1. Roger Faligot, *Britain's Military Strategy in Ireland: The Kitson Experiment* (Brandon/Zed Press, 1983), p. 83. The journalist Duncan Campbell cites the British government definition of Psy-ops: 'planned psychological activities in peace and war directed towards the enemy, friendly and neutral audiences, in order to create behaviour favourable to the achievement of political and military objectives': 'Still Dark in Paranoia Gulch', in *War and Words: The Northern Ireland Media Reader*, ed. by Bill Rolston and David Miller (Belfast: Beyond the Pale, 1996), pp. 191-96 (p. 192). Roger Faligot has also written a novel about the H-Block struggle: *Bloc H, ou la ballade de Colm Brady* (Lyon, Editions Jacques-Marie Laffont, 1981), which he dedicated to the memory of two republican activists on the issue, Miriam Daly and Martin McKenna.
2. Ray O'Hanlon, 'Letter from New York: A bad week for spooks, spies and 'diplomats'', *Irish News*, 1 June 1999.
3. Jack Holland, *The American Connection* (Dublin: Poolbeg, 1987), p. 56.
4. Joe McMinn, 'In defence of Field Day: talking among the ruins', *Fortnight*, No. 224, 9 September 1985, pp. 19-20.
5. Robert Johnstone, *Fortnight*, 2 December 1985, p. 19.
6. James O'Hara, reviewing *Irish Studies: a general introduction* (Gill and Macmillan, 1988) for *Fortnight*, 21 November 1988, p. 21.
7. Giles De La Mare, 'Publishing: Time Present and Time Future', in *Publishing Now: A definitive assessment by key people in the book trade*, ed. by Peter Owen (Peter Owen Publishers, 1993), p. 19.
8. Alex Hamilton, 'Top Hundred Chart of 1993 Paperback Fastsellers', in *Writers' and Artists' Yearbook* (London: A & C Black, 1994), p. 256.
9. *Ibid.*, p. 256.
10. Marjory Alyn, *The Sound of Anthems* (New York: St Martin's, 1983); Iris Murdoch, *The Philosopher's Pupil* (1983); Mary Tanquay, *Run With the Hare* (Ontario: Coram Publishing, 1983).
11. Linda Anderson, *To Stay Alive* (London: Bodley Head, 1984); Lynn Reid Banks, *Maura's Angel* (London: Dent, 1984); Elizabeth Gibson, *The Water is Wide* (London: Hodder and Stoughton, 1984); Jennifer Johnston, *The Railway Station Man* (London: Hamish Hamilton); Mary Ann Sullivan, *Child of War* (New York: Holiday House, 1984); Una Woods, *The Dark Hole Days* (Belfast: Blackstaff, 1984).
12. Joe McMinn, *Fortnight*, 24 June 1985, p. 17.
13. Fiona Barr, 'Afraid to move outside the cave', *Fortnight*, No. 205, June 1984, p. 25. For a useful discussion on the distinction between feminist literature and women's literature read Elaine Showalter, 'The Feminist Critical Revolution', in *Imagining Women: Cultural Representations and Gender*, ed. by Frances Bonner *et al* (Polity Press/OU, 1992), pp. 73-78.
14. Frances Molloy, *No Mate for the Magpie* (London: Virago, 1985); Mary Beckett, *Give Them Stones* (London: Bloomsbury, 1987).
15. See Liz Curtis's discussion about the media portrayal of Margaret McKearney in *Ireland: the Propaganda War: the British media and the 'battle for hearts and minds'* (Pluto Press, 1984), pp. 122-24. Later, in a review of Reg Gadney's *Just When We Are Safest* (London: Faber, 1996), Eoghan Corry was to remark on the fictional exploitation of the theme: 'Patriot Games [top IRA bomber Maureen O'Dwyer: pp. 168-69], The Crying Game, Mairead Farrell's tabloid dubbing as the 'Queen of Terror' and Donna Maguire's high heels, somebody should write a thriller based on the British fascination with IRA women', *Andersonstown News*, 20 April 96, p. 21.
16. To give some examples, Colin Leinster's *The Outsider*, was made into a Paramount film, 1980; Jennifer Johnston's *Shadows on Our Skin* was dramatised for the BBC, 1980; and her 1984 novel, *The Railway Station Man* was made into a film in 1991 starring Julie Christie; Gerald Seymour's *Harry's Game*, was dramatised for TV in 1982; John Montague scripted his short story 'The Cry' for the BBC in 1984; Bernard MacLaverty's novel, *Cal* became a film of that name in 1983; and a film starring Mickey Rourke and Liam Neeson appeared in 1987 based on Jack Higgins *A Prayer for the Dying*.
17. Liz Curtis, 'A Catalogue of Censorship: 1959-1993', in *War and Words: The Northern Ireland Media Reader*, ed. by Bill Rolston and David Miller (Belfast: Beyond the Pale Publications, 1996), pp. 265-328; Martin McLoone, 'Drama Out of a Crisis: BBC Television Drama and the Northern Ireland Troubles', in *Broadcasting in a Divided Community: Seventy Years of the BBC in Northern Ireland*, ed. by Martin McLoone (Belfast, Institute of Irish Studies, QUB, 1996), pp. 73-104.
18. Liz Curtis, 'The Reference Upwards System', in *War and Words: The Northern Ireland Media Reader*, ed. by Bill Rolston and David Miller (Belfast: Beyond the Pale Publications, 1996), pp. 80-95 (pp. 83-4).
19. Hugo Meenan, *No Time for Love* (Dingle: Brandon, 1987).

20. *Iris*, No. 10, July 1985, p. 41. The three winning stories were Roy Walsh's 'The Street', John MacElhinney's 'Change', and Seamus Leonard's 'A Close Call'.
21. Jack Higgins, *Touch the Devil* (London: Collins, 1982).
22. Higgins did, however, publish at least one novel during this nine-year gap containing a brief reference to the Troubles: *Solo* (1980; published in the USA as *The Cretan Lover*).
23. Higgins (1982), p. 14.
24. *Ibid.*, pp. 15-6.
25. According to Michael Farrell, the term 'green fascists' was first used against the Provos by the Official IRA after they ended their military campaign in May 1972: *Northern Ireland: The Orange State* (London: Pluto, 1980 [1976]), p. 294.
26. Higgins (1982), p. 55.
27. *Ibid.*, p. 70.
28. *Ibid.*, p. 75.
29. *Ibid.*, p. 46.
30. *Ibid.*, p. 36.
31. *Ibid.*, p. 37.
32. *Ibid.*, pp. 25-6.
33. *Ibid.*, p. 198.
34. Jack Higgins, *Confessional* (London, Collins, 1985).
35. *Ibid.*, p. 21.
36. See also Bernard MacLaverty's short story *Walking the Dog* (Jonathan Cape, 1994) in which 'haitch' and 'aitch' distinguish Catholic and Protestant respectively.
37. Higgins (1985), p. 57.
38. *Ibid.*, p. 77.
39. *Ibid.*, p. 139.
40. *Ibid.*, e.g., p. 133
41. Bernard MacLaverty, *Cal* (Belfast, Blackstaff, 1983).
42. *Ibid.*, p. 19.
43. *Ibid.*, p. 19.
44. *Ibid.*, p. 22.
45. *Ibid.*, p. 23.
46. *Ibid.*, p. 23.
47. *Ibid.*, p. 26.
48. *Ibid.*, p. 44.
49. *Ibid.*, p. 103.
50. *Ibid.*, p. 122.
51. *Ibid.*, p. 73.
52. *Ibid.*, p. 73.
53. *Ibid.*, p. 81.
54. Stephen Watt, 'The Politics of Bernard MacLaverty's *Cal*', *Eire-Ireland*, 28,3 (1993), pp. 130-146 (p.130).
55. MacLaverty, p. 92.
56. *Ibid.*, p. 93.
57. *Ibid.*, p. 101.
58. *Ibid.*, p. 102.
59. *Ibid.*, p. 92.
60. M.S. Power, *The Killing of Yesterday's Children* (London: Chatto and Windus, 1985), *Lonely the Man Without Heroes* (London: Heinemann, 1986), and *A Darkness in the Eye* (London: Heinemann, 1987).
61. Liz Curtis, 'A Catalogue of Censorship' (1996), p. 295. Curtis cites examples of television programmes with an Irish theme being re-scheduled so as not to offend the sensitivities of the British viewing public in the wake of IRA actions: screenplays as seemingly innocuous as Ken Loach's *Hidden Agenda* and Neil Jordan's *Angel* were pulled by Channel 4 in March 1993 in the wake of the Warrington bomb (pp. 265-328). A more recent example, was when Channel 4 postponed, because of Canary Wharf, the release in the UK of the film *Nothing Personal*, based on Daniel Mornin's novel *All Our Fault*, 1991 (Hugh Linehan, 'Green on the screen makes a critic see red', *Irish Times*, 18 May 1996).
62. Power (1985).
63. *Ibid.*, pp. 209-10.
64. *Ibid.*, p. 114.
65. *Ibid.*, p. 28.
66. Maurice Leitch, *Poor Lazarus* (MacGibbon and Kee, 1969).
67. Power (1985), p. 27.
68. *Ibid.*, p. 247.
69. Stephen Bygrave, 'Romantic poems and contexts', in *Romantic Writings*, ed. by Stephen Bygrave (Routledge/Open University, 1996), pp. 3-46 (p. 25).
70. Power (1985), p. 42.
71. *Ibid.*, p. 251.
72. *Ibid.*, p. 97.
73. *Ibid.*, p. 99.
74. *Ibid.*, p. 101.
75. *Ibid.*, p. 118.
76. *Ibid.*, p. 118.

77. *Ibid.*, p. 150.
78. *Ibid.*, pp. 121-2.
79. *Ibid.*, p. 174.
80. *Ibid.*, p. 70.
81. *Ibid.*, p. 190.
82. *Ibid.*, p. 262.
83. M.S. Power, *A Darkness in the Eye* (London: Heinemann, 1987).
84. *Ibid.*, p. 1.
85. *Ibid.*, p. 3.
86. *Ibid.*, p. 132.
87. A.F.N. Clarke, *Contact* (London: Secker and Warburg, 1983), p. xi.
88. *Ibid.*, p. 30.
89. Gerald Seymour, *Field of Blood* (London: Collins, 1985).
90. *Ibid.*, p. 18.
91. *Ibid.*, p. 102.
92. *Ibid.*, p. 218.
93. *Ibid.*, p. 17.
94. *Ibid.*, p. 28.
95. *Ibid.*, p. 34.
96. Antony Beevor, *Inside the British Army* (London, Corgi, 1991).
97. Seymour (1985), p. 40.
98. *Ibid.*, p. 65.
99. *Ibid.*, p. 79.
100. Jerry Palmer, 'Mickey Spillane: a reading', in *The Manufacture of News*, ed. by Stanley Cohen and Jock Young (London: Constable, 1973), pp. 302-313 (p. 318).
101. Quoted in Jerry Palmer's *Potboilers: Methods, Concepts and Case Studies in Popular Fiction* (London and New York: Routledge, 1991), p. 25.
102. David Miller, 'Introduction', *Don't Mention the War: Northern Ireland, Propaganda and the Media* (London: Pluto, 1994), p. 4.
103. Catherine Sefton, *Island of Strangers* (London: Hamish Hamilton, 1983), pp. 65-6.
104. Catherine Sefton, *Starry Night* (Magnet Books, 1987 (1986)). Winner of the Other Award.
105. *Ibid.*, pp. 104-5.
106. Glenn Patterson, *Fatlad* (London: Chatto and Windus, 1992).
107. Sefton (1986), p. 34.
108. Lynn Reid Banks, *Maura's Angel* (London: Dent, 1984).
109. Mary Ann Sullivan, *Child of War* (New York: Holiday House, 1984).
110. Stephen King, *Danse Macabre* (Macdonald, 1981), p. 18.
111. Des Wilson, *Democracy Denied* (Dublin: Mercier Press, 1997), pp. 153-54.
112. *Children in Conflict: a study of Belfast children* by Morris Frazer, Senior Registrar in Psychology at Belfast Royal Hospital for Sick Children (London, Secker and Warburg, 1973); *Children and the Troubles: Children in Northern Ireland*, ed. by Joan Harbinson (Stranmillis College Belfast, 1983): 'research, mainly by psychologists, on maladjusted children and the political socialisation of children'; *Children at War* Joan Harbinson, (London, New English Library, 1984); *Children of the Troubles* (Marshall Pickering, 1986), by Peter Jennings and Maggie Durran; Ed Cairns (ed.), *Caught in the Crossfire: Children and the Northern Ireland Conflict* (Belfast: Appletree Press/Syracuse Univ., 1987); and more recently, *Children of 'The Troubles': Our Lives in the Crossfire of Northern Ireland* (Washington Square Press, 1997), by Laurel Holliday, award-winning author of *Children of the Holocaust: Their Secret Dreams*.
113. Ruth Hooley (ed.), *The Female Line: Northern Irish Women Writers* (Belfast, Northern Ireland Women's Rights Movement, 1985).
114. Jennifer Johnston, *The Railway Station Man* (London: Hamish Hamilton, 1984).
115. Deirdre Madden, *Hidden Symptoms* (London: Faber and Faber, 1986).
116. Mary Beckett (1987) p. 125.
117. *Ibid.*, p. 121.
118. Other novels in which reference is made to the killing of the three Scottish soldiers: Terence De Vere White, *The Distance and the Dark* (1973); John Feeney, *Worm Friday* (1974); Gerald Seymour, *Harry's Game* (1975); John Morrow, *The Confessions of Proinsias O'Toole* (1977).
119. Beckett, p. 124.
120. *Ibid.*, p. 131.
121. *Ibid.*, p. 131.
122. *Ibid.*, pp. 141-42.
123. P.A. Foxall, *The Face of Fury* (London: Robert Hale, 1982).
124. Frank Herbert, *The White Plague* (New York: Putnam, 1982).
125. Des Wilson, *The Demonstration* (Belfast: the author, 1982).
126. In Walter Hegarty's novel *The Price of Chips* (London: Davis-Poynter, 1973), for example, which gives a middle class nationalist perspective on the Battle of the Bogside, the state violence witnessed radicalises Finbarr O'Kane.
127. Des Wilson, *An End to Silence* (Cork: Mercier Press, 1985).
128. Wilson (1982), p. 3.
129. *Ibid.*, p. 24.

130. *Ibid.*, p. 36.
131. *Ibid.*, p. 36.
132. *Ibid.*, pp. 50-1.
133. *Ibid.*, p. 112.
134. *Ibid.*, p. 123.
135. G.F. Newman, *The Testing Ground* (London: Michael Joseph, 1987).
136. *Ibid.*, p. 2.
137. Liz Curtis, *A Catalogue of Censorship* (1996), p.288.
138. *Ibid.*, pp. 289-290.
139. Tom Clancy, *Patriot Games* (Collins, 1993 [1987]). Incidentally, two previous novels are similarly titled: John De St Jorre and Brian Shakespeare's *The Patriot Game* (1973), discussed in Chapter Five; and George V. Higgins's *The Patriot Game* (1982). The theme possibly derives from Dominic Behan's song of that title: 'My name is O'Hanlon/My age is sixteen/My home is in Monaghan/That's where I was weaned/I learned all my life cruel England to blame/Which made me a part of the Patriot Game.' Curiously, you may still hear republican supporters singing that song believing it to be pro-republican when, as the lyric suggests, it is opposed to the use of a romanticised view of history and of nationalism to inculcate a hatred of England among young people. The song is about Fergal O'Hanlon, who was killed in action during the 1950's Border Campaign.
140. Clancy, p. 5.
141. *Ibid.*, p. 5.
142. *Ibid.*, p. 18.
143. *Ibid.*, p. 22.
144. *Ibid.*, p. 48.
145. Tom Clancy, 'My Views on Unity', *Irish America*, January, 1988, pp. 15-17.
146. *Sunday Times*, 26 July 1998, p. 21.
147. Clancy (1988), p. 17.
148. *Ibid.*, p. 16.
149. *Ibid.*, p. 17.
150. Hugo Meenan (1987).
151. *Ibid.*, p. 15.
152. *Ibid.*, p. 27.
153. *Ibid.*, pp. 60-1.
154. *Ibid.*, p. 61.
155. *Ibid.*, p. 91.
156. *Ibid.*, p. 100.
157. *Ibid.*, p. 259.
158. *Ibid.*, p. 259.
159. Frank Whitney, *Iris*, No. 12, 1988, pp. 68-9.

Chapter 7 - A Scenario for Peace: 1988 - 93

1. Cited in Henry Patterson, *The Politics of Illusion: A Political History of the IRA* (London: Serif, 1997), p. 202.
2. *Ibid.*, p. 203.
3. *Ibid.*, p. 217.
4. *Ibid.*, p. 219.
5. Ronan Bennett, 'An Irish Answer', *Guardian*, 16 July 1994.
6. Dean R. Koontz, *Midnight* (USA: G.P. Putnam's Sons, January 1989).
7. Danny Morrison, *Fortnight*, September 1995, p. 23.
8. Brendan Bradshaw, 'Nationalism and historical scholarship in modern Ireland', *Irish Historical Studies*, Vol. XXVI, No. 4 (November 1988), pp. 329-51.
9. Cited by Joe Cleary in 'Fork-Tongued on the Border Bit': Partition and the Politics of Form in Contemporary Narratives of the Northern Irish Conflict', *South Atlantic Quarterly*, Vol. 95, No.1 (Winter 1996), pp. 227-276 (p. 234).
10. Elizabeth Bouché, 'No big thrill', *Fortnight*, No. 312, December 1992, p. 46.
11. Two articles are particularly useful in explaining the role of 'revisionism' at this time: Peter Berresford Ellis, 'Revisionism in Irish historical writing: The new Anti-Nationalist School of Historians', *Iris*, No. 14, August 1990, pp. 36-43; and Martin Spain, 'The Betrayal of 1916 – Revisionism Exposed', *Iris*, No. 15, Easter 1991, pp. 7-10.
12. Thomas Kuhn, in *The Structure of Scientific Revolutions*, argues that our knowledge of reality is not accumulative but plural; that is, instead of there being a universally assimilated incremental growth of knowledge there are instead communities who share sets of accepted concepts, or a paradigm in Kuhn's schema, and who express and understand the world from that vantage. In this model, scientific history is divisible 'into periods of steady development with one set of accepted concepts, called a paradigm, and periods of revolutionary change when the reigning paradigm is replaced by another in a way that he likens to a gestalt switch. In these periods the paradigms compete with each other, a conflict likened to that occurring in Darwinian evolution': in *The Fontana Dictionary of Modern Thinkers*, p. 413.
13. Alistair Renwick,...*last night another soldier...* (London: Information On Ireland, 1989).
14. Danny Morrison, *West Belfast* (Dublin: Mercier, 1989).
15. Danny Morrison in a private letter dated 25 August 1998.

16. Ronan Bennett, *The Second Prison* (London: Hamish Hamilton, 1991); Robert McLiam Wilson, *Ripley Bogle* (London, Andre Deutsch, 1989); Glenn Patterson, *Fatlad* (London: Chatto and Windus, 1992).

17. Richard Deutsch, ''Within Two Shadows': The Troubles in Northern Ireland', in *The Irish Novel in Our Time*, ed. by Patrick Rafroidi and Maurice Harmon (PUL, 1976), pp. 131-154 (p. 151).

18. Brian Moore, *Lies of Silence* (London: Bloomsbury, 1990).

19. Joan Lingard: 8; Maurice Leitch: 7; Martin Waddell (Catherine Sefton): 2 (5); Bernard MacLaverty: 6; Colin Bateman: 4; Jennifer Johnston: 4; Danny Morrison: 4; David Park: 4; M.S. Power: 4. Jack Higgins (Harry Patterson): 14 (1); Bartholomew Gill: 5; Gerald Seymour: 5; Robert Charles: 4, and Terence Strong: 4, are not Irish – and Higgins, of course, has roots in Ireland.

20. Gavin Esler, *Loyalties* (London: Headline, 1990); Graham Hurley, *Reaper* (London: Macmillan, 1991); Gordon Stevens, *Provo* (London: Harper Collins, 1993).

21. Frederick Forsyth, *The Deceiver* (Transworld, 1991).

22. Hanna Wakefield, *A February Mourning* (London: Women's Press, 1990).

23. Paulo Freire, *Pedagogy of the Oppressed* (Penguin, 1972).

24. Unpublished paper on the history of the prison struggle written by republican prisoners in Long Kesh, p.16.

25. *Ibid.*, p. 18.

26. Laurence McKeown, 'Very Important Person', *An Glór Gafa* (Autumn, 1989).

27. Felim O'Hagan, 'The second last time he cried', *An Glór Gafa* (Spring, 1990).

28. Jim McVeigh, 'The Rosary', *An Glór Gafa* (Spring, 1991),

29. Pádraig Wilson, 'The Buffer Zone', *An Glór Gafa* (Summer, 1993).

30. Paddy O'Dowd, 'Two Wheels from Amsterdam, *An Glór Gafa* (Autumn, 1995).

31. Renwick, p. 49.

32. *Ibid.*, p. 95.

33. *Ibid.*, p. 38.

34. *Ibid.*, p. 163.

35. *Ibid.*, p. 177.

36. *Ibid.*, p. 186.

37. Morrison, p. 114.

38. *Ibid.*, p. 127.

39. *Ibid.*, p. 141.

40. *Ibid.*, pp. 142-3.

41. Gerry Adams, *The Street and Other Stories* (Dingle: Brandon, 1990).

42. Ronan Bennett, *The Second Prison* (London: Hamish Hamilton, 1991).

43. Ronan Bennett, *Overthrown by Strangers* (London: Penguin, 1993 [Hamish Hamilton, 1992]), p. 24.

44. *Ibid.*, p. 226.

45. Eve Patten, 'Fiction in conflict: Northern Ireland's prodigal novelists', in *Peripheral Visions: Images of Nationhood in Contemporary British Fiction*, ed. by I.A. Bell (Cardiff: University of Wales Press, 1995), pp. 128-148 (p. 130).

46. Robert McLiam Wilson, *Ripley Bogle* (London, 'Andre Deutsch, 1989).

47. Edna Longley, *The Living Stream: Literature and Revisionism in Ireland* (Bloodaxe, 1994), p. 64.

48. Candida Crewe, 'Biting the bullet', *Times Magazine*, 7 September 1996, p. 21.

49. *Selections from the Prison Notebooks of Antonio Gramsci*, ed. by Quintin Hoare and Geoffrey Nowell-Smith (London: Lawrence and Wishart, 1971), p. 324.

50. McLiam, Wilson (1989), p. 83.

51. *Ibid.*, pp. 91-2.

52. Moore, p. 11.

53. Shervington, Sharon, 'Any of us could be hostages', *New York Times*, 2 September 1990.

54. Moore, p. 49.

55. Frederick Forsyth, *The Deceiver* (Bantam, 1991). Forsyth subsequently published *The Fist of God* (USA: Bantam hardcover, June 1994), which though dealing with the Gulf War contains an apparent justification for the murders of fourteen civil rights marchers by British Paras on Bloody Sunday: '...since Bloody Sunday of January 1972 the IRA tended to avoid the Paras like the plague' [p82].

56. *Ibid.*, p. 281.

57. *Ibid.*, p. 245.

58. *Ibid.*, p. 246.

59. *Ibid.*, p. 241.

60. For example: John Stalker, *Stalker* (Harrap, 1988); Paul Foot, *Who Framed Colin Wallace?* (Macmillan, 1989); Fred Holroyd, *War Without Honour* (Hull: Medium, 1989); Martin Dillon, *The Dirty War* (Hutchinson, 1990); Raymond Murray, *The SAS in Ireland* (Mercier, 1990); Mark Urban, *Big Boys' Rules: The SAS and the Secret Struggle against the IRA* (London: Faber, 1992).

61. Gavin Esler, *Loyalties* (London: Headline, 1990).

62. *Ibid.*, p. 79.

63. *Ibid.*, p. 242.

64. *Ibid.*, p. 242.

65. *Ibid.*, p. 242.

66. *Ibid.*, p. 100.

67. *Ibid.*, pp. 159-160.

68. All the more absurd in light of Douglas Hurd's revelation that the media ban was introduced to pacify Margaret Thatcher who wanted to renegotiate the border and to repatriate the nationalist populations from the areas retained for unionism.

69. Graham Hurley, *Reaper* (London: Macmillan, 1991).
70. *Ibid.*, p. 83.
71. *Ibid.*, p. 255.
72. *Ibid.*, pp. 85-6.
73. Gordon Stevens, *Provo* (London, Harper Collins, 1993).
74. Stevens (1993), p. 185.
75. *Ibid.*, pp. 124-5.
76. *Ibid.*, p. 403.
77. Lionel Shriver, *Ordinary Decent Criminals* (Harper Collins, 1992; originally published in the USA as *The Bleeding Heart* [New York: Farrar, Strauss & Giroux, 1990]), p. 128.
78. *Ibid.*, pp. 38-9.
79. *Ibid.*, p. 172.
80. *Ibid.*, p. 106.
81. John Arden, *Cogs Tyrannic* (London: Methuen, 1991).
82. Wakefield, pp. 83-4.
83. *Ibid.*, p. 84.
84. *Ibid.*, p. 88.
85. *Ibid.*, pp. 100-101.
86. *Ibid.*, p. 119.
87. *Ibid.*, p. 123.
88. *Ibid.*, pp. 147-8.

Chapter 8 - Troubled Resolutions: 1994 - 99

1. Eamonn Mallie and David McKittrick, *The Fight For Peace: The Secret Story Behind the Irish Peace Process* (London, Heinemann, 1996), p. 284.
2. Martin Amis, *Heavy Water and Other Stories*; Nicholas Blincoe, *Manchester Slingback*; Fiona Bullen, *From Pillar to Post*; Tom Clancy, *Rainbow Six*; Jude Collins, *Only Human and other stories*; Robert Cremin, *A Sort of Homecoming*; Ann Doughty, *Stranger in the Place*; Carlo Gebler, *Frozen Out* and *How to Murder a Man*; Hugo Hamilton, *Sad Bastard*; Maurice Leitch, *The Smoke King*; Ardal O'Hanlon, *The Talk of the Town*; Ian Rankin, *The Hanging Garden*; and Eamonn Sweeney, *Waiting for the Healer*.
3. Jack Holland, *Walking Corpses* (Dublin: Torc, 1994).
4. Patrick Quigley, *Borderland* (Dingle: Brandon, 1994).
5. David Park, *Oranges from Spain*; *The Healing*; *The Rye Man* (all published in London by Jonathan Cape in 1991, 1992 and 1994 respectively); and *Stone Kingdoms* (Phoenix, 1996).
6. David Park, *The Times* (23 May 1996).
7. Martin Dillon, *25 Years of Terror* (Bantam, 1996), p. 341.
8. David M. Kiely, *The Angel Tapes* (Belfast, Blackstaff, 1997).
9. James Kennedy, *Silent City* (London: Heinemann, 1998). James Kennedy is a pseudonym of the Waterford-born thriller writer Jim Lusby.
10. *The Serpent's Tail* (London: Richard Cohen Books, 1995) is Martin Dillon's first novel. He is better known for his reportage of the conflict: *Political Murder in Northern Ireland* (co-written with Dennis Lehane: Penguin, 1973); *Shankill Butchers* (Arrow, 1985); *The Dirty War* (Arrow, 1990); *Stone Cold* (Arrow, 1993); *25 Years of Terror* (Bantam, 1996).
11. *Ibid.*, p. 18.
12. Martin Dillon, *Irish News*, 24 November 1995.
13. Dillon, *The Serpent's Tail*, p. 50.
14. Sue Corbett, 'Writer set for summer blockbuster', *Sunday Life*, 23 June 1996.
15. Danny Morrison, 'Dillon's wonderland', *Fortnight*, January 1996, p. 35.
16. *Ibid.*, p. 35.
17. Brendan Hughes, 'Headlines grabbed – facts distorted', *AP/RN*, 7 July 1990, p. 12.
18. Dillon, pp. 140-1.
19. *Ibid.*, p. 212.
20. *Ibid.*, p. 288.
21. *Ibid.*, p. 291.
22. *Ibid.*, p. 291.
23. *Ibid.*, p. 228.
24. Morrison, *Fortnight*, p. 35.
25. Dermot Healy, *A Goat's Song* (London: Harvill, 1994); Patrick McCabe, *The Dead School* (Picador, 1995); Seamus Deane, *Reading in the Dark* (London: Jonathan Cape, 1996); Edna O'Brien, *House of Splendid Isolation* (London: Weidenfeld and Nicholson, 1994).
26. Ronan Bennett, *The Catastrophist* (Headline Review, 1998).
27. Healy, pp. 352/53.
28. McCabe (1995), p. 48.
29. *Ibid.*, p. 143.
30. *Ibid.*, p. 145.
31. *Ibid.*, p. 146.
32. *Ibid.*, pp. 148-9.

33. Sebastian Barry, *The Whereabouts of Eneas McNulty* (Picador, 1998).
34. Eoghan Corry, *Andersonstown News*, 7 March 1998.
35. Robert McLiam Wilson, *Eureka Street* (London: Secker and Warburg, 1996).
36. Cited by John O'Mahony, 'Troubles in mind', *Guardian*, 7 July 1993.
37. The apparent abbreviation, OTG, is unexplained and perhaps meaningless, and in the novel is mysteriously daubed on walls throughout Belfast as a piece of absurdist agit-prop. A year after the novel's publication, a *Sunday Life* front page headlined that 'Life imitates art' (10 August 1997). The tabloid reported that Pastor Clifford Peoples, then a member of FAIT, confessed to a 'graffiti spree', painting 'Ichabod' (apparently Hebrew for 'the glory of God has departed') on walls in the Shankill Road area. Peebles is currently held in Maghaberry Prison on charges connected to dissident Loyalist activity.
38. Edna Longley, *Fortnight*, October 1996, p. 34.
39. Hugh Kenner's term for works influenced by Joyce.
40. Edna Longley, *The Living Stream: Literature and Revisionism in Ireland* (Bloodaxe, 1994), p. 98.
41. Wilson (1996), p. 324.
42. *Ibid.*, p. 324.
43. *Ibid.*, p. 383.
44. Louise Doherty, 'Why the last laugh is on 'extremists'', *Irish News*, 31 August 1996.
45. Wilson (1996), p. 222.
46. *Ibid.*, p. 231.
47. McCabe (1995), p. 145.
48. Robert McLiam Wilson, 'Cities at War', *Irish Review*, No. 10 (Spring 1991), p. 95.
49. Wilson (1996), p. 257.
50. *Ibid.*, p. 267.
51. Lionel Shriver, *Ordinary Decent Criminals* (London, Harper Collins, 1992), p. 229.
52. Phelim McAleer, 'Author goes road of Joyce and Beckett', *Irish News*, 28 November 1996.
53. Eugene McEldowney, *A Kind of Homecoming* (London, Heinemann, 1994).
54. *Ibid.*, p. 44.
55. *Ibid.*, p. 194.
56. Russell Braddon, *The Progress of Private Lilyworth* (London: Michael Joseph, 1970).
57. Shaun Clark, *Underworld* (Coronet, 1997).
58. Colin Bateman has quickly established his credentials as the most prolific of Irish writers whose works feature the Troubles. Besides *Divorcing Jack* (London, Harper Collins, 1995), he produced in rapid succession *Cycle of Violence*, *Of Wee Sweetie Mice and Men*, *Empire State*, and *Maid of the Mist* (all Harper Collins, 1995, 1996, 1997 and 1998 respectively).
59. Daniel Easterman, *Day of Wrath* (London, Harper Collins, 1995).
60. Rebecca Tinsley, *The Judas File* (Headline, 1996).
61. Douglas Hurd, *The Shape of Ice* (London: Little, Brown, 1998).
62. *Ibid.*, p. 37.
63. Keith Baker, *Inheritance* (London: Headline, 1996).
64. Peter Cunningham, *Tapes from the River Delta* (London: Century, 1995).
65. Ian Watson, *Oracle* (London, Gollancz, 1997).
66. Ian McDonald, *Sacrifice of Fools* (London, Gollancz, 1996).
67. Paul Anthony, *The Fragile Peace* (London: James Publishing, 1996).
68. Eddy Shah, *Fallen Angels* (Corgi, 1995 [1994]).
69. *Ibid.*, p. 15.
70. *Ibid.*, p. 25.
71. *Ibid.*, p. 10.
72. *Ibid.*, p. 26.
73. *Ibid.*, p. 123.
74. *Ibid.*, p. 519.
75. James Kennedy, *Armed and Dangerous* (London: Heinemann, 1996).
76. Tom Foote, *Undertow* (Knockeven Press, 1998).
77. Murray Davies, *The Drumbeat of Jimmy Sands* (London, Harper Collins, 1999).
78. Terence Strong, *Rogue Element* (London: Heinemann, 1997).
79. Reg Gadney, *Just when we are safest* (London: Faber and Faber, 1996).
80. Marian Urch, *Violent Shadows* (London: Headline, 1996).
81. Patrick McCabe, *Breakfast on Pluto* (Picador, 1998).
82. Terence Strong, *The Tick Tock Man* (London: Heinemann, 1994).
83. Hugo Barnacle, *Day One* (Quartet, 1998).
84. Louise Doughty, *Crazy Paving* (London: Touchstone, 1995).
85. 'Paperback Preview', *Bookseller* (October 1995).
86. Simon Weston and Patrick Hill, *Cause of Death* (London: Little, Brown '22-Books', 1996).
87. Philippa Kennedy, 'The Making of a Hero', *Daily Express* (30 September 1995).
88. *Ibid.*
89. Art MacEoin and Mairtin Mac Diarmada, 'Getting High on Lies: IRA drug myths exposed', *AP/RN* (22 August 1991).
90. Ron McKay, *The Catalyst* (New English Library, 1991).
91. However, Benedict Kiely's *Proxopera* (London: Gollancz, 1977) mentions 'protection racketeers'.
92. Elliot Cannon, *Stand By To Shoot* (London: Robert Hale, 1973).
93. James Hawes, *A White Merc with Fins* (Jonathan Cape, 1996).

94. Jack Higgins, *Drink with the Devil* (Michael Joseph, 1996).
95. Deirdre Purcell, *Sky* (Dublin: Townhouse, 1995).
96. Shaun Hutson, *White Ghost* (London: Little, Brown & Co, 1994).
97. *Ibid.*, p. 242.
98. *Ibid.*, p. 282.
99. *Ibid.*, p. 103.
100. *Ibid.*, p. 104.
101. *Ibid.*, p. 105.
102. Simon Conway, *Damaged* (Canongate, 1998).
103. John Newsinger, 'Our Boys in the North', *Irish Studies*, No. 6 (Autumn 1996), pp. 34-37.
104. Shaun Clarke, *Soldier E: Sniper Fire in Belfast* (Maidstone: 22 Books, 1993).
105. Peter Morton, *Emergency Tour* (William Kimber, 1989); Michael Asher, *Shoot to Kill* (Guild Publishing, 1990); Johnny Cooper, *One of the Originals* (Pan, 1991); Mark Urban, *Big Boys' Rules* (Faber, 1992); Paul Bruce, *The Nemesis File* (Blake, 1995); Harry McCallion, *Killing Zone* (Bloomsbury, 1995); Andy McNab, *Immediate Action* (Bantam, 1995); Tony Geraghty, *The Irish War* (Harper Collins, 1998); Tom Read, *Free Fall* (Little, Brown, 1998).
106. Scott Graham, *Violent Delights* (Blake Publishing Ltd, 1997).
107. Liam Clarke, 'Nairac's 'lover' claims MI5 fixed his murder', *Sunday Times*, 14 February 1999.
108. Shane Paul O'Doherty, *The Volunteer: a former IRA man's true story* (Fount, 1993); Eamon Collins, *Killing Rage* (1997); Martin McGartland, *Fifty Dead Men Walking* (1997); and in 1999 McGartland published a subsequent exposé of how he alleges he was set up by his British intelligence handlers; Raymond Gilmour, *Dead Ground: Infiltrating the IRA* (Little, Brown and Co, 1998); Sean O'Callaghan, *The Informer* (1998).
109. Gerald Seymour, *Harry's Game* (London: Collins, 1975).
110. P.A. Foxall, *Face of Fury* (London: Robert Hale, 1982).
111. Kevin Dowling, *Interface: Ireland* (London: Barrie and Jenkins, 1979).
112. Liz Curtis, *Ireland: the Propaganda War: the British media and the 'battle for hearts and minds'* (Pluto Press, 1984), p. 83.
113. Chris Ryan, *Stand By, Stand By* (London: Century, 1996).
114. *Guardian*, 19 September 1996.
115. Andy McNab, *Remote Control* (Bantam Press, 1997).
116. *Sunday Times*, 27 September 1998.
117. Chris Ryan, *Zero Option* (London: Century, 1997).
118. Kate Nicholl, *Express on Sunday*, 26 June 1998.
119. John Gray, *Irish News* (9 January 1996 [first published in the Guardian]).
120. Seamus Mac Annaidh, *An Deireadh* (1996).
121. Mairtin Ó Muilleoir, *Ceap Cuddles* (1996).
122. Aodh Ó Canainn, *Tearmann na gColœr* (Cló Iar-Chonnachta, 1999).
123. Tarlach Ó hUid, *Adios* (1975); Annraio Ó Liathain, *Nead na gCreabhar* (Dublin: Sairseal and Dill, 1977); and Breandan Ó Doibhlin, *An Branar gan Cur* (Skerries: Gilbert Dalton, 1979). Alan Titley argued that in Ireland 'there is no real popular literature of patriotic military justification', citing Ó Liathain's novel as an exception for its portrayal of 'Irish special agents tracking down SAS bombers': 'Rough Rug-headed Kerns: The Irish Gunman in the Popular Novel', *Eire-Ireland*, Vol. 15, No. 4 (Winter, 1980), pp. 15-38 (p. 22).
124. Philip Robinson, *Wake the Tribe O'Dan* (The Ullans Press, 1998).
125. Richard Crawford, *The Minstrel Boy* (London: Heinemann, 1994).
126. James McKeon, *Operation Pontiff* (Cork: Acorn Press, 1994).
127. Eoin McNamee, *Resurrection Man* (London: Picador, 1994). The character Victor Kelly, a member of a loyalist gang, similar to the Shankill butchers in mid-1970s' Belfast, could be modelled on the Butchers' alleged leader, Lenny Murphy.
128. Glenn Patterson, *Black Night at Big Thunder Mountain* (London: Chatto and Windus, 1995).
129. Rebecca Tinsley, *The Judas File* (Headline, 1996).
130. William Trevor, 'Lost Ground', *After Rain* (Viking, 1996).
131. Jo Bannister, *No Birds Sing* (St Martin's Press, 1997).
132. Adrian McKinty, *Orange Rhymes with Everything* (New York: William Morrow, 1997).
133. Geoffrie Beattie, *The Corner Boys* (London, Gollancz, 1998).
134. Daniel Silva, *The Marching Season* (Weidenfield and Nicolson, 1999).
135. Bill Rolston, 'Mothers, whores and villains: images of women in novels of the Northern Ireland conflict', *Race and Class*, 31, 1 (1989), pp. 41-57 (p. 47).
136. Sean P. Murphy, *Foreign Chains* (Dublin: 1996).
137. Danny Morrison, *The Wrong Man* (Dublin: Mercier, 1997).
138. Gerry McGeough, *Defenders* (Monaghan: Seesvu Press, 1996).
139. Declan Moen, 'Enclosure', *Racconti? Ireland '96: Short stories from Ireland, Italy, France* (Belfast: Beyond the Pale Publications, 1996).
140. Reviews of the genre might be a worthy area for scrutiny; such a study might elicit some interesting insights into the partiality of the reviewers or journals concerned, for example, when compared to the contemporary record of the events alluded to in the novels.
141. Danny Morrison, *The Wrong Man* (Dublin: Mercier, 1997).
142. Liz MacPherson, 'Morrison finds his freedom in words', *Irish News*, 25 February 1997.
143. Mary Holland, 'Morrison wields pen to fight free of conflict', *Observer*, 2 March 1997.
144. Wilson, 'Cities at War' (1991), p. 95.
145. Kate Fearon, 'J'accuse', *Fortnight*, September 1997, p. 35.
146. Eugene McEldowney, 'Hearts of gold, bullets of lead', *Irish Times*, 28 March 1997.

147. Alannah Hopkin, 'At the heart of the action', *Sunday Tribune*, 2 March 1997.
148. Arthur Koestler, 'Conflict and Plot', in *The Writer's Book*, ed. by Helen Hull (New York: Barnes and Noble, 1956), pp. 69-74 (p. 69).
149. John Dunlop's *A Precarious Belonging: Presbyterians and the Conflict in Ireland* (Belfast, Blackstaff, 1995), p. 124.
150. Kevin Boyle and Tom Hadden, *Northern Ireland: The Choice* (London: Penguin, 1994), p. 7.
151. Padraig O'Malley, *The Uncivil Wars: Ireland Today* (Belfast: Blackstaff, 1983), p. 287.
152. Gerry McGeough, *Defenders* (Monaghan: Seesvu Press, 1998).
153. Gerry McGeough, *The Ambush and other stories* (Jay Street Publishers, 1996).
154. McGeough (1998), p. 153.
155. *Ibid.*, p. 15.
156. *Ibid.*, p. 131.
157. *Ibid.*, p. 3.
158. *Ibid.*, p. 29.
159. David M. Thomas, *Anger's Violin* (Dingle: Mount Eagle, 1998).
160. Stella Bingham, 'Take 5 Detective Novels', *Express on Sunday* (1 November 1998).
161. *Popular Fiction and Social Change*, ed. by Christopher Pawling (London: Macmillan Press, 1984), p. 14.
162. *Ibid.*, p. 14; Gramsci's defined 'common sense' in a particular way: 'Stone Age elements and principles of a more advanced science, prejudices from all past phases of history at the local level and intuitions of a future philosophy which will be that of a human race united the world over': *Selections from Prison Notebooks*, p. 324.
163. Pawling, p. 4.

Chapter 9 - Conclusion: The Uncreated Subject

1. John Pilger, *Heroes* (London, Pan, 1987), p. 485.
2. See the front page and editorial of *AP/RN*, 20 August 1992.
3. *AP/RN*, 'Book ban opposed at writer's festival', 23 September 1993.
4. Quoted in Niall Blaney, *Irish News*, 13 August 1997.
5. Peter King, *Terrible Beauty* (USA: Roberts Rinehart, May 1999).
6. *Kirkus Reviews*, 15 March 1999.
7. Jenny Bell, 'Ireland's genial book trade statesman hangs up his boots', *The Bookseller* (16 June 1995), p. 13.
8. Edna O'Brien interviewed in *Banned in Ireland*, edited for Article 19 by Julia Carson (London: Routledge, 1990), pp. 69-79 (p. 76).
9. *Ibid.*, p. 76.
10. Terry Eagleton, *Literary Theory: An Introduction, 2nd edn* (Oxford: Blackwell, 1996), p. 104.
11. In 'Is Nothing Sacred', Salmon Rushdie's Herbert Read Memorial Lecture which, because of the fatwa, was delivered in his absence at the Institute of Contemporary Arts on 6 February 1990 by Harold Pinter.
12. John Sutherland, *Fiction and the Fiction Industry* (Athlone Press, 1978), p. 229.
13. *Ibid.*, p. 186.
14. *Andersonstown News*, 'New chapter is opening for A'town author', 30 March 1996.
15. Sean P. Murphy, in a letter dated 21 July 1998.
16. Peter Berresford Ellis, *The Rising of the Moon* (London: Methuen, 1987).
17. I am grateful to Aly Renwick, who taped an interview with Peter Berresford Ellis on 30 May 1998, asking questions supplied by me, as well as contributing his own views.
18. *Ibid.*
19. Derek Parker, in a letter dated 1 July 1998.
20. Berresford Ellis interviewed on tape. He also wrote an article in the *Irish Democrat* (December 1988) concerning the treatment of Titley's novel.
21. *Ibid.*
22. In a letter from Steve MacDonogh, Mount Eagle Publications, Dingle, Co. Kerry, 19 February 1998.
23. Berresford Ellis interviewed on tape.
24. *Ibid.*
25. *Ibid.*
26. Ronan Bennett, *Guardian*, 16 July 1994.
27. Interviewed by Helen Meany, *Irish Times*, 10 August 1995.
28. Ronan Bennett, *The Catastrophist* (Review, 1998), p. 312.
29. *Ibid.*, p. 294.
30. Edna O'Brien (1990), p. 76..
31. Chris Weedon, *Feminist Practice and Poststructuralist Theory* (Cambridge: Blackwell, 1987), p. 21.
32. Francis Stuart, *Memorial* (London: Martin Brian and O'Keefe, 1973), p. 237.
33. Since completion of the bibliography for my doctoral thesis, I haven't been able to do an exhaustive update to include titles published after 1999. The following six novels, all published in 2000, however, do suggest that the heterogeneity of narrative approaches to the conflict that is an increasingly marked feature of the genre as I have argued is set to continue: Gretta Curran Browne, *Ordinary Decent Criminal*; Ruth Dudley Edwards, *The Anglo-Irish Murder*; Stephen Fry, *The Stars' Tennis Balls*; James Hawes, *Dead Long Enough*; Jack Higgins, *Day of Reckoning*; and Eamonn Sweeney's *The Photograph*.
34. Joseph McMinn, 'Contemporary Novels on the 'Troubles'', *Études Irelandaises* (No. 5, December 1980), pp. 113-121 (p. 121).

Bibliography

Adams, Gerry. *The Politics of Irish Freedom*. Dingle: Brandon, 1986

Ashley, Bob (ed). *The Study of Popular Fiction: a Source Book*. London: Pinter Publishers, 1989

Beevor, Antony. *Inside the British Army*. Corgi, 1991

Beresford, David. *Ten Men Dead*. HarperCollins, 1994

Bishop Patrick and Eamonn Mallie. *The Provisional IRA*. Corgi, 1988

Boggs, Carl. *Gramsci's Marxism*. London: Pluto Press, 1976

Boyce, D. George. *Nationalism in Ireland*. Croom Helm, 1982

Boyle, Kevin and Tom Hadden. *Northern Ireland: the Choice*. Harmondsworth: Penguin, 1994

Boyle, Kevin, Tom Hadden and Paddy Hillyard. *Ten Years On in Northern Ireland*, Cobden Trust, 1980

Bradshaw, Brendan. 'Nationalism and historical scholarship in modern Ireland'. *Irish Historical Studies*, vol. xxvi, no. 4, November 1988, pp. 329-351

Brady, Anne and Brian Cleeve. *A Biographical Dictionary of Irish Writers*. Lilliput Press, 1985

Brown, Joseph. 'The Literature of Violence: the Writer and Northern Ireland', in E. Sullivan et al. (eds). *Conflict in Ireland*. *Gainesville*, Florida: Florida University, 1976, pp. 155-168

Butler, David E. *The Trouble with Reporting Northern Ireland: the British State, the Broadcast Media and Nonfictional Representation of the Conflict*. Avebury, 1995

Bygrave, Stephen. 'Romantic poems and contexts', in Stephen Bygrave (ed). *Romantic Writings*, Routledge/Open University, 1996, pp. 3-46

Campbell. Flann. *The Dissenting Voice*. Blackstaff, 1991

Carson, Julia (ed). *Banned in Ireland: Censorship and the Irish Writer*. Routledge, 1990

Cash, John D. *Identity and conflict: the Structuration of Politics in Northern Ireland*, Cambridge University Press, 1996

Chatman, Seymour. *Story and Discourse*. London: Cornell University Press, 1978

Chomsky, Noam. 'The Manufacture of Consent', in James Peck (ed). *The Chomsky Reader*. London: Serpent's Tail, 1998, pp. 121-136

Clark, Giles. *Inside Book Publishing*. Routledge, 1994

Cleary, Joe. "'Fork-tongued on the Border Bit": Partition and the Politics of Form in Contemporary Narratives of the Northern Irish Conflict'. *South Atlantic Quarterly*, vol. 95, no. 1, winter 1996, pp. 227-276

Cockburn, Claud. *Bestseller: the Books that Everyone Read, 1900-1939*. Sidgwick and Jackson, 1972

Coleman, Janet. 'St Augustice: Christian political thought at the end of the Roman Empire', in *Plato to NATO: Studies in Political Thought*. BBC Books, 1984, pp. 30-6·

Connolly, James. *Labour in Irish History*. Bookmarks, 1987

Coogan, Tim Pat. *The IRA*. Fontana, 1980

Coogan, Tim Pat. *The Troubles*. London: Arrow, 1996

Cronin, John. 'Ulster's alarming novels'. *Eire-Ireland*, vol. 4, no. 4, 1969, pp. 27-34

Cronin, Sean. *The McGarrity Papers*. Anvil, 1972

Crusias, T.W. *Discourse: a Critique and Synthesis of Major Theories*. New York: Modern Language Association, 1989

Curtis, Liz. *Ireland: the Propaganda War*. London: Pluto Press, 1984

Curtis, Liz. *Nothing but the Same Old Story: the Roots of Anti-Irish Racism*. London: Information on Ireland, 1985

Curtix, Liz. *The Cause of Ireland: From the United Irishmen to Partition*. Belfast: Beyond the Pale Publications, 1994

Dangerfield, George. *The Damnable Question: a Study in Anglo-Irish Relations*. London: Quartet Books, 1979

De La Mare, Giles. 'Publishing: Time Present and Time Future', in Peter Owen (ed). *Publishing Now: a Definitive Assessment by Key People in the Book Trade*. Peter Owen Publishers, 1993

De Saussure, Ferdinand. 'Course in General Linguistics', reproduced in Stuart Sim (ed). *Art: Context and Value*. Open University, 1992, pp. 366-377

Deutsch. Richard. 'Within Two Shadows': the Troubles in Northern Ireland, in Patrick Rafroidi (ed). *The Irish Novel in Our Time*. PUL, 1976, pp. 131-154

Dillon, Martin. *Shankill Butchers*. Arrow, 1985

Dillon, Martin. *Stone Cold*. Arrow, 1993

Dillon, Martin. *25 Years of Terror*. Bantam, 1996

Dillon, Martin and Dennis Lehane. *Political Murder in Northern Ireland*. Penguin, 1973

Drabble, Margaret and Jenny Stringer (eds). *The Concise Oxford Companion to English Literature*. Oxford: OUP, 1990

Dunlop. John. *A Precarious Belonging: Presbyterians and the Conflict in Ireland*. Belfast: Blackstaff Press, 1995

Eagleton, Terry. *Literary Theory: an Introduction, second edition*. Oxford: Blackwell, 1996

Eagleton. Terry. *Ideology: an Introduction*. Verso, 1991

Ellils, Peter Berresford. *A History of the Irish Working Class*. London: Pluto Press, 1985

Faligot, Roger. *Britain's Military Strategy in Ireland: the Kitson Experiment*, Brandon/Zed Press, 1983

Fanon, Franz. *Black Skin, White Masks*. New York: Grove Press, 1967

Farrell, Michael. *Northern Ireland: the Orange State*. London: Pluto Press, 1980 [1976]

Farrell, Michael (ed). *Twenty Years On*. Brandon, 1988

Foster, John Wilson. *Forces and Themes in Ulster Fiction*. Dublin: Gill and Macmillan, 1974

Freire, Paulo. *Pedagogy of the Oppressed*. Penguin, 1972

Hamilton, Alex. 'Top Hundred Chart of 1993 Paperback Fastsellers', in *Writers' and Artists' Yearbook*. London: A & C Black, 1994

Harwood, Jeremy et al. *Ireland – Our Cuba?* London: Monday Club, 1970

Hersey, John. 'The Novel of Contemporary History', in Helen Hull (ed), *The Writer's Book*. New York: Barnes and Noble, 1956

Hicken, Mandy and Ray Prytherch. *Now Read On ... A Guide to Contemporary Popular Fiction*. Gower, 1990

Hoare, Quintin and Geoffrey Nowell-Smith (eds). *Selections from the Prison Notebooks of Antonio Gramsci*. London: Lawrence and Wishart, 1971

Hogan, Robert (ed). *The Macmillan Dictionary of Literature*, 1980

Holland, Jack. *The American Connection*. Dublin: Poolbeg, 1987

King, Stephen. *Danse Macabre*. Macdonald, 1981

Helm, David (ed). *State and Societies*. Basil Blackwell, 1983

Kelly, Henry. 'Northern Ireland: beginning or end?' *Eire-Ireland*, vol. 7, no. 1, 1972

Kircaldy, John. 'English Cartoonists, Ulster Realities'. *Eire-Ireland*, autumn 1981, pp. 27-42

Kitson, Frank. *Low Intensity Operations*. London: Faber, 1971

Koestler, Arthur. 'Conflict and Plot', in Helen Hull (ed), *The Writer's Book*. New York: Barnes and Noble, 1956, pp. 68-74

Lloyd, David. *Anomalous States: Irish Writing and the Post-Colonial Moment*. Lilliput Press, 1993

Longley, Edna. *The Living Stream: Literature and Revisionism in Ireland*. Bloodxe, 1994

Longley, Michael (ed). *Causeway: the Arts in Ulster*. Gill and Macmillan, 1971

Lyons, F.S.L. *Culture and Anarchy in Ireland: 1890-1939*. OUP, 1982

Mallie, Eamonn and David McKittrick. *The Fight for Peace: the Secret Story behind the Irish Peace Process*. Heinemann, 1996

Maxwell, D.E.S. 'Imagining the North: violence and the writers'. *Eire-Ireland*, vol. 8, no. 2, summer 1973, pp. 91-107

McArdle, Dorothy. *The Irish Republic*. Irish Press Ltd, 1951

McCann, Eamonn. 'The British Press and Northern Ireland', in Stanley Cohen and Jock Young (eds). *The Manufacture of News*. London: Constable, 1973, pp. 242-261

McCann, Eamonn. *War and an Irish Town*. Pluto, 1980

McCracken, Scott. *Pulp: Reading Popular Fiction*. Manchester University Press, 1998

McGuire, Maria. *To Take Arms: a Year in the Provisional IRA*. London: Macmillan, 1973

MacKillop, James. 'Ulster Violence in Fiction, in E. Sullivan et al. (eds). *Conflict in Ireland*. Gainesville, Florida: Florida University, 1976, pp. 130-152

McLoone, Martin. 'Drama Out of a Crisis: BBC Television Drama and the Northern Ireland Troubles', in Martin McLoone (ed). *Broadcasting in a Divided Community: Seventy Years of the BBC in Northern Ireland*. Institute of Irish Studies, QUB, 1996, pp. 73-104

McMahon, Sean and Jo O'Donoghue (eds). *The Mercier Companion to Irish Literature*. Mercier Press, 1998

McMinn, Joe. 'Contemporary novels of the "troubles"', *Études Irlandaises*, no. 5, December 1980, pp. 113-121

Merry, Bruce. *Anatomy of the Spy Thriller*. Dublin: Gill and Macmillan, 1977

Metscher, Priscilla. *Republicanism and Socialism in Ireland*. Lang, 1986

Miller, David. 'Introduction', *Don't Mention the War: Northern Ireland, Propaganda and the Media*. London: Pluto Press, 1994

Morrison, Danny, in Martin Collins (ed). *Ireland After Britain*. London: Pluto, 1985

Newsinger, John. 'Our Boys in the North'. *Irish Studies*, no. 6, autumn 1996, pp. 34-37

O'Brien, Conor Cruise. 'Introduction', *Edmund Burke: Reflections on the Revolution in France*, Penguin,

O'Brien, Edna, interviewed in Julia Carson (ed). *Banned in Ireland: Censorship and the Irish Writer*. Routledge, 1990, pp. 69-79

Ó Dochartaigh, Niall. *From Civil Rights to Armalites: Derry and the Birth of the Irish Troubles*. Cork University Press, 1997

O'Malley, Padraig. *The Uncivil Wars: Ireland Today*. Belfast: Blackstaff, 1983

Palmer, Jerry. 'Mickey Spillane: a Reading, in Stanley Cohen and Jock Young (eds). *The Manufacture of News*. London: Constable, 1973, pp. 302-313

Palmer, Jerry. *Potboilers: Genesis and Structure of a Popular Genre*. London: Edward Arnold, 1978

Patten, Eve. 'Fiction in Conflict: Northern Ireland's prodigal novelists', in I.A. Bell (ed). *Peripheral Visions: Images of Nationhood in Contemporary British Fiction*. Cardiff: University of Wales Press, 1995, pp. 128-148

Patterson, Henry. *The Politics of Illusion: a Political History of the IRA*. London: Serif, 1997

Pawling, Christopher (ed). *Popular Fiction and Social Change*. London: Macmillan, 1984

Pilger, John. *Heroes*. London: Pan, 1987

Purdie, Bob. 'Was the civil rights movement a republican/communist conspiracy?' *Irish Political Studies*, 3, 1988, pp. 33-41

Republican POWs. 'Questions of History'. *AP/RN*, 1987

Rolston, Bill. 'Mothers, whores and villains: images of women in novels of the Northern Ireland conflict'. *Race and Class*. vol. 31, no. 1, 1989, pp. 41-57

Rolston, Bill and David Miller (eds). *War and Words: the Northern Ireland Media Reader*. Belfast: Beyond the Pale Publications, 1996

Rothenberg, Jerome. 'American Indian Poetry and the "Other Traditions"'. *The New Pelican Guide to English Literature*. Volume 9: American Literature. Penguin, 1988

Scanlon, Margaret. 'The unbearable present: northern Ireland in four contemporary novels'. *Études Irlandaises*, no. 10, December 1985, pp. 145-161

Showalter, Elaine. 'The Feminist Critical Revolution', in Frances Bonner et al. (eds). *Imagining Women: Cultural Representations and Gender*. Polity Press/Open University, 1992, pp. 73-78

Sim Stuart. 'Structuralism and post-structuralism', in Oswald Hanflung (ed). *Philosophical Aesthetics: an Introduction*. Blackwell, in association with the Open University, 1992, pp. 405-439

Smith, Henry Nash. *Virgin Land: the American West in Symbol and Myth*. Harvard University Press, 1971

Smyth, Gerry. 'The Novel and the North', in *The Novel and the Nation: Studies in the New Irish Fiction*. London: Pluto Press, 1997, pp. 113-143

Sutherland, J.A. *Fiction and the Fiction Industry*. Athlone Press, 1978

Sutherland, John. *Bestsellers: Popular Fiction of the 1970s*. Routledge and Kegan Paul, 1981

Thompson, John B. *Ideology and Modern Culture: Critical Theory in the Era of Mass Communication*. Oxford: Polity, 1990

Titley, Alan. 'Rough rug-headed kerns: the Irish gunman in the popular novel'. *Eire-Ireland*, vol. 15, no. 4, winter 1980, pp 15-38

Walsh, Dermot P.J. *The Use and Abuse of Emergency Legislation in Northern Ireland*. Cobden Trust, 1983

Watt, Stephen. 'The politics of Bernard MacLaverty's Cal'. *Eire-Ireland*, vol. 28, no. 3, 1993, pp. 130-146

Weedon, Chris. *Feminist Practice and Poststructuralist Theory*. Cambridge: Blackwell, 1987

Welch, Robert (ed). *The Oxford Companion to Irish Literature*. Osford: Clarendon Press, 1996

Whelan, Kevin. *The Tree of Liberty*. Cork University Press, 1996

Wilson, Des. *An End to Silence*. Cork: Mercier Press, 1985

Wilson, Des. *Democracy Denied*. Cork: Mercier Press, 1997

Wilson, Robert McLiam. 'Cities at war'. *Irish Review*, no. 10, spring 1991, pp. 95-98

Other Publications

Adams, Gerry. 'Republicanism and socialism'. *Fortnight*, September 1983

Barr, Fiona. 'Afraid to move outside the cave'. *Fortnight*, 205, June 1984, p. 25

Bell, Geoffrey. 'Without bitterness: an interview with Edna O'Brien', *Fortnight*, 47, 5 October 1972, pp. 19-20

Bell, J. Bowyer. 'The troubles as trash: shadows of the Irish gunman on an American curtain'. *Hibernia*, 22 January 1978, p. 22

Bell, Jenny. 'Ireland's genial book trade statesman hangs up his boots'. *The Bookseller*, 16 June 1995, pp. 12-13

Bennett, Ronan. 'An Irish answer'. *The Guardian*, 16 July 1994

Bingham, Stella. 'Take five detective novels', *Express on Sunday*, 1 November 1998

Boland, Eavan. 'The northern writers' crisis of conscience'. *Irish Times*, 12-14 August 1970

Bouche, Elizabeth. 'No big thrill'. *Fortnight*, 312, December 1992, p. 46

Caldwell-Wood, Naomi and Lisa A. Mitten. '"I" is not for Indian: the portrayal of Native Americans in books for young people. Program of the ALA/OLOS, Subcommittee for Library Services to American Indian People, American Indian Library Association, Atlanta, 29 June, 1991

Carty, Ciaran. 'Poor wee boy, indeed'. *Sunday Tribune*, 11 June 1995

Clancy, Tom. 'My views on unity'. *Irish America*, January 1988, pp. 15-17

Clarke, Liam. 'Nairac's "lover" claims MI5 fixed his murder'. *Sunday Times*, 14 February 1999

Corbett, Sue. 'Writer set for summer blockbuster'. *Sunday Life*, 23 June 1996

Crewe, Candida. 'Biting the bullet'. *Times Magazine*, 7 September 1996, p. 21

Dawe, Gerald. 'Old bones of contention'. *Fortnight*, 151, July 1977, p. 13

Deane, Seamus. 'The writer and the troubles'. *Threshold*, no. 25, summer 1974, pp. 13-17

Doherty, Louise. 'Why the last laugh is on "extremists"'. *Irish News*, 31 August 1996

Ellis, Peter Berresford. 'Shamrock in the sky'. *Irish Democrat*, November 1987, p. 2

Ellis, Peter Berresford. 'Revisionism in Irish historical writing: the new anti-nationalist school of historians'. *Iris*, no. 14, August 1990, pp. 36-43

Fearon, Kate. 'J'accuse'. *Fortnight*, September 1997, p. 35

Hoggart, Richard. 'Ulster: a turn-off TV subject'. *Listener*, 28 February 1980, pp. 261-262

Holland, Jack. 'A northern view'. *Irish Echo*, 20-26 May 1998

Holland, Mary. 'Morrison wields pen to fight free of conflict'. *Observer*, 2 March 1997

Hopkin, Alannah. 'At the heart of the action'. *Sunday Tribune*, 2 March 1997

Hughes, Brendan. 'Headlines grabbed – facts distorted'. *An Phoblacht/Republican News*, 7 June 1990, p. 12

Kennedy, Philippa. 'The making of a hero'. *Daily Express*, 30 September 1995

Linehan, Hugh. 'Green on the screen makes a critic see red'. *Irish Times*, 18 May 1996

MacEoin, Art and Mairtin Mac Diarmada. 'Getting high on lies: IRA drug myths exposed'. *An Phoblacht/Republican News*, 22 August 1991

MacPherson, Liz. 'Morrison finds his freedom in words'. *Irish News*, 25 February 1997

McAleer, Phelim. 'Author goes road of Joyce and Beckett'. *Irish News*, 28 November 1996

McEldowney, Eugene. 'Hearts of gold, bullets of lead'. *Irish Times*, 28 March 1997

McLaughlin, Brighid. 'The lonely torment of John Broderick', *Sunday Independent*, 29 March 1998, pp. 1, 6

McMinn, Joe. 'In defence of Field Day; talking among the ruins'. *Fortnight*, no 224, 9 September 1985, pp. 19-20

Morrison, Danny. 'Dillon's wonderland'. *Fortnight*, January 1996, p. 35

Nelson, Sarah. 'Oceans of Krapp'. *Fortnight*, no 136, 5 November 1976, p. 7

O'Hanlon, Ray. 'Letter from New York: a bad week for spooks, spies and "diplomats"'. *Irish News*, 1 June 1999

O'Mahony, John. 'Troubles in mind'. *The Guardian*, 7 July 1993, pp. 4-5

O'Neill, Una. '1979 paperbacks: flimsy covers for the same lies'. *An Phoblacht/Republican News*, February 1980

O'Rourke, peter. 'Remembering the past: republican papers amalgamate'. *An Phoblacht/Republican News*, 19 January 1995

Ormsby, Frank. 'John Morrow'. *Fortnight*, 5 February 1971, p. 20

Rolston, Bill and Robert Bell. 'Literature of the "Troubles"'. May 1996; Available from the Linen Hall Library, Belfast

Rushdie, Salman. 'Is nothing sacred?' Herbert Read Memorial Lecture, delivered in his absence at the Institute of Contemporary Arts on 6 February 1990 by Harold Pinter

Shara, Louise. 'Thugs and hooligans'. *Fortnight*, no. 325, February 1994, p. 18

Shervington, Sharon. 'Any of us could be hostages'. *New York Times*, 2 September 1990

Sinn Féin. *Constitution and Rules*. 1983

Sinn Féin. *A Scenario for Peace*. 1987

Sinn Féin. *Towards a Lasting Peace*. 1992

Spain, Martin. ' The betrayal of 1916 – Revisionism exposed'. *Iris*, no. 15, Easter 1991, pp. 7-10

Sutherland, John. 'Bounty hunter'. *London Review of Books*, 17 July 1997, pp. 26-27

Taylor, Peter. *Provos*, part 2

Appendix A: Category (a) novels by year of first publication

1970: 6
Menna Gallie, *You're Welcome to Ulster*
Peter Leslie, *The Extremist*
Joan Lingard, *The Lord on Our Side*
Joan Lingard, *The Twelfth Day of July*
Lee MacKenzie, *Hadleigh*
Martin Waddell, *A Little Bit British*

1971: 5
James Barlow, *Both Your Houses*
Russell Braddon, *The Progress of Private Lilyworth*
James Carrick, *With O'Leary in the Grave*
Tom McIntyre, *Through the Bridewell Gate*
James Wood, *Road to Canossa*

1972: 5
David Brewster, *The Heart's Grown Brutal*
Robert Crawford, *Whip Hand* (Hugh C. Rae, 1974)
Shaun Herron, *Through the Dark and Hairy Wood*
Jack Higgins, *The Savage Day*
Joan Lingard, *Across the Barricades*

1973: 16
Bob Aylott, *Cry for Tomorrow*
Harry Barton, *Yours Till Ireland Explodes, Mr Mooney*
Elizabeth Boyle, *Obsession*
Jimmy Breslin, *World Without End, Amen*
Elliot Cannon, *Stand By to Shoot*
John De St Jorre & Brian Shakespeare, *The Patriot Game*
Peter Dickinson, *The Green Gene*
June Drummond, *Bang! Bang! You're Dead!*
Walter Hegarty, *The Price of Chips*
Shaun Herron, *The Whore Mother*
Jack Higgins, *A Prayer for the Dying*
Joan Lingard, *Into Exile*
Ned Nicholl, *No More Leprechauns*
James A. Philips, *Joe Gall: the Shankill Road Contract*
Francis Stuart, *Memorial*
Terence De Vere White, *The Distance and the Dark*

1974: 8
Harry Barton, *Yours Again, Mr Mooney*
Robert Charles, *The Hour of the Wolf*
Jon Cleary, *Peter's Pence*
Peter Driscoll, *In Connection with Kilshaw*
John Feeney, *Worm Friday*
Michael Kenyon, *A Sorry State*
Donald Seaman, *The Bomb That Could Lip-read*
George W. Target, *The Patriots*

1975: 12
Brian Ball, *Keegan: No-Option Contract*
Robert Charles, *The Flight of the Raven*
Max Franklin, *Hennessy (The Fifth of November)*
Douglas Hurd, *Vote to Kill*
Joan Lingard, *A Proper Place*
Brian Marriner, *A Splinter of Ice*
David Martin, *The Task*
Ian Kennedy Martin, *Regan*
Ian Kennedy Martin, *The Sweeney*
Edith Morrison, *Joy in the Troubles*
Edward A. O'Neill, *The Rotterdam Delivery*
Gerald Seymour, *Harry's Game*

1976: 20
Anthony Burton, *The Coventry Option*
Robert Charles, *The Scream of a Dove*
Gerard De Villiers, *Belfast Connection*
P.A. Foxall, *Inspector Derben's War*
John Hale, *Lovers and Heretics*
Oliver Jacks, *Assassination Day*
Joan Lingard, *Hostages to Fortune*
James Lund, *The Ultimate*
Sam McBratney, *Mark Time*

Eugene McCabe, *Victims: A Tale from Fermanagh*
Naomi May, *Troubles*
Robin Moore, *The Kaufman Snatch*
Malachi O'Doherty, *Belfast Story*
Chapman Pincher, *The Eye of the Tornado*
Philip Prowse, *Death of a Soldier*
Gerald Seymour, *The Glory Boys*
Dennis Sinclair, *The Third Force*
Paul Theroux, *The Family Arsenal*
Peter Van Greenaway, *Suffer! Little Children*
Jon Manchip White, *The Robinson Factor*

1977: 20
Patrick Aalben, *The Grab*
James D. Atwater, *Time Bomb*
Colin Bennett, *Night Moves by Armour*
Robert Byrne, *The Tunnel*
James Carroll, *Madonna Red*
Peter Carter, *Under Goliath*
Kevin Casey, *Dreams of Revenge*
Robert Cawley, *Friend or Foe?*
Robert Charles, *The Prey of the Falcon*
P.A. Foxall, *Inspector Derben and the Widow Maker*
B. M. Gill, *Target Westminster*
Michael Hilliar, *Come Dance With Me*
Jennifer Johnston, *Shadows on Our Skin*
Benedict Kiely, *Proxopera*
Bob Langley, *Death Stalk*
David Martin, *The Ceremony of Innocence*
John Morrow, *The Confessions of Proinsias O'Toole*
Ritchie Perry, *Dead End*
Donald Seaman, *The Committee*
Francis Stuart, *A Hole in the Head*

1978: 14
James Carroll, *Mortal Friends*
Ray Connolly, *News Death*
John Cowell, *The Begrudgers*
Clive Egleton, *The Mills Bomb*
James Forman, *A Fine, Soft Day*
Bartholomew Gill, *McGarr and the Politician's Wife*
Clifford Hanley, *Prissy*
John Hardesty, *The Killing Ground*
Andrew Lane, *Forgive the Executioner*
Bob Langley, *The War of the Running Fox*
Nick McCarty, *Spearhead*
Michael McNamara, *The Dancing Floor*
Lucille Redmond, *Who Breaks Up the Old Moons to Make New Stars*
Martin Walker, *The Infiltrator*

1979: 18
Patrick Adams, *Everything Can Be OK*
David Bellin, *The Children's War*
Stewart Binnie, *Across the Water*
Iain Blair, *Hooligan's Rant*
Robert Cawley, *Shockwave*
John Chapman, *City War*
Kevin Dowling, *Interface Ireland*
Bartholomew Gill, *McGarr and the Dublin Horse Show*
Des Hamill, *Bitter Orange*
David Hanley, *In Guilt and in Glory*
Palma Harcourt, *A Sleep of Spies*
Christopher Hawke, *For Campaign Service*
David Hayward, *The Provo Link*
Andrew Lane, *The Ulsterman*
Michael McNamara, *The Sovereign Solution*
Richard Montague, *Frank Faces of the Dead*
Walter Nelson, *The Minstrel Code*
Surrey Smith, *A Gun for Delilah*

1980: 16
G.J. Arnaud, *Colonel Dog*
Ambrose Clancy, *Blind Pilot*
Colm Connolly, *The Pact*

Guiy De Montfort, *All the Queen's Men*
Lee Dunne, *Ringmaster*
Brian Garfield, *The Paladin*
David Grant, *Emerald Decision*
Norma Harrs, *A Certain State of Mind*
Colin Leinster, *The Outsider*
Brian O'Connor, *The One-Shot War*
Uinsin O'Donovan, *Rag Shadows*
Julia O'Faolain, *No Country For Young Men*
Joseph Rosenburg, *Death Merchant: the Shamrock Smash*
Gerald Seymour, *The Contract*
Peter Spain, *Blood Scenario*
Norman Stahl, *The Assault on Mavis A*

1981: 14
Roy Bradford, *The Last Ditch*
Mildred Downey Broxon, *Too Long a Sacrifice*
Susan Cheever, *A Handsome Man*
Russell Claughton, *The Long Good Friday*
Nelson DeMille, *Cathedral*
Jack Holland, *The Prisoner's Wife*
Alan Judd, *Breed of Heroes*
Maurice Leitch, *Silver's City*
Peter McDonald, *One Way Street*
Valerie Miner, *Blood Sisters*
Michael North, *Mission to Ulster*
R.W. Porter, *Kiss and Kill*
Ian St James, *The Balfour Conspiracy*
Arden Winch, *Blood Money*

1982: 12
P.A. Foxall, *The Face of Fury*
Frank Herbert, *The White Plague*
George V. Higgins, *The Patriot Game*
Jack Higgins, *Touch the Devil*
Rupert Holloway, *The Terrorist Conspiracy*
John Milne, *Tyro*
John Morrow, *The Essex Factor*
Hardiman Scott, *Operation 10*
Terence Strong, *Whisper Who Dares*
Julian Symons, *The Detling Murders*
Steve White, *The Fighting Irish*
Des Wilson, *The Demonstration*

1983: 8
Marjory Alyn, *The Sound of Anthems*
Antony Beevor, *The Faustian Pact*
A.F.N. Clarke, *Contact*
Tom Gibson, *A Wild Hope*
Bartholomew Gill, *McGarr and the PM of Belgrave Square*
Ted Harriot, *No Sanctuary*
Bernard MacLaverty, *Cal*
Mary Tanquay, *Run With the Hare*

1984: 15
Linda Anderson, *To Stay Alive*
Lynn Reid Banks, *Maura's Angel*
Elizabeth Gibson, *The Water is Wide*
Bartholomew Gill, *McGarr and the Method of Descartes*
Pete Hamill, *The Guns of Heaven*
Dermot Healy, *Fighting with Shadows*
Desmond Hogan, *A Curious Street*
Richard Hugo, *Last Judgement*
Jennifer Johnston, *The Railway Station Man*
Peter Ransley, *The Price*
John Rowe, *Long Live the King*
Mike Shelley, *The Last Private Eye in Belfast*
Ian St James, *The Killing Anniversary*
Mary Ann Sullivan, *Child of War*
Una Woods, *The Dark Hole Days*

1985: 12
Colin Dunne, *Rat Catcher*
Jack Higgins, *Confessional*
John Howlett, *Orange*
Grace Ingoldby, *Across the Water*
Philip Kerrigan, *Dead Ground*
Donall MacAmhlaigh, *Schnitzer O'Shea*
Dominic McCartan, *Operation Emerald*
Frances Molloy, *No Mate for the Magpie*
William Paul, *Seasons of Revenge*
M.S. Power, *The Killing of Yesterday's Children*
Gerald Seymour, *Field of Blood*
James Shannon, *A Game of Soldiers*

1986: 15
Linda Anderson, *Cuckoo*
Albert J. Countryman, *The Streets of Derry*
M. Gilliland, *The Free*

Desmond Hogan, *A New Shirt*
P.J. Kavanagh, *Only By Mistake*
Peter Lauder, *Noble Lord*
Don MacNaughton, *They Stayed a Soldier*
Deirdre Madden, *Hidden Symptoms*
Chris Ould, *A Kind of Sleep*
Roger Parkes, *Riot*
Sean Patrick, *Maureen's Ireland*
M.S. Power, *Lonely the Man Without Heroes*
Allan Prior, *Her Majesty's Hit Man*
Catherine Sefton, *Starry Night*
Terence Strong, *Dragon Plague*

1987: 20
Evelyn Anthony, *A Place to Hide*
Evelyn Anthony, *No Enemy But Time*
Campbell Armstrong, *Jig*
Mary Beckett, *Give Them Stones*
Mary Bringle, *Death of an Unknown Man*
Mary Bringle, *The Man in Moss Coloured Trousers*
Jim Case, *Cody's Army: Belfast Blitz*
Tom Clancy, *Patriot Games*
Michael Gilbert, *Trouble*
Peter Harris, *A Solitary Terrorist*
James Kelly, *The Marrow from the Bone*
Stephen Leather, *Pay Off*
Maurice Leitch, *Chinese Whispers*
Joan Lingard, *The Guilty Party*
Hugo Meenan, *No Time for Love*
James Murphy, *Juniper*
G.F. Newman, *The Testing Ground*
M.S. Power, *A Darkness in the Eye*
Catherine Sefton (Martin Waddell), *Shadows on the Lake*
David Thompson, *Broken English*

1988: 8
John Brady, *A Stone of the Heart*
Michael Chaplin, *Act of Betrayal*
Eoin McNamee, *The Last of Deeds*
Antony Melville-Ross, *Shaw's War*
S[arah].J. Michaels, *Summary Justice*
Julie Mitchell, *Sunday Afternoons*
Glenn Patterson, *Burning Your Own*
Catherine Sefton, *Frankie's Story*

1989: 18
Philippa Blake, *Looking Out*
John Brady, *Unholy Ground*
Richard Burns, *Why Diamond Had to Die*
R.W. Jones, *The Green Reapers*
Joe Joyce, *Off the Record*
Denis Kilcommon, *Serpent's Tooth*
John Loftus & Emily McIntyre, *Valhalla's Wake*
Patrick McCabe, *Carn*
Tom McCaughren, *Rainbows of the Moon*
Vincent MacDowell, *An Ulster Idyll*
Peter Maas, *Father and Son*
Pat Molloy, *A Legacy of Demons*
Danny Morrison, *West Belfast*
Frederick Nolan, *Sweet Sister Death*
Aly Renwick, *...last night another soldier...*
Catherine Sefton, *The Beat of the Drum*
Eileen Sherman, *Victor's Place*
Robert McLiam Wilson, *Ripley Bogle*

1990: 21
Don Anderson, *Heatshield*
Dermot Bolger, *The Journey Home*
John Brady, *Kaddish in Dublin*
Peter Burdon, *Warrior's Son*
Gavin Esler, *Loyalties*
Fergus Finlay, *A Cruel Trade*
Niki Hill, *Death Grows on You*
Shaun Hutson, *Renegades*
James Hynes, *The Wild Colonial Boy*
Russell Celyn Jones, *Soldiers and Innocents*
Joe Joyce, *The Trigger Man*
Jonathan Kebbe, *The Armalite Maiden*
Kitty Manning, *The Between People*
Brian Moore, *Lies of Silence*
Frederick Nolan, *Designated Assassin*
Timothy O'Grady, *Motherland*
Kenneth Royce, *Exchange of Doves*
Lionel Shriver, *The Bleeding Heart* (*Ordinary Decent Criminals*,
    1992)
Alan Spence, *The Magic Flute*
Hanna Wakefield, *A February Mourning*
Stuart White, *The Shamrock Boy*

1991: 22
John Arden, *Cogs Tyrannic*
Ronan Bennett, *The Second Prison*
Dan Binchy, *The Neon Madonna*
George Brown, *Ringmain*
Susan Crosland, *Dangerous Games*
Frederick Forsyth, *The Deceiver*
David Hegarty, *Short Storm*
Jack Higgins, *The Eagle Has Flown*
Graham Hurley, *Reaper*
Evelyn James, *Taking the Forbidden Road*
Frank Kippax, *The Butcher's Bill*
Mary Leland, *Approaching Priests*
Thomas McCarthy, *Without Power*
Ron McKay, *The Catalyst*
Paul Mann, *The Traitor's Contract*
S.J. Michaels, *Dieback*
Daniel Mornin, *All Our Fault*
Victor O'Reilly, *Games of the Hangman*
M.S. Power, *Come the Executioner*
Jan Roberts, *A Blood Affair*
Patrick Ruell, *The Only Game*
Deborah Valentine, *Fine Distinctions*

1992: 20
Ronan Bennett, *Overthrown by Strangers*
Bernard Cornwell, *Scoundrel*
Mary Costello, *Titanic Town*
Ita Daly, *All Fall Down*
Julian Desser, *Soap Star Kidnapped*
Joe Donnelly, *The Shee*
Randy Lee Eickhoff, *The Gombeen Man*
Richard Grindal, *The Tartan Conspiracy*
Ken Gross, *Hell Bent*
Jack Higgins, *Eye of the Storm*
Henry H. Howley, *The Making of an Assassin*
Frank Kippax, *Other People's Blood*
Stephen Leather, *The Chinaman*
Henry McCallion, *Double Kill*
Jane McLoughlin, *Coincidence*
Brian Morrison, *A Cause for Dying*
David Park, *The Healing*
Glenn Patterson, *Fatlad*
Kenneth Royce, *A Wild Justice*
Gerald Seymour, *The Journeyman Tailor*

1993: 16
James Adams, *Taking the Tunnel*
Mary Breasted, *Why Should You Doubt Me Now?*
Shaun Clarke, *Soldier E, SAS: Sniper Fire in Belfast*
Patrick Coogan, *The General*
Richard Crawford, *Fall When Hit*
Peter Cunningham, *Who Trespass Against Us*
Angela Doherty, *Constant Friends*
Briege Duffaud, *A Wreath Upon the Dead*
Jack Higgins, *Thunder Point*
Blair McMahon, *Nights in Armour*
Paul Mann, *The Britannia Contract*
Frank Palmer, *Bent Grasses*
William Rocke, *Operation Birdie*
Gordon Stevens, *Provo*
Edward Toman, *Shambles Corner*
Paul Watkins, *The Promise of Light*

1994: 27
George Brown, *Sacrifice*
Roger Cottrell, *The Orpheus Programme*
Richard Crawford, *The Minstrel Boy*
Conor Cregan, *With Extreme Prejudice*
James Daniel, *They Told Me You Were Dead*
James Douglas, *The Clearing*
Tom Faulkner, *The Machiavellian Legacy*
Dermot Healy, *A Goat's Song*
James Heneghan, *Torn Away*
Jack Higgins, *On Dangerous Ground*
Jack Holland, *Walking Corpses*
Shaun Hutson, *White Ghost*
Colbert Kearney, *The Consequence*
Stephen Leather, *The Long Shot*
Eugene McEldowney, *A Kind of Home Coming*
James McKeon, *Operation Pontiff*
Eoin McNamee, *Resurrection Man*
Kirk Mitchell, *Blown Away*
Edna O'Brien, *House of Splendid Isolation*
David Park, *The Rye Man*
Patrick Quigley, *Borderland*
David Rice, *Blood Guilt*
Sean Rooney, *Early Many a Morning*
Ras Sewell, *A Basketful of Sleepers*
Eddy Shah, *Fallen Angels*

Terence Strong, *The Tick Tock Man*
Glover Wright, *Headhunter*

1995: 26
John Arden, *Jack Juggler and the Emperor's Whore*
Colin Bateman, *Divorcing Jack*
Colin Bateman, *Cycle of Violence*
Sean Martin Blain, *The Java Man*
Phil Clarke, *Featherbed*
Johnson Courts, *Collusion*
Peter Cunningham, *Tapes from the River Delta*
James Daniel, *Out of the Strong*
Eamon Delaney, *The Casting of Mr O'Shaughnessy*
Martin Dillon, *The Serpent's Tail*
Louise Doughty, *Crazy Paving*
Daniel Easterman, *Day of Wrath*
Pat Gray, *The Political Map of the Heart*
John Hands, *Brutal Fantasies*
Jack Higgins, *Angel of Death*
Graham Hurley, *Sabbathman*
Patrick McCabe, *The Dead School*
Eugene McEldowney, *Stone of the Heart*
Gareth O'Callaghan, *Dare to Die*
Kate O'Riordan, *Involved*
Rhonda Paisley, *Lost Fathers*
Glenn Patterson, *Black Night at Big Thunder Mountain*
Deirdre Purcell, *Sky*
John Quinn, *Generations of the Moon*
Ian Rankin, *Mortal Causes*
Michael Shea, *Spin Doctor*

1996: 33
Paul Anthony, *The Fragile Peace*
Keith Baker, *Inheritance*
Jo Bannister, *No Birds Sing*
Colin Bateman, *Of Wee Sweetie Mice and Men*
Colin Bennett, *The Entertainment Bomb*
Theresa Breslin, *Death or Glory Boys*
Sam Brian, *Winter's Return*
Sean Colm, *Letter to Glenn*
James Daniel, *Kisses of the Enemy*
Seamus Deane, *Reading in the Dark*
Daniel Easterman, *Night of the Apocalypse*
Michael Foley, *The Road to Notown*
Reg Gadney, *Just When We Are Safest*
James Hawes, *A White Mercs with Fins*
Jack Higgins, *Drink with the Devil*
James Kennedy, *Armed and Dangerous*
Stephen Leather, *The Double Tap*
Ian McDonald, *Sacrifice of Fools*
Eugene McEldowney, *The Sad Case of Harpo Higgins*
Deirdre Madden, *One by One in the Darkness*
Julie Moffett, *The Double-Edged Blade*
Sean P. Murphy, *Foreign Chains*
Ruth Padel, *Fusewire*
David Park, *Stone Kingdoms*
Chris Petit, *The Psalm Killer*
Chris Ryan, *Stand By, Stand By*
Eamonn Sweeney, *Waiting for the Healer*
Gordon Thomas, *Poisoned Sky*
Leslie Thomas, *Kensington Heights*
Rebecca Tinsley, *The Judas File*
Marian Urch, *Violent Shadows*
Simon Weston & Patrick Hill, *Cause of Death*
Robert McLiam Wilson, *Eureka Street*

1997: 18
Colin Bateman, *Empire State*
Seán Beecher, *The Fastnet File*
Shaun Clarke, *Underworld*
Anne Doughty, *A Few Late Roses*
Lois Gould, *No Brakes*
Jack Higgins, *The President's Daughter*
Shaun Hutson, *Knife Edge*
Paul Harvey Jackson, *McCluskey (serialised in Figments)*
David M. Kiely, *The Angel Tapes*
Eugene McEldowney, *Murder at Piper's Gut*
Adrian McKinty, *Orange Rhymes with Everything*
Bernard MacLaverty, *Grace Notes*
Andy McNab, *Remote Control*
Danny Morrison, *The Wrong Man*
Chris Ryan, *Zero Option*
Terence Strong, *Rogue Element*
Ian Watson, *Oracle*
Stewart J. Wilson, *The Gobbins*
1998: 21
Alex Ashe, *An Acceptable Level of Violence*
Hugo Barnacle, *Day One*
Sebastian Barry, *The Whereabouts of Eneas McNulty*
Colin Bateman, *Maid of the Mist*

Geoffrey Beattie, *The Corner Boys*
Ronan Bennett, *The Catastrophist*
Tom Bradby, *Shadow Dancer*
Shaun Clarke, *Red Hand*
Evelyn Conlon, *A Glassful of Letters*
Simon Conway, *Damaged*
Frank Delaney, *Desire and Pursuit*
Tom Foote, *Undertow*
Mark Harris, *My Sweet Irish Rose*
Douglas Hurd, *The Shape of Ice*
James Kennedy, *Silent City*
Joan Lingard, *Dark Shadows*
Patrick McCabe, *Breakfast on Pluto*
Gerry McGeough, *Defenders*
Dan Mahoney, *Once In, Never Out*
David M. Thomas, *Anger's Violin*
Mark Urban, *The Linguist*

1999: 14
Patrick Corcoran, *Last Light Breaking*
Murray Davies, *The Drumbeat of Jimmy Sands*
Frances Fyfield, *Staring at the Light*
Jack Higgins, *The White House Connection*
Peter King, *Terrible Beauty*
Stephen Leather, *The Bombmaker*
Michael Ledwidge, *The Narrowback*
K.T. McCaffrey, *Revenge*
Gemma O'Connor, *Time to Remember*
Glenn Patterson, *The International*
Henry Porter, *Remembrance Day*
Daniel Silva, *The Marching Season*
Katharine Weber, *The Music Lesson*
Sylvester Young, *What Goes Around*

Appendix B: Novels published each year by category

	(a)	(b)	(c)	(d)	Total	(e)	(f)
1960	2				2	1	1
1961			0				
1962	1	1			2	1	
1963		1		1	2		
1964	1	1			2		
1965	1			3	4	1	
1966	2				2		
1967	1			1	2	1	
1968				1	1		
1969	2			1	3	2	
	[10]	[3]	[0]	[7]	[20]	[6]	[1]

Post-1969 titles per year: (a) novels, (b) short stories, (c) non-English, (d) questionable: Total; (e) category (a) novels by Irish, (f) category (a) novels by women:

	(a)	(b)	(c)	(d)	Total	(e)	(f)
1970	6			1	7	3	3
1971	5			2	8	2	
1972	5	3			8	1	1
	[16]	[4]	[0]	[3]	[23]	[6]	[4]
1973	16	1	1		18	4	3
1974	8		4	2	14	2	
1975	12		1	1	14	1	2
	[36]	[1]	[6]	[3]	[46]	[7]	[5]
1976	20	1		2	23	2	2
1977	20		3		23	6	2
1978	14	3			17	1	1
1979	18	3	1	2	24	3	1
1980	17	5		3	25	3	2
1981	14		1	1	16	4	2
	[103]	[12]	[5]	[8]	[128]	[19]	[10]
1982	12	3		1	16	2	
1983	8	3		3	14	1	2
1984	15				15	5	6
1985	12	10		5	27	5	2
1986	15	2	1	3	21	6	2
1987	20	2		3	25	6	6
	[82]	[20]	[1]	[15]	[118]	[25]	[18]
1988	8	11		1	20	5	2
1989	18	2		4	24	6	3
1990	21	5		3	29	5	3
1991	22	4		5	31	9	5
1992	20	12			32	5	3
1993	16	3		2	21	6	3
	[105]	[37]	[0]	[15]	[157]	[36]	[19]
1994	26	4		6	36	11	1
1995	26	6		5	37	12	4
1996	33	4	3	3	43	11	6
1997	18	5		2	25	7	2
1998	21	4		14	39	12	2
1999	14	1	1	5	21	2	4
	[138]	[24]	[4]	[35]	[201]	[55]	[19]
Total	480	98	16	79	673	148	75

Index